Information Technology and Indigenous People

Laurel Evelyn Dyson
University of Technology, Sydney, Australia

Max Hendriks
University of Technology, Sydney, Australia

Stephen Grant
University of Technology, Sydney, Australia

INFOSCI

Informati[illegible]e [illegible]ishing

Hershey • Lon[illegible] • Singapore

Acquisitions Editor: Michelle Potter
Development Editor: Kristin Roth
Senior Managing Editor: Jennifer Neidig
Managing Editor: Sara Reed
Copy Editor: Mike Goldberg
Typesetter: Marko Primorac
Cover Design: Lisa Tosheff
Printed at: Integrated Book Technology

Published in the United States of America by
Information Science Publishing (an imprint of Idea Group Inc.)
701 E. Chocolate Avenue
Hershey PA 17033
Tel: 717-533-8845
Fax: 717-533-8661
E-mail: cust@idea-group.com
Web site: http://www.idea-group.com

and in the United Kingdom by
Information Science Publishing (an imprint of Idea Group Inc.)
3 Henrietta Street
Covent Garden
London WC2E 8LU
Tel: 44 20 7240 0856
Fax: 44 20 7379 0609
Web site: http://www.eurospanonline.com

Library of Congress Cataloging-in-Publication Data

Information technology and indigenous people / Laurel Evelyn Dyson, Max Hendriks, and Stephen Grant, editors.
p. cm.
Summary: "This book provides theoretical and empirical information related to the planning and execution of IT projects aimed at serving indigenous people. It explores cultural concerns with IT implementation, including language issues & questions of cultural appropriateness"--Provided by publisher.
Includes bibliographical references and index.
ISBN 1-59904-298-3 (alk. paper) -- ISBN 1-59904-299-1 (softcover : alk. paper) -- ISBN 1-59904-300-9 (ebook : alk. paper)
1. Indigenous peoples--Computer network resources. 2. Information technology--Social aspects. 3. Internet--Cross-cultural studies. I. Dyson, Laurel Evelyn, 1952- II. Hendriks, Max A. N. III. Grant, Stephen, 1965-
GN380.I58 2006
303.48'33--dc22

2006015055

British Cataloguing in Publication Data
A Cataloguing in Publication record for this book is available from the British Library.

All work contributed to this book is new, previously-unpublished material. The views expressed in this book are those of the authors, but not necessarily of the publisher.

Information Technology and Indigenous People

Table of Contents

Section IV: Applications Transforming Communities

Preface

There is a growing interest in information technology (IT) by indigenous peoples around the world. Indigenous peoples see this as a means of preserving their traditional cultures for future generations as well as providing their communities with opportunities for economic and social renewal. There are many potential benefits that indigenous peoples can enjoy from information technology, including e-commerce and employment opportunities, better education and service delivery and enhanced communication.

However, in an age dominated by information technology, indigenous peoples have often found themselves separated by the digital divide. The cost of the new technologies, the geographic isolation of many communities, low levels of computer literacy and lack of awareness of how the technologies might serve indigenous goals and interests have led to this low adoption of the technology. There are also many cultural concerns, particularly related to the management of indigenous knowledge, language issues and questions of cultural appropriateness.

Recognition of these constraints will be necessary before indigenous peoples gain full access to the new technologies and all the benefits that they bring. Governments, indigenous community leaders, non-government service providers and educators are looking for solutions to these problems. They are looking for information to guide their policy making. This book is a step towards achieving this.

This book is an essential tool for community leaders, policy makers, researchers, educators and students involved with policy decisions related to indigenous communities. Topics covered provide both theoretical and empirical information. The topics emanate from a broad cross section of the research community and practitioners, and explore many interesting ideas and opinions that give voice to indigenous peoples on the role of information technology in their lives. About half the contributors are indigenous, and the remainder, have worked with indigenous communities for many years. The book will enable the reader to make informed decisions for planning and action in indigenous IT-related areas.

Contributions to the book are global. All continents where there are major indigenous communities are represented: North and South America, Australia, Asia, the Pacific and Africa. Many different peoples are included, such as the Orang Asli of Malaysia, the Maori of Aotearoa (New Zealand), the Yanomi community of the Amazon, the Wendat-Wyandotte Nation of Canada, the Himba people of Namibia and the Torres Strait Islanders of Australia.

The book is organized into chapters and short case studies which provide examples of IT implementations that have been successful in serving indigenous needs and goals. The articles show how information technology can be developed to fit indigenous culture and social practices, rather than forcing indigenous peoples to adapt to information technology.

Section I: Indigenous People and Information Technology: Issues and Perspectives

In the first section of the book we present chapters which address general issues regarding indigenous peoples and information technology. These include questions of indigenous adoption and participation in information technology, globalization issues and concerns of power and control.

The opening chapter, *Portals and Potlatch,* comes from Canadian authors Carol Leclair and Sandi Warren. Appropriately enough, it consists of a conversation reflecting the oral form of communication that characterizes most indigenous cultures. They discuss protocols for knowledge sharing using information technology which are based on an indigenous ethic of exchange and reciprocity, and founded on respect for the elders and for intellectual property. The authors stress the importance of context in traditional communication and show how context can also be created around online knowledge. As the Potlatch ceremonies of First Nations involve transfer of knowledge in a process of creating shared meaning, so information technology portals can provide a collective reality if they are grounded in indigenous principles and law. An important insight to come from these authors is the readiness of indigenous peoples to adopt new technology — to "steal fast horses" — if it can serve their communities' goals.

Juan Francisco Salazar is also interested in the reality of cyberspace for indigenous peoples. *Indigenous Peoples and the Cultural Construction of Information and Communication Technology (ICT) in Latin America* explores issues of indigenous adoption and control of the new digital technologies which go beyond simplistic discussions of the digital divide. He points out that many indigenous communities and organizations have established a Web presence in order to pursue activities as diverse as political advocacy, e-commerce, biodiversity research and the creation of a coordinated pan-indigenous movement. The communities assert their right to decide on what terms they will engage with the Internet and new media, redefining technology and conceiving of it differently from other populations.

In *Indigenous Knowledges and Worldview: Representations and the Internet*, Judy Iseke-Barnes and Deborah Danard take a different approach, focusing on many of the problematic issues surrounding the Internet and the way in which indigenous peoples are portrayed on Web sites. In particular, they note three aspects: commodification, by which indigenous peoples are reduced to stereotypes to sell products, the power over representations of indigenous peoples which is exercised by non-indigenous institutions and the distance which separates indigenous peoples from those who are seeking to define them. These misrepresentations produce destructive outcomes for indigenous peoples, no less serious than past practices of colonization. The authors call on indigenous peoples, particularly Web artists, to find new ways of using information technology which will support indigenous identities and communities.

Robyn Kamira is also interested in issues of control or, more specifically, governance. In her chapter, *Kaitiakitanga and Health Informatics: Introducing Useful Indigenous Concepts of Governance in the Health Sector,* she draws on the Maori concept of Kaitiakitanga, an idea which includes guardianship, stewardship and responsibility. She notes that after many decades of unsuccessful attempts to improve Maori health, more control is needed by Maori over health data and other information which impact their well-being. Indigenous perspectives must be included into public policy since Western approaches have failed indigenous peoples. Though she places her arguments for indigenous concepts of governance within the area of health informatics — her particular field of interest — they might well be applied to any area of information technology which impacts the lives of indigenous peoples.

Victor Giner Minana reports on quite a different topic: UNESCO's project *ICTs for Intercultural Dialogue (ICT4ID)*. During the 2004-2005 biennium UNESCO sponsored five pilot projects with the San people of southern Africa, the Himba of Namibia, the Pygmy Forest People of Gabon in central Africa, the Quechua in Peru and various indigenous peoples in Bolivia. The projects fostered indigenous cultural resources and dialogue with the outside world through developing the communication capacities of the people using a range of information and communication technologies, including digital film making, multimedia exhibitions and the digitization and repatriation of archives. The results of the pilot projects are currently being evaluated prior to the implementation of more projects over the next two years.

The final three case studies which conclude this section all provide a portrait of what information technology means to indigenous peoples and how it has transformed their lives. Pauline Hui Ying Ooi interviews five indigenous information technology undergraduates in her study, *ICT and the* Orang Asli *in Malaysia.* So far, the involvement of the Orang Asli with information technology is very small due to lack of education, the high cost of computer equipment and lack of basic infrastructure in their villages. However, they are generally willing to accept new technologies as long as the technologies do not threaten their traditional values. As the younger generations gain formal education, adoption of computer technology is likely to increase.

In *My Life with Computers on a Remote Island* and *How Computers Came into My Life*, two authors from Dauan Island in the Torres Strait, Bethalia Gaidan and Margaret Mau, describe how they learnt to use a computer and the changes that information technology has made to their lives. Bethalia Gaidan narrates how she used to have to travel to the main island by dinghy, small plane and then ferry in order to do the payroll before computerized payroll systems were introduced: At low tide she would wade through the mud to get to the boat, or in bad weather it would be dangerous to travel. Margaret Mau tells of the trials and tribulations of learning how to use computers as she assumed positions of responsibility in the government of her island and the council that oversees the region. For both women, living and working on one of the most remote islands in the world, computers have made a huge difference. As Margaret Mau says, "They make the world become your oyster."

Section II: Technology in Education

This section explores the ways information technology is being used as an educational tool from an indigenous perspective. Even when indigenous peoples have access to the same education as non-indigenous peoples, they often experience difficulties as a result of isolation, culturally inappropriate educational programs and learning styles. Information technology allows these difficulties to be addressed in innovative and interesting ways.

Christopher Robbins explores the problems of educating diverse indigenous populations scattered on many distant islands in the South Pacific in his chapter, *Developing Culturally Inclusive Educational Multimedia in the South Pacific.* After expansive research, three major recommendations for instructional design were suggested: "learning in wholes," the encouragement of observation and imitation and the use of vernacular metaphors and local languages. From these principles, multimedia was developed, thereby allowing students at the University of the South Pacific to develop and grow according to their own cultures, and teachers were encouraged to add local content.

In quite a different vein, the accessing of Internet banking services by indigenous peoples is described by Fiona Brady in her chapter, *Learning to Internet Bank.* Communities in the Torres Strait, due to their isolation in the Far North of Australia, have little or no opportunity to visit banks. Their need for this service provides the impetus to develop the skills required, as all alternatives are prohibitively expensive. Online banking — for many people today taken for granted — provides a rich learning experience for these peoples. The study provides a useful lens to view the process of technology skill acquisition, which the author interprets from a number of theoretical perspectives.

Michael Donovan, in his chapter *Can Information Communication Technology Tools be Used to Suit Aboriginal Learning Pedagogies?*, addresses the need to design programs that address educational outcomes for indigenous students. He notes a coincidence between ICT pedagogy and aboriginal pedagogy, and therefore suggests that ICT can be a useful tool to improve aboriginal education. He proposes "Outcamp" learning centres, placed in remote communities: These centres would provide Internet access with up to 15 computer terminals in a comfortable environment, allowing students to access a server where information is managed, with the support of an education facilitator. Programs could be designed to cater for the individual needs of these students and contextualize learning within their community setting.

Instructional design and technology (ITD) is discussed by Wanjira Kinuthia in her chapter, *Instructional Design and Technology Implications for Indigenous Knowledge: Africa's Introspective.* In particular she looks at indigenous knowledge as a resource, and investigates its place within the educational design process. She suggests that indigenous knowledge should be integrated into instructional design, thereby recognising that knowledge is dynamic, and reflects the culture to which it belongs.

Education, driven by the allied need to improve health programs, is the basis for the case study by Gale Goodwin Gómez, *Computer Technology and Native Literacy in the Amazon Rain Forest.* The Yanomani Intercultural Education Program was linked to the village health program, which at the time had high infant mortality rates as a result of epidemics of communicable diseases and malaria. Some 32 villages and over 400 students now participate in the programs. An interesting outcome is the production by teachers of teaching materials and newsletters.

Effective Maori teaching and learning and effective e-learning are examined in the case study by Terry Neal, Andrea Barr, Te Arani Barrett and Kathie Irwin in *Toi Whakaoranga: Maori and Learning Technology*. The progress made in the past using culturally appropriate educational content was seen to be under challenge by the potentially monocultural new e-learning environment, To address their concerns, workshops were conducted to develop appropriate Maori e-learning content and training.

Indigenous peoples have traditions of story telling and oral communication which are essential to their learning environment. How these stories are being recorded and placed on CD-ROM for use in educational environments form the basis of Ella Inglebret, Susan Rae Banks, D. Michael Pavel, Rhonda Friedlander and Mary Loy Stone's case study: *Multimedia Curriculum Development Based on the Oral Tradition*. Allowing indigenous peoples to speak, and using the multimedia medium, is preserving this rich cultural experience.

The development of a Pre-IT course at the University of Technology, Sydney, Australia, is the study by Stephen Grant, Max Hendriks and Laurel Evelyn Dyson in *The Indigenous Pre-IT Program*. From earlier modelling of a similar approach for indigenous students to study law, this course provides a bridge for students to enter tertiary education in the field of information technology. With the course offered successfully twice to date and a third planned for 2006, this is a successful ongoing program.

The use of problem-based-learning (PBL) for indigenous Australians has been the basis for the piloting and implementation of problem-based e-learning (PBeL). Rosemary Foster and Michael Meehan, in *Problem-Based Online Learning and Indigenous Tertiary Education: Reflections on Implementation*, explore the issues and limitations associated with this form of e-learning. Access to online computing and multimedia generally is explored.

Language and cultural recovery are investigated by Tish Scott in *Student Technology Projects in a Remote First Nations Village*. Here the year 6/7 students were given several community-based projects which were the result of research and field trips. From these, six short multimedia presentations were produced by the students. It was seen that through the use of digital technologies culture could be acknowledged, preserved, revitalised and shared.

Russell Gluck and John Fulcher, in *Draw-Talk-Write: Experiences and Learning with Indigenous Australians that are Driving the Evolution of Word Recognition Technology,* explore the use of a large variety of electronic media for indigenous Australians to use in their own language to tell stories. The equipment used includes electronic white boards, tablets, scanners, digital voice recorders, computers and word recognition engines. By using these means, orally rich people can share their language with others and build understanding.

Section III: Cultural Preservation and Revitalisation

Indigenous cultures around the world are under threat. Many communities no longer live on their traditional lands and much of the knowledge is now held by older people, who are concerned that the culture is not being passed on to the younger generation. Many indigenous languages are also threatened, with few remaining fluent speakers. Traditional knowledge and language resources are often stored away in museums and libraries, placed there by anthropologists and linguists in the past, but largely inaccessible to the indigenous owners.

The multimedia capabilities, storage capacity and communication tools offered by information technology provide new opportunities to preserve and revitalize indigenous cultures and languages, and to repatriate material back to communities from national cultural institutions. In particular the graphical, video and audio facilities of multimedia speak directly to cultures which are principally rooted in spoken language, music, dance, ceremony and visual forms of artistic expression. In this section we present three startlingly different approaches to indigenous living cultural archive systems and also a selection of projects aimed at ensuring that indigenous languages continue into the future.

One of the most successful indigenous cultural database systems that has been implemented to date is described by Martin Hughes and John Dallwitz in *Aṟa Irititja: Towards Culturally Appropriate IT Best Practice in Remote Indigenous Australia*. This system was developed expressly for the Anangu people, who live in the environmentally challenging desert regions of Central Australia, but it has also been adopted by a number of other communities. The development process was careful and painstaking, involving Anangu participants at every stage in order to ensure that the resulting interface, database, security and hardware were culturally and environmentally appropriate. An interesting feature of the Aṟa Irititja database is the mobile workstation, which is heat-proof, dust-proof, mouse-proof, equipped with an uninterruptible power supply and which can be wheeled around or placed on the back of a truck and taken anywhere the community wish to use it, indoors or out. The authors question standard IT best practice and show how "everything we think we know, believe is essential, or take for granted as axioms" must be set aside when designing systems which truly meet the needs of indigenous peoples.

There are other approaches to building indigenous living cultural archives. Brett Leavy, in *Digital Songlines: Digitising the Arts, Culture and Heritage Landscape of Aboriginal Australia*, illustrates a radically different approach which uses games-engine technology and data gathered from global positioning systems to create three-dimensional virtual environments in which the user can discover indigenous culture, stories and artefacts. The design of the system reflects the fundamental link between the land and indigenous culture. It has an extremely attractive interface and high levels of interactivity with figures in the landscape. At present the system is in the prototype phase, but has several potential market applications including indigenous heritage management, education, tourism and entertainment.

Katina Michael and Leone Dunn present another approach in *The Use of Information and Communication Technology for the Preservation of Aboriginal Culture: The Badimaya People of Western Australia*. They suggest interactive vector-based maps as a portal to multimedia content and digitized document and photographic archives. Since the focus of their work has been linguistic, they propose the Badimaya lexicon as a directory for organizing the multimedia resources. Since most of the people now live away from their traditional lands, the development of systems like these is very important in maintaining a link with their culture.

Given the crisis in many indigenous languages today, systems developers and linguists are teaming up to design programs to help revitalize these threatened languages and ensure that the younger generation have the opportunity to learn them. As one Tagish elder says, language is the "root and heart of our culture." In *Indigenous Language Usage in a Bilingual Interface: Transaction Log Analysis of the Niupepa Web Site*, Te Taka Keegan, Sally Jo Cunningham and Mark Apperley describe a Web site which provides access to Māori newspaper articles. The analysis reveals usage patterns which have implications for the design of similar sites. Importantly, their study shows that Māori and bilingual speakers are making considerable use of the Web site and therefore a great need exists for resources such as this.

The range of different indigenous language systems being implemented around the world is best seen in a series of short case studies. Kate Hennessy and Patrick J. Moore, in *Language, Identity, and Community Control: The Tagish First Voices Project*, describe a Canadian attempt from the Yukon to undo the assimilationist educational practices of the past which forbad Tagish and Tlinglit children from speaking their language. The Tagish tongue has only one remaining fluent speaker, but a database and Web site allowing community members to read while they listen to sound recordings is helping to address this issue.

An Australian project is described by Daryn McKenny, Baden Hughes and Alex Arposio in *Towards an Indigenous Language Knowledge Base: Tools and Techniques from the Arwarbukarl Community*. Twenty people are learning the Arwarbukarl language of the Hunter Valley region north of Sydney using linguistic knowledge management software available via the Web or on CD, which incorporates text, graphics, audio and video to create a rich learning experience.

Glenn Auld reports on a project from the remote north of Australia in *Ndjébbana Talking Books: A Technological Transformation to Fit Kunibídji Social Practice*. Ndjébbana is spoken by only 150 people, but is being passed on to the children through innovative, multimedia "talking books" which play recordings of stories while at the same time highlighting the words displayed on a simple-to-use touch screen.

Interactive multimedia is again the foundation of *A Talking Dictionary of Paakantyi*, described by David Nathan and available on CD-ROM. This case study illustrates how language projects evolve in consultation with indigenous participants into far richer outcomes than originally anticipated, in this instance with the addition of insightful explanations of Paakantyi usage supplied in English by the community members and incorporated into the dictionary.

The final study, by Gary Holton, Andrea Berez and Sadie Williams, centres on *Building the Dena'ina Language Alaska Archive*. This archive provides otherwise unavailable copies of audio recordings and documents of the Dena'ina Athabascan language of Alaska. It is helping to revitalize a language which had ceased to function in daily communication and, by incorporating best practice methodologies of digital preservation, is ensuring that the language materials will be an enduring and permanent resource for the community.

Section IV: Applications Transforming Communities

This section explores the ways in which computer systems are being designed specifically with indigenous peoples and their special needs in mind. Though indigenous peoples employ many of the same types of applications that non-indigenous peoples use — for example, financial and accounting packages to help them run businesses, word processing programs to write letters and other documents; and e-mail, mobile phone and text messaging technology for communication — indigenous peoples also have particular requirements which systems design must take into account.

In the first chapter of this section, *Ethnocomputing with Native American Design*, Ron Eglash explores an aspect of indigenous life which is of great interest to most indigenous communities around the world, that of art. He shows how computer simulation tools such as the Virtual Bead Loom and the SimShoBan basketry simulation can be used to help school students learn about traditional Native American art and at the same time express their individual creativity. Moreover, since the tools exploit mathematical concepts embedded in these art practices, students learn about mathematics at the same time. The tools demonstrate how good design practices which respect indigenous culture and involve collaboration with indigenous communities can yield positive results in a number of areas.

An application of information technology which is receiving a great deal of focus at the moment is GIS — geographic information systems. Given the strong attachment to the land that indigenous peoples traditionally have and the dispossession that many suffered in the process of colonization, these systems have a huge potential to either assist or hinder indigenous claims to legal title over their countries. In *Cut from the Same Cloth: The United States Bureau of Indian Affairs, Geographic Information Systems, and Cultural Assimilation*, Mark H. Palmer takes the more pessimistic view that GIS is being used as yet another tool in the assimilation of Native Americans. He argues strongly that communities are not being allowed to participate fully in modern cartography. The maps being produced therefore do not truly reflect Native American cultural landscapes, geographic knowledge and place names.

Andrew Turk, on the other hand, in *Representations of Tribal Boundaries of Australian Indigenous Peoples and the Implications for Geographic Information Systems*, assumes a more positive view, seeing GIS as an important tool in furthering indigenous land claims and access to resources. He explores how indigenous concepts of boundary — often more indeterminate than Western approaches — might be properly represented in systems which incorporate social and ethical issues in their design. He foresees the development of a truly indigenous GIS which faithfully reflects the culture and beliefs of native peoples.

Given the poverty and lack of local employment opportunities that characterize many communities, economic development of indigenous communities is particularly important. Remoteness is a significant factor here, and e-commerce provides a means of overcoming distance by giving direct access to global markets for indigenous products and services. Roger W. Harris, Doug Vogel and Lars H. Bestle, in their chapter *E-Community-Based Tourism for Asia's Indigenous Peoples*, demonstrate how community-based tourism is assisting indigenous peoples in the Asian region earn tourist dollars without having to go through intermediaries. Currently there is a boom in world tourism and the Internet is restructuring tourism distribution channels, allowing easy access for computer literate "geo-tourists" who are searching for more experiential, village-based tourism products. People like the Kelabit in Sarawak, Malaysia, are pioneering this community-based e-tourism. It allows communities to operate tourism on their own terms, enjoy a fair share of the profits and remain on their traditional homelands.

Some short case studies on a range of applications serving indigenous needs conclude this section. In *Computerised Tests of Brain Function for Use with Indigenous Peoples*, Sheree Cairney and Paul Maruff describe a program in the area of indigenous health called CogState. This has been developed to assess cognitive function in cases of drug abuse and mental illness. It allows patients who live in remote areas and have difficulty in accessing hospital testing facilities to be assessed using a simple program based on card games, an activity that is popular with many aboriginal people. The program allows them to remain in their community and can be administered under a tree, on a verandah or even on the beach. It is a good case of information technology adapting to indigenous needs and circumstances.

Shigenobu Sugito and Sachito Kubota present their *Alliance Project: Digital Kinship Database and Genealogy* — a system designed specifically for recording indigenous family relationships. These relationships are typically characterized by strong lateral interconnections rather than the vertical trees usual in Western genealogies. Because of the different way that indigenous peoples view their genealogy, systems which have been designed in the West to catalog such relationships are totally inappropriate. Software such as Alliance is important in helping indigenous peoples gain recognition of their identity, particularly where they were removed from their traditional lands, and is also being used in establishing land rights since these are often related to kinship.

Marcia Langton, Odette Mazel and Lisa Palmer give an overview of the *Agreements Treaties and Negotiated Settlements Database*, which provides an online gateway to resources to assist in policy-making, governance and other issues relating to agreements formed between indigenous peoples and governments, companies and other organizations. Like the other systems described above, it is appropriate to indigenous culture and serves a specific indigenous need. One can imagine in time other specialist computer applications arising to fill a full range of indigenous requirements.

Section V: Linking Communities and Improving Access

Isolation marks many indigenous communities. This can be either geographic or social isolation. Access to ICT is limited because indigenous peoples often live in remote regions, far from major communications infrastructure. Social factors prevent access to technology available to the wider community. Without ICT, indigenous peoples are often denied communication with the outside world and with each other. They are denied access to a range of government and non-government services, such as education, health, justice, welfare, banking and commercial services. They are also denied access to national and global markets for sale of their arts, crafts and tourism services.

Essentially, ICT can reduce the disadvantage of location for remote communities. However, a number of issues need to be addressed before these benefits can be realized because the very remoteness of the communities, their small populations and environmental challenges mean that implementation of technology is difficult and costly. In Section V we showcase some of the projects and technologies which have been successful in linking communities together and improving access.

Anne Daly reports on a common approach to overcoming access problems for poor communities in her chapter *The Diffusion of New Technologies: Community Online Access Centres in Indigenous Communities in Australia.* Community technology centres, or telecentres, provide indigenous peoples with access to computer technology and the Internet by spreading costs across the community and so increasing affordability. Through interviews with centre managers, indigenous community members and service providers, she considers factors which make centres successful. These include a strong commitment by the community to the development and ongoing management of the centre, a close integration of the centre to community activities (including development goals and cultural activities) and the funding of training for staff and community members.

Another approach to improving access is outlined in Laurel Evelyn Dyson's *Wireless Applications in Africa.* A range of wireless technologies are delivering cost effective services in a continent where traditional, wired infrastructure is lacking, where populations are often itinerant, literacy levels are low and there is little money to spend on technology. Four implementations are examined to demonstrate how new approaches to mobile design are producing culturally and environmentally appropriate technology: the Himba's satellite-based mobile telephone network, Cyber Sherpherd, Cybertracker and WorldSpace satellite Internet radios. Wireless devices offer portability to semi-nomadic peoples, can be designed with graphical interfaces and menus to suit the literacy levels of people coming from an oral culture and may well provide a real option for indigenous peoples all around the world.

Overcoming geographic isolation often requires new, innovative technological approaches. Mehran Abolhasen and Paul Boustead, in their case study *UHF-Based Community Voice Service in Ngannyatjarra Lands of Australia*, show how a new radio network is providing communication in one of the remotest and most challenging desert environments in the world. The Ultra-High Frequency radios are smaller, more portable devices than what was previously available and are run off a community-owned network that allows free calls and is therefore cost-effective.

An important implementation in remote Australia in recent years is the *Cape York Digital Network,* detailed by 'Alopi Latukefu in his case study. This network addresses the "tyranny of distance" and lets a number of indigenous communities achieve some independence and control of their communication needs via a high bandwidth network. A number of services are offered including Internet banking and videoconferencing, which allows virtual "visits" to family members in prison. One innovate facility is the Indigenous Stock Exchange, which encourages investment in indigenous enterprises.

Though governments often see providing infrastructure as the key issue in overcoming disadvantage for isolated indigenous communities, projects which do not include social factors are likely to fail. Ryan Sengara describes the *Redfern Kids Connect* project which operates in an inner city neighbourhood of Sydney, Australia. Here it is not geographic isolation, but rather high levels of socio-economic disadvantage which keep aboriginal children from accessing information technology. The project addresses this by fostering positive interactions and relationships within a computer laboratory context.

A computer lab is also the setting for J. David Betts's case study, *Community Computing and Literacy in Pascua Yaqui Pueblo*. Located near Tucson, Arizona, the Pascua Yaqui community have learnt computer skills, improved school achievement and developed new literacies, as people interact in the lab in English, Spanish and Yaqui, their native tongue. The computer clubhouse has become a drop-in centre for youth, who work with mentors on multimedia projects, robotics, graphics, video and animation, and there is also a music studio. The project shows the potential for well-developed programs to build social capacity on a number of fronts which go well beyond basic computer literacy.

The final contribution in our book by Linda Sioui illustrates how information and communication technologies can be used to link communities once problems of access are overcome. *Reunification of the Wendat/Wyandotte Nation at a Time of Globalization* shows how the Internet is allowing indigenous peoples to reconnect and reform their communities out of the diaspora which resulted from colonial policies antagonistic to indigenous sovereignty and well-being. The Wendat First Nation, originally from Ontario, Canada, were dispersed from their homelands to Quebec, Oklahoma, Kansas and Michigan, but have now formed virtual groups such as Wendat Gathering, Wendat Longhouse and Longhouse Women, which allow daily communications. It illustrates how information technology can be used as a force for good to overcome the injustices of the past, how it can serve indigenous goals for self-determination and how it can ensure the continuation of indigenous cultures and indigenous languages in the modern world.

Section I

Indigenous People and Information Technology: Issues and Perspectives

Chapter I

Portals and Potlatch

Carol Leclair, Wilfred Laurier University, Canada

Sandi Warren, Trent University, Canada

Abstract

The authors are Métis scholars and members of the Métis Women's Circle. The Métis Women's Circle is a not-for-profit, national organization that represents approximately 200 aboriginal women of Métis and mixed heritage from across Canada. The Circle offers services and programs to develop and share Métis communities' knowledge with their people and the broader Canadian public. This chapter represents a dialogue between the authors regarding the protocols for information technology as seen from their indigenous worldviews.

Introduction

It is easier to predict the technology than the application of the technology; and it is easier to predict the application than its social impact. To attempt to foretell the meaning of all this in terms of human values is hardest of all (Rothmann & Mosmann, 1976, p. 406).

Our society is in the midst of a debate. We are trying to determine whether technology can be controlled and directed toward the betterment of humankind or whether it will lead to the restriction of human liberty (Rothmann & Mosmann, 1976, p. 9).

Protocols for Information Technology from an Indigenous Worldview

[Sandi]: I came across the above quotes several years ago, when I was studying information technology (IT) as a chosen career. In the late 1970s, as one of many industry analysts, I began to ponder the ethics associated with knowledge sharing, particularly the level of responsibility required by information developers in a global context. However, like many IT professionals, I continued my work with little input from our aboriginal communities. As a consequence, the information technology era has advanced and operated within a narrow philosophical, structural and intellectual framework, as defined by a Eurocentric worldview.

Thirty years later, the debate regarding information technology and its social impact surfaces once again within our communities, as we reach out to share indigenous knowledge within a framework of exchange and reciprocity.

[Carole]: As communally based peoples, we have always sought to bring wealth and possessions to the people. To have is to share. Sharing is both an economic necessity and a prized virtue. No native culture I'm aware of is indifferent to the impoverishment of the community. Our Métis Women's Circle mandate is to support, educate and empower our community. To do this, our leaders seek cross-cultural strategies to interact as equals with universities, government and scientific bodies to develop our resources. It's good to think about our ancestors and how they cared for the people, overcoming many obstacles by their resourceful, intelligent and hard-working approach to life.

I met elder and educator Oscar Kawagley (Yupiaq) at a CASTS (Canadian Aboriginal Science & Technology Society) Conference, in the summer of 2003. During our personal conversation, we talked about the use of science and technologies. His view is that we should be teaching our youth both traditional ways and western skills, so that when the youth travel outwards to the wider world they can carry their "specific cultural mandates regarding the ways in which the human being is to relate to other human relatives and the natural and spiritual worlds" (Kawagley, personal communication, Summer 2003). So, if we remain close to our aboriginal traditional thought worlds, we will continue to use our powerful minds to stay awake and aware to our surroundings. At that same conference, Jennifer Morrison presented a session entitled "Coyote Goes Virtual." In her talk she asked the question, "What if a First Nation had the power and capability to link their knowledge with scientific knowledge about the land on their terms?" She described the merging of PEM (predictive ecosystem modeling) with Nlaka'pmx GIS (geographic information system) data, the breaking down of barriers and the development of a new virtual reality whereby the Chiefs will be able to build future management options for the Nation's forests.

Nancy Maryboy (Navaho) is a professor in the Department of Physics and Astronomy at Northern Arizona University. She is developing an Internet-based course on Native American Astronomy. She shares her people's ancient knowledge of the Navaho night sky and tells the stories of the constellations, their names and how they came to be. She gives national and international presentations on the juxtaposition of native knowledge, quantum consciousness, western science and the protocols of conducting indigenous research. Dr. Maryboy sat with a panel of experts at the end of last years' CASTS conference. She was cautioned by one of the non-native experts that she ought to formally document the broader contextual and ceremonial elements of Navaho cosmology, since it would likely disappear in future. She gently made the point that certain knowledge must remain within the Navaho people's possession and that she was very confident that they could be entrusted with its preservation, as they had done so for thousands of years.

[Sandi]: Our contemplation of information technology and its social impact appears to fall into two perspectives within our communities....

The first perspective seeks to utilize information technology for sharing knowledge and resources as a means to increase the capacity and capability of the community, either through e-commerce, e-learning or via a community Web portal. The argument is that the inclusion of knowledge networks raises the demand for technology and communication infrastructures that provide vehicles to the world, foster culture and tradition, maximize resources, increase services, enhance organizational and individual development and create wealth (Sixdion, 1997, p. 19). Furthermore, partnerships and technology-based solutions equalize the playing field for small or rural communities by providing access to governments, schools, health institutions, social services or business partners. Consequently, an equalization of the playing field reduces brain-drain of talented aboriginal youth and professionals, who leave for more competitive opportunities (Hqnet, 2002).

The second perspective cautions against situating indigenous knowledge, among a platform of social and intellectual hierarchies, power relationships and other discursive frameworks, which feed the embedded histories and misunderstandings of indigenous peoples, through stereotypes, which create "Pan-Indian" or simplified characteristics of a people (Dei, Hall, & Rosenberg, 2002, p. 7). The concern challenges the platform developers and network systems' ability to distinguish authentic and inauthentic resources (Fee, 1995, p. 245). Consequently, it may be difficult to distinguish who is writing as "other" or who may be deliberately or unknowingly espousing events from a perspective located in a dominant ideology (Fee, 1995, p. 244).

[Carole]: David Kanatawakhon (Mohawk) tells me that the word for computer in Mohawk is "kawennarha" — in English, "hanging words" — a literal description of how the words appear on a computer screen, no lines, just words hanging in space. He has no difficulty using email in Mohawk since the language relies less on visual images than precise language use. He argues that "language is the way in which you deliver yourself to the world," and so, the value of relationship, embedded in language, is expressed with greatest clarity in native languages. Native traditional knowledge is a high-context system. This means that how knowledge is acquired is critically important, since we are responsible for healthy relationships between humans and the object, whether a plant, another animal or an energy. Low-context cultural systems express no such responsibility. Similarly, Philip H. Duran (Twa Pueblo), from the Northwest Indian College, shares with us that an Indian Paradigm of science includes these concepts:

> *[A]ll things are related, the system is of cycles, reciprocity, natural (vs. written) law is at premium, renewal, all matter is vibrating energy, mysteries are part of the universe (accepted as nature's gifts and as something only the heart can access), there is constant change.* (Duran, 2003)

[Sandi]: These perspectives call for strengthening of indigenous knowledge(s) through protocols that respect the intellectual property of elders, community members and indigenous research. The fortification is grounded by traditional relationships, which recognize a reciprocal responsibility by the receiver and the custodian of the knowledge to the knowledge itself, which extends beyond either person (Battiste [Micmac], 2000, pp. 135-136). Without a commitment to reciprocity, respect and responsibility, information technology risks a breach of communal and individual rights, as well as claims of appropriation and infringement of cultural integrity.

These risks surfaced in the broader public domain of the information network during the advancement of the knowledge evolution. In 1996, the U.S. Senate drafted a report regarding security in cyberspace, which identified a security culture that has left people vulnerable to hacker technologies and fraud. As an outcome, ethical cyberspace community development was proposed (Palloff & Pratt, 1999, p. 44). The goal was to create a balance between open dialogue and a cautionary approach, which maintains integrity and security.

A cautionary attitude is shared among aboriginal communities. Historically, aboriginal identity and worldviews were only understood from the Eurocentric legacy of anthropology and social analysis (Henderson [Chickasaw], 2000, p. 255). This legacy has shaped decisions within Eurocentric society that perpetrated a primitive perception of indigenous knowledge systems, in terms of their structure, process and philosophy.

[Carole]: As for concerns over authentic and inauthentic sources, I think that our oral traditional protocols continue to guide us. Web sites, which claim to offer native knowledge, are scrutinized through some of the basic concepts embedded in oral tradition. I check for clear statements of who is writing, identifying self, family, place, of how you come to know from your own experience, or who has passed on the information and how this person has demonstrated knowledge in the past. When I look at Métis Web sites, I use my intellect and my intuition, (another word for wisdom or experience) to assess the usefulness of the site. We acknowledge that for hundreds of years now, we have been "in the pot, trying not to melt." Luckily, a hallmark of most traditional cultures is their success at adapting and changing with conditions.

[Sandi]: Pan-Indianism goes beyond acting together, to build on existing traditions, or to replace them entirely. Those who fight for tribal integrity have deep concerns about the erosion of tradition, the corruption of the teachings which make them distinct. While I respect this concern, I also note that pan-Indianism is not always to be viewed with suspicion, since many urban aboriginal peoples would be lost without a Native Friendship Center or broader access to indigenous cultures to nurture them when they have lost their family of origin. From what I observe, there is still great respect among native nations for diversity, for self-determination. The value of respect is made real in the daily responses to life.

[Carole]: Some years ago when I was young and learning my Anishnaabe ways, I was sitting with a Haudenosaunee woman and expressing my confusion over a certain protocol to be used for one who has died. My friend sat quietly, nodding encouragement as I struggled to remember what I'd been taught. I thought it odd that she didn't join in with suggestions, "you know, maybe it goes like this, or that," the usual kind of helpful dialogue. Today I understand and acknowledge her gentle refusal to speak in error about another Nation's traditions as the value of respect in practice.

Our relatives from different tribal backgrounds have often chosen to act in concert, to join together as close allies. For millennia our economies were conservative and largely stationary. During the fur trade period, Cree and Assinaboine quickly became merchants and seized business opportunities to trade inland with many other native nations. Cree culture experienced profound social transformations as they went from canoe-based to horse-based, from fur trappers to provisioners and buffalo-hunters over a very short time. For hundreds of years my Saulteaux/Métis world experienced this clash between natural communities and new capitalism, between "the new technological juggernaut and plain people trying to make a home along with our tribal relatives" (Howard, 1952, p. 6). So I would say that we have much experience in "going with the flow," in "stealing fast horses" from western ingenuity.

[Sandi]: Subsequently, the introduction of indigenous information technology portals, grounded by protocols based upon indigenous practices for ceremonies, go beyond prediction, emancipation and deconstruction responses to colonization. These portals, articulate a re-acculturation process by influencing new agendas and understanding of indigenous and Eurocentric thought.

[Carole]: We have guidance from the peoples of the Six Nations' Kahswentha (Two Row Wampum), which was intended as an agreement that native peoples should keep their own laws, customs and ways and the settler nations should keep their own laws, customs and ways. It was the intention of this agreement that neither nation would try to make compulsory laws or interfere with one another, although interaction was expected. Groups such as The Alaska Native Science Commission have taken a leadership role in the development of guidelines, which scientists and others must use when interacting with native communities. Native scientists are aware of how important the appropriate context is when using a piece of knowledge. We can borrow the expression, "autonomous appropriation" (Aikenhead, 1997) to describe the careful distinction between appropriating western knowledge without assimilating to western ways of valuing the world.

[Sandi]: My initiation to the Teachings of the Potlatch introduced me to a commitment to how knowledge, story, resources and/or economy are transferred from one person(s) to another, through principles of respect, responsibility and reciprocity. As background, the Potlatch Teachings serve as a venue, which narrate and transfer ownership of economic and ceremonial privileges from one community member to others. As such, Potlatch Ceremonies are social occasions to mark a significant event in aboriginal family or community. Traditionally, Western aboriginal communities along the coast of Canada and the United States were associated with this practice. Some Eastern Nations practiced similar ceremonies, often called "give-away" ceremonies, which fit the intent and meaning of the potlatch.

[Carole]: Respect prevents me from speaking as an insider authority about Potlatch, but I can make some observations from my own perspective. I'm told

that Potlatch is a Chinook word meaning "to give." I can think of Potlatch metaphorically as a Haida information technology, a kind of "data storage" through family-owned dances, objects, stories, songs and ceremonies. Many witnesses confirm and preserve an organic process. Of course there are many other dimensions to Potlatch, which are properly held by the community and not shared globally. Historically, potlatch ceremonial material has been confiscated and sold to collectors worldwide. This could be analogous to computer hacking and theft of data. We know how difficult a process of repatriation of cultural materials continues to be. I imagine the repatriation of information will be very difficult. The U'mista Cultural Center Web site does a fine job of offering information while protecting sacred knowledge.

[Sandi and Carole]: By participating in give-away [Potlatch] ceremonies with members of the Métis Women's Circle, we recognize that gifts represent the intangible and tangible relationship between mind, emotion, spirit and body, embodied in the relationship between the donor and recipient of the exchange (Leclair, 2003, p. 142). In this manner, the relationship creates shared meaning, which both members seek to create, sustain and grow through interdependency and reciprocity.

[Sandi]: In this context, information networks create a "space" for sharing stories, values, customs and experiences, which represent the roles and responsibilities of self and community. Individuals and the community participating in the "space" articulate a shared meaning through a process that facilitates an exchange between the internalization of meaning and the externalization of actions and behaviours. This exchange creates a phenomenology about indigenous knowledge that is associated with specific ways of knowing and being, which are constructed as a collective reality for the individual and the community (Little Bear, 2000, p. 77).

Similarly, "portals" provide an opportunity for resource and knowledge-transfer. The word "portal" is derived from the Latin word *porta*, which translates to "gate". In the strictest sense of the word, anything that acts as a gateway to anything else is a portal. From a technology standpoint, portals increase the participation of a large "network" of people through shared information or resources.

The portals create avenues that enable indigenous communities to articulate community systems, such as justice, education, health and other social priorities that have relevance for their people (Giroux, 1997, p. 227). The participating members recognize that the process of re-acculturation involves an appreciation of diverse traditions, histories and identities (1997, p. 268). Specifically, the community negotiates the socio-cultural relations and structures that reflect the complex experiences of aboriginal communities within the broader context (in this instance, the information network community) (Freire, 1970, p. 153).

[Carole]: When I think of gates or doorways, I imagine those Medicine Wheel doorways. The teachings of the Medicine Wheel can be useful as we develop technological systems for articulating community systems, transfer of knowledge and re-acculturation. We know that the Eastern Doorway (Waabinong) offers the energy of vision, which can be used to help in our search for knowledge, for establishing goals and determining our needs. We can turn to the Southern Doorway (Zhawinong) for the gifts of knowledge skills, understanding human language, sensitivity to the feelings of others and our own nurturing through interactions with physical and spiritual places. The Western Doorway (Niingabiianong) can help us with self-awareness, reflection on our experiences, values and strengths. The Northern Doorway (Giiwetinong) gives us the gift of accomplishment. We can learn how to evaluate our performance in practical situations. There are myriad layers of teaching in this ancient concept, and I have sketched a bare outline of how useful these concepts can be if we use them as grounding in embracing western ways.

[Sandi]: If information technology serves as a "doorway" for indigenous peoples to negotiate and share knowledge, we must ensure that information technology principles respect a definition for indigenous knowledge that is grounded by indigenous theories for constructing identity and empowering change.

Knowledge is a community resource. It defines and drives the community. It's interconnected[ness], it's multifaceted and multidimensional, it's revered, and it's language, communication and history. It's collective memory. It's captured and maintained for future generations. It's a reflection of life experience. It's acquired listening and being empathetic. It's wisdom, strength and leadership. It's a strategic resource. It's the power of a good mind. It's imperfect. It's a gift bestowed by the Creator. (T. Maracle, cited in National Aboriginal Health Organization Report, February 5, 2001)

Maracle's definition suggests that knowledge is a fundamental character, a social process, and the foundation that guides our everyday life, whether we are consciously aware of the process or not (Berger & Luckmann, 1967, p. 14). Consequently, knowledge represents a common or shared expression of our social and cultural relations (Warmoth, 2000, p. 4). Within a concept of indigenous worldview, knowledge, language, consciousness and social order are understood as four complementary perspectives that require time and a lifetime of experiences to cultivate ways of being and knowing (Henderson, 2000, p. 261).

By incorporating the concepts of organic or natural laws into principles for creating indigenous information portals, the model observes a practice which honours information from various sources, such as environmental observations, dreams, visions, ceremonies, communion with spirits of nature and time spent with Elders. This practice supports an indigenous way of being and knowing through behaviours and actions that regard all things as Sacred (Cajete [Tewa Nation], 2000, p. 190).

In accordance, indigenous knowledge systems, which generate shared meaning and action, begin with our narratives and our experiences. In exchange, our collective narratives and stories nurture a shared knowledge, which has high meaning and generates high actions within the community (NAHO, 2001, p. 3). Within an information technology application, knowledge has the potential to generate and share indigenous narratives, stories and experiences as a source of meaning that is "lived and made transparent in everyday relations, rituals and activities" (NAHO, 2001, p. 3).

In her text, *The Knowledge Evolution: Expanding Organizational Intelligence*, Verna Allee describes a knowledge archetype that suggests a movement away from a single person having data toward a community of wisdom-keepers (Allee, 1997, p. 45). Specifically, the knowledge evolution demonstrates a movement outward from a single repository of data, to more integrated patterns of information, knowledge, meaning, philosophy, wisdom and union (Allee, 2003). The increased community knowledge facilitates problem-solving more quickly, by building on the experiences of others, articulated as learning communities.

Aboriginal information networks utilize harmony, trust, sharing and kindness as a similar model which guides relationships, establishes rules and recognizes categories for necessary actions (Henderson, 2000, p. 273). Under the principles of responsibility and reciprocity, phenomenology (of experiences) is influenced by aspects of knowing, which are derived from all creation. Pam Colorado (Oneida) articulates this distinction as an integral part of indigenous knowledge systems, which she identifies as indigenous science (Colorado, 1988). This concurs with Henderson's premise that aboriginal knowledge systems move beyond concepts of subject and object and into a complexity of a state of community that is reflective of all creation (Henderson, 2000, p. 264).

The complex institutions, which have continued to exist in our communities as various models of political, economic, social and cultural knowledge systems, are characterized as interconnected and multidimensional (Champagne, 1989, pp. 2-13). Subsequently, aboriginal responses and ability to negotiate the "mainstream" exist through well-developed and complex traditional decision-making structures, which can serve as guidelines for current information network structures and protocols.

The implication is an interpretation of indigenous societies as sophisticated participants rather than victims of an imperial hegemonic power. Battiste argues that aboriginal knowledge systems have been undermined and discredited through cognitive imperialistic presentations of indigenous societies and historical events. She advocates for the re-visioning of aboriginal communities and our knowledge systems from an indigenous perspective (Battiste, 1998, pp.16-27).

Supportively, Champagne (Chippewa) challenges the passive or understated image of indigenous peoples in society, which presents the focus of indigenous responses as actions associated with coping with the colonial systems. Instead, aboriginal societies are recognized as strategists, who develop specialization and institutionalization processes as innovative responses to the social, political, normative, economic and cultural changes brought about through contact with Eurocentric institutions (Champagne, 1989, p. 3). In this context, these strategies are deliberate efforts to preserve the cultural and national autonomy, as well as to create options for sustaining a collective resistance (1989, p. 14).

By articulating an information technology protocol, based on indigenous theories associated with proactive measures for addressing change, we begin to build a legacy of indigenous change models and associated characteristics that is reflective of our ways of knowing, being and doing. These models provide a benchmark for contemporary information networks.

As community theorists, it is our responsibility to facilitate the creation of models based upon experiences which observe natural patterns, through the linkage of theory, strategy and action. These patterns are influenced by the environment as a component of aboriginal thought and identity (Henderson, 2000, p. 252). For our community, we envision that these models reflect a worldview that is "not a description of reality but an understanding of the processes of change and ever-changing insights about diverse patterns and styles of flux" (Henderson, 2000, p. 265).

An information technology protocol developed for and by aboriginal communities articulates a specific voice that represents the diversity and complexity of our aboriginal nations. By proposing models based on strategic differentiation, we introduce the concepts of certain institutional configurations that facilitate adaptation of social change as well as other configurations that present obstacles to change (Champagne, 1989, p. 10).

In this sense, the information protocols represent a complex process with features from both deconstruction and construction theory. These protocols facilitate the reclaiming of our histories, social structures, political and cultural vocabularies that define and shape our individual and collective identities (Giroux, 1997, p. 198).

The protocols enable community development efforts to operationally address the day-to-day re-traditionalization of programs, while establishing long-term scenario planning to strategically position the community's internal capacity and capability. The long-term scenarios create portals for indigenous information sharing while facilitating our communities' adaptations to on-going societal, economical, political and cultural influences. From this perspective, we foresee a proposed indigenous information technology that builds upon our communities' skills as strategists, who negotiate social priorities that have contemporary and future application for our people, while safeguarding values and norms, which are relevant to one's community.

[Carole]: Our nations have the gift of beautiful speech, a gift, which persists even through the dimming effect of the English language. Our material creativity has been taken up and imitated worldwide. I read recently that our Métis beaded moccasins will be walking down New York fashion runways this year. Anishnaabe wisdom questions where we stand with respect to the Seven Fires prophecies. Has that Fourth Fire come to pass where the light-skinned race brings new knowledge and technologies which can be joined with native knowledge to produce a mighty and healthy nation? We understand the warnings of our wise ones that a headlong rush into embracing western sciences and technologies will result in disaster for the earth and for the nations if the. In the past we did not have the option of choosing between vanguard technology and a rearguard community (Cook, 2001). Today we do have more choices to make. I leave the discussion to wiser ones to decide whether we are children of the Fourth or Seventh Fire, but I do observe that scientists of integrity are interested in learning our indigenous science views. Hope for the future lies in bringing the two elements together to create the kind of thinking we must develop if we are to solve the problems, which reductionist science and capitalism have created.

References

Aikenhead, G. S. (1997). Toward a First Nations cross-cultural science and technology curriculum. *Science Education*, *81*, 217-238.

Allee, V. (1997). *The knowledge evolution: Expanding organizational intelligence.* Boston: Butterworth-Heinemann.

Allee, V. (2003). *Knowledge complexity framework.* Retrieved September 18, 2004, from http://www.vernaallee.com/library%20articles/Knowledge%20Complexity%20Framework(c).htm

Battiste, M. (1998). Enabling the autumn seed: Toward a decolonized approach to aboriginal knowledge, language, and education. *Canadian Journal of Native Education, 22*(1), 16-27.

Battiste, M. (2000). *Reclaiming indigenous voice and vision.* Vancouver: University of British Columbia Press.

Berger, P., & Luckmann, T. (1967). *The social construction of reality.* New York: Anchor Books.

Cajete, G. (2000). Philosophy of native science. In *Native science: Natural laws of interdependence.* Santa Fe, NM: Clear Light Publishers.

Champagne, D. (1989). *American Indian societies: Strategies and conditions of political and cultural survival* (Cultural Survival Report No. 3). Cambridge, MA: Cultural Survival Inc.

Colorado, P. (1988). Bridging native and western science. *Convergence, 21*(2/3), 49-68.

Cook, R. (2001). *The challenges of globalization.* Retrieved November 5, 2004 from, http://www.trilateral.org/annmtgs/trialog/trlgtxts/t55/coo.htm

Dei, G. J. S., Hall, B. L., & Rosenberg, D. G. (2000). Introduction. In G. J. S. Dei, B.L. Hall, & D. G. Rosenberg (Eds.), *Indigenous knowledges in global context: Multiple readings of our world* (pp. 3-17). Toronto: University of Toronto Press.

Duran, P. (2003). Address to Native Science Symposia at the 2003 AAAS Annual Meeting. Retrieved January 18, 2005, from http://www.tapestryweb.org/aaas/participants.html

Fee, M. (1995). Who can write as other? In B. Ashcroft, G. Griffiths, & H. Tiffin (Eds.), *The post colonial studies reader* (pp. 242-245). New York & London: Routledge.

Freire, P. (2003). *Pedagogy of the oppressed* (30th anniversary edition). New York: Continuum International Publishing Group.

Giroux, H. (1997). *A pedagogy and the politics of hope: Theory, culture, and schooling* (Critical studies in educational theory). Boulder, CO: Westview Press.

Henderson, J. Y. (2000). Post colonial ghost dancing: Diagnosing European colonialism; & Ayukpachi: Empowering aboriginal thought. In M. Battiste (Ed.), *Reclaiming indigenous voice and vision* (pp. 57-76; 248-278). Vancouver: University of British Columbia Press.

Howard, J. (1952). *Strange empire: Louis Riel and the Metis people.* New York: William Morrow and Company.

HQNet (company profile). (2002). Retrieved September 12, 2004, from http://www.hqnet.on.ca/

Leclair, C. (2003). *Métis environmental knowledge: La tayr pi tout le moond.* Unpublished doctoral dissertation, Faculty of Environmental Studies, York University, Toronto.

Little Bear, L. (2000). Jagged worldviews colliding. In M. Battiste (Ed.), *Reclaiming indigenous voice and vision* (pp. 77-85). Vancouver: University of British Columbia Press.

National Aboriginal Health Organization (NAHO). (2001). *Establishing a leading knowledge-based organization.* Retrieved March, 2004, from http://www.naho.ca/english/pdf/about_knowlege_based_organization.pdf

Palloff, R. M., & Pratt, K. (1999). *Building learning communities in cyberspace: Effective strategies for the online classroom.* San Francisco: Jossey-Bass.

Rothman, S., & Mosmann, C. (1972). *Computers and society* (2nd ed.). Science Research Associates Inc.

Simonelli, R. (2003, Summer). Spirit and reason reunite at the AAAS. *Winds of Change, 18*(3), 36-40.

Sixdion Inc. (1997). *The strategically positioned first nation.* Report for Indian and Northern Affairs and the Indian Taxation Advisory Board.

U.S. Senate Permanent Subcommittee on Investigations. (1996). *Security in cyberspace: Staff statement* (Hearings June 5). Retrieved November 3, 2005, from http://www.fas.org/irp/congress/1996_hr/s9606052.htm

Warmoth, A. (2000). Social constructionist epistemology. Retrieved September 13, 2003, from http://www.skaggs-island.org/commdev/epistemology.html

Chapter II

Indigenous Peoples and the Cultural Construction of Information and Communication Technology (ICT) in Latin America

Juan Francisco Salazar, University of Western Sydney, Australia

Abstract

Indigenous media have become an intensely debated subject in discussions of cultural diversity and access to information and communication technologies (ICTs). In many circles, the question of the equitable and affordable access to communication and information has begun to be conceptualized as integral to human rights and as an essential element in the foundation of a knowledge and/or information society. The purpose of the chapter is to analyse current approaches to indigenous ICT practices in Latin America by examining several case studies that explore, enliven and criticize the often ethnocentric discussions of the digital divide. The analysis is placed in the context of the rise of coordinated indigenous movements in Latin America, the wave of media privatisation in the region and the impact of IT policy and reform. It argues that, beyond consideration of the social impact of ICT on indigenous cultures, it is also relevant to consider the cultural construction of new technologies of information and communication in order to better understand the ways in which indigenous peoples adopt and make use of new digital technologies according to traditional knowledge and systems of law. The chapter concludes by supporting the need for self-identification of local practices and knowledge within the communities in order to design adequate strategies to gain benefit from the use of ICTs.

Introduction

Today, halfway through the first decade of the twenty first century, it is outstanding to see that a large number of indigenous organizations, collectives, groups, tribes and nations worldwide have been able to set up their presence on the World Wide Web. Moreover, several indigenous organizations actively use various information technologies for different purposes on an everyday basis, ranging from political advocacy to electronic commerce, film and television marketing or biodiversity research. Nevertheless, despite increasing access to information and communication technologies, indigenous peoples worldwide have made it clear that the promotion of the Internet by governments and non-governmental organizations alike may constitute yet another exercise in control and coercion. If digital division is cultural exclusion, digital inclusion has not necessarily meant cultural inclusion. In this regard, the dynamics of visibility/invisibility of indigenous peoples in the information society remain as complex an issue as ever before.

An important example of this is the inclusion of indigenous peoples in discussions on the information society, like the ones that took place as part of the World Summit on the Information Society (WSIS) in Geneva in 2003 where a Declaration of Indigenous Peoples and the Information Society and a Programme of Action were articulated. On that occasion it was made clear that indigenous peoples do not seek inclusion in the information society at the expense of their civil rights, cultural identities, ancestral territories or bio-resources. Moreover, it must be indigenous peoples themselves who decide on how and when they access and use new technologies.

Keeping these broad issues in mind, this chapter examines current literature and proposals on the topic, particularly those calling for new frames for action regarding the technological, cultural and policy use of ICTs by indigenous peoples in Latin America and the Caribbean. While we may celebrate the possibilities for developing new social literacy, political alliances and independent cultural production, at the same time we must understand that indigenous peoples are still faced and confronted with a paradox of media power and control, particularized by the fact that technology may be disruptive of traditional knowledge if exerted as an imposed gadget.

In the following pages it is argued that the indigenising of digital information and communication technologies is a clear example of what might be called the cultural construction of information technology. Culture is not only shaped by technology, but also determines its use and value. The increasing appropriation of ICTs by indigenous organizations and individuals in Latin America in the past decade can only be grounded in new processes of ethnic resurgence sweeping the region, and has to do with finding efficient ways for intra-communal communication and ways to communicate and inform the broader societies within which indigenous nations live. More importantly for the Latin American case, ICTs have been constructed as useful technologies for the formation of a new "pan-indigenous discourse" (Bengoa, 2000, p.138) and also an incipient pan-American indigenous public sphere. What is striking in the international indigenous movement in recent years is that the indigenous demands of today have moved from mere complaint to compound proposals. In other words, they have stepped forward from complaint and objection to the proposal for a world of decentralised but coordinated autonomies (Lara, 1999). For this reason, to consider the impact of ICT on indigenous peoples is certainly a critical issue, yet we should not overlook the impact of culture on technology and the implications of the indigenising of IT. Therefore, I propose to consider indigenous media as a socio-technical system of relations where technology becomes a cultural construction appropriated according to relevant cultural codes and social relations.

In the following pages I have summarized some of the critical issues in Latin America today in relation to indigenous peoples and the information society. In examining a range of literature on the topic, I refer to broader questions of, first, how indigenous peoples feel incorporated into the information society, and second, up to what point ICTs offer fresh possibilities for empowerment to indigenous peoples. Both have direct relation to more complex concerns of ethnic citizenship and political autonomy.

Indigenous Peoples, ICT, and Research

Much of the emphasis of the existing literature that explores indigenous peoples and information technology has dealt with the negative or positive impacts of ICTs on indigenous peoples. Little work has been done to understand the cultural constructions of technology or what the "cultural impact" of indigenous knowledge on IT may be in the near future. Recent literature examining indigenous peoples and ICTs in Latin America and the Caribbean has been important in defining those aspects of the "information paradigm" that have helped promote indigenous marginalisation in regard to what some called the "digital revolution" (Hernandez & Calcagno, 2003; Monasterios, 2003; Forte, 2002; Delgado, 2003; Becker & Delgado, 1998; Pilco, 2000; Salazar, 2002). The expansion of digital capitalism has often resulted in the commodification of indigenous identities, which are pushed to overcome issues such as lack of electricity in remote areas, geographical isolation, lack of technical know-how, absence of regulatory legal frameworks or low degree of connectivity in some areas.

The question of digitalisation of knowledge is particularly critical as new digital information and communication technologies offer alternative possibilities — from cultural recuperation, revival and political mobilisation, to questions of cultural autonomy and indigenous rights to artistic and intellectual property. In many cases, information technology has proven to be a useful tool beyond a symbolic field of struggle to become, in certain cases, an option for the construction of alternative spheres of public debate, or what Fraser (1993) has called "counter public spheres" in reference to the limitations of the original concept of public sphere put forward by Jurgen Habermas. The latter may not be appropriate to understand the way "ethnic citizenship" has been absent in most constructions of the public sphere in modern states.

The first academic references to indigenous peoples and the Internet in Latin America began coming out in the late 1990s, mostly analysing the impact of the Zapatistas use of the medium after the uprising of 1994 as part of their political and cultural program against the expansionism of the Mexican State (Froehling, 1997; Knudson, 1998; Cleaver, 1998; Becker & Delgado, 1998; Barnhardt-Park, 2000; Villarreal & Gil, 2001). These were primarily academic examinations of a new phenomenon, written in English and targeting mainly a small section of politically aware English-speaking academics.

Since then, several other documents have been published in several languages including indigenous languages. One of the first was written by Sami Pilco, an indigenous woman from Ecuador as part of a postgraduate degree at the University of Bergen, Norway. This document written in 2000 may be regarded as one of the first critical analyses from an indigenous perspective of the challenges of IT to indigenous peoples in Latin America. What is interesting in

Pilco's early analysis is her critical problematization of the "democratic" nature of the Internet, the logic of IT towards consumerism and profit and the challenges that ICTs pose to indigenous peoples. This work is definitely the first attempt to systematize different experiences of indigenous appropriation of the Internet in Latin America and critically analyses the politics of representation (and self-representation) of indigenous peoples in cyberspace. The study concluded that with notable exceptions, most Internet sites with indigenous content were produced by international NGOs as a way of promoting indigenous development and as part of technology transfer programs of European cooperation agencies, but only a few were produced by indigenous peoples themselves. This has changed in recent years as several indigenous organizations have become autonomous in their use of the Internet.

More recently, in what is perhaps the most comprehensive analysis of indigenous peoples' access to IT in Latin America, Hernandez and Calcagno (2003) have written a significant case outlining the opportunities, challenges and possible paths for indigenous peoples' involvement in the information society. The document, elaborated by the United Nations Economic Commission for Latin America and the Caribbean (ECLAC) and the Institute for Connectivity in the Americas (ICA), is a serious and respectful attempt to develop a typology of indigenous Internet sites in Latin America, and a summary of the modes that indigenous communications may take within a Latin American "information society."

In their study, Hernandez and Calcagno (2003) distinguish Web sites by the ethnic origin of their creators, by the level of representation of the institutions, by the geographical location of the creators, by the origin of the funding agent, by the language used on the Web site and by the main interests or subject matter of the Web site. In the first instance, the authors include two variants. First, those Web sites developed by non-indigenous peoples, generally intellectuals, foundations, academic institutions, governmental organizations, social science professional associations and NGOs. These have an emphasis on disseminating historical, social, political, linguistic, ecological, ethnic and technical information; legislation; and denouncements against actions that threaten territories, organizations and people, as well as human and cultural rights. Second, there are Web sites produced by indigenous peoples, as in the case of those developed by local grassroots organizations, NGOs and associations that coordinate the activities of various regional, national and international ethnic organizations. The primary objective of these sites is "to use the Web to display the presence and points of view of the indigenous organizations about topics of interest for the communities: globalization, the economy, indigenous politics, relations with the national society and transnational businesses, cosmology, history, art, native language courses, dictionaries, grammars, etc." (Hernandez & Calcagno, 2003, p. 11).

More importantly, the document promotes a practical framework for action by way of a regional strategy for the reduction of the *information marginalization* of indigenous communities. This regional strategy is put into practice through specific programs for indigenous access to the new information and communication technologies, which in turn are based in the demands of the communities themselves. The study clearly acknowledges that the digital divide has become a new form of indigenous cultural exclusion. However, it moves beyond the critical study of the impacts of ICT to an attempt to incorporate the specific cultural variables of indigenous peoples' appropriation and use of IT.

First, in this regard, the study emphasizes the need for respecting community organizations, social and communal solidarities and indigenous law in the design of consensual policies and actions that correspond to concrete means of reduction of the social phenomenon of information exclusion.

Second, there is the assumption that the principle of self-determination — where a community or nation plays an active role in its own development and is capable of making its own decisions in matters of "national" interest — is intimately tied to the principle of self-management. Self-management of ICTs refers to the ability "to learn the concrete tasks that require the gradual incorporation of the population and the indigenous communities into the digitalization process" (Hernandez & Calcagno, 2003).

The Poetics of Information and Communication Technologies

In this section of the chapter I put forward some theoretical considerations before going on to look at several case studies of indigenous peoples' use of IT. I propose an examination of the "poetics" of information technology or, in other words, the process of media *making*. A poetics of ICT is therefore concerned with the way media comes into being and functions in a given community, group or culture through its practice, or poiesis. It is concerned with the way social practices of technology are grounded in cultural politics and social action, generally rooted in local social solidarities. This poiesis, or making of communication technologies, is both a process and product of cultural representation. Therefore, the term ICT should be understood more in a practical way, as a form of action, and not exclusively in a technical way, as the incorporation of material gadgets or tools into indigenous peoples' lives. By acknowledging that indigenous engagements with digital technologies of information and communication have their own logic, then the structuralization of indigenous information technology in Latin America can be contextualized in broader processes of cultural activism, including the new processes of ethnic resurgence originating primarily since 1992 onwards.

In attempting to decolonize research on indigenous peoples and information technology from the often ethnocentric assumptions of development and technology transfer, it must be assumed that the appropriation of a new technology is ultimately a process of negotiation between different constituencies and the creation of content is ultimately a social process. Thus, indigenous media production in general and the appropriation of new technology in particular shouldn't be seen as isolated phenomena, but as inserted in historical conditions and placed in intertextual and intercultural frames of reference, like the struggle of the Mapuche against the logging companies in Chile, the Zapatistas against the Mexican State or the Ashaninka in Peru as a way to defend their biodiversity rights against the onslaught of American transnational companies.

Indigenous Peoples and the Uses of ICT in Latin America

In 1998, only 0.8% of the population in Latin America had access to the Internet. In 2004, more than 55 million users — or 10% of the total population — had access, marking the single most important increase worldwide. Among these users, 50% are located in urban centres of Brazil, while the previous year Uruguay and Chile had the highest levels of internet penetration in the region, with 34% and 29% respectively. However, despite exponential growth, the average cost of Internet access in most Latin American and Caribbean countries is still much higher than the average connection in the U.S., Canada, Australia, Japan or western European countries. This growth may be partly explained by the strong wave of privatisation of the Latin American telecommunication markets during the early 1990s, leading to an explosion of new technologies, new services and an influx of new market players, including also the move by several states to become part of the "information revolution."

The wave of privatisations, deregulation and liberalization of the information and telecommunication sectors during the last two decades, together with a reorientation of foreign cooperation development funding towards programs dealing with new information and communication technologies and a more active role of public policy and state involvement, have paved the way for more innovative implementations of ICT initiatives in indigenous communities, ranging from literacy to political activism and e-commerce. Many initiatives have sprung from indigenous organizations themselves, who have been able to access IT through their own means. Lets us look, then, at some important examples of the favourable use of ICTs by indigenous organizations in Latin America.

ICT Access and Literacy

Information technology literacy has become a critical aspect of the incorporation of indigenous cultures into the information society, as shown by a variety of pilot programs in different countries in the region. One of the most notable cases in recent years has been the Telematic Network for Indigenous Populations begun in 2000 simultaneously in Bolivia, Peru, Ecuador and Colombia. The pilot project is funded by the United Nations and coordinated by INKARRI, a non-governmental organization and indigenous documentation centre with headquarters in the Basque country. Since its inception, the project has sought the systematization of mechanisms for the appropriation of telematic technology and computer science by indigenous organizations. The five-year plan (under review in 2005) has aimed at strengthening local capacities through promotion of a more democratic participation, the latter stimulated by shared access to ICTs through public or collective telecenters in rural and peripheral-urban areas. What seems really critical in this initiative is the emphasis on the self-identification of local practices that benefit through the use of the ICTs, which in turn has encouraged the appropriation and use of new digital, computer-based technologies within the communities.

Another similar initiative began around the same time (1999), the Internet Radio for Ashaninka Aboriginal Communities in Peru, which promotes computer literacy and community access through telecentres for over 60 Ashaninka communities in the Peruvian Sierra. The Ashaninka project — funded by IDRC, the Canadian International Development and Research Centre, through one of its PAN Americas initiatives — has been strongly motivated by new forms of self-management offered by the new technologies and the opportunities for the production of content; this in turn has fostered processes of appropriation and training of indigenous ICT users. Through the use of high frequency Internet radio, over 60 Ashaninka communities, located in a relatively extensive area of the Peruvian Andes, have been able to establish a network of intra-communal information that ranges from cultural revival to protection of native rights to natural resources and traditional medicine. In addition, e-commerce is promoted, whereby the communities are able to sell products — such as coffee — in big urban centres such like Lima. The project has also become an important way for the Ashaninka to fight for traditional knowledge of medicinal plants and the access to their ancestral environment resources, which have been seriously threatened by the activities of large foreign transnational companies.

ICT and E-Commerce

The issue of e-commerce is not unique to the Ashaninka communities of Peru. Otavalo communities in northern Ecuador have established important businesses in Europe, where they market weavings and other crafts. Another example is the pilot project Virtual Bolivian Market, financed by the International Telecommunication Union in 1999. This is an innovative project of indigenous e-commerce that aims to supply indigenous and peasant communities with e-commerce tools, such as an online purchasing portal that allows visitors to buy various products, including music, handicrafts and food.

The commercial use of IT in indigenous communities is still marginal and, despite these cases, the Internet is yet to become a technology for profit. Up until now, IT has been primarily an instrument of political advocacy and cultural activism, as it has allowed for wide ranging and fast circulation of information.

ICT and Political Advocacy

When looking at the shaping of ICT for political activism and advocacy, it is important to remark the ways in which ICTs have been constructed as fields of symbolic struggle all over the region (Bonilla, 2000). Some of the best known cases of indigenous organizations that have made effective use of ICT for political purposes are the Zapatistas in Chiapas, Mexico and the Confederation of Indigenous Nations of Ecuador (CONAIE). The CONAIE was formed in 1988 and is today one of the strongest indigenous organizations in the world. Computer networking played a pivotal role when the CONAIE was able to coordinate and organize mass mobilizations of indigenous peoples and peasants during the massive protests of 1997 and 2000, both of which led to the ousting of Ecuadorian presidents. Similar events have occurred in Bolivia with the rise of Aymara ethno-nationalism in recent years. In Panama, some Kuna communities have forged institutional partnerships with international environmental NGOs to work towards the preservation of their traditional resources and environment, and, in similar circumstances, indigenous groups in Colombia have made useful exercise of information technology to arrest the offensive of transnational oil companies and the onslaught of both the guerrilla and paramilitary forces. In Bolivia a new project by CIDOB, the Confederation of Indigenous Peoples of Eastern Bolivia, is creating an information system (database and Web site) to work on claims by Bolivian indigenous groups regarding their land rights. The information is collected through CIDOB's regional offices, and is used to inform the indigenous groups as to the state of their claims and to obtain information in relation to conflicts and negotiations regarding indigenous land.

In this regard, Bolivia is at the forefront of indigenous peoples' use of new technologies. The country has been one of the regional centres for indigenous media production in recent years, for example, hosting the regional office of CLACPI, the Latin American Indigenous Council of Film, Video and Communications. The Bolivian Plan of Indigenous Audiovisual Communications, designed in 1996 after a regional meeting of CLACPI in La Paz, constitutes a concrete outcome of a long process by which several indigenous and peasant organizations in Bolivia established a long-term scheme of audiovisual communication in conjunction with CEFREC, an independent Film Education Centre. Mainly working with video, but recently with new technologies as well, it is interesting to note how indigenous peoples in Bolivia have been able to begin inserting their cultural narratives into broader spheres, based on their ancestral forms of communication and representation. Through this scheme, a varied and thriving indigenous media practice has emerged, establishing the foundation for a series of exchange practices at the national level that allow for the continuation of traditional forms of oral and collective memory. As such, video has come to be conceptualised as a tool for empowerment and as a tactic to elaborate an ambitious strategy for cultural survival, promoting a more democratic and multicultural participation in the mass media.

In Chile, the Mapuche movement has also been active in the use of ICT for creating alternative public spheres of debate. Mapuche organizations and individuals, both in Chile and abroad, have constructed a remarkable digital network of Web sites and online communication. These organizations have vehemently embraced the Internet as a viable tactic for building a counter-hegemonic discourse that has started to impact the national public sphere. These instances stand out as notable cases of radical indigenous media practices which I argue can be seen as a strong yet incipient indigenous (Mapuche) public sphere. Today there are at least twenty-five distinctive Mapuche Web sites, some hosted in Chile, many others in countries like Sweden, the Netherlands, the United Kingdom, France, Germany, Belgium and Spain. Most of these sites have been used as vehicles of expression for processes of "rebellious communication" (Downing, 2001) as well as mobilisation originating at the community level (see also Salazar, 2003). To support the argument that one of the primordial uses of the Internet for the Mapuche has been to develop an oppositional public sphere, I will focus here only on those cases that I believe have played a key role. In general terms, the Mapuche Web sites have continued to bare witness to the legacies of the military dictatorship, even after fifteen years of democratic administration. Examples of this are the neo-liberal policies impacting negatively on indigenous peoples and the environment, or the infliction of the anti-terrorist law of 1979 — designed under the military dictatorship of General Augusto Pinochet to counter Marxist guerrillas — on Mapuche peasants and activists. The Mapuche Web sites have been crucial in showing images of police abuse, the action of paramilitary groups and the militarisation of rural communities in the south. They have raised fresh claims over the control, production and circulation of images and the ownership of media and communications outlets. In general, the Mapuche online network is a locus without a centre and without vertical control with the potential to host a "free and influential public space, a sphere of social action not separate but fully linked to and a protagonist in conflicts and antagonisms" (Carlini, 1996, in Bentivegna, 2002, p. 59).

The Future Ahead: Indigenous Communication Rights

The social impact of ICTs on indigenous populations has been a critical issue in recent years. The chapter has summarized some of the current issues, literature and contexts of use regarding indigenous peoples and ICTs in Latin America. It has been argued that to move beyond the "impact of technology on society" approach, we need to attend to the cultural constructions of technology and the way indigenous groups may use, appropriate, conceive and image technology differently than other populations. Questions of self-determination that have been so important within indigenous movements worldwide need also to apply to communication. Further research on the topic should focus more on examining ways of developing autonomous indigenous communications and self-management. As indigenous communities gain increasing access to ICT in coming years, researchers, advocates and policy makers will also need to put more attention to the design of appropriate regulatory frameworks to ensure indigenous communication rights and to open truly intercultural information spaces. This begins with the design and implementation of programs aimed at reducing computer illiteracy and at promoting favourable attitudes for the incorporation of the ICTs within communities and organizations based on principles of indigenous knowledge and law. The incorporation of indigenous languages within these new frameworks will be of critical importance in deploying a new configuration of indigenous communications.

Moreover, indigenous peoples around the world have a broad range of knowledge with high potential commercial value for national and transnational corporations. This has been demonstrated through a series of international studies and reports by non-governmental groups and indigenous organizations that have shown the critical importance of implementing intellectual property rights to such knowledge so that local and indigenous communities can have an instrument to fight against "piracy" by foreign companies and researchers. As has been shown in the case studies mentioned in this chapter, ICTs will have critical importance in promoting a more equitable distribution of profits from the commercialization of indigenous knowledge, whether it be of plants with medicinal properties, television programs or alternative farming practices.

References

Barnhart-Park, A. (2000, March). *alt.Indigenous.electronic-(re)sources.* Paper presented at the Annual Meeting of the Latin American Studies Association, Miami.

Becker, M., & Delgado, G. (1998). Latin America: The Internet and indigenous texts. *Cultural Survival Quarterly 21*(4). Retrieved May 11, 2006, from http://209.200.101.189/publications/csq/csq-article.cfm?id=1455

Bengoa, J. (2000). *La emergencia Indígena en América Latina. Santiago.* Chile: Fondo de Cultura Económica.

Bentivegna, S. (2002). Politics and new media. In L. Lievrouw & S. Livingstone (Eds.), *Handbook of new media: Social shaping and consequences of ICT* (pp. 50-60). London: Sage.

Bonilla Urvina, M. (2000). *Investigando las nuevas tecnologías de información y comunicación (NTIC) como campos de lucha simbólica en América Latina y el Caribe.* Quito, Ecuador: Facultad Latinoamericana de Ciencias Sociales (FLACSO).

Cleaver, H. M. Jr. (1998, Spring). The Zapatista effect: The Internet and the rise of an alternative political fabric. *Journal of International Affairs*, *51*(2), 621-640.

Delgado, G. (2003, March). Solidarity in cyberspace: Indigenous peoples online: Have new electronic technologies fulfilled the promise they once seemed to hold for indigenous peoples? The answers are yes, and no. In NACLA, *Report on the Americas*, *35*(5), 49-53.

Downing, J. D. H. (2001). *Radical media: Rebellious communication and social movements.* London: Sage.

Forte, M. (2002). "We are not extinct": The revival of Carib and Taino identities, the Internet, and the transfomation of offline Indigenes into online "N-digenes." In *Sincronia: An Electronic Journal of Cultural Studies.* Department of Letters, University of Guadalajara, Mexico.

Fraser, N. (1993). Rethinking the public sphere: A contribution to the critique of actually existing democracy. In B. Robbins (Ed.), *The phantom public sphere* (pp. 1-32). Minneapolis: University of Minnesota Press.

Froehling, O. (1987). The cyberspace "war of ink and Internet" in Chiapas, Mexico. *The Geographical Review*, *87*(2), 291-307.

Hernández, I., & Calcagno, S. (2003). *Indigenous peoples and the information society in Latin America and the Caribbean: A framework for action*. Santiago, Chile: CEPAL.

Knudson, J. W. (1998). Rebellion in Chiapas: Insurrection by Internet and public relations. *Media, Culture & Society*, *20*(3), 507-518.

Lara, S. (1999). YANAPANAKU: Propuesta de organización y construcción de la red global de solidaridad. Retrieved November 3, 2005, from http://funredes.org/mistica/castellano/ciberoteca

Monasterios, G. (2003). Usos de Internet por organizaciones Indígenas (OI) de Abya Yala: Para una alternativa en políticas comunicacionales. *Revista Comunicación*, *122*, 60-69.

Pilco, S. A. (2000). *La red de Internet y los Pueblos Indíigenas de América Latina: Experiencias y perspectives.* Institute for Media Studies, University of Bergen, Norway. Retrieved November 3, 2005, from http://www.nativeweb.org

Salazar, J. F. (2002). Activismo Indígena en América Latina: Estrategias para una construcción cultural de tecnologías de información y comunicación. In *Journal of Iberian and Latin American Studies*, *8*(2), 61-79. Melbourne, Australia: La Trobe University.

Salazar, J. F. (2003). Articulating an activist imaginary: Internet as counter public sphere in the Mapuche movement, 1997-2000. In *Media International Australia, incorporating Culture and Policy*, *107*, 19-30. Brisbane, Australia: Griffith University.

Villarreal, T. & Gil, G. (2001). Radical Internet use: Two case studies. In J. D. H. Downing (Ed.), *Radical media: Rebellious communication and social movements*. London: Sage.

Chapter III

Indigenous Knowledges and Worldview: Representations and the Internet

Judy Iseke-Barnes, University of Toronto, Canada

Deborah Danard, University of Toronto, Canada

Abstract

This chapter explores how representations of indigenous peoples on the Internet and other media are contextualized according to an outsider worldview, and that much of the information about indigenous peoples accessed through virtual media lack the original context in which to position the information. This means that the information is completely distanced from the indigenous peoples whom the information is purported to represent. This is problematic when representations of indigenous peoples are defined by dominant discourses which promote bias and reinforce stereotypes. With the increase of technology and the race to globalization, symbols are being reconstructed and redefined to connect and create a global identity for indigenous peoples. The consequences of this further the current practices of erasing and reconstructing indigenous history, language, culture and tradition through control and commodification of representations and symbols. This removal from history and community ensures continued silencing of indigenous voices. Although these misrepresentations continue to frame the discourse for indigenous peoples in Canada, it is time for indigenous peoples to reclaim and resist these representations and for outsiders to stop creating social narratives for indigenous peoples which support western hegemony.

Introduction

Indigenous representations based on an indigenous worldview have historically been under the control of indigenous peoples; for example, picture writings or pictographs, recorded histories on skins, birch bark, pottery and rocks reflecting oral histories. Story-telling, myths, legends, songs and ceremonies are the means of ensuring indigenous knowledges are passed from one generation to the next. Recorded histories of indigenous peoples are found throughout the world (Mallery, 1972). Today, contemporary indigenous artists continue to engage in representational practices not only to record current and historic events but to critique political realities and as forms of personal expression. Artists use many modern means of expression such as canvas, paper, sculpture, film, photography, radio, music, electronic media and the Internet. Other indigenous artists continue to use more traditional art forms (beading, leather work, porcupine quill work, etc.) as forms of healing and expression.

However, others, both indigenous and non-indigenous, use these potentially expressive forms to supply a trade market in more imitative practices. This result is in the loss of control of representation of distinct indigenous nations across North America and globally. These representational practices may impact public perceptions of what it means to "be Indian," and project images that have been broadly adopted to generalize misrepresentations of all indigenous peoples. Consequences of these representational practices, which are ongoing in Canada, include erasure or reconstruction of indigenous histories, languages, cultures and traditions. Canada has continued to use romanticized representations of "Indians" as commodities of entertainment (Iseke-Barnes, 2005) and to support the Canadian national identity of being connected to the land (Mackey, 2002). This has been primarily systemic and rooted in all levels of society (vertical and horizontal, internal and external as well as within and outside communities and nations), including the national government (Adams, 1999). In media and popular discourse, indigenous peoples have been represented by non-indigenous peoples as culturally inferior and unable to provide for themselves. These representations function to strengthen Canada's right to define who is and is not Canadian and to control what can and cannot be considered indigenous (Doxtator, 1988).

Representations of indigenous peoples and practices are being reconstructed and redefined to create a global identity through the increased use of technology and in the race to globalization. Systemic representational practices, such as those described above, may be accelerated and their destructive outcomes broadened through the Internet (Iseke-Barnes, 2002; Iseke-Barnes & Sakai, 2003; Iseke-Barnes, 2005).

This chapter provides examples of resistance to colonial discourses by indigenous peoples but cautions that there are risks, with the increasing commercialization of the Internet, that dominant discourses might prevail. Readers are challenged to consider how representational practices contribute to growing problems, and also how they might be transformed in order to contribute to solutions.

Commodification

When indigenous representations are taken out of their cultural context and interpreted through the dominant culture, interpretations will inevitably support the beliefs and biases in which the dominant culture communicates. This means that when one culture interprets another it generally obscures rather than clarifies meaning. "Native reality is grounded in the kaleidoscopic experience of being inscribed as subaltern in the history of others and as subject to one's own heritage. For Indians, these are placements built upon contradictory social imaginaries, representation of otherness prescribed by the missionary, the merchant, the military" (Valaskakis, 1993, p. 158).

This has led to the appropriation of indigenous symbols for the purpose of wealth accumulation, both historically within the tourist and commercial art markets and today through the Internet. Indigenous symbols and representations in this new world order become commodities. For example, dream catchers, which were specific to indigenous peoples in North America, are now produced in other countries by peoples who have no historical or cultural context to make this product (e.g., http://www.sacredart.com/dreamcatchers.html; http://www.native-languages.org/dreamcatchers.htm; http://www.dreamcatcher.com; http://allclassifieds.com.au; http://www.crystalinks.com/dreamcatcher.html; or just search for dream catchers for sale through a Web search engine to find hundreds of thousands of sites). This mass production and marketing via the Internet creates exploitation of cultural symbols and practices. The cultural significance of the dream catcher is erased. It simply becomes a commodity.

An earlier version of this process engaged indigenous women in making standardized products for sale in markets overseas — for example moccasins had to be produced in a standard design and structure so they could be mass marketed in the early 1900s. Today, however, there is no longer a desire or need for these indigenous women artists as these items are mass produced and marketed by companies who replicate indigenous designs through the labor of non-indigenous workers or, ironically, indigenous workers from another country. Marketing has extended to the Internet (e.g., http://www.minnetonkamoccasinshop.com; http://www.sofmoc.com; http://www.native-languages.org/moccasins.htm; http://shopping.yahoo.com; http://www.trademe.co.nz), and this further removes the goods from the women who created them for their own people.

Moreover, there is a trend amongst popular culture celebrities in the United States of America to wear mukluks — a type of leather boot originally made by indigenous peoples in Canada. These are also available on the Internet (http://www.focusonstyle.com/style-pack/mukluks.htm; http://www.harperlee.co.uk/ourproducts.html). Some of these Web sites describe mukluks as "made by Canadian Indians," with substantially increased prices when these "authenticity" claims are attached. These Web sites further exploit the productions and creativity of indigenous peoples in Canada.

This control of representations of indigenous cultures limits the expression and perception of indigenous symbols, designs and history and indigenous worldviews and knowledges. It creates a negative cycle where indigenous peoples may adapt their art to comply with tourist and commercial markets in order to receive "fair" market value, or indeed *any* market value for their products. However, this practice constitutes another control of indigenous representations of indigenous culture and limits expression. Significantly, indigenous peoples' worldviews become shaped by what the external society expects and demands of them. For indigenous survival, indigenous peoples must adapt, assimilate and accommodate. Furthermore, these controlled representations do not afford copyright to the indigenous peoples whose symbols and designs are incorporated into products such as moccasins and mukluks made in other countries and sold in tourist markets.

The use, misuse and abuse of indigenous representation are also created through trademarks. These trademarks are used to sell non-indigenous commodities, such as butter sold by Land O Lakes using the image of an "Indian maiden" (http://www.landolakes), Indian Motorcycles (http://www.indianmotorcycle.com) and high school, professional and college sports teams such as the Red Skins and Braves (http://www.aistm.org/1indexpage.htm). Trademark abuse instituted in the pre-Internet era has since been transferred to the Internet via Web sites promoting these products.

Medicines are now currently marketed through the use of indigenous actors in "traditional" attire suggesting natural products are associated with indigenous peoples, e.g., Lakota products sold at http://www.aworldofgoodhealth.com/american-indian-lakota-prostate.htm. These appropriated and grossly misrepresented images promote racial stereotypes and may disrupt valid perceptions of indigenous peoples and worldviews that are rooted in indigenous histories, cultures and languages.

Stuart Hall (1997) explains that meaning is produced through representational systems we refer to as languages. He explains that we use "signs to symbolize, stand for or reference objects, people and events" as well as "reference imaginary things and fantasy worlds or abstract ideas which are not in any obvious sense part of our material world" (Hall, p. 28). Hall further explains that within mainstream articulations of representational practices, "commodity racism" (Hall, p. 239) engages representations of the "other" in order to define and market a product based on a reduction of the "other cultural group" to a few essential characteristics which are fixed in meaning — a stereotype. The stereotypes produced are then associated with a product. Dominant culture retains the right and holds the power to define, classify and reduce cultural groups to stereotypes and to use these reductions to market and sell products. Stereotypes are often based on "binary oppositions" which polarize "extreme opposites" producing "absolute difference between human "types" or species" (Hall, p. 243). For example, indigenous peoples may be perceived as "nature" to dominant society's "culture/civilization." These practices split what is acceptable from what is unacceptable and externalize what is unacceptable. Differences between varying groups are naturalized, which functions to fix difference and ensure that these differences are closed to change or reinterpretation (Hall, p. 245). This commodity racism and stereotyping of indigenous culture is evident in the Internet examples previously cited.

The Power to Control Representations

The desire to control representations of indigenous peoples lies in the need of the dominant society to maintain its power. Edward Said (1978) describes this process as it applies to the production and maintenance of ideas about Asia in his discussion of "Orientalism." Similarly, Gerald Vizenor (1972), a mixed-blood Ojibway scholar, describes the term Indian as an invention. One of Vizenor's acts of resistance to this invention and the dominant stereotype associated with it is his substitution of "indian" for Indian and his use of *oshki anishinabe*, which is an Ojibway expression meaning roughly "we the people of mother earth," and either refers specifically to the Ojibway people or to all indigenous peoples. He explains that:

The dominant society has created a homogenized history of tribal people for a television culture. Being an indian is a heavy burden to the oshki anishinabe *because white people know more about the* indian *they invented than anyone. The experts and cultural hobbyists never miss a chance to authenticate the scraps of romantic history dropped by white travelers through* indian country *centuries ago. White people are forever projecting their dreams of a perfect life through the invention of the indian — and then they expect an* oshki anishinabe *to not only fulfill an invention but to authenticate third-hand information about the tribal past.* (Vizenor, 1972, pp. 15-16)

Stereotypes of indigenous peoples, which have been promoted around the world, are maintained to support the beliefs and biases of western society and exercise control. Galleries and museums that have "acquired" (stolen) indigenous objects maintain the power to interpret them. For example, ceremonial objects, such as a bison hide pictograph robe, are displayed and interpreted on the Web site of the Glenbow Museum in Calgary, Alberta, Canada (http://pages.prodigy.net/jzeller/storyrobe/srobe.htm#robe). The museum says it is "of the Plains First Nations" (something like describing the words of a great French scholar as European), rather than naming the national affiliation of the stories and people recorded in this document.

The Story Robe uses pictograph images like written words to record specific times and community events, no less so than the written words of English-speaking nations. Story Robes are historical recordings of patterns of social relationships to the land and between people. Wars, deaths, negotiations and treaties were documented. The indigenous historians recorded hunting success, weather patterns, droughts and interrelationships. Indigenous leadership used this information to make community and indigenous nation decisions.

As visitors to the Web site, we can read about these Story Robes, but we cannot enter the community of origin. We cannot know the ways that this history continues to live in the lives of the present generations and those of the future. The historical knowledge is portrayed as belonging *only* to the past (the vanishing Indian) rather than belonging to the present and future survival of indigenous peoples. To avoid this, it is important on museum Web sites to "integrate what native people write about their past … [W]hat native people currently believe about their history may provide valuable insights into the significance of that history" (Trigger, 1988, p. 35). It is important that indigenous peoples are not denied their traditional roles of taking care of these items and being responsible for protecting and transmitting the history and the stories for the next generation "and for seven generations into the future." On this Web site there is no evidence of this occurring.

Distance

What happens when the need to control and exploit indigenous peoples is translated into cyberspace and information technology? Loretta Todd, a Cree filmmaker and theorist, explains that:

> *Western culture seems to want everything, to go everywhere. Wants that seem endless ... The desire to know, seek new experience, take new journeys, create light, has somehow grown from a flame to a forest fire that burns everything in its way ... Of course, in a world with a legacy of colonialism, the hunger of Western culture is threatening and frightening. We have had to feed that hunger, with the furs of animals and flesh of fish and the gold and silver of our lands and ourselves as fearsome mysteries in the West's drama of itself.* (Todd, 1996, p. 184)

There appear to be no boundaries to the need of the West to conquer and control.

Cyberspace and information technology are limitless in their potential as the modes of transmission for the dominant society to continue colonization practices. Information accessed through the Internet has no context in which to position it and is distanced from the indigenous peoples that it purports to represent. Linda Smith (1999), a Maori indigenous scholar, describes distance as an ongoing part of colonization. She explains that it is "one of the concepts through which Western ideas about the individual and community, about time and space, knowledge and research, imperialism and colonialism can be drawn together" (p. 55). She explains that through colonization, "the individual can be distanced, or separated, from the physical environment, the community. Through the controls over time and space the individual can also operate at a distance from the universe" (p. 55). In this way the individual is separated from his/her self, family, community, nation, land and universe. They are further separated from their history, culture, language and traditions. This complete separation of the self—physically, mentally, emotionally and spiritually—is the true nature of the colonial process.

The fragmentation of indigenous peoples' worldview and existence continues in cyberspace at a distance from those who are being represented. This distance encourages alienation and separation, rather than unifying and connecting people together. "The alienated psyche of western man and woman cannot find relief in cyberspace and virtual reality. You can go anywhere, be anyone — but you are still alone" (Todd, 1996, p. 193). Indigenous peoples have always seen themselves as connected to all of life and all of our relations. In contrast, rather than recognizing our natural connection to all life, cyberspace fabricates connections, further alienating our connection to the universe. The artificial structure of cyberspace reflects western thought, which is fragmented and disconnected, yet strives for dominance over humanity to find meaning. "A fear of the body, aversion of nature, a desire for salvation and transcendence of the earthly plane has created a need for cyberspace" (Todd, 1996, p. 182). "The Web" embodies this alienation of western thought.

Fragmenting and distancing colonial thought from colonial practices ensured that "crimes" committed against humanity were justified as necessary for colonization and, ultimately, civilization to prevail. Smith explains that "both imperial and colonial rule were systems of rule which stretched from the centre outwards to places which were far and distant. Distance again separated the person in power from the subjects they governed. It was all so impersonal, rational and extremely effective" (pp. 55-56). In such a process, distance also implies separation of those in control and who have power from those without the means to control their own realities. The Internet, in encouraging distance, also encourages power and separation of those who are represented from the very representations which "write" them/us. Globalization is the ultimate expression of this colonial process. The Internet is powerful and instrumental in carrying this out.

Information represented on the Internet is distanced from its context. Perhaps this lack of context makes it appear neutral. This supposed neutrality may make the information seem more acceptable. But for indigenous peoples, who are represented and defined by non-indigenous peoples on the Internet, the information is not neutral or acceptable when it is filtered through perspectives which promote bias and reinforce stereotypes.

Conclusion

Representational practices generated in mainstream discourse produce destructive outcomes for indigenous peoples. These practices — associated with colonization — continue through the Internet today, furthering the destructive process (Iseke-Barnes, 2002; Iseke-Barnes & Sakai, 2003; Iseke-Barnes, 2005). Commercialization and its associated commodification and stereotyping continue to assail indigenous peoples. Dominant society continues to use the

Internet to exert its control over images of indigenous peoples, art, production and creativity.

Colonization, and its ongoing practice in society and through information technology, produces distance — between the individual and their environment, between those doing the representing (mainstream) and those being represented (indigenous people), between indigenous peoples and their communities, between indigenous peoples and their knowledge and art, and between indigenous peoples and their sense of self — in all aspects including physical, emotional, mental and spiritual. The outcome is that the history, culture, identity and tradition of indigenous peoples are being eroded, erased and reconstructed. The genuine loss of indigenous knowledge and diversity of thought is shifting the world towards a singular hegemonic structure, and towards globalization of thought, control and a singular world order. The value of life is being replaced by the value of commodities and resource accumulation for the dominant society.

How will indigenous peoples ever restore their rightful place in a world they are custodians of if this symbolic violence and colonial power is not challenged? How will we ensure that the race for globalization does not mean erasure and rewriting of indigenous peoples' knowledge and worldviews? According to Valaskakis (1993):

We stand apart, living together in an increasingly hostile and distrustful social reality in which land, sovereignty and self-determination are ever more urgent in the lived experience of native people. We stand opposed, unaware that we are all rooted to each other in the construction and the appropriation of the contradictory Indian social imaginaries which make native sovereignty and self-determination so important to understand and so difficult to achieve. (p. 167)

Shannon Thunderbird, a member of the Coast Tsimshian First Nation and a significant indigenous artist and educator in Canada, explains on her Web site that:

Once great and vibrant indigenous cultures are now being embraced through a rebirth of ancient art and music. ... This is what pride in indigenous culture is all about, beautiful art works, music and dance produced in a sacred and respectful manner that celebrates the vibrancy and texture of an ancient civilization that still resonates today in the care and trust of those who have followed in the footsteps of their ancestors and learned the old ways in order to produce works that speak to a contemporary world. (All My Relations, www.shannonthunderbird.com/indigenous_art.htm)

Thunderbird, like many other indigenous artists, uses her Web site for anti-colonial education and to promote indigenous art used for its true intention. She challenges the role of museums in relegating indigenous art into seclusion and creating "artifacts" from indigenous productive activities, noting that "many tribal groups were looted of their precious items by over-zealous collectors." In addition, she advocates for the recognition and acknowledgement of native art as "fine art and not just craft or artefact," and notes that newer exhibits in regional and national museums are starting to change the way indigenous peoples are represented. Further, Thunderbird's discussion brings to light the questions: How will we be remembered? By whom? Or is it worse not to be remembered? And, who will control how we are remembered?

It is not the sole responsibility of indigenous peoples to continually inform western society of their colonial narratives. It must become the responsibility of western society to (1) transform themselves; (2) begin to decolonize their own structures and systems; (3) look closely at themselves; and (4) find other ways to construct their identities rather than through attempts to control and define indigenous peoples.

Indigenous peoples have always seen themselves as connected to all of life, engaging the past, present and future simultaneously. Is information technology a competent resource to ensure our natural connection to life, a life to be experienced, shared and recorded by indigenous people; bringing knowledge from the past, building on the present and creating a solid foundation for the seven generations into the future?

Through the creativity of indigenous peoples, new ways of using information technology can and will be generated which result in the support of our identities and communities. Perhaps there are examples of this creativity and these positive outcomes in the remainder of this volume.

References

Adams, H. (1999). *Tortured people: The politics of colonization*. Penticton, BC: Theytus.

Doxtator, D. (1988). *Fluffs and feathers: An exhibit of the symbols of Indianness: A resource guide*. Brantford, ON: Woodland Cultural Centre.

Hall, S. (1997). *Representation: Cultural representations and signifying practices*. London: Sage Books.

Iseke-Barnes, J. (2002). Aboriginal and indigenous peoples' resistance, the Internet, and education. *Race, Ethnicity, and Education*, *5*(2), 171-198.

Iseke-Barnes, J. (2005). Misrepresentations of indigenous history and science: Public broadcasting, the Internet, and education. *Discourse: Studies in the Cultural Politics of Education*, *26*(2), 149-165.

Iseke-Barnes, J., & Sakai, C. (2003). Indigenous knowledges, representations of indigenous peoples on the Internet, and pedagogies in a case study in education: Questioning using the Web to teach about indigenous peoples. *Journal of Educational Thought*, *37*(2), 197-232.

Mackey, E. (2002). *The house of difference: The cultural politics and national identity in Canada*. Toronto: University of Toronto.

Mallery, G. (1972). *Picture-writing of the American Indians* (2 vols). Canada: General Publishing.

Said, E. (1978). *Orientalism*. New York: Random House.

Smith, L. T. (1999). *Decolonizing methodologies: Research and indigenous peoples*. London: Zed Books.

Todd, L. (1996). Aboriginal narratives in cyberspace. In M. A. Moser & D. Macleod (Eds.), *Immersed in technology: Art and virtual environments* (pp. 179-194). Cambridge, MA: MIT Press.

Trigger, B. (1988). The historian's Indian: Native Americans in Canadian historical writing from Charlevoix to the present. In R. Fisher & K. Coates (Eds.), *Out of the background: Readings on Canadian native history*. Toronto: Copp Clark Pittman.

Valaskakis, G. G. (1993). Postcards of my past: The Indian as artefact. In V. Blundell, J. Shepherd, & I. Taylor (Eds.), *Relocating cultural studies: Developments in theory and research* (pp. 155-170). London: Routledge.

Vizenor, G. (1972). *The everlasting sky: New voices from the people named the Chippewa*. New York: Crowell-Collier Press.

Chapter IV

Kaitiakitanga and Health Informatics: Introducing Useful Indigenous Concepts of Governance in the Health Sector

Robyn Kamira, Paua Interface Ltd. &
Rangatiratanga Canvases Ltd., New Zealand

Abstract

Indigenous contributions to governance in health informatics can be drawn from cultural concepts such as Kaitiakitanga, which implies guardianship, stewardship, governance and responsibility roles. This chapter explores Kaitiakitanga, its potential implementation in the Aotearoa (New Zealand) health sector, and its contributions to our thinking. After decades of unsuccessful attempts to positively shift the status of health for Maori, we must ask whether more control by Maori over information about Maori will make a difference. Kaitiakitanga enables us to explore Maori perspectives and insights about health and information and calls for stronger inclusion of Maori in decisions. It acts as a guideline to address ongoing and complex issues such as collective ownership, the responsible publication of data and whether benefits in health for Maori can be explicitly declared and met.

Introduction

This chapter discusses the potential of indigenous concepts of governance within a contemporary health informatics setting. Health informatics is an evolving socio-technical and scientific discipline. It deals with the collection, storage, retrieval, communication and optimal use of health data, information and knowledge (hereafter referred to simply as "information").[1] The discipline attempts to assure quality healthcare for the community it serves.

Governance can be situated alongside health informatics, especially when considering the ethics, values and quality issues that impact on the care of people. Central to governance is decision-making and the process through which a group with delegated decision-making authority will direct their collective efforts. Governance involves multiple stakeholders to whom decision-makers are accountable: Governance in New Zealand's (Aotearoa's) health sector deals with relationships between the Crown (Ministries, Government agencies, delegated authorities, etc.), communities, Maori and individuals. Governance also applies to guardianship over information in the best interests of stakeholders, and involves achieving both "desired results and achieving them in the right way" (IOG). Since the *right way* is largely shaped by the cultural norms and values of the stakeholders, there can be no universal template for good governance. Information technology is significantly redefining governance by providing enhanced opportunities to collaborate with and influence policy makers. Similarly, information technology changes accountabilities by opening new possibilities for the dissemination of information about the performance of government, district health boards and providers.

Indigenous contributions to governance in health informatics can be drawn from cultural concepts such as Kaitiakitanga, which implies guardianship, stewardship, governance and responsibility roles. This chapter explores Kaitiakitanga, its potential implementation in the Aotearoa health sector and its contributions to our thinking. After decades of unsuccessful attempts to positively shift the status of health for Maori, the indigenous peoples of Aotearoa, we must ask whether more control by Maori over information about Maori will make a difference. Kaitiakitanga can introduce a stronger position on ethics, values and quality when managing health data and optimize the benefits for both Maori and non-Maori alike.

Further, the inclusion of Kaitiakitanga concepts in governance structures, processes and roles in New Zealand's health sector in recent years points to a growing acceptance of indigenous input. For example, the establishment of the Cervical Screening's Kaitiaki Group as a legislated body (MOH, 2002a), and the Northern Region Hepatitis Consortium's Treaty Relationship Company model (C. Bullen, personal communication, 2003) are examples where indigenous ideas are perceived by their supporters to add value to governance.

The chapter specifically addresses collective ownership, collective privacy, responsible publishing and benefit. Kaitiakitanga implies that Maori will participate in *decisions* about health informatics and information technology, and influence policies and laws that support concepts of traditional protection, ownership and benefit that go beyond current laws and policies.

A Maori Perspective on Information Technology

Definitions of information technology need not be limited to those found in academic or information technology industry journals. Potentially, any means of storing, analyzing and disseminating information can be included — *even our minds* (Kamira, 2002, p. 4). Maori concepts such as *Matauranga*, or intelligence, and *hinengaro*, or the mind, offer broader definitions and enhance what is generally understood about information technology. Matauranga refers to education and intuitive intelligence, and is linked to the divine. Hinengaro is the mind, the thinking, knowing, perceiving, remembering, recognizing, feeling, abstracting, generalizing, sensing, responding and reacting (Pere, 1991, p. 32). They are both vessels for knowledge.

Indeed, the broader Maori perspectives, such as those above, inform us why concepts of information technology as the information technology *industry* sees it are not only within the reach of Maori, but are also too simplistic since they do not include wider concepts of knowledge and understanding (Kamira, 2002, p. 5). It also explains why information technology is of great importance to Maori since the ancestor Tane-nui-a-rangi retrieved the *baskets of knowledge* from a celestial abode while coping with many dangers along the way (Barlow, 1991, p. 156), and that the dissemination of knowledge is thus a matter of great ritual and responsibility.

Colonization, Tiriti (Treaty of Watangi) and Relevance for Health Informatics

It was the Maori version of the Treaty of Waitangi, "Te Tiriti O Waitangi," that was signed by chiefs at Waitangi on February 6, 1840 and subsequently in other locations. It is New Zealand's founding document. While debate is ongoing regarding its status and implementation, the legal status of the Treaty is not enforceable as there is an absence of statutory incorporation (TPK, 2001b, p. 16).[2] Therefore, governance models that are based on the Treaty are dependent on the application of moral obligations of the Crown and the recognition of principles.

The Hunn report (1961) first highlighted the failings of the Crown to meet its Treaty obligations to Maori. The government has attempted unsuccessfully since then to rectify the situation by focusing on socio-economic improvements for Maori. Yet, Maori continue to feature disproportionately in almost all of the negative statistics including unemployment, education, health, housing, domestic abuse and crime (Hunn, 1961; Williamson, 2001, p. 1; TPK, 2003). Particularly, the poor state of Maori health is well documented (MOH, 2002b, p. 2) and has sustained its negative status over many decades. Colonization clearly undermined the economic and social base of Maori society and resulted in mass dislocation and loss of land, language and spirituality: This has led to urgent calls for reclamation and protection of Maori "assets," including land, natural resources, language, belief systems, processes, etc. Active reclamation and protection of those assets are facilitated by movements such as Te Kohanga Reo (language nests), the Waitangi Tribunal and Maori authorities, etc. This call also applies to health and wider concepts of well being. As a result, Maori health provider groups aspire to become key providers for Maori and often coin the phrase "by Maori, for Maori" in the belief that other health services are not focused or responsive to the needs of Maori (Kamira, 1999-2000, p. 2).

Health informatics captures the need for technological capacity amongst all health providers, but access to that capacity for Maori providers is yet to be addressed fully. Anecdotal evidence suggests that the skills and equipment required for Maori providers to fully participate in health informatics is lacking (Kamira, 1999-2000, p. 14). Recent reports indicate that Maori are not participating in information technologies to the extent of other New Zealanders (TPK, 2001a; Infometrics, 2001).

However, there is some evidence that Maori are beginning to enter the information technology industry (Infometrics, 2001, TPK, 2001a), and that they are forming professional and interest groups.[3] These shifts towards "mastery" of information technology will eventually enable Maori to make well-informed decisions in health informatics. However, while it is an aspiration to build capacity in information technology in the broadest sense (Korowai Groups, 2002), this is some time away.

This leads us to the following questions:

1. Does the health sector enable Maori to make decisions about their health, or does it prefer to "look after" Maori?
2. What technological capacity would need to be available to Maori providers to assist aspirations to provide effective health care to Maori?
3. In the absence of technological capacity, what ways can Maori influence decisions about technology and health for their benefit?

What is Kaitiakitanga?

Data—anonymous or not—has enormous spiritual and cultural significance for Maori, so it may require more attention and protection than generally given (MOH, 2001, p. 3). One way to provide this is to exercise the customary practices of Kaitiakitanga.

Kaitiakitanga (and the person or group who performs the Kaitiakitanga role – Kaitiaki), implies guardianship, protection, care and vigilance of data about Maori that is collected, stored and accessed. It introduces the idea of an inter-generational responsibility and obligation to protect, and enables the use of mechanisms such as *tapu*, the setting apart or restriction of knowledge or things, and *rahui*, the necessity to conserve, protect or restrict (Kamira, 2002, p. 22).

As governance decisions impact Maori and since the "right way" to govern is largely shaped by cultural norms and values of stakeholders, it is critical to extend current governance ideas if Maori are to successfully implement their Kaitiakitanga responsibilities. However, indigenous governance issues are complicated. For example (adapted from IOG):

1. What form(s) of indigenous governance are appropriate to the 21st century and suitable to the needs of indigenous peoples?
2. What is the appropriate balance between contemporary and traditional forms of governance for indigenous peoples?
3. What are appropriate strategies for creating indigenous capacity to successfully manage their governance responsibilities today?

It is important that members of governance or kaitiaki groups have an understanding of the historical, cultural and social complexities in which Kaitiakitanga perspectives are grounded.

Kaitiakitanga and Health Informatics Issues

The advantages of obtaining statistical information about health for Maori are clearly to profile groups — that will assist in developing effective policies and assist Maori to better manage their own health (MOH, 2002b, p. 23). However, decades of negative statistics indicate that gathering this information does not measurably achieve health gains for Maori.

1. Is data and information being gathered without producing *knowledge* that will generate benefits?
2. How would concepts of Kaitiakitanga in health informatics make any positive difference?

The following sub-headings provide some insights.

Data and Statistics

The publication of negative statistics over many decades undermines Maori and their health and produces few benefits. Negative statistics invoke the concept of *Takahia*, the act of trampling, often used to describe being belittled. Government databases collect abundant data about Maori: The data is analyzed and published, and Maori are profiled through statistical findings that continue to reinforce the most negative stereotypes. Currently, health informatics and statistics that are generated from databases symbolize disadvantage for Maori, who are busily curbing continuous socio-economic decline. The Maori experience of information technology that is in the control of others is the repeated reinforced perception of failure (Kamira, 2002, p. 22).

This is not to say that ethnicity data or data which identify particular Maori groups should not be collected. However, the accuracy through to the eventual publication of such data should be, ideally, constructive. Kaitiakitanga through the idea of *mana* — power or influence — can refocus the way that statistics are generated and published and demand a more productive and benefit-focused model.

Intellectual Property, Collective Ownership and Privacy

Kaitiakitanga introduces the idea of *tiaki*. Tiaki is to look after and guard and is a responsibility or an obligation rather than a right due to ownership. It enables a less exploitive relationship to exist where data about Maori are for the purpose of improvement and benefit first and foremost. Maori see the issues of intellectual property as a subset of these broader rights of ownership and include concepts of collective ownership. Collective ownership in health informatics can imply that grouped data about a collective such as a *hapu*, or an extended family tribal group, are owned by that collective. In turn, this implies their rights to make decisions about that data and benefit from that data.

In contrast, Western law defines intellectual property as outcomes of ideas or processes that are the result of human intervention — that is, knowledge created from the mind (Mead, 1997). Intellectual property laws both here and internationally tend to focus on commercial *ownership* and are inadequate as a way to protect indigenous collective knowledge. Until the fundamental ownership issues raised by Maori under the Treaty of Waitangi are mirrored in legislation, the best that can be achieved is interim recognition of Maori values and rights to participate in decision-making within the limits of the existing system (Putahi Associates, 1999).

Similarly, the Maori concept of privacy can encompass both the individual and the collective. An individual can have their privacy protected via the Privacy Act 1993. However, a *hapu*, or extended family tribal group, may feel they have a right to collective privacy that is not currently supported by legislation. Collective privacy is a means to protect data and information about groups of people rather than individuals, and is a key issue when data collection occurs on identifiable groups that wish to manage or control data about themselves.

First Beneficiaries

Kaitiakitanga introduces the idea of *awhina* — to assist or benefit. The ability to give what is truly needed without an expectation of reward means a clearer focus on more beneficial activities and responsible allocation of resources. The premise is that if Maori provide data then they should benefit from that data.

Some situations may prevent Maori from becoming the first beneficiaries. For example, limited participation by Maori providers in health informatics due to insufficient computer equipment or a lack of technological skills may be a barrier. Some Maori providers may need to rely on others to provide information, or they may only have access to information that has been collected for other purposes and does not focus on Maori, nor contain the detail required to initiate effective action (Kamira, 1999-2000, p. 14).

Mechanisms to promote Maori as first beneficiaries may include:

1. Protocols around grouped data with the input of Maori stakeholders that *require* benefits to be identified as criteria for collection and publication.
2. The development of initiative(s) when grouped data about Maori are identified to develop standards on the collection and use of data, and standards regarding real benefits that are more actively promoted and delivered.

The Strategy

Mastery

While there is little *evidence* that information technology has positive and long-term impacts on the socio-economic status of people, the perception throughout the world is that information technology is a key driver for improving the world's socio-economic conditions (Riley, 1999), and that to ignore it will perpetuate or lead to even further disparities amongst the world's poorest and richest nations (UN, 2002). Maori will not be in a position to find out whether this is a *truth* for them unless they move from a passive role to mastery (Kamira, 2002, p. 17).

Apirana Ngata, a scholar and the first Maori university graduate in 1894, wrote in his granddaughter's autograph book (Huta, 2001):

E tipu e rea mo nga ra o tou ao
To ringa ki nga rakau a te pakeha
Hei oranga mo to tinana
To ngakau ki nga taonga a o tipuna Maori
Hei tikitiki mo tou mahunga
To Wairua ki te Atua
Nana nei nga mea katoa

Grow up o tender youth in days of your life
Your hands grasp hold of the tools of the Pakeha
For your material well being

Your heart to the treasures of your Maori ancestors
As a plume for your head
Your spirit to God
The creator of all things

This well known passage captures the desire and the ability of Maori to acquire the knowledge of other cultures (of the Pakeha, or non-Maori) and is an important strategy for operating in a contemporary world, and for the uptake of information technology that would potentially improve health for Maori.

Using the Treaty / Tiriti Productively

The Ministry of Health's WAVE report (MOH, 2001, p. 3) states that the Treaty of Waitangi established a Crown obligation for Maori to enjoy a health status at least as good as that enjoyed by non-Maori. Further, it states that the government is committed to fulfilling its obligations to Maori to support self-determination for whanau (extended families) and Maori organizations. Kaitiakitanga can assist the Crown to achieve this obligation.

While Te Tiriti O Waitangi was signed and subsequently breached, attempts to bring it into a contemporary context have seen some progress. Concepts such as equity, partnership, collective ownership and protection (Treaty Articles II and III) can be expressed in relation to governance. Specifically, Maori are partners in the treaty and as such:

1. Article II guarantees Maori control and enjoyment of their valued possessions — tangible and intangible. This includes their health.
2. Article III affords Maori the attainment of equal human and social rights and privileges. The treaty implies that the *right* to good health can be exercised as per Article III regarding equity.

Validating and Promoting Maori Concepts

Health informatic projects are an opportunity to discover what gains can be made if Maori are actively involved in decisions through Kaitiakitanga. Aspirations of *tino rangatiratanga* — the ability to make decisions and control one's direction — are supported by Plumptre and Graham (1999), who conclude that three factors determine why some Native American tribes develop and some do not.

They are:

1. Having the power to make decisions about their own future;
2. Exercising that power through effective institutions; and
3. Choosing the appropriate economic policies and projects.

Identifying the possible contributions from Maori through Kaitiakitanga and then incorporating them into health informatics will help to promote, protect and validate the assets (knowledge and skills) that Maori have and, importantly, may change the current negative health status that has become the norm.

How Kaitiakitanga Would Work Today

Treaty as a Framework

The Treaty of Waitangi can be implemented in current day activities as a localized and living model for Maori to apply tino rangatiratanga (decision making and control). It can act as a framework by which the appropriateness of decisions made during the development and implementation of health informatics projects can be assessed against Articles II and III of the Treaty.

Recognizing Existing Structures

Existing Maori structures also perform governance and Kaitiakitanga roles through Runanga (Maori authorities, trusts or similar organizations). These are legitimate structures often established by mandate and should not be undermined, but instead utilized where appropriate for health informatics projects. Maori governance roles will usually extend to a holistic range of areas along a continuum of well-being that extends far beyond the narrow constructs of health and all of its sub-categories.

Kaitiaki Groups

Kaitiaki groups would have overview roles to look after data, information and knowledge sourced from, or about, Maori. These groups would set ethical, value and quality guidelines. Ideally, participation of a Kaitiaki group would begin at the initiation stage of an IT project through to implementation and post-implementation.

The following points regarding establishing such a group are useful:

1. The membership and appointment of Kaitiaki groups is significant and Maori stakeholders would determine the appropriate type of Maori representation.
2. The position of Kaitiaki groups as a part of, or aside from, broader governance groups is significant as accountabilities and relationships are determined.
3. Kaitiaki group members should have decision-making powers and be informed on all issues, not just perceived Maori ones. This ensures Maori are defining what is of interest and prevents inappropriate filtering of information.
4. The issue of accountability is linked to risk. Kaitiaki groups would take into account the different levels of risk, the shared-risk and the authority it would accept or have delegated to it.

Kaitiaki Members

Kaitiaki members would represent stakeholder groups that would in turn expect them to pursue aspects of tino rangatiratanga (decision making and control). Kaitiaki members would be responsible for, and would ensure a focus on:

1. The treaty;
2. Safety and protection of Maori individuals and collectives; and
3. Benefit to Maori individuals and collectives.

Conclusion

Health informatics will need to include concepts of governance and Kaitiakitanga alongside its medical, technology and social discourses. Modern concepts of Kaitiakitanga can enable:

1. Maori to be explicitly identified as first beneficiaries of health informatics where relevant;
2. Recognition of collective ownership, use, access, analysis and interpretation of data; and
3. Recognition of collective privacy as a valid form of control for grouped data. (Kamira, 2002, p. 23)

Kaitiakitanga contributes useful indigenous ideas that add value to governance and potentially may result in a health gain for Maori in the long term as they make decisions about information that will be expected to return benefits. Maori can, through Kaitiakitanga, actively and effectively influence policies and laws that support the protection and ownership of data and information towards improving health benefits.

References

Barlow, C. (1991). *Tikanga whakaaro: Key concepts in Maori culture.* Oxford, New York and Melbourne: Oxford University Press.

Bellinger, G., Castro, D., & Mills, A. (n.d.). Data, information, knowledge, and wisdom. Retrieved May 30, 2004, from http://www.outsights.com/systems/dikw/dikw.htm

Duffy, A. P., Barrett, D. K., & Duggan, M. A. (2001). *Report of the ministerial inquiry into the under-reporting of cervical smear abnormalities in the Gisborne region.* Retrieved September 14, 2005, from http://www.csi.org.nz/report/download.htm

Hunn, J. K. (1961). *Report on the Department of Maori Affairs.* Wellington, NZ: Government Printer.

Huta, J. (2001). A Maori perspective. *CTC Bulletin, 17*(2), April. Retrieved December 28, 2004, from http://www.daga.org/cca/ctc/ctc01-04/ctc0104h.htm

Infometrics. (2001). *The digital divide and Maori.* Retrieved December 28, 2004 from, www.nzmis.org.nz

IOG (Institute on Governance). (n.d.) Retrieved November 3, 2005, from http://www.iog.ca

Kamira, R. (1999-2000). (Combined Report). *The kidZnet project: Guiding cultural and ethical issues for Iwi*, 1999; *Report for Iwi cultural and ethical issues in kidZnet,* 2000. Retrieved December 28, 2004, from www.pauainterface.com

Kamira, R. (2002). *Te Mata o te Tai — The edge of the tide: Rising capacity in information technology of Maori in Aotearoa.* Paper presented at the *Fourth International Information Technology in Regional Areas Conference*, Rockhampton, Australia. Retrieved May 28, 2004, from www.pauainterface.com

Korowai Groups (The). (2002). *Maori information and communication technologies strategic plan.* Aotearoa.

Mead, A. T. P. (1997). Cultural and intellectual property rights of indigenous peoples of the Pacific. In *Cultural and intellectual property rights: Economic, politics & colonisation* (vol. 2, pp. 22-30).

MOH (Ministry of Health). (2001). *The WAVE project, from strategy to reality*, Wellington, NZ. Retrieved December, 28, 2004, from http://www.moh.govt.nz

MOH (Ministry of Health). (2002a). *Review of the health (cervical screening (Kaitiaki)) regulations 1995*, Retrieved March 25, 2004, from http://www.moh.govt.nz

MOH (Ministry of Health). (2002b). *He Korowai Oranga: Maori health strategy*. Wellington, NZ: Ministry of Health.

Orange, C. (1987). *The Treaty of Waitangi*, Wellington, NZ: Allen & Unwin.

Pere, R. T. (1991). *Te Wheke: A celebration of infinite wisdom*. Gisborne, NZ: Ao Ako Global Learning New Zealand Limited.

Plumptre, T., & Graham, J. (1999). *Governance and good governance: International and aboriginal perspectives*. Canada: Institute on Governance. Retrieved December 25, 2004, from http://www.iog.ca

Putahi Associates Ltd. (1999). *Maori and the patenting of life form inventions: An information paper produced by the patenting of life forms focus group for the Ministry of Commerce,* Wellington, NZ: Patenting of Life Forms Focus Group.

Riley, L. A., Nassersharif, B. N., & Mullen, J. (1999). *Assessment of technology infrastructure in native communities.* Washington, DC: Report for Economic Development Administration, U.S. Department of Commerce.

TPK (Te Puni Kokiri). (2001a). *Maori access to information technology*. Wellington, NZ.

TPK (Te Puni Kokiri). (2001b). *He Tirohanga o Kawa ki Te Tiriti O Waitangi: A Guide to the principles of the Treaty of Waitangi as expressed by the Courts and the Waitangi Tribunal*. Wellington, NZ.

TPK (Te Puni Kokiri). (2003). *Maori in New Zealand*. Wellington, NZ: Ministry of Maori Development. Retrieved December 28, 2004, from http://www.tpk.govt.nz/maori/default.asp

UN (United Nations). (2002). CSTD Panel on *Indicators of technology development*. Room XXVI, Palais des Nations, Geneva, Switzerland. Retrieved June 7, 2004 from, http://www.unctad.org/stdev/un/p1-02.html

Williamson, A. (2001). Emancipatory learning via the Internet: A model for reducing Maori socio-economic exclusion in Aotearoa/New Zealand. In W. Kim, T. W. Ling, Y. J. Lee, & S. S. Park (Eds.), *The human society and the Internet: Internet related socio-economic issues*. Berlin, Germany: Springer.

Endnotes

1 While there are a multitude of definitions for data, information and knowledge, this is a favourite of the author. Data are raw and have little significance beyond itself. Information is data that have been given meaning by way of relational connection; it provides answers to "who," "what," "where" and "when" questions. Knowledge is the appropriate collection of information, such that its intent is to be useful; it answers "how" questions (Bellinger, Castro, & Mills, n.d.).

2 A political analysis of the Treaty is not provided, as there are many appropriate and more in-depth sources of information available such as TPK (2001b) and Orange (1987).

3 E.g., Te Waka Wahine Wa-hangarau: Society for professional Maori women in information technology. Note, there are at least three Maori IT groups in the country.

Case Study I

ICTs for Intercultural Dialogue (ICT4ID)

Victor Giner Minana, UNESCO ICT4ID Programme, Spain

This case study will focus on UNESCO's cross-disciplinary programme spanning the sectors of communication and culture, "Information and Communication Technologies for Intercultural Dialogue: Developing Communication Capacities of Indigenous Peoples (ICT4ID)." It will show a general overview of the five ongoing pilot projects. This programme aims at preserving indigenous peoples' cultural resources by fostering access to ICT. These are the expected results:

- Indigenous community representatives trained in media content production and ICT use.
- Indigenous cultural content produced for television, radio and news media.
- Awareness raised at an international level of indigenous creativity.

- Advocacy made for the importance of cultural diversity and its expression through ICTs.
- Reinforcement of intercultural dialogue through the inclusion of indigenous peoples' cultural expressions in mainstream knowledge societies.

In order to achieve these objectives, the programme has begun to implement five pilot projects worldwide. These five projects can be divided into two groups: the first group of projects focusing on the audiovisual and the second group consisting of two projects related to multimedia.

Audiovisual Projects

The projects of the first group (audiovisual) are being implemented in Peru, Bolivia and Gabon. These projects have three phases: training, production and broadcasting. During the first phase, indigenous representatives are trained in audiovisual techniques. The training also includes classes in indigenous culture, focusing on topics such as history, artistic expression and narrative skill. In the second phase the participants film documentaries which allow them to express their view of the world through the audiovisual tool. Afterwards, during the third phase, this work is broadcasted nationally and internationally. This phase is very important because its objective is to show other social groups the tasks carried out by the indigenous populations and therefore, by doing so, achieving an intercultural dialogue.

These three projects have all concluded the first phase. A first survey has been carried out among the trainees who participated in the project in Peru. This project takes place in Villa El Salvador, a district in Lima inhabited by the Quechua population which began to migrate in the forties from the Sierra to the capital. The target group of the project is the second generation of Quechuas living in Villa El Salvador — children of the migrants who have grown up in an environment consisting of two cultures and two worlds.

The training has been highly appreciated by the 14 students who took part. They have emphasized the importance of the classes of Quechua culture (they had never studied it before) and the fact that the work that they will film in the second phase of the project will be seen abroad. Even if most of them had no prior experience in audiovisual techniques, they have easily learnt the basic audiovisual language. Nevertheless they are aware of the high price of the audiovisual equipment, which hinders them from feeling comfortable using it.

Multimedia Projects

In the second group (related to multimedia) there are two projects. The first one takes place in Namibia and its target population is the Himba people. The second one takes place in South Africa and its beneficiaries are the San people. There is a close collaboration between both project managers.

The "Kaoko Local Knowledge Living Archive project" (Namibia) aims to revive the oral history of the Himbas through several activities. They are:

- The production of the documentary "Katjira's Dream: Memory, Land and Ancestors in the Land of Kaoko" by Doxa Productions.
- Setting up of an ICT centre in Kaoko, which will also be a base station for the mapping and recording of the oral history of the Kaoko people. Along with this, the centre and its ICT facilities will provide information in areas such as education, political representation, HIV, cattle diseases and tourism. Cornelius Tijuma, a Himba who has worked with Doxa Productions in the last few years, has been trained in order to be able to train other Himbas in ICT and to manage the ICT centre.
- The production of an interactive DVD-ROM by a multidisciplinary team consisting of anthropologists, filmmakers and DVD designers who will work together to create a living archive of the Himba oral culture which will be made accessible to them.

The "San Interactive Archive, Training and Heritage Management" project aims to train and enable the San people to manage their cultural heritage and express their own cultural contents through audiovisual media and multimedia. As a first step, the San representatives were trained in cultural management. As a second step, the community will produce a DVD on the San people dealing with the loss of their land in 1935. In the long run, by making use of all the audiovisual archives that the project coordinators have gathered during the last years of fieldwork, it will be possible to organise and conceptualise all these audiovisual and multimedia materials into interlinked interactive archival packages which could be used to create local-content productions, such as documentaries, short narratives, animations and DVDs in collaboration with the representatives of the San communities.

In this paper the five ongoing pilot projects of ICT4ID have been presented. The programme is currently at the midpoint, so it is too early to assess its results, even if the first outcome has been successfully achieved. It is likely that UNESCO will decide to extend this programme which would allow the implementation of more projects taking advantage of the lessons learnt during the implementation of these five projects.

Case Study II

ICT and the Orang Asli *in Malaysia*

Pauline Hui Ying Ooi, Intel Technology Penang, Malaysia

Orang Asli means the "Original People" in the Malay language. Nowadays, they are classified into three large groups: Senoi, Negrito and proto-Melayu, which further break down into various tribes. Although many still live in the rural areas, some youth have been fortunate enough to venture life in the city by pursuing higher education or seeking employment. A few information technology undergraduates from the Orang Asli community of Malaysia were interviewed via e-mail on the subject of information and communication technology (ICT) among the local indigenous peoples.

Senyeorita, Rubycca, Jeneta, Zue and Khairol were all born in Peninsular Malaysia. They came from different Orang Asli tribes, namely the Semelai, Temuan and Semai. The culture, lifestyle and beliefs of their communities had an impact in shaping their identities. Seneyorita described the Orang Asli people as shy due to limited exposure to the outside world. As for Khairol, having lived near the forests surrounded by nature, the Semelai culture had shaped him to appreciate nature which gave him a feeling of harmony.

The Orang Asli in Malaysia are socio-economically and culturally marginalised, although most respondents felt that the development of indigenous peoples in Malaysia was fairly good considering Malaysia is one of the developing countries. Besides the digital divide, there are other issues which have led to an erosion of their cultural identity. The respondents stated that the land problem was one of the issues faced by the Orang Asli. Other major problems include the poor education system, health, poverty, sanitation and clean water supply. According to Khairol, some conservative Orang Asli were unwilling to accept development and disregard the significance of education for the younger generation. A high dropout rate also contributes to low participation in education among the Orang Asli children (Mokshein, 2004).

With regard to the digital divide, Jeneta explained that besides being computer illiterate, the high cost of computer gadgets were among the technological issues faced by the Orang Asli. Rubycca also commented that it was impossible for the people to use the latest technology, as some of the villages do not even have basic necessities, including power supply and education. Khairol, Senyeorita and Zue agreed that the lack of exposure to ICT among the people could contribute to the wider technology gap.

ICT is a growing industry in Malaysia. Over the years, the industry has provided employment opportunities for its citizens, which also explicitly explains the increasing number of higher institutions offering ICT-related courses to encourage more students into this stream. While Zue, Senyeorita and Rubycca got involved in ICT because courses were offered at the university, Khairol and Jeneta chose ICT for other reasons. Jeneta was encouraged by her family and friends to get involved in ICT. Khairol was inspired by the rapid growth of technology globally, and he believed that ICT plays an important role in every aspect of life. In response to the opportunities offered by ICT to further the goals and interests of the Orang Asli community, the IT undergraduates were confident that it would improve the quality of life, knowledge and work performance of their people. ICT will also help to bridge the gap in education and economic status between Orang Asli and other ethnic races.

None of the respondents thought that ICT would pose a threat to their community. In fact, they were positive about the Orang Asli willingness to accept new technologies. However, Zue emphasized that the acceptance of technologies among the people without seeing it as a threat was greatly dependent on their exposure and the way technology was presented to them. Khairol said that some Orang Asli from the Semelai tribe were still unwilling to accept advancement in their lives because they assumed that it will threaten the chastity of Semelai people as well as the customs, culture, and beliefs of other communities. All respondents said the potential ICT users among the Orang Asli community would possibly be the younger generations who received formal education.

The government, jointly with other organizations, has been organizing programmes to introduce ICT in rural areas. It is an ongoing process, which has ample room for development. Some of the suggestions given included giving workshops, presentations and seminars on ICT in Orang Asli villages as part of exposure measures, making ICT a core subject in school, supplying necessary equipment and a "One family one computer" campaign by introducing attractive packages. In 2003, it was reported that, with assistance from the United Nations Development Program and the Department of Orang Asli Affairs, Malaysia, the indigenous Temuan people in Pahang state were fortunate to have a solar power generator in their village. Although there was no school nearby, Temuan youngsters were learning how to read and write using solar powered computers. (Temuan take to technology transfer, 2003). Today, there are still several Orang Asli villages that are deprived of this privilege.

In conclusion, the indigenous peoples' involvement in information technology is still very small. Education is the primary factor that leads the community towards accepting information technology. However, other major problems such as poverty, a poor education system, health and sanitation should be overcome first before information technology is introduced to the indigenous community.

Acknowledgment

I would like to thank Senyeorita, Rubycca, Jeneta, Zue and Khairol for their participation and contribution to this case study. Special thanks to Dr. Laurel Dyson for her guidance and advice.

References

Mokshein, S. E. (2004). *Education for sustainable development (ESD) in Malaysia: An overview.* Putrajaya, Malaysia: Educational Planning and Research Division, Ministry of Education.

Temuan take to technology transfer. (2003, November 6). *The Sun*, 24.

Case Study III

My Life with Computers on a Remote Island

Bethalia Gaidan,
Dauan Island Community Council, Australia

I have spent most of my life in the Torres Strait in Far North Queensland, Australia. There are 17 inhabited islands spread across the strait with populations from less than 30 to several thousand. It is a remote and isolated area.

There were no computers at the school I went to. The first time I used computers was when I enrolled in a teaching course in the city and I learnt to word process my assignments. That was the only application I used.

I started working at the community council on my home island but the community wanted me to have business qualifications, so I went to the Technical and Further Education (TAFE) College on Thursday Island where I learnt Microsoft Office programs: Word, Excel and Access. From there I travelled to another remote community and I learnt how to use the banking machines.

Then I went back to my island and started working at council again. At that time all work was done manually. While I had been working at the other community I had seen printed payslips, so I started asking about doing our payroll on a computer. When the opportunity to learn how to do it came up, I was one of the first people to join the training program. We used to take our payroll documents into the regional centre (by dinghy to the airstrip on the neighbouring island, small plane and then ferry to Thursday Island) each fortnight. There, we would learn the program while running our pay. We could then collect the cash from the bank and return home the next day. This was often a challenge: On low tides we could not get the dinghy to the landing and had to walk through the mud; or the weather would make it risky to travel in a small boat.

I did this until there was an air accident and I was too nervous to fly any more. We found it was possible to do bank transfers over the telephone line. When the time came to set it up, however, there was only the payroll clerk and myself, so we had to sort it out using telephone help from the bank. We then had to learn how to use the program.

Working on a regular basis at the office in Thursday Island had given me an opportunity to see how they had set out their computers and how they used their network. When the time came for us to move into our new council chambers, I decided on a similar system.

I attended training in hardware maintenance because it cost too much to fly a technician up to fix small problems. After the training, I could telephone him and he could talk me through the process of installing a new part or troubleshooting the problem. I like working with the hardware; I find it interesting to test and replace parts in order to get the computer working again. The technician also gave us an overview of other applications of technology: We saw PowerPoint, Internet searching, Publisher, FrontPage, graphics and clipart before we had them on our computers, so we knew what they could be used for when we did get them.

I wanted technology for my workplace because it could make jobs easier for staff and I wanted to share what I had learnt. We have all learnt how to play games as well as the work-related programs. When I see someone doing something different on the computer I ask them about it, then I go and try to do it.

I have helped people in the community to set up their own Internet banking accounts using one of the office computers because otherwise they would have to pay the $30 per transaction charge at the local store to transfer money, or have to send their card, with a trusted person, to another island to get cash when we run out on our island. I have also encouraged my staff to help people, especially older people, to use services which are now only available over the telephone or Internet. I have also always made the computer available to the Health Centre, so they can print notices, and the church, where we would print the service for them. We let people who are doing assignments for training courses use the computer as well. Although I have allowed fairly free access to the system, we have not had problems with inappropriate use. I tell people that if they go to pornographic sites using a council computer and our network gets a virus then they will have to pay for the repairs.

Our Internet connection was initially a slow, intermittent, expensive, hourly-rate dial-up running off one computer: We used it only for getting online forms and it had a council e-mail account. We now have a one-way satellite connection which is reliable. The Internet has opened my eyes to a lot of possibilities: For the first time we can look up information easily. At home my daughter downloads the latest music and movies. All staff now have an email address and we use it all the time. So much work is done through the email that I have to check it every day.

I like technology: With it I can have information about or access to anything I can think of searching for. However, I would like computers to be more reliable, because it is very expensive for those of us in remote areas to get our own computers fixed.

I have built my knowledge about technology from looking at what other people and workplaces do, attending training courses and surfing the Internet. I have to teach myself how new software programs and hardware work. My next challenge is to learn how to use our new video conferencing unit so we can offer this service to the community.

Case Study IV

How Computers Came into My Life

Margaret Mau, Dauan Island Community Council,
Torres Strait Regional Authority & Island Coordinating Council, Australia

My earliest experience with anything to do with information technology was the electric typewriter. That was in 1977 when I attended the Cairns Business College for a year. In that same year, I was recommended as a trainee to the Commonwealth Education Department where I learned how to work a telex machine.

Computers came into my life in the form of a word processor when I worked for Comalco at Weipa. I did not operate this machine, but I watched its operation with fascination. Yet it did not impress me in any way at all to learn how to use it and, back then, I did not ever think it could evolve into what computers are today.

In 1989 I worked for Torres Strait Gold on Horn Island as the accounts payee clerk. The accounts system was on a computer into which I would enter invoice data. At the end of each month, I would pay accounts on the computer, which paid accounts on a monthly basis only and printed out the cheques as well. (When is Dauan Island Council getting one of these software programs?) I was called in to work on a Saturday one time and the operations manager asked me to type a letter on the computer. I steadfastly refused and asked for the electric typewriter to be brought out. At that time I still had no knowledge of how to operate a computer. Terms such as "software," "Excel," "Word," etc., had me in a state of confusion. I typed the letter and made photocopies to file instead of "saving" it.

I was formally introduced to computers when I was elected as chairperson of Dauan Island Council in March 1997. That was when all administration staff had visions of me doing irreparable damage to the office computers. Beth (CEO) always blamed me when things went wrong with the computers. She would sit at a computer and if something was wrong would say, "Margaret, have you been using this computer?"

The first thing I learned on computers was how to access games, then I progressed to using Microsoft Word to type my own letters, notices, etc., as I was not fortunate enough to have my own secretary. Through this process I learned that you did not have to make copies to save or file in a cabinet as it could be done on the computer. Great, I thought, less paper lying around the place and no filing. But for some reason when I wanted to bring up that particular document, I could never find it. I'd forgotten where I'd saved it.

During my term as chairperson I had the opportunity of being enrolled with my fellow councillors to do a basic computer training course at the Technical and Further Education (TAFE) College on Thursday Island. It was very interesting and I learned that the computer is a tool to help us in our daily lives and can do just about anything you want done and, if you could afford it, you can have one custom made and designed to cook, clean, iron and be the housemaid, wife and mother in your absence.

I feel that for isolated communities such as ours, computers are our link to the outside world. The use of Internet Explorer provides that link for us. Everyone can use a computer, even those with limited or no experience — take it from me, I speak from life experiences.

There is also the downside of computers, where if something really does go wrong with it, the cost of repair is extreme unless you know how to fix it yourself. The downside of Internet Explorer also is frightening to me in the way of "chat rooms." My children want me to put a computer in our home — which I refuse. The amount of coverage on the television news about children being exploited by adults and news of pedophiles loose on the Internet just scares the hell out of me — even if we are isolated.

In conclusion, computers are the future and with the right knowledge, restrictions, uses, etc., they become your friend and ally — THEY MAKE THE WORLD BECOME YOUR OYSTER.

Section II

Technology in Education

Chapter V

Developing Culturally Inclusive Educational Multimedia in the South Pacific

Christopher Robbins, Rhode Island School of Design, USA
& The University of the South Pacific, Fiji

Abstract

This chapter explores how educational technology can be developed according to indigenous learning approaches of the South Pacific. It is based on an expansive research and development project conducted 2003-2004 at The University of the South Pacific (USP). After an introduction to several aspects of indigenous South Pacific learning approaches and their usage in the formal learning sector, I make several recommendations for instructional technology design based on these principles, illustrated with examples of educational technology projects that apply these recommendations. Specifically, we follow educational multimedia efforts at USP that enable learning in wholes, encourage observation and imitation and utilize vernacular metaphors and languages. This includes recommendations for interface design, interaction design and decentralized content localization.

Introduction

Information technology plays a vital but contentious role in tertiary education in the South Pacific. Although many students must rely on information technology for higher education, there are concerns regarding the intrinsic cultural biases of, and unbalanced access to, educational technology in the region (Matthewson, 1994; Thaman, 1997; Va'a, 1997; Wah, 1997). Approximately half of the 15,000 students of The University of the South Pacific (USP) study through USP's Distance and Flexible Learning (DFL) Centers, a network of mini-campuses in 12 island-nations (Cook Islands, Fiji, Kiribati, Marshall Islands, Nauru, Niue, Samoa, Solomon Islands, Tokelau, Tonga, Tuvalu and Vanuatu) linked through VSAT satellite (USP DFL Unit, 2004). These students negotiate audio and video conferences, Web-based group activities, interactive CD-ROMs, video broadcasts of lectures, email, faxes and even CB radio as they communicate with their teachers and fellow students.

While educational technology offers distance students a higher degree of interaction with their educational materials, lecturers and fellow students, it can also introduce additional cultural biases into their already imported education system. The cultural gaps between USP's formal education system and the diverse South Pacific cultures of USP's staff and students has been widely documented (Lockwood, Roberts, & Williams, 1998; Thaman, 1997; Va'a, 1997, 2000; Wah, 1997). Closing these gaps through culturally inclusive curricula and pedagogy has become an institutional priority. Recently, the University's focus on culturally relevant pedagogy has broadened to include the instructional design of educational technology.

As part of this initiative, The University of the South Pacific Media Centre, with funding from the Japan International Cooperation Agency (JICA), completed a project that examined how educational multimedia can be designed according to the learning approaches of the South Pacific. In the study (Robbins, 2004), we captured the views of Pacific educationists through a series of interviews and a review of academic literature covering indigenous pedagogy in the South Pacific. We conducted interviews, employed questionnaires and usability tests with staff and students from the 12 member-nations of USP to find applications of regional learning approaches to the development of educational technology and built an educational CD-ROM to audit and illustrate the findings.

In this chapter I outline several recommendations and applications of these findings, focusing on how educational multimedia can be made culturally relevant to the South Pacific.

The goal of this chapter is not only to enable technological fluency by helping developers create educational multimedia designed specifically for the region, but also to ensure that the technology promotes indigenous approaches and values, rather than submerging them under dominant technological hegemonies.

Pedagogic Focuses for Educational Technology Developers in the South Pacific

This chapter concentrates on three regional pedagogic focuses relevant to educational technology in the region:

1. Enable learning in wholes (Thaman, 1992; Yorston, 2002);
2. Encourage observation and imitation (Lima, 2003; Pagram, Fetherston, & Rabbitt, 2000; Taufe'ulungaki, 2003; Thaman, 1999; Yorston, 2002); and
3. Utilize vernacular metaphors and languages (Afamasaga, 2002; Pagram, Fetherston, & Rabbitt, 2000; Taafaki, 2001; Taufe'ulungaki, 2003; UNESCO, 1992).

Enabling learning in wholes, or preserving "the big in the small," arises time and again as a key component of South Pacific learning approaches (Mel, 2001; Harris, 1992; Thaman, 1992; Yorston, 2002). The key concept is that rather than segmenting learning activities into distinct conceptual units, ideas are approached as they can be applied within the context of larger tasks (Thaman, 1992; Yorston, 2002). In other words, rather than master each step consecutively, learners witness and then imitate the whole, attaining the desired goal through trial and error (Mel, 2001). To preserve the whole, complex activities are tackled as "successive approximations" of the final product rather than as "sequenced parts" (Harris, 1992, p. 38). For example, in learning a musical piece using this method, a band would play the entire piece through until they had mastered it, as opposed to repeating individual refrains.

A nuance of learning in wholes is that in each step, the focus is on the specific context of the task or idea and its relevance to the broader goal, as opposed to working from generalizations towards instances of universals (Thaman, 2003; Va'a, 1997).

In educational technology, this approach has ramifications for information architecture and interface design, suggesting navigation processes that are more task than concept-focused, and content-display that continues to present the wider context while students explore details.

Closely related to the concept of learning in wholes is the process of observation and imitation, as both approaches originate from task-based learning exercises applied in "real world" settings. However, while learning in wholes translates well from traditional contexts to formal education settings, observation and imitation can manifest itself less desirably as rote memorization and surface learning (Landbeck & Mugler, 1994). Tying observation and imitation activities to application rather than memorization can encourage deep learning (Landbeck & Mugler, 1994). In other words, showing how a concept can be applied to something the student already knows can situate the knowledge more deeply than having students memorize sets of tasks or terms.

Teaching from students' own cultural contexts can be difficult with a population as diverse and distributed as that served by USP, and is further confounded by the colonial history and post-colonial legacy of formal education in the region (Petaia, 1981; Thaman, 2000b, 2003; Wah, 1997). Most textbooks used at USP are published in Europe and North America, and utilize examples from the cultures in which the books are produced (Thaman, 2000a). Despite efforts to create culturally relevant learning materials at USP, it can be incredibly difficult to choose examples and metaphors that make sense in all 12 countries served by the University:

Some of the course writers only use examples from the countries they know. If you look at sourcebooks, most use examples from Fiji and Samoa — a staff-member at the USP Solomon Island DFL Centre. (Robbins, 2004, p. 29)

The exam paper had to do with kava. It was like double-dutch to us... Most of the examples are very Fijian. We don't have veggie markets. We don't have military management. I have to pick something we can identify with — a staff-member at the USP Nauru DFL Centre. (Robbins, 2004, p. 29)

In addition to local metaphors, there is also a need for local languages in educational materials. Vernacular languages play a vital role in this officially English-speaking University. As a lecturer at the Samoa Campus confessed, "after class, when there are no other English-speaking students around, they ask me to explain in Samoan" (Robbins, 2004, p. 16). A program assistant's comments at the Tuvalu DFL Centre clarified, "all students understand English, it's just when it comes to tutoring, or when a point needs to be understood subtly, the students and the tutors prefer to exchange in the local language" (Robbins, 2004, p. 16).

Regional research has shown that using vernacular language aids comprehension (Pagram, Fetherston, & Rabbitt, 2000; Taafaki, 2001; Taufe'ulungaki, 2003) and deeper learning (Kalolo, 2002) where English alone can fail, and is also important for purposes of cultural preservation (Afamasaga, 2002; Sami, 2004; Taufe'ulungaki, 2003; Veramu, 2004).

Taken together, these pedagogic foci indicate that educational technology in the South Pacific should utilize vernacular metaphors, examples and languages, and should be presented in a way that enables learning in wholes using activities that rely on observation and imitation.

Applications of Indigenous Learning Approaches to Educational Technology in the South Pacific

In this section, I discuss how the aspects of South Pacific learning approaches outlined earlier can be applied to the development of culturally inclusive educational multimedia. Specifically, I explore how interventions at the following design levels can help achieve our pedagogic goals:

1. **Interface level:** enable learning in wholes;
2. **Interaction level:** encourage observation and imitation; and
3. **Content level:** utilize vernacular metaphors and languages.

Interface Level: Enable Learning in Wholes

The solutions we have created to enable learning in wholes are primarily interface-based, maintaining the big picture while focusing students on specifics. I discovered one very simple way to preserve "the big in the small" while looking for something else entirely. As part of our 2003-2004 study (Robbins, 2004), we asked 155 students of USP to choose between two Web designs (Figure 1). The goal was to determine whether the students would feel more comfortable with contextual, inline navigation (links within the body of the text), or with a separate menu listing the links apart from the body. I expected students to prefer the simpler, inline approach (labeled "L"), as this is closer to the layout of books, and so would be more familiar to them than the Web-derived navigation menu. However, my hunch was proven unequivocally wrong: 93% of the students preferred the menu navigation, labelled "O" (X^2 (2, N = 155) = 250.90 $p < 0.0001$). Students appreciated that the separate menu neatly summarized the longer text, and allowed them to jump directly to points of interest without losing their place.

Figure 1. Navigation preference (Robbins, 2004, used with permission)

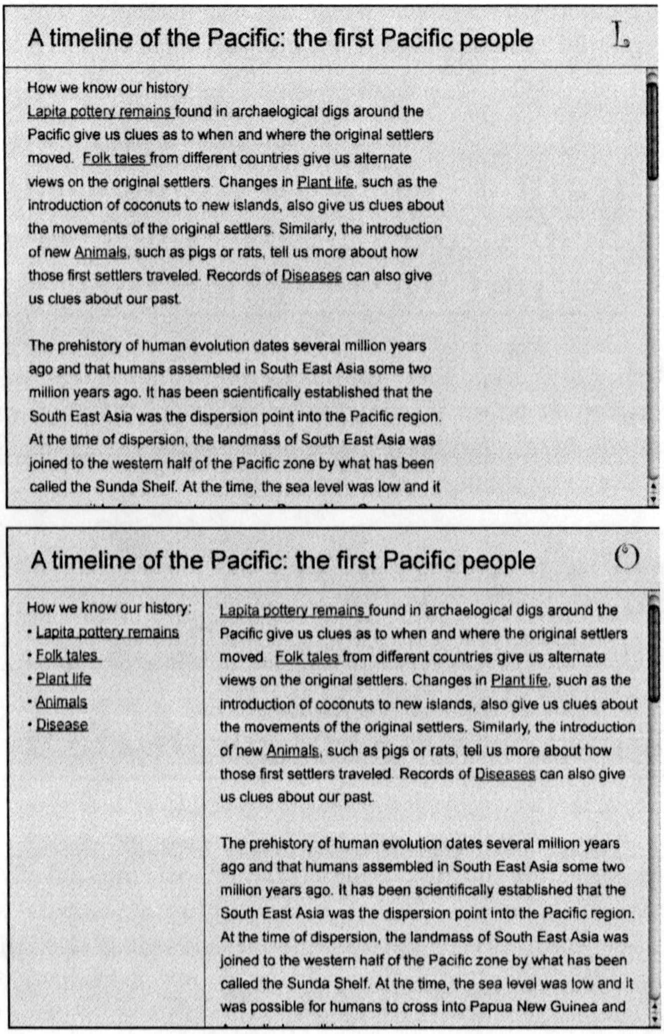

A graphical corollary involves presenting concepts through "layers of simplicity" that offer increasing levels of detail to the students without muddying the overall purpose of the graphics. In other words, the basic lesson or overall theme of the image is always clear, even when students have drilled into details of the graphic or animation. For example, in Figure 2 we present the student with a simple initial layer of information (arrows showing immigration patterns), augmented with

Figure 2. Using layers of simplicity on a map/timeline to show immigration patterns into the South Pacific (Robbins, 2004, used with permission)

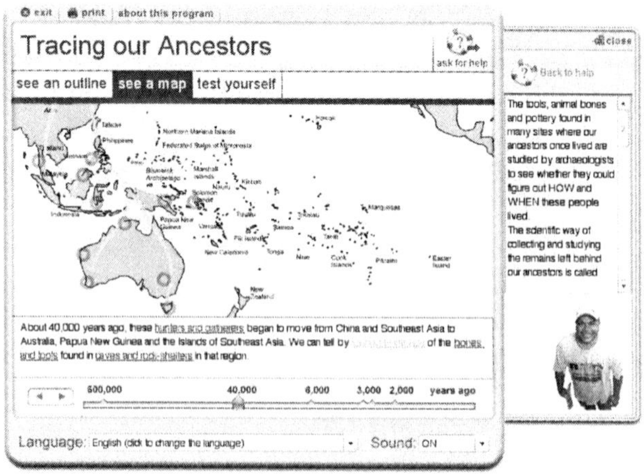

deeper layers of information (descriptions of archaeological remnants at different sites or related stories from regional oral histories) that the student can access by clicking sections of the map/timeline with his or her mouse.

Interaction Level: Encourage Observation and Imitation

While preserving the whole plays a role in determining the organization of content in the interface, observation and imitation have applications when designing the deeper interactivity and functionality of an educational technology project. Designing these interactions around observation and imitation enables students to act on instructions within the learning interface. For instance, in Figure 3, instructions are overlaid on the active interface, rather than being provided in separate instruction screens, so that students seeking help are shown exactly what to do, where to click and how to do it, rather than merely being provided with instructions.

By programming timers that automatically demonstrate the options for the user after a period of inactivity, this same approach can be used to help students with a tendency to "freeze" when confused, and has many applications to lab simulations.

Figure 3. Instructions are paired with an overlay showing how to act on the instructions within the interface itself (Robbins, 2004, used with permission)

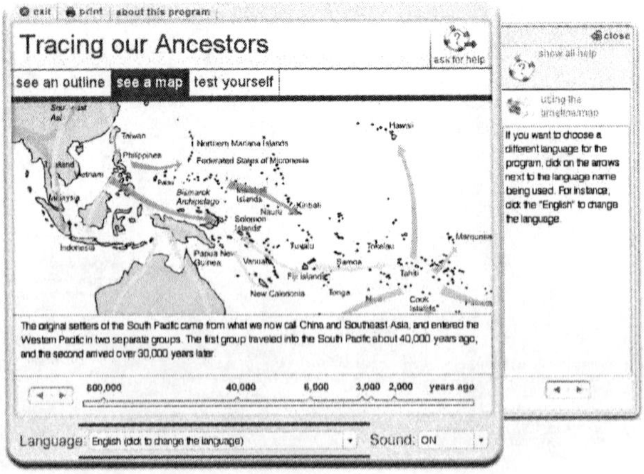

Content Level: Utilize Vernacular Metaphors and Languages

The most obvious way that educational technology can be made culturally inclusive is by including the cultures of students and teachers in the educational content. This is true anywhere in the world, but is a particular focus at USP because of the wide gaps between the cultures of the educational institution, students, teachers and educational technology developers.

As USP caters to 12 distinct island-nations, providing truly local illustrations for every concept is incredibly difficult. However, by designing educational multimedia so that teachers and students can provide cultural context themselves, educational technology developers can create flexible toolsets that decentralize the contextualization process.

One such solution is the virtual peer, which uses regional examples as "seed-questions" to encourage students to contribute their own explanations. In Figure 4, peers representing different cultures in the South Pacific discuss aspects of the Internet using metaphors from their home countries. Clicking the "show me" button brings up an animation, illustration or audio clip, so the interface is not dominated by text.

To further situate the learning to the student's own circumstances, the student is asked to make his or her own descriptions of the concept (Figure 5). These

Figure 4. A virtual peer gives his or her own descriptions of the concepts in local terms (Robbins, 2004, used with permission)

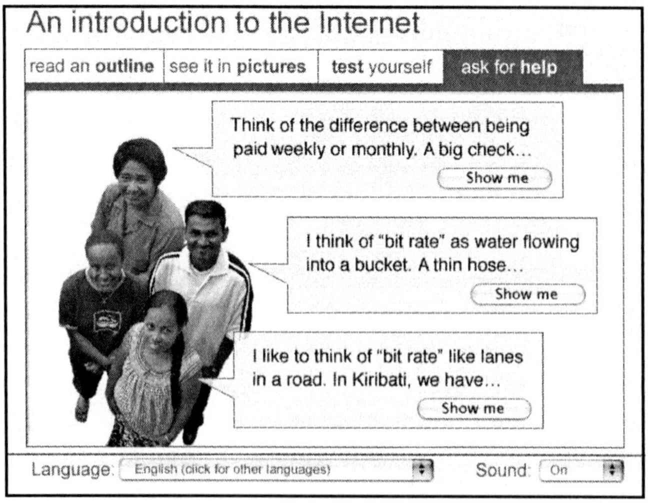

Figure 5. The student is asked to make his or her own metaphors to describe streaming media (Robbins, 2004, used with permission)

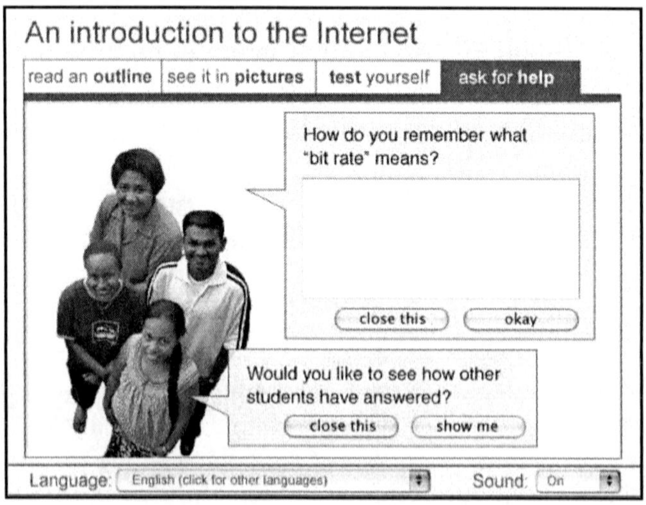

answers are saved on the computer for future iterations of the program, allowing other students to view each other's perspectives.

Another approach to creating flexible educational multimedia relies on the file structure rather than the interface. For instance, in order to create multilingual and multicultural educational multimedia at USP, we have employed an open-

Figure 6. A three-tier file structure for multilingual multimedia (Robbins, 2004, used with permission)

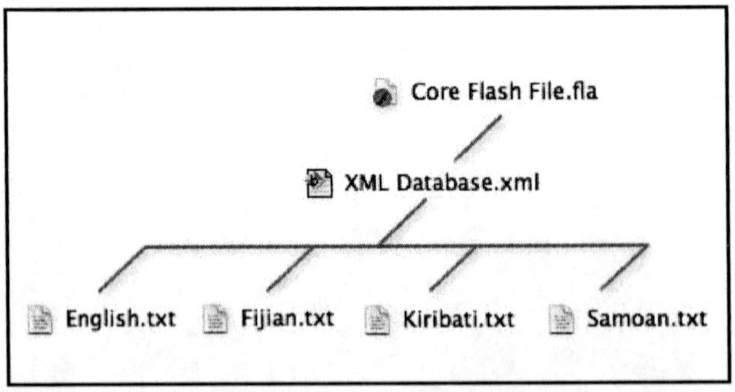

source, three-tier file structure to help staff and students customize their learning materials themselves. Separating the core multimedia from all supporting image, text and audio files makes these updates easier to achieve. Figure 6 shows how this approach can be used to create an open framework for multilingual multimedia. Each language is given its own text file so that students and teachers need only make edits to existing text files to add additional languages and metaphors. The language files are inserted into the educational multimedia at runtime so that the materials are flexible and current.

An additional benefit of the three-tier file structure is that presenting the images, audio files, videos and animations separately encourages their re-use in other media, aiding accessibility as well as customization of the media. The approach can also make the separate elements of a multimedia project (text, images, video and audio) available for re-use in other projects and media, along the lines of learning objects in object-oriented instructional design (Ahern & Van Cleave, 2002; Parrish, 2004; Wiley, 2000).

Additionally, translating entails more than simply changing the language; it involves translating the stories, devices, examples and metaphors to correlates that are meaningful within the culture of the language of translation. As such, developing educational technology that can be easily localized enables deeper reflection rather than surface memorization, encouraging students to think about their learning materials within their own cultural contexts while simultaneously creating culturally relevant educational media for future students.

While the approaches I have mentioned are tied to specific courseware, other methods for providing cultural context focus more broadly on cross-curricula databases of educational content from a variety of cultures. USP's multimedia database (http://mdb.usp.ac.fj) and cultural curriculum development initiative are the beginnings of multicultural learning toolsets for the South Pacific, with the promise of freely accessible educational media from various cultures of the region.

Conclusion

In order to help ensure that educational technology is built according to the cultures of the South Pacific rather than relying on de facto standards of the technology developers, the following suggestions are useful to consider:

- Offer opportunities for contextualization of the educational media, utilizing decentralized methods that enable "on-the-fly" staff and student input. Such approaches can be front-end, such as virtual peers from several countries who present examples and explain concepts using terms from their own backgrounds, or back-end, involving open file-structures that enable localization of supporting media files.
- Ensure that materials preserve the whole while offering specific anchors. For instance, long text should be accompanied by quick summaries that link to different parts of the main text. Graphical interfaces should present concepts through "layers of simplicity," in which details are available to the students without confusing the overall purpose of the graphics or the interface.
- Utilise modeling rather than separate instructions, enabling students to act on any instructions or practice any skills within the learning interface. For instance, overlay instructions on the active interface rather than providing separate instruction screens for help sections or lab simulations.
- Provide vernacular translations or glossaries within the educational multimedia. For ease of translation, save language files as separate text documents so that translators can make edits to the multimedia using simple word-processors, and need not know how to use multimedia development software.

This list is by no means exhaustive. Our own USP study (Robbins, 2004) explored how educational multimedia can help students with regard to computer access, reticence with authority figures, group learning, content-display and usability. Other studies have explored the role of terminology, multiple-modes and representational form (McCloughlin, 1999); icons and visual metaphors (Evers, et al., 1999); design and content-flow (Hedberg & Brown, 2002) and institutional/industrial collaboration (Kisum, 2003) in developing culturally inclusive educational technology.

The aspects of indigenous approaches to educational technology covered in this chapter were chosen because they reflect a broad scope of the educational technology development process (interface, interaction and content), and because their immediate applicability to a wide variety of educational technology can promote their further development in the educational technology community. Likewise, this chapter does not focus on differences between individual nations in the region, as such distinctions were beyond the scope and sample size of the original study, but rather on shared approaches that can be applied throughout the region.

References

Afamasaga, T. (2002). Personal reflection on education in Samoa. In F. Pene, A. Taufe'ulungaki, & C. Benson (Eds.), *Tree of opportunity: Rethinking Pacific education* (pp. 96-101). Suva, Fiji: University of the South Pacific Institute of Education.

Ahern, T. C., & Van Cleave, N. K. (2002). Utilizing open source and object oriented paradigms in instructional technology. *World Multiconference on Systemics, Cybernetics and Informatics*. Retrieved January 11, 2005, from http://www.ux1.eiu.edu/~cfnkv/Papers/SCI2002_OpenSource.pdf

Evers, V., Kukulska-Hulme, A., & Jones, A. (1999). Cross-cultural understanding of interface design: A cross-cultural analysis of icon recognition. In E. del Galdo & G. Prahbu (Eds.), *Proceedings of the International Workshop on Internationalisation of Products and Systems*. Rochester, NY. Retrieved August 9, 2004, from http://www.swi.psy.uva.nl/usr/evers/IWIPSFinal.pdf

Harris, S. (1992). "Going about it the right way" — Decolonising aboriginal school curriculum processes. In B. Teasdale & J. Teasdale (Eds.), *Voices in a seashell: Education, culture and identity* (pp. 37-53). Suva, Fiji: The University of the South Pacific Institute of Pacific Studies.

Hedberg, J. G., & Brown, I. (2002). Understanding cross-cultural meaning through visual media. *Education Media International, 39*(1), 23-30.

Kalolo, K. (2002). A Tokelau perspective. In F. Pene, A. Taufe'ulungaki, & C. Benson (Eds.), *Tree of opportunity: Rethinking Pacific education* (pp. 104–06). Suva, Fiji: University of the South Pacific Institute of Education.

Kisum, S. (2003). Selected country papers: Fiji (2). *Multimedia and e-learning: A new direction for productivity promotion and enhancement* (report of the APO Seminar on Multimedia for Productivity Promotion and Enhancement (with special focus on e-learning)). The Asian Productivity Organization, Japan. Retrieved January 12, 2005 from, http://www.apo-tokyo.org/00e-books/07.eLearning.htm

Landbeck, R., & Mugler, F. (1994). *Approaches to study and conceptions of learning of students at the USP*. Suva, Fiji: University of South Pacific Centre for the Enhancement of Learning and Teaching (CELT).

Lima, R. (2003). Educational ideas of the Noole (Solomon Islands). In K. H. Thaman (Ed.), *Educational ideas from Oceania: Selected readings* (pp. 120-125). Suva, Fiji: The University of the South Pacific Institute of Education, in association with the UNESCO Chair of Teacher Education and Culture.

Lockwood, F., Roberts, D. W., & Williams, I. (1998). Improving teaching at a distance within the University of the South Pacific. *International Journal of Educational Development*, *8*, 265-270.

Matthewson, C. (1994). Whose development, whose needs? Distance education practice and politics in the South Pacific. *Journal of Distance Education*, *9*(2), 35-47. Retrieved January 11, 2005, from http://cade.athabascau.ca/vol9.2/09_matthewson.html

McLoughlin, C. (1999). Culturally inclusive learning on the Web. *Proceedings of the teaching learning forum 1999,* The University of Western Australia (pp. 272-277). Retrieved January 12, 2005, from http://lsn.curtin.edu.au/tlf/tlf1999/mcloughlin.html

Mel, M. A. (2001). Interfacing global and indigenous knowledge in evaluation and assessment in information technologies. *Educational innovation for development: Interfacing global and indigenous knowledge*. Report of the Sixth UNESCO–ACEID International Conference on Education (pp. 61-66). Retrieved June 19, 2004, from www.unescobkk.org/ips/ebooks/%20documents/aceidconf6/themetwo.pdf

Pagram, J., Fetherston, T., & Rabbitt, E. (2000). Learning together: Using technology and authentic learning experiences to enhance the learning of distance education students. *Proceedings of the Australian Indigenous Education Conference,* Australia. Retrieved August 13, 2003, from http://www.kk.ecu.edu.au/sub/schoola/research/confs/aiec/papers/jpagram02.htm

Parrish, P. E. (2004). The trouble with learning objects. *Educational Technology Research and Development, 52*(1), 49-67.

Petaia, R. (1981). Kidnapped. *The Mana annual of creative writing, 1*(3). Suva, Fiji: Mana Publications.

Robbins, C. (2004). *Educational multimedia for the South Pacific*. Suva, Fiji: JICA ICT Capacity Building at USP Project. Retrieved January 11, 2005, from http://www.grographics.com/fiji/AccessUsability-ICTResearch/research-report/Education-Multimedia-for-the-South-Pacific_Robbins.pdf

Sami, G. (2004). Decolonizing our mind: Rationale, challenges and coping strategies. *Panel at the Fiji Institute for Educational Research.* The University of the South Pacific, Suva, Fiji, January 7, 2004.

Taafaki, I. (2001). *Effecting change and empowerment: Library/information studies training through distance education in the Marshall Islands* (Internal Document). Marshall Islands: University of the South Pacific Distance and Flexible Learning Centre.

Taufe'ulungaki, 'A. M. (2003). Vernacular languages and classroom interactions in the Pacific. In K. H. Thaman (Ed.), *Educational ideas from Oceania: Selected readings* (pp. 13-35). Suva, Fiji: The University of the South Pacific Institute of Education, in association with the UNESCO Chair of Teacher Education and Culture.

Thaman, K. H. (1992). Looking towards the source: A consideration of (cultural) context in teacher education. *Directions 27, 14*(2), 3-13.

Thaman, K. H. (1997). Considerations of culture in distance education in the Pacific Islands. In L. Rowan, L. Bartlett & T. Evans (Eds.), *Shifting borders: Globalisation, localisation and open and distance education* (pp. 23-43). Geelong: Deakin University Press.

Thaman, K. H. (1999, November). Of teachers and lecturers: Understanding students' cultures. *Centrepoint* (4) (pp. 1-2). Centre for the Enhancement of Learning and Teaching), The University of the South Pacific, Fiji Islands.

Thaman, K. H. (2000a, October 25-27). Open and flexible learning for whom? Rethinking distance education (Keynote address). *14th Annual Conference of the Asian Association of Open Universities (AAOU),* Manila, Philippines. Retrieved January 14, 2004, from http://www.friends-partners.org/utsumi/gu-l/early-2001/1-31-a.html

Thaman, K. H. (2000b). Decolonising Pacific studies: Indigenous knowledge and wisdom in higher education (Plenary address). *Pacific Studies 2000,* University of Hawaii at Manoa, Honolulu.

Thaman, K. H. (2003). A conceptual framework for analysing Pacific educational ideas: The case of Tonga. In K. H. Thaman (Ed.), *Educational ideas from Oceania: Selected readings* (pp. 73-8). Suva, Fiji: The University of the South Pacific Institute of Education, in association with the UNESCO Chair of Teacher Education and Culture.

UNESCO. (1992). Recommendations of the conference "Education for Cultural Development" Rarotonga. In B. Teasdale & J. Teasdale (Eds.), *Voices in a seashell: Education, culture and identity* (p. 7). Suva, Fiji: The University of the South Pacific Institute of Pacific Studies.

USP DFL Unit. (2004). *Distance and flexible learning at USP: About us.* Retrieved January 4, 2005, from http://www.usp.ac.fj/dfl/aboutus.htm

Va'a, R. (1997). Cultural accountability in the USP science courses at a distance. In L. Rowan, L. Bartlett, & T. Evans (Eds.), *Shifting borders: Globalisation, localisation and open and distance education* (pp. 83-97). Geelong: Deakin University Press.

Va'a. R. (2000). *Appropriate telecommunication and learning technology for distance education in the South Pacific* (Report of a project funded by NZODA). Suva, Fiji: Pacific Islands Regional Association for Distance Education, the University of the South Pacific.

Veramu, J. (2004, January 7). *Decolonizing our mind: Rationale, challenges and coping strategies.* Panel at the Fiji Institute for Educational Research, The University of the South Pacific, Suva, Fiji.

Wah, R. (1997). Distance education in the South Pacific: Issues and contradictions. In L. Rowan, L. Bartlett, & T. Evans (Eds.), *Shifting borders: Globalisation, localisation and open and distance education* (pp. 69-82). Geelong: Deakin University Press.

Wiley, D. A. (2000). Connecting learning objects to instructional design theory: A definition, a metaphor, and a taxonomy. In D. A. Wiley (Ed.), *The instructional use of learning objects* [Online version]. Retrieved January 11, 2005, from http://reusability.org/read/chapters/wiley.doc

Yorston, F. (2002). *Learning to teach in Samoa. Master's of teaching internship case from four months in Samoa in 1999.* The University of Sydney, Australia. Retrieved January 15, 2004, from http://alex.edfac.usyd.edu.au/acrosscurric/Paradise/POP/centre_intern.html#An%20example%20of%20how%20effective

Chapter VI

Learning to Internet Bank

Fiona Brady, Central Queensland University, Australia

Abstract

The increasing deployment of technology is changing the way services are delivered. New technologies require people to learn new procedures to do the same things they were doing previously as well as to learn to use entirely new services. Business has made little accommodation for the diversity of users and their situations as the use of technology increases and the human interface with its client's decreases. This study looks at how indigenous peoples in a remote area access Internet banking services. Internet banking is a discrete technological skill that has been effectively acquired without outside assistance or direction: this makes it a useful lens to view the process of technology skill acquisition.

Introduction

This is a study of how indigenous peoples in a remote community have taught themselves to use Internet banking. I give a brief literature review to situate the theories I am using to discuss my findings. I establish this project as effective learning and then focus on the characteristics of the learners, the training method and the context of learning. Some very strong themes are apparent: the importance of personal networks, the central position of the workplace as the location as well as the facilitator of learning and the place of personal agency to take up opportunities to learn.

The project is presented as an exploratory one to see how such a situation aligns with existing theories on adult learning, indigenous learning and workplace learning.

Methodology

This research is conducted as an ethnographic case study and includes some quantitative data analysis. The data collection follows a multiple method approach, including initial exploratory observation, interview and informal conversations. A questionnaire was used as a supportive technique for the qualitative findings. The participant sample was representative of the active Internet bank users; it does not include those people who enlisted others to do their Internet banking for them. The research was conducted on site.

Literature Review

There are a range of theories that offer partial explanations for the situation of this project.

Knowles developed a concept of adult learning distinguishing between how children and adults learn. He called this "andragogy" and argued that the life experiences of adults are a rich resource for self-directed problem solving groups (1985). His work underpins a range of work-based learning theories which make the further distinction between how workers learn and how people learn in institutions. Mitchell and Young (2001), outlining the derivation of work-based learning theories, identify key researchers in this field as Mezirow (1981),

Kolb (1984), Marsick (1987), Boud (1997) and Garrick (1998). Adult learning theory is also used in work on aboriginal learning (ANTA, 2004).

Activity theory, or more properly the cultural-historical theory of activity, is a general learning theory. It works on the relationship between human agents and objects of environment as mediated by cultural means, tools and signs. The founders of this theory were Lev Vygotsky, A. N. Leont'ev and A. R. Luria in the 1920s and 1930s. This theory provides structure for a socio-cultural work-based learning approach. Mitchell and Young (2001) include Billet (1993, 1994), Lave and Wenger (1991), Vygotsky (1978) and Wenger and Snyder (2000) as the main researchers using this approach. In this chapter I draw on Stephen Billet's work. Billet challenges the distinction between institutional, or formal, learning and workplace, or informal, learning.

Aboriginal learning style is another approach, whose primary source in Australia is Stephen Harris in *Culture and Learning: Tradition and Education in Northeast Arnhem Land*, published in 1980. Harris identified five areas characteristic of indigenous learning: learning by observation; learning from life experiences; learning by trial and error; focus on skills for specific tasks; and emphasis on people and relationships. Harris' work was particularly influential in raising awareness of the importance of a contextualized system and style of learning. Other researchers in this field include Nichol and Robinson (1999), Nichol (2002) and Malin (1990). Hughes and More (1997) provide an international perspective.

Whilst theorists of indigenous learning agree that indigenous peoples are culturally and linguistically very diverse within Australia, as well as differing from rural to urban settings (Nichol & Robinson, 1999; Nichol, 2002; Nakata, 2000; Gelade & Stehlik, 2004; Robertson, 2004), they claim an essential indigenous learning style or at least sufficient common factors to make it useful to talk about one (Hughes & More, 1997).

Substantial work has been done under social justice auspices to develop resources and curriculum for teachers of indigenous students. These contain practical strategies based on learning styles theory as well as aboriginal learning styles and adult learning principles (Robertson, 2004; ANTA, 2004). This work is supported by reports that critically look at the impact of context and location on indigenous learning outcomes (Gelade & Stehlik, 2004).

Background

The project takes place on a small remote island with a population around 120. Radio, television, video and stereo ownership is nearly universal. Every household has or has had a telephone. Private computer ownership is limited, so although satellite and dialup Internet access is available, fast and reliable, few households can access it. The school and the council are the only workplaces with Internet access, and only one other workplace has a computer. There is limited availability of newspapers and there is no library.

Neighbouring island communities are at a similar technological level but neighbouring villages in Papua, New Guinea have little technological development.

There is a primary school on the island, however, children must go away to boarding school for secondary education. The post school training available on the island is generally work related.

The banking services are limited to telephone banking, EFTPOS, Internet banking and credit card. Money transfers may be done at businesses on the island at a cost of between $11 and $30 per transaction.

Internet Banking Sites

Participants in the project used a number of different banks; however there are general features of their Internet Web sites. Though the "log on" section may be hyperlinked to a tutorial (only one bank has an interactive test-drive tutorial), or troubleshooting area, it always has a local call telephone number for assistance. Different banks' "Help" are not interactive but they may be hyperlinked to a text glossary. Financial awareness training is included on the bank sites; however, it is primarily designed for school children. The sites also offer some "tools" to calculate such things as time and cost of loans or savings plans, information about other bank services and may also have finance-related news updates and newsletters.

Results

Participant Profile

All project participants are currently employed. Of the participants, 29% are currently enrolled in job-related training courses and 57% have completed a post compulsory education award.

Participants identified a variety of places where they had learnt their computer skills:

- 86% of participants identified work as one of the places;
- 71% learnt at school;
- 57% identified learning at a training course on the island; and
- 57% identified learning their technology skills in training off the island also.

All participants had computer skills prior to using Internet banking, and 71% owned their own computer. However, at the time of writing, 57% stated that their computer was not working.

Of the island population, 17.5% regularly use computers; this exceeds the 2001 census figures of 4.5% of the indigenous population in the Torres Strait region using computers (Arthur, 2003). This percentage compares with an Australia-wide rate of 17.3% for Torres Strait Islanders who use computers (including Torres Strait Islanders who live on the mainland), although it is well below the non-indigenous Australia-wide rate of 44% for computer usage (Arthur, 2003).

Participants came to know of Internet banking from a variety of sources:

- 57% heard about it through their personal network (the questionnaire did not ask the location of this person);
- 14% read bank advertising;
- 29% were introduced to it in a professional development activity; and
- 14% saw it being done.

Once they were aware of Internet banking:

- 86% went to the Web site to read about it;
- 14% asked other people; and
- 14% telephoned the bank (participants could indicate more than one source of information).

Participants demonstrated a combination of strategies to learn Internet banking:

- 29% learnt from a friend;
- 14% did the online tutorial;

- 43% just went in and started to work through the process on the live Web site; and
- 14% observed someone else doing it.

In all, 71% were independently learning.

Effective Learning

It is important for the scope of this project to establish that this process represents effective learning. I have used Kirkpatrick's (1994) four-level model for assessing training effectiveness to evaluate this project. This model includes evaluation of the impact of the project on the surrounding community, and it has been effective for evaluating online training and information technology projects. Specific questions were included in the questionnaire for this purpose.

Level 1 Reaction to the Training Process

- 71% found Internet banking easy to use; and
- 29% took some time to work it out but now find it easy.

They said they liked it because it was easy.

Level 2 Amount Learnt

Participants identified the following things they had learnt to do in Internet banking:

- all 100% check account balance, check statement and transfer to another person's account;
- 71% are paying bills and transferring between own accounts; and
- 14% used the scheduling of transactions facility, the search for bank fees facility, other bank services, money management information, viruses and security and how to minimize transaction fees.

To access the online banking program participants had already used a diverse range of skills, such as information seeking, problem solving, navigating, that is, making associative or referential links, comprehension to sort information for relevance and processing knowledge from both graphical and textual information (McKavanagh et al., 1999).

Level 3. Transfer, or Amount of Material Learnt that Participants Actually Use

This is established use:

- 43% report using Internet banking every week;
- 29% every fortnight; and
- 29% every month.

Participants' responses show that they are very focused on Internet banking primarily for checking their accounts and transferring funds on an ad hoc basis. Very low to zero ranking was given to doing banking tutorials or accessing other information about bank services. Fifty-seven percent report setting up their own additional bank accounts for Internet banking.

Level 4. Value to the Community

The ability to Internet bank has been of benefit to more than just the individuals concerned. The participants have helped and taught others the process: 29% reported helping more than 10 other people to do Internet banking. Those who help report that they spend more time doing banking for other people than on their own. The people they help may be on the same island or family members on other islands; they may be older and not want to deal with technology, or find it difficult to access technology. This sharing of skills has been reported as a learning "multiplier effect" in other communities (Gelade & Stehlik, 2004)

All participants report that Internet banking saves them money in fees. Eighty-six percent report being able to send money to family, and 43% report accessing off-island shopping as advantages of Internet banking. Participants comment that it gives them choice and the potential to do more shopping off island. Fifty-seven percent report that Internet banking enables them to manage their money better; better money management could be considered an aspect of community capacity building. Evaluating from these four perspectives indicates this to be effective "training."

Discussion

The project has elements of workplace learning, indigenous learning styles and adult learning theory. Between them, these theories address the characteristics of the learner, the training methods and content as well as the context of delivery.

Characteristics of the Learner

The participant profiles show this group is not representative of the community as a whole. They are all employed people, which means they are working out technical and administrative problems daily. They have completed or are in training, so they are experienced learners developing skills over time using a variety of training sources. As government employees they are used to dealing with European culture and English language, so language is not the barrier to learning that other remote indigenous students may face (Gelade & Stehlik, 2004).

The adult learning approach states that adults are autonomous and self directed, goal oriented and relevancy oriented (they need to know why they are learning something), are practical problem solvers and have accumulated life experiences (Blackmore, 1996). The study confirms the participants are showing these characteristics and that this online learning suited them.

Aboriginal learning theorists add both insight and contradictions. Traditionally skills were learned by observation, imitation and real life practice and from an oral tradition linking song, site, skin and ceremony (Nichol & Robinson, 1999). The historical model indicates the importance of learning in context and of personal links with information. Nichol (2002, p. 7) summarizes the characteristics of aboriginal learners now as "holistic, imaginal, (through observation and imitation rather than verbalisation), kinaesthetic, cooperative, contextual and person oriented." This project exemplifies aspects of all of these learning styles. However, while participants were reliant on personal links for the concept of Internet banking, there was a strong preference toward independent learning and privacy.

Where successful learning has occurred we can see adult learning and indigenous learning styles evident. However, what makes learners choose to take up, or to make, opportunities to learn this particular skill? Motivation is important; a "lack of clear goals" has been offered as a reason for poor learning outcomes in training programs (Bowman, 2004; Gelade & Stehlik, 2004). In this project participants identified saving money in transaction fees and having choice and control of their finances as benefits of Internet banking. In interview, they reported that their reason for learning Internet banking was because it was easy. The choice to learn is complex and not entirely conscious; Billet describes it as a person's agency and, within that, active agency. Agency determines their engagement with the social world; each person's worldview is shaped by their history and experiences, values and beliefs and, from this, individuals will decide whether they will engage with workplace learning opportunities (Billet, 2001).

Individual choice to learn is internal and learners have a learning style preference, but the nature of the training and the context of the training are also fundamental considerations in making that choice.

Training Methods

The bank site and banking tutorial for connecting to Internet banking are consistent with just in time (JIT) learning. This approach is used to deliver training to workers on the job rather than in traditional classroom training. Workers use online tutorials, interactive CD-ROMs and other tools to access the information they need to solve the particular problem they have at the time. Features of this approach are learner control, time and place independence and functional use of information. It is a constructivist model where learners actively construct knowledge by integrating new information and experiences into their existing knowledge. This approach aligns with adult learning principles, and this mode has been identified as a way to make training more culturally appropriate for indigenous peoples, with its focus on skills for specific tasks (Robertson, 2004; Gelade & Stehlik, 2004).

Critics of JIT argue that these models transform learners and consumers into individuals who understand what they need, where to find it and how to use it (Riel, 2001). JIT suits some learners but it may further disadvantage those who have less developed analytical or critical skills. In this study we see participants selectively accessing information and learning particular skills. The results show that they took what they already knew, a service that they had previously used in different form, but did not explore far beyond, even though they were in an information rich environment relevant to their banking interests.

Riel (2001) argues that the enormous amount of information on the Internet ultimately increases our dependence on each other. This study shows the importance of a personal link to information: most people found out about it from a friend, which in such an isolated region is a significant finding.

The bank site design presupposes users will already be familiar with the Internet, the procedures and terms of banking and be motivated to persevere with the process through their need to access their accounts. Participants in the study have responded very positively to the bank Web sites and their learning experience. No problems or suggestions for improvement have been made either in interview or questionnaire.

Context of Learning

The two aspects of extreme remoteness and very small population are important in this project. The community is too small to support specialist staff for services; the few staff employed must be generalists, and the community is too isolated for easy sharing of skills and training from outside. Location is recognised as a determining factor for opportunities and choices for education (Gelade & Stehlik, 2004). It affects the literacy, language, attendance, health and self esteem of the learners (NLLIA, 1996), and the availability of teachers and trainers.

The workplace in this project is both the site of learning and the place where the technology is accessed. Billet (2002) explores ways of understanding workplace participation as learning experience. In this project the workplace provides a nexus of the learner, site and participation, or context, for learning.

Billet uses a range of conceptual bases; however, they all focus on relations between individual cognition and the social sources of knowledge and contribution to learning. He argues that workplaces are sites of social practice and identifies three factors that affect learning: inter-psychological processes between individual and social partners, artefacts, symbols and the physical environment; workplace affordance; and the agency of the learner. He describes learning as co-participative, that is, both how the workplace affords participation and how individuals elect to engage with the work practice and therefore learn (Billet, 2001b).

Billet argues that opportunities for learning are distributed by "factors such as workplace cliques, affiliations, gender, race, language or employment standing and status" (2001a, p. 89), and that individuals' engagement with the workplace is a "product of their personal history or ontogeny, which is shaped by their social experiences" (2001b, p. 99). In this study, the ability to do Internet banking is closely tied to opportunities to access computers in the office. Council employees have access to their work computers but some "outsiders" access the computers also. These "outsiders" may have access on the basis of family or personal links, but there is also a sort of professional network operating in that some employees from other organisations may access the computers.

Billet (2001, p. 98) gives examples of the affordance a workplace offers as access to other workers, time to practice and learn, inclusion in knowledge sharing, discussion groups, access to knowledge, implementation of training programs, encouragement, attitude and skills of co-workers and opportunity to practice. Affordance may be more or less active.

This workplace is shown to have active affordance in that non-work related learning and use of computers by staff is openly encouraged in the understanding that the skills people learn on the computer in non-work activity will be transferable to the work situation. There is also an established pattern of skill sharing and even some degree of competition in learning new skills with software.

Future Study

This exploratory study has shown the value of using a range of perspectives. Future work would look at a framework, such as activity theory, to tie the perspectives together. The workplace is a significant factor in this situation and future work should include a more detailed study of aspects of Billet's workplace learning approach in relation to this workplace.

Conclusion

This project has looked briefly at characteristics of learners, the training program and the context in which it occurs. Each area has provided insight and reinforces the idea that learning can not be studied apart from the context in which it occurs.

Some very strong themes are apparent: personal networks were the impetus for people to start the process, the workplace was important for access to both equipment and to willing and skilled support and the place of personal agency to choose to take up this learning opportunity.

Workplaces in remote areas are sites for information, ICT skills and knowledge acquisition, opportunities for ad-hoc learning, English language practice, a reliable computer system and the opportunity to attend training on and off the island. In a remote area workplaces are relatively more important than workplaces in urban areas because such opportunities are so limited.

Studies of this nature are important to trace the impact of increasing use of ICT on different sectors of society. This study has indicated some of the issues faced by people in a remote area to develop skills and gain access to IT equipment. ICT-enabled bank services have allowed the bank to transfer the major cost and responsibility of providing the banking service to the community, thus leaving people in remote areas vulnerable to exploitation. People in this community are fortunate in that they have a workplace which offers active affordance for learning technology and active, altruistic family and community members to perform bank services for them.

References

Arthur, W. (2003). *Torres Strait Islanders in the 2001 census* (CAEPR Discussion Paper No. 255/2003). Canberra: Australian National University.

Australian National Training Authority. (2004). *Gettin' into it!: Working with indigenous learners.* Melbourne, Australia: Australian Training Products Limited.

Bevan, F. (1999, December). Discovering learning strategies learners develop using hypermedia systems. *Changing practice through research: Changing research through practice. Proceedings of 7th Annual International Conference on Post Compulsory Education and Training,* Surfers Paradise Australia (Vol. 1, pp. 64-74). Brisbane: Centre for Learning and Work Research.

Billet, S. (2001a, December 3-5). A critique of workplace learning discourses: Participation in and continuity of practice. *Knowledge demands for the new economy. Proceedings of 9th Annual International Conference on Post Compulsory Education and Training,* Surfers Paradise, Australia (Vol. 1, pp. 85-92). Brisbane: Centre for Learning and Work Research.

Billet, S. (2001b, December 3-5). Workplace pedagogic practices: Participatory factors on localized arrangements. *Knowledge demands for the new economy. Proceedings of 9th Annual International Conference on Post Compulsory Education and Training* (Vol. 1, pp. 93-101). Brisbane: Centre for Learning and Work Research.

Billet, S. (2002, July 9-12). *Co-participation at work: Understanding learning through work education.* Paper presented at 11th National VET training research conference, Brisbane, Australia. Retrieved May 5, 2004 from, http://ncver.edu.au/newsevents/events/papers/trconf11.html

Blackmore, J. (1996). *Pedagogy: Learning styles.* Retrieved February 5, 2005, from http://granite.cyg.net/~jblackmo/diglib/styl-a.html

Bowman, K. (Ed.). (2004). *Equity in vocational education and training: Research readings.* Adelaide, Australia: National Centre for Vocational Educational Research.

Gelade, S., & Stehlik, T. (2004). *Exploring locality: The impact of context on indigenous vocational education and training aspirations and outcomes.* Adelaide: National Centre for Vocational Educational Research.

Harris, S. (1990). *Two-way aboriginal schooling: Education and cultural survival.* Canberra: Aboriginal Studies Press.

Hughes, P., & More, A. (1997). *Aboriginal ways of learning and learning styles*. Paper presented at the Annual conference of the Australian Association for Research in Education, Brisbane, December. Retrieved February 1, 2005, from www.aare.edu.au/97pap/hughp518.htm

Kirkpatrick, D. L. (1994). *Evaluating training programs: The four levels*. San Fransisco: Berrett-Kohler.

Knowles, M. S. (1985). *Andragogy in action: Applying modern principles of adult learning*. San Fransisco: Jossey-Bass.

Malin, M. (1990). Why is life so hard for aboriginal students in urban classrooms? *Aboriginal Child at School, 18*(1), 9-29.

McKavanagh, C. W., Kanes C., Bevan F., Cunningham A., & Choy, S. (1999, December). A conversational framework for the evaluation of Web-based flexible learning in VET. *Changing practice through research: Changing research through practice. Proceedings of 7th Annual International Conference on Post Compulsory Education and Training* (Vol. 1, pp. 1-11). Brisbane: Centre for Learning and Work Research.

Mitchell, J., & Young, S. (2001). *A new model of work-based learning in the Australian VET sector*. Retrieved February 10, 2005, from http://www.ReframingtheFuture.net

Nakata, M. (2000). History, cultural diversity and English language teaching. In B. Cope & M. Kalantzis (Eds.), *Multiliteracies: Literacy, language and the design of social futures*. South Melbourne: Macmillan.

National Languages and Literacy Institute of Australia. (1996). *Report of National Child Literacy and ESL Project, 1*. Melbourne, Australia: Teaching and Curriculum Centre.

Nichol, R. (2002, September). *To grow up in the ashes: Researching indigenous pedagogy in aboriginal Australia*. Paper presented at 9th International Conference on Hunting and Gathering Societies, Edinburgh.

Nichol, R., & Robinson, J. (1999). Reconciling indigenous pedagogy and SOSE. *Ethos, 2*(2), 1-7.

Riel, M. (2001). *Education in the 21st century: Just in time learning or learning communities*. Retrieved April 30, 2005, from http://www.gse.uci.edu/mriel/jit-learning

Roberston, R., Sclanders, M., Zed, J., & Donaldson, H. (2004). *Working with diversity: Quality training for indigenous Australians*. Brisbane, Australia: Australian National Training Authority.

Chapter VII

Can Information Communication Technological Tools be Used to Suit Aboriginal Learning Pedagogies?

Michael Donovan, University of Newcastle, Australia

Abstract

Indigenous peoples are some of the most disadvantaged groups globally; Australian aboriginal and Torres Strait Islander communities are no different. Much of their lack of success can be related to the inappropriate educational practices directed at them through non-indigenous pedagogical filters of the Australian educational systems. There is a need for some pedagogical change to suit the needs and learning pedagogies of aboriginal and Torres Strait Islander students. By accessing information communication technologies (ICT), aboriginal and Torres Strait Islander communities can improve their educational outcomes. They can design educational programs with aboriginal pedagogies at the forefront to suit their needs using ICT. Outcamp ICT learning centres, placed where aboriginal communities can gain easy access to them and staffed with educators who can help facilitate the development of learning skills, are one solution to improving educational achievement.

Introduction

Indigenous peoples are some of the most disadvantaged groups globally. When using any social indicator, indigenous communities will always be noted at the negative end. Ole Henrik Magga, Chair of the United Nations (UN) Permanent Forum on Indigenous Issues, states that, "[I]t is absolutely clear that with every indicator, with every statistic... on education, livelihood, economy, you name it... the indigenous groups are the lowest; in every country they are far below the average" (Logan, 2004).

Aboriginal and Torres Strait Islander communities are no different; much of their lack of success can be related to the inappropriate educational practices directed at them through non-aboriginal pedagogical filters of the Australian educational systems.

Aboriginal Educational History and the Current Situation

The history of aboriginal education is marked by aboriginal students being denied quality education and the process of attempting to assimilate them into the values of the wider non-aboriginal community (Heitmeyer, 2001).

When viewing aboriginal educational history, you can understand why statistical evidence of aboriginal students' records can be so negative in comparison to non-aboriginal students' records. Levels of retention and attendance are always down when comparing aboriginal to non-aboriginal students. For example, the retention rate for aboriginal students in Australia is relatively poor, with 38% of aboriginal students going through to senior years of school education; this is compared to 79% of non-aboriginal students (NSW Aboriginal Education Consultative Group, 2004). Some answers to why aboriginal students do not complete these years are generally directed towards racism and culturally inappropriate curriculum (McConnochie, 1998). When reviewing literacy and numeracy benchmarks, aboriginal students are again presented less than their non-aboriginal counterparts, such as only 72% of aboriginal students compared to 90% of all students reaching the National literacy benchmarks in Year Three and this gap increasing by Year Five of primary school (NSW Aboriginal Education Consultative Group, 2004). Since the establishment and recorded collection of basic skills testing (BST) results in the early 1970s, aboriginal students' results have constantly been lower than their non-aboriginal counterparts. These gaps can be viewed on a larger scale, such as with an International review of educational standards of 42 Nations where Australia overall was placed fourth but aboriginal Australians placed 30 first, expressing the wide gap between aboriginal and non-aboriginal educational standards (Australian Government, 2002). Through my own 13 years of experience within the field of aboriginal education, I have seen countless programs, policies and curricula developments to attempt to decrease these educational failings with very limited, if any, significant success.

The policies and the outcomes within aboriginal education are controlled completely from state or Commonwealth Government bodies. State governments develop programs and the Commonwealth Government supplies support funds for the running of these aboriginal-specific programs. In 2004 there was no direct funding from NSW State Government budgets directly focusing on aboriginal educational needs. There has been very limited aboriginal input throughout the development of aboriginal education policy or programs. Even today, when the understandings of self-determination are consistently recommended by professionals who report for the Australian Government in education related fields, the involvement given to aboriginal communities is almost nonexistent. The Australian Government consistently ignores the advice from education professionals who suggest giving greater power to aboriginal people in relation to the development of policy and programs to suit aboriginal students' educational needs.

Significant factors that contribute to the poor educational outcomes of aboriginal students are the limited involvement of aboriginal and Torres Strait Islander peoples throughout educational reform (Robertson, Dyson, Norman, & Buckley, 2003). Aboriginal peoples have only in the recent past been able to present their perspectives on the educational developments that are directed towards themselves and their communities. Generally, most of the educational direction has come from a paternalistic point of view of non-aboriginal society, ignoring the influence of their own cultural filters in muddying the educational experience of aboriginal students with the non-aboriginal educational systems.

Acknowledging Aboriginal Pedagogy

The recognition of difference in learning preferences of aboriginal and Torres Strait Island students and the recognition of the need for change is important when developing appropriate educational programs. Gore (1997) notes:

...the incredible "continuity in pedagogical practices" over time despite decades of educational reform. That is, despite a constant flow of new techniques and new curriculum, new ways of understanding learning and new forms of work organisation in schools, there appear to be some aspects

of pedagogical relations and pedagogical practice which have altered little during the past century.

Designing the learning so students can be involved in their own learning experiences is a key issue. Aboriginal pedagogies focus towards the more significant learning styles of aboriginal students and allow students to gain a full understanding of the learning experience. Dodson, cited in Herbert (1998), highlights that aboriginal students are currently being placed through inappropriate systems that are unsuitable to their needs and in which aboriginal pedagogies are not the focus:

We have our own unique ways of knowing, teaching and learning which are firmly grounded in the context of our ways of being. And yet we are thrust into the clothes of another system designed for different bodies, and we are fed ideologies which serve the interests of other peoples.

Fraser (2004) reinforces these comments in his research on aboriginal pedagogy suggesting that, "good indigenous pedagogy is right for all students but not all pedagogy is good for indigenous students."

Many authors who have worked on the identifying of an aboriginal pedagogy have crossed over similar content (Heitmeyer, 2001; Hughes, 1997; Halse, 1999; Craven, 1996; Herbert, 1998; Wyatt, 1998; Harris, 1994). Herbert (1998), in defining aboriginal pedagogy, sees it as having many elements:

I cannot see it as a single entity... the complexities inherent in considering the commonality of the aboriginal experience within the context of our diversity of life experiences means that, for me, an essential element in trying to understand what it is that we are trying to define, is to appreciate its plurality... I think in terms of a common pedagogy underpinning a range of aboriginal pedagogies... I believe it is equally important to acknowledge that there are common threads, aspects of aboriginal pedagogies which, in my opinion, provide the important links... the defining elements which clearly place these pedagogies within the aboriginal realm... Education is an holistic process which is concerned with the overall needs of the individual as a member of the group. Educational needs are perceived as being linked to survival of both the individual and the group.

Engaging the learner in the educational experience is a key element when designing appropriate learning experiences. Heitmeyer (2001, pp. 222) states that:

Educators acknowledge that the most effective way of teaching any concept is to move from the child's known world and to lead them into the unknown... they are disadvantaged at the outset if their learning environment has no similarities to their known world... it is telling Aboriginal students that their ways of doing and knowing are not worthy of recognition... There is more than one correct way of knowing and doing that will lead to successful educational outcomes.

Aspects of aboriginal pedagogy acknowledge that aboriginal students value their place within the group, actively working within peer or group learning experiences; that the placing of learning tasks in the context of the aboriginal student's life or cultural experience will increase the student's motivation and that the development of a space for experimentation or self-investigation will increase their confidence towards that task and allow learning to deal with real-life issues.

Aboriginal pedagogies are becoming recognised as connections to learning for aboriginal students (Hughes, 1997; Heitmeyer, 2001; Herbert, 1998; Harris, 1994; Halse, 1998). But as Halse (1998) suggests, these pedagogies are generalisations: They will connect to many but may not connect to all aboriginal students. Recognising this need and designing educational experiences to cater for individual difference is necessary, thereby connecting more completely to a greater diversity of learning styles. The use of aboriginal pedagogical practices will be positive in maintaining the very distinct aboriginal cultural practice of the group but must be accompanied by an acknowledgment of some diversity in learning styles.

Aboriginal Communities Acceptance of ICT Tools

I have noted through my experiences with aboriginal students, both young and old, that multimedia and ICT are readily accepted, being used creatively and passionately. This suggests an effective partnership between aboriginal learning styles and the pedagogical qualities of ICT tools. My focus in this article will be to examine this partnership and how, by accessing ICT, aboriginal and Torres Strait Islander communities can improve their educational outcomes.

ICT Pedagogy

In my research into the field of the effective use of ICT pedagogies, I have seen that this is still a developing field of understanding. Many of the authors I have examined highlight their understandings in relation to either specific projects or a certain student body, and there appear to be many similarities within their understandings of the use of ICT pedagogies. Some of these pedagogical qualities include the flexibility of this learning tool, the ability to contextualise the learning to suit individual or small group needs, the use of ICT tools in self-directed or peer-directed learning tasks and the ability to develop a space for learning where students can interact and experiment on the learning tasks (Loveless, 2000; Morozov, 2004; Dede, 2005; Jones, 2002; Wonacott, 2002). Loveless (2000, p. 340) highlights some of these pedagogical qualities when using ICT tools effectively:

...a range of teaching strategies was observed in interactions between teachers and children engaged in digital arts activities — including technician and facilitator; questioner and consultant; publisher and promoter; and collaborator and networker.. Effective capability with ICT depends not on techniques, but on the context in which the experience is embedded.

The flexibility of ICT tools has been noted by several theorists. Nunan (1999) highlights the connections between ICT flexibility and preferred educational models: "Part of the attraction of flexible delivery for many educationalists is to link the term with student centred learning, self directed learning, activity learning, problem based learning, open learning, learner controlled instruction and the like."

Dede (2005) highlights that the use of ICT pedagogical models has many benefits for learners in that you can adapt the educational programs to suit the learners' needs:

Increasingly, people want educational products and services tailored to their individual needs rather than one-size-fits-all courses of fixed length, content, and pedagogy. Whether this individualization of educational products is effective depends both on the insight with which learners assess their needs and desires and on the degree to which institutions provide quality customized services rather than Frankenstein-like mixtures of learning modules.

Aboriginal Education and ICT Pedagogy

When comparing aboriginal and ICT pedagogical systems, there are many overlapping commonalities and, when used effectively, many aspects of the ICT pedagogy would work with aboriginal students. Table 1 examines some comparable features of these two pedagogies.

ICT tools can be used to support various aspects of aboriginal and Torres Strait Islander education. Oliver (1999) highlights the capability of ICT to fit with aboriginal pedagogies: "content is flexible, outcomes-oriented and unstructured. The activities are global and anchored, contextualised and authentic. The implementation is teacher as coach, collaborative learning, with integrated assessment."

ICT tools can also be used to support the mobile or transient state of living of many aboriginal students in contemporary aboriginal society. Through family obligations and commitments, many aboriginal families will, at times, move frequently from one area to another, one school to another. These changes can affect the flow of many of these students' educational progression. ICT tools have the ability to continue students' educational programs and maintain a connection with learning tasks. Through the capability of ICT tools to contact centrally stored files from multiple access points and to interact with sequenced educational programs or unfinished projects, students may progress through educational tasks with limited disruption to their learning.

The concept of ongoing lifelong education is possible by using ICT tools to support aboriginal students' educational progression. As an aboriginal adult educator, considering learning as a lifelong experience is an aspect of my culture that I present to the learners. ICT tools can support aboriginal students' lifelong education through distance education programmes, access to information via the Internet, communication with other learners or the establishment of learning communities where understandings and experiences can be shared.

Table 1. Aboriginal and information communication technology pedagogies comparison

Aboriginal pedagogy	ICT pedagogy
Learning through experiencing concepts	Learning through experimentation
Peer or group learning	Can allow group space
Space for own investigation	Allows them to investigate in their own time
Adapt to local context	Learning can be contextualised
Community can direct aspects in their local practices	Learning can be flexible and the design can adapt tasks to specified outcomes

Considering Change

As highlighted earlier, aboriginal and Torres Strait Islander students are statistically the most educationally disadvantaged student cohort (Australian Government, 2002; NSW Aboriginal Education Consultative Committee, 2004). There is a definite need for some positive change to address this situation. When examining the similarities between ICT and aboriginal pedagogies, the connections are positive points in the development of effective learning experiences for aboriginal students. They both work on the basis of supporting the learner to be self-directed, taking responsibility for their personal learning with some guidance from an educational facilitator who designs tasks that are contextually significant to the student's life.

Future Trends: Outcamps

An "Outcamp," or ICT learning centre, would need to be established to allow an aboriginal community to gain access to ICT systems and online learning environments. This centre of both human and technological resources would be established to provide support to aboriginal students. The primary focus of these centres would be to position them for easy access by the aboriginal community and to ensure that the people feel comfortable within this environment. Heitmeyer (2001) highlights the importance of this in the development of any learning environment designed for aboriginal students.

The educational setup would suit online learning environments for isolated aboriginal communities that would have approximately 10 to 15 computer terminals with online access and some storage space on a server for the management of the information presented to students. Any number of training or educational programs could be progressing at any one time. Within the Outcamps, the only human resource needed to support the students would be a person with some educational experience to help facilitate the development of learning skills, particularly with experience in the support of aboriginal learning styles, not an expert to pass on the knowledge. Shaw, cited in Morozov (2004, p. 20), supports this idea, stating that these educational agents should have, "enough understanding of the educational context in order to be able to play certain roles in education scenario and interact with learners during the education course." There would also be a need for some technical expertise in the maintenance of the computer network, but this could be maintained from an external or online source.

The flexibility of choice offered by Outcamps aptly suits the concept of community learning. Aboriginal communities could choose the resources online to suit their academic program and community needs. Students could follow a thread of knowledge that may not have been prescriptively set in an institution as the established program within a degree or degree major. The content and process would be unique to that group of learners. With education institutions using generic outcomes, the education facilitator at the Outcamp, or the coordinator of the education program, could adjust the learning tasks or outcomes to directly relate to the learner's home community.

If effectively coordinated, the aboriginal students could work within educational frameworks that highlight their culture as an important learning tool, contextualising the learning experiences to support local community development or train individuals with skills that are needed within the learners' community. The information literacy skills gained by these students upon the successful completion of an online course would be very empowering, both for them and their communities.

The Outcamps would suit isolated communities. Isolation includes more than remoteness: These communities could be isolated by distance or by social barriers in an urban setting. The seclusion from access to mainstream facilities is just as real in both cases and the need for access to these systems can be as desperate in both. Aboriginal students and their communities would be able to access information globally and participate in global indigenous politics, allowing their voices to be heard outside their immediate environments on the global stage.

Conclusion

There is substantial evidence to show a need for improvement in the educational achievements of aboriginal students. This is not a recent incident and it has been acknowledged since the early 1970s, when records of standardised Basic Skills Tests results began to be maintained showing a significant educational gap between aboriginal students and the rest of the student population. Even with significant targeted funding and specific programming towards aboriginal education, these results have not significantly changed for the better.

The development of effective change for the benefit of aboriginal students is a must and can be brought about through the use of ICT tools, which can complement aboriginal students' preferred learning styles. With the use of Outcamp centres, small aboriginal community-based educational learning spaces can support the educational experiences of aboriginal students, designed with the direction of their community and entrenched within the objectives of educational programs being undertaken.

Educators who have a clear understanding of aboriginal pedagogies can facilitate the learning experience presented to the students or support their understanding of the learning tasks. Self-directed educational tasks that focus on the student or their community's needs will place the learning experience in context for the students, heightening the motivation and importance of that experience for them. By using interactive multimedia tools, the learning experience can cater to a variety of learning styles, dominance being given to the oral, visual or kinaesthetic; the presentation of outcomes can be examined in multiple formats, not just embedded in text.

Our communities can only become more self-determining with the application of this new technology into their learning environment. But the ICT tools are only part of this solution: curriculum design must include the aboriginal students' needs. This combination of using ICT tools to support educational needs, together with programs developed with aboriginal pedagogical qualities at the forefront, will empower aboriginal communities to become self-determining in their educational experiences.

References

Australian Government. (2002). *National report to parliament on indigenous education and training.* Canberra, Australia: Canberra Government Printers. Retrieved June 10, 2002, from http://www.dest.gov.au/schools/publications/subject.htm#Indigenous_Education

Craven, R. (1996). *Teaching the teachers [kit]: Indigenous Australian studies.* Oatley, Australia: School of Teacher Education, UNSW.

Dede, C. (2005). Planning for neomillennial learning styles shifts in students' learning style will prompt a shift to active construction of knowledge through mediated immersion. *Educause Quarterly, 28*(1), 7-12.

Fraser, A., & Hewitt, K. (2004, May 7). *Aina is the textbook: Good Indigenous pedagogy speaks of country as that which sustains and establishes the foundation of knowledge.* Paper presented at the 10th Annual PASE Conference, New York.

Gore, J. (1997). Who has the authority to speak about practice and how does it influence educational inquiry? *The Australian Association for Research in Education Conference, Brisbane.* Retrieved March 29, 2005, from http://www.aare.edu.au/97/gorej305.htm

Halse, C., & Robinson, M. (1999). Towards an appropriate pedagogy for aboriginal children. In R. Craven (Ed.), *Teaching aboriginal studies* (pp. 199-213). St. Leonards, Australia: Allen & Unwin.

Harris, S., & Marlin, M. (1994). *Aboriginal kids in urban classrooms*. Wentworth Falls, Australia: Social Science Press.

Heitmeyer, D. (2001). The issue is not black and white: Aboriginality and education. In J. Allen (Ed.), *Sociology of education: Possibilities and practices*. Katoomba, Australia: Social Science Press.

Herbert, J. (1998). *Making the links*. Aboriginal Pedagogy Conference, Perth, Western Australia. Retrieved April 1, 2005, from http://www.eddept.wa.edu.au/abled/Pedagogy/jherbert.htm

Hughes, P., & More, A. J. (1997). Aboriginal ways of learning and learning styles. *Australian Association for Research in Education*, Brisbane. Retrieved March 29, 2005, from http://www.aare.ed.au/97/hughp518.htm

Jones, C. (2002). The dichotomy of the conquering hero: Looking for the pedagogy in ICT. *Society for Information Technology and Teacher Education International Conference* (Vol. 1, pp. 52-58). Retrieved April 1, 2005, from http://dl.aace.org/10650

Logan, M. (2004). Indigenous children's survival tied to aboriginal culture. *Terraviva, 12*(33), 4-9. Retrieved April 1, 2005 from, http://www.un.org/esa/socdev/unpfii/pfii/TERRAVIVA%20article%20Magga.htm

Loveless, A. M. (2000). Where do you stand to get a good view of pedagogy? *Journal of Technology and Teacher Education, 8*(4), 337-342.

McConnochie, K., Hollingsworth, D., & Pettman, J. (1998). *Race and racism in Australia*. Redfern, Australia: Hogbin Poole Printers.

Morozov, M., Tanakov, A., & Bystrov, D. (2004). A team of pedagogical agents in multimedia environment for children. *Educational Technology & Society*, *7*(2), 19-24.

NSW Aboriginal Education Consultative Group & NSW Dept of Education & Training, (2004). *The report of the review of aboriginal education, Yanigurra muya: Ganggurrinyma taarri guurulaw yirringin.gurray, Freeing the spirit: Dreaming an equal Future*. Sydney, Australia: NSW Department of Education & Training.

Nunan, T. (1999, July 8-12). *Flexible delivery: What is it and why is it a part of current educational debate?* Paper presented at the Higher Education Research and Development Society of Australasia Annual Conference—Different Approaches: Theory and Practice in Higher Education, Perth, Australia. Retrieved June 4, 2000, from http://www.lgu.ac.uk/deliberations/flex.learning/nunan_content.html

Oliver, R. (1999, July 8-12). *Online teaching and learning: New roles for participants*. In *Internationalisation, Flexible Learning, & Technology Conference,* Pre-conference online discussion paper, Monash University. Retrieved June 4, 2000, from http://www.monash.edu.au/groups/flt/1999/online.htm

Robertson, T., Dyson, L. E., Norman, H., & Buckley, B. (2002). *Increasing the participation of indigenous Australians in the information technology industry*. Sydney, Australia: University of Technology. Retrieved April 1, 2005, from http://project.it.uts.edu.au/ipit/ipitp-report.pdf

Wonacott, M. E. (2002). *Blending face-to-face and distance learning methods in adult and career-technical education* (Practice Application Brief No. 23). ERIC clearinghouse on adult, career & vocational education, Columbus, Ohio. Retrieved April 1, 2005, from http://www.cete.org/acve/docgen.asp?tbl=pab&ID=113

Wyatt, K. (1998). *A strategy for reconciliation within the schooling system*. Aboriginal Pedagogy Conference, Perth, Western Australia. Retrieved April 1, 2005, from http://www.eddept.wa.edu.au/abled/Pedagogy/kwyatt.htm

Chapter VIII

Instructional Design and Technology Implications for Indigenous Knowledge: Africa's Introspective

Wanjira Kinuthia, Georgia State University, USA

Abstract

It is fairly accurate to assume that societies are facing a paradigm shift from industrial to information society, and a transition from information to knowledge society. This shift has impacted the nature of the relationship between society, knowledge and technology. It is also valid to assume that knowledge is a resource. This chapter discusses instructional design and technology from Africa's indigenous knowledge perspective. It is not the intent necessarily to dichotomize indigenous and non-indigenous knowledge structures. Rather, the objective is to rationalize the place of indigenous knowledge by addressing the context of usage, challenges and dilemmas, and provide a rationale and suggestions for instructional integration.

Introduction

In Africa, as elsewhere, much has been written about information and communication technology (ICT), even though it has been too expensive, complicated or outside everyday culture for many indigenous peoples (Adam & Wood, 1999; Herselman & Britton, 2002; Sonaike, 2004). Specifically, ICT (mis)application is well noted, as is the direct and indirect influence that it has on society (Gibson, O'Reily, & Hughes, 2002; Liberman, 2003; Reiser, 2001). These dynamics influence the distribution of knowledge and *its* (mis)application. While a persuasive argument is presented here for the integration of indigenous knowledge (IK) into the curriculum and for proposed instructional and pedagogical practices, no suggestion is made that either will go uncontested or will be seamlessly validated. It is, however, argued that when making instructional decisions it is pertinent to acknowledge IK structures.

Instructional design and technology (IDT) is guided by theories and models that direct the development of instructional sequencing. It encompasses analysis of learning and performance problems, design, development, implementation, evaluation and management of instructional and non-instructional processes and resources. Instructional goals are accomplished through systematic procedures and various instructional media (Reiser, 2001). ICT, on the other hand, refers to computers, software, networks and related systems that allow users to access, analyze, create, exchange and use data, information and knowledge. If successfully implemented and maintained, the infrastructure brings together people in different places and time zones with multimedia tools for data, information and knowledge management (Herselman & Britton, 2002). Interestingly, the growing awareness of IDT has coincided with increased ICT application (Dillion, 2004; Reiser, 2001). However, as Dillon observes, ICT has no theoretical foundation of its own and has applied theories developed in education, while IDT utilizes both educational and technological theories.

In this chapter, the term "indigenous peoples" is used holistically to refer to multiple groups in Africa and their interaction with introduced Western-influenced education systems. The term is contrasted with "non-indigenous" knowledge. While the term "knowledge" is used singularly, the position of this chapter is that there is not a single ideal of "knowledge" and that each group has its own understanding and interpretation of "knowledge." Likewise, the term "peoples" reflects multiple groups. Although the term "Africa" is also used broadly, the diverse nature of the continent is recognized, as are the shared histories and processes. Therefore, this chapter is written with the recognition that many "knowledges" exist in the context of Africa's "peoples"

It is not the intention of the chapter to diminish the role of "Western" education. Rather, it is an attempt to contextualize IDT within a context of IK that utilizes

ICT, and suggests ways that both knowledge structures can be merged to accommodate learners. The discussion is an introspective of Africa's IK structures, instructional implications and challenges facing the integration process. Recommendations and suggestions for implementation are also presented.

Contextualizing Africa's Indigenous Knowledge Structures

Around the world, indigenous peoples face difficulties in gaining adequate recognition. Likewise, indigenousness as a concept fails to attain the status it deserves (Miller, 2003). Maybury-Lewis (2002) observes that there is no clear-cut distinction between indigenous peoples and other localized ethnic groups. Who then are indigenous peoples? The term is ambiguous because a majority of the peoples are "indigenous" in the sense of having been born [there] and descended from those who were born [there].

While there are several definitions, most describe indigenous peoples as those social groups that are culturally identified and maintain historical continuity with their ancestry. This continuity is in the forms of their organization, culture, self-identification, and languages (Dei, 2000a, 200b; Semali & Kincheloe, 1999). Another definition views them as descendants of those who have been marginalized, for example the Basarwa of Botswana and the Maasai of Kenya and Tanzania, by major powers and dominant groups (Mammo, 1999; Maybury-Lewis, 2002; McGovern, 1999; Wangoola, 2000). In both cases, indigenous peoples have maintained a lifestyle that sets them apart from the rest of society, and have traditionally been subordinated and marginalized by unequal economic, political, and social structures (Wangoola, 2000).

Maybury-Lewis (2002) and Miller (2003) make an observation that in Africa, the difference between "indigenous peoples," "ethnic groups" and "minority groups" is difficult to discern. In fact, as noted by Miller, some argue that the concept of "indigenous" is inappropriate in Africa because the situation is too complex, there are too many potential Indigenes, and identities are too tangled. On the contrary, Semali (1999) argues that for residents of Africa, IK is not as elusive as suggested. In presenting the case of Tanzania, Semali notes that what is elusive is the fact that knowledge structures have not been systemically documented or taught in formal settings. Inadvertently, these knowledge structures are gradually being forgotten and replaced by formal education and technology. Despite the alleged nebulosity in definition, indigenous peoples make up about 5% of the world population (Maybury-Lewis, 2002). In Africa, this number accounts for 30 million nomadic peoples. Yet another statistic estimates 1.2% of the population in Africa as indigenous (Miller, 2003).

Like the term indigenous peoples, IK has multiple descriptors, many of which refer to the unique, traditional and local knowledge existing within and developed around the specific conditions of local peoples resulting from their long-term geographical residence. This knowledge is part of the cultural heritage and histories and preserves a way of life and serves social interests. Such knowledge systems are cumulative and represent generations of experiences. Recognition of the embedded nature of culture to the situational, historical and political context supports the argument that the term "indigenous" is not a detached concept. It can then be inferred that the ability to use these knowledge forms is pertinent to peoples' understanding of themselves and their world, and will have an influence on their education systems (Dei, 2000a; Mosha, 1999; Wangoola, 2000). Thus, IK is cultural knowledge in its broadest form (Dei, 2000a, 2000b; Robyn, 2002; Semali, 1999). This brings us to the understanding that Western-style education and a history of colonization led to instances where indigenous populations were excluded from participation in introduced education systems due to a lack of consensus as to what constitutes knowledge (Wangoola, 2000).

Incorporating Indigenous Knowledge: Conflicts, Challenges and Complexities

The interface between instruction and IK is rarely the focus of attention in post-colonial African education systems, and the transfer of IK from the learners' everyday life to formal instruction is not necessarily encouraged. Nonetheless, IK is about what local people know and do, and have done for generations (Mammo, 1999; Semali, 1999; Wangoola, 2000). A challenge encountered is the facilitation, recognition and validation of the legitimacy of IK as a pedagogical, instructional and communicative tool due to:

1. indigenous educators being discounted as having valuable expertise;
2. an underlying fear that introduction of indigenous content is potentially identifiable with the dominant indigenous group;
3. the notion that diverse cultures with differing opinions can create conflict;
4. the fact that introduced systems of education may not allow for cultural differences, as acknowledged by both indigenous and non-indigenous educators; and
5. the limits of oral knowledge transition to literate forms.

Paradoxically, the maintenance of multiple cultural identities in the instructional process simultaneously serves the needs of indigenous peoples and informs non-indigenous learners (Mosha, 1999; Semali, 1999). Yet, as stated by Semeli (1999) and indicated in Table 1, few attempts have successfully implemented localized, indigenized curricula.

Indigenous Knowledge and Technology

Depending on availability and access, perceived benefit and economic capacity, indigenous groups have historically taken advantage of new technologies. Such decisions are generally taken as positive progression, but it also infers leaving some things behind (Lieberman, 2003). In the Zimbabwe case cited by Lewis (2000), technology education assumed new status after independence but takes on different names at different times and phases of the education system. For example, at the primary level, the focus is on agriculture, and at the secondary level, on woods and metals.

For those that are unable to cross the so-called "digital divide," ICT is yet another means to marginalize indigenous groups (Cavallo, 2000; Herselman & Britton, 2002). Moreover, when misapplied, the consequences of ICT can be repercussive: When it is introduced to indigenous groups it brings along mass media, popular culture and global languages that can potentially conflict with local traditions. Paradoxically, these same technologies also provide users with new tools that can be used to preserve, promote and strengthen their culture (Lieberman, 2003). The challenge with ICT is to make it relevant to the user, not to assume that it is in great demand by all peoples; users should be aware of the "alternatives" available (McGovern, 1999; Sillitoe, 1999). Successful participation is impractical when potential users do not know what the alternatives are (Herselman & Britton, 2004). In many countries, ICT adoption involves a

Table 1. Reasons for lack of indigenous knowledge integration

- Lack of political motivation to deal with contradictions between intentions and practical applications of the curriculum
- Reliance on foreign aid that stipulates curriculum planning
- Reliance on macro planning that ignores local needs and disparities
- Inappropriate research methods
- Failure to incorporate African instructional methodologies
- Limited funding to support Indigenous education research
- Alienation of intellectuals from their own culture

substantial learning cycle, level of investment, continuous change and reliance on donor resources that are often presented with strings attached. This creates dependencies that inadvertently result in underutilization of existing technology, reinforced by inappropriate instructional application and tools (Adam & Wood, 1999).

Africa, by its sheer nature, has many ethnicities and Indigenes. Localized relevance of IK, therefore, has significant bearing on the organization of knowledge and ICT incorporation (Dei, 2001b; McGovern, 1999; Sillitoe, 2002). Two aspects can potentially complicate integration:

1. the uniqueness of IK in a particular culture does not imply consensus with other cultural or indigenous groups' knowledge structures; and
2. in this highly transient "global" lifestyle, it is not uncommon for IK to be influenced by non-indigenous knowledge.

Examples from Ghana and Ethiopia, Dei (2000b) and Mammo (1999), demonstrate complexities when syllabi are not designed with these aspects in mind at inception. Lewis (2000) draws on the example of Nigeria, where obstacles result in lack of indigenous capacity to assimilate, adapt and/or create technology.

Incorporating Indigenous Knowledge: Future and Promises

A question posed is by McLoughlin and Oliver (2000): "Is cultural pluralism even possible in designing instruction?" Instruction that acknowledges and incorporates multiple cultural perspectives regardless of the instructional content may qualify as culturally pluralistic. It then becomes the task of educators to contextualize cognitive, social, cultural and pedagogical elements. Is meaningful integration of indigenous and non-indigenous forms of instruction therefore possible? It can be argued that to blend local knowledge into formal education fallaciously assumes that indigenous education systems represent an easily definable body of knowledge ready for extraction and incorporation (Cavallo, 2000; Mosha, 1999).

Underutilization of ICT signals the need for indigenous capacity-building (Adam & Wood, 1999). Dillon (2004) and Jones (2001) outline the purposes for ICT integration in instruction as:

1. intrinsic individual development;
2. improving the economy of a people, and
3. immersion into a culture.

As part of the cultural immersion, learners are introduced to technology so that they can understand it and be able to participate in it at some level. Technology therefore stands alongside other ways that culture is represented. Jones presents the argument that if technology is indeed integral to our world, learners need to understand how it shapes that world and education should prepare them to do this by dealing with the underlying technical, social, ethical, political and economic issues.

While investment in ICT alone cannot yield results, it follows that well-implemented ICT has the potential to bring theory closer to instructional practice. For instance, Higgs, Higgs, and Venter (2003) argue that for development to occur in the South African context, indigenized innovations and knowledge systems should be considered in higher education curricula. Several projects demonstrate the benefits of carefully integrated technology and cultural content (Gibson et al., 2002; Reiser, 2001). ICT is being used to enhance education by including emerging technologies such as e-learning and multimedia classrooms (Herselman & Britton, 2002). There are various examples of blended IK, ICT and Web resources used to present cultural information published by indigenous groups for a global audience, chat rooms in indigenous languages and CD-ROMs for learning indigenous languages (Lieberman, 2003). Kenyatta University in Kenya, for example, houses the African Virtual University. It also houses the Culture Village, an outfit that blends Western and local cultures where learners are presented with opportunities to explore both technical and cultural dimensions.

To help learners acquire critical thinking skills and question the absence of indigenous literature in the curriculum, pedagogical and instructional practices that target indigenous concerns and issues should include:

1. Developing an awareness of IK: learners should be exposed to processes that acknowledge the sources of empowerment and disempowerment in society. They must also acknowledge their capacity to engage in self-reflective knowledge production. This is accomplished through open discussions with learners, use of indigenous guest speakers, resources, displays and field trips to indigenous communities and participation in cultural celebrations, all of which are placed in appropriate histories and contexts.

2. Developing advocacy and support networks to promote indigenous educators.
3. Developing sustainable community action, including linkages and guidance from the communities.
4. Addressing pertinent issues at a political level.

These strategies must define the guiding principles, objectives and goals, establish a plan of action and develop resource lists. An understanding of probable outcomes and change agents responsible for executing action plans must also be considered (McLoughlin & Oliver, 2000).

Pedagogical, instructional and communicative approaches to synthesizing different knowledge structures should allow learners to produce and control knowledge about themselves and their communities. Therefore, they must resonate with *their* culture and traditions as a basis for contributing to a universal knowledge system in a process that is viewed as both intergenerational and holistic (Cavallo, 2000; Mosha, 1999; Reiser, 2001). This necessitates a systemic change process; one that incorporates synthesized, multiple, collective and collaborative dimensions of knowledge. As stated by Herselman and Britton (2002), when considering the possibility, viability and desirability of ICT as an educational vehicle, it is important to examine political, social and individual interests as demonstrated in Table 2.

There is a need to form links that merge instructional skills with technical and scientific knowledge. Facilitating meaningful communication between ICT investigators and indigenous communities is therefore pertinent to establishing what ICT may have to offer them (Mundy & Compton, 1995). Communicative processes should inform this process, otherwise local participation is likely to have limited impact. The communicative approach encourages reciprocal flow

Table 2. Suggestion for indigenous knowledge integration

• Formalized agencies to oversee Indigenous instructional systems • Developing curricula that respect and promote Indigenous values, philosophies, and ideologies • Developing culturally sensitive and inclusive curricula • Establishing fair and equal evaluation and assessment • Promoting Indigenous languages in instruction • Establishing parameters and ethics of Indigenous education research • Establishing Indigenous education standards

of ideas, information and mutual decision-making (Mundy & Compton, 1995; Grenier, 1998; Viergever, 1999).

Interest in IK is growing beyond the anthropological documentation of cultures. In recognition of the importance of this need for continued research, literature in IDT, for example, is exploring applications of cultural knowledge. The research sets out to make connections between local peoples' understandings and practices and those of outside researchers (Viergever, 1999; Reyner, 1999; Semali, 1999). It also aims to contribute to long term positive change and promote cultural inclusiveness (Abdullah & Stringer, 1999; Grenier, 1998; Sillitoe, 1998). The success of research therefore depends on the appropriateness of approaches and recognition of existing sociopolitical and cultural constraints (Viergever, 1999).

Mosha (1999) presents exemplars of how the Chagga of Tanzania assimilate learning opportunities as everyday interaction and teachable moments. He describes the instructional process and its fundamental virtues, and proposes that modern education should also give equal emphasis to spiritual development and intellectual growth. Mosha thus proposes that for instructional programs to be truly effective in Tanzania or elsewhere, they should be holistic and unrelenting in their quest to educate the entire being. This applies also to instructional programs that incorporate ICT.

It can be argued that instructional processes that address the needs of indigenous peoples are bound to be more effective and meaningful to both the indigenous and non-indigenous learners. Thus, transferring and sharing of knowledge should not be about coming up with technological fixes to [their] problems, or passing along ICT for [them] to adopt. It should be about acknowledging that they have their own effective knowledge, resources, and practice management systems (Sillitoe, 1998). To promote a positive impact, ICT should be central to instructional processes that stimulate critical thinking and that are supported simultaneously by research as a means to providing insightful feedback (Adam & Wood, 1999).

Incorporating IK into IDT assumes that coexistence of different knowledge structures is conceivable, and that while they can complement each other, they may be in conflict. To avoid fallacious dichotomization of knowledge structures, it is important to understand that the past continues to influence the present and the present influences the narration of the past. Because different knowledge systems represent different points on a continuum, it is necessary to work toward synthesis of the different systems, both indigenous and non-indigenous. ICT dissemination should be a continuous search for jointly negotiated advances rather than as a top-down imposition. It should seek systematic accommodation of IK in research on technological interventions. While this is not an easy task, it is one that requires formulation of strategies that meet demands and challenges: cost-effective, time-effective, insightful, readily intelligible to non-experts yet not compromising expectations (Sillitoe, 1998; Viergever, 1999).

Conclusion

This chapter does not intend to imply that each culture must translate the other's conceptions or test itself according to another's standards. Indigenous and non-indigenous perspectives must be considered alongside each other. IK does not set aside other knowledge structures. Rather, a hybrid of the knowledge forms is advocated because different bodies of knowledge continually influence each other and demonstrate the interrelated dynamics of all knowledge systems. Ethnocentric dangers arise when comparing and contrasting knowledge forms, imputing inappropriate concerns and predetermining problems that may or may not exist. It must be also recognized that knowledge is relative to the cultural context, and what may be appropriate in one context may not suit another.

A collaborative dimension of knowledge speaks to the diversity of histories, events and experiences that shape our view of an interconnected world. When advocating incorporation into technology, one must be aware of the challenges, nuances, contradictions and contestations. With the consensus that knowledge is not a static entity, IK needs to be an integral part of the ongoing co-creation and re-creation of instructional knowledge.

References

Abdulah, J., & Stringer, E. (1999). Indigenous knowledge, indigenous learning, indigenous research. In L. M. Semali & J. L. Kincheloe (Eds.), *What is indigenous knowledge? Voices from the academy* (pp. 143-155). New York: Falmer.

Adam, L., & Wood, F. (1999). An investigation of the impact of information and communication technologies in sub-Saharan Africa. *Journal of Information Science, 25*(4), 307-318.

Cavallo, D. (2000). Emergent design and learning environments: Building on indigenous knowledge. *IBM Systems Journal, 39*(3-4), 768-781.

Dei, G. J. (2000a). Rethinking the role of indigenous knowledges in the academy. *International Journal of Inclusive Education, 4*(2), 111-132.

Dei, G. J. (2000b). African development: The relevance and implications of "indigenousness." In G. J. Dei, B. L. Hall, & D. G. Rosenberg (Eds.), *Indigenous knowledges in global contexts: Multiple readings of our world* (pp. 70-86). Toronto, ON: University of Toronto.

Dillon, P. (2004). Trajectories and tensions in the theory of information and communication technology in education. *British Journal of Educational Studies, 52*(2), 138-150.

Gibson, I. S., O'Reily, C. O., & Hughes, M. I. (2002). Integration of ICT within a project-based learning environment. *European Journal of Engineering Education, 27*(1), 21-30.

Grenier, L. (1998). *Working with indigenous knowledge: A guide for researchers*. Ottawa, ON: International Development Research Centre.

Herselman, M., & Britton, K. G. (2002). Analysing the role of ICT in bridging the digital divide amongst learners. *South African Journal of Education, 22*(4), 270-274.

Higgs, P., Higgs, L. G., & Venter, E. (2003). Indigenous African knowledge systems and innovation in higher education in South Africa. *South African Journal of Higher Education, 17*(2), 40-45.

Jones, A. (2001). Theme issue: Developing research in technology education. *Research in Science Education, 31*, 3-14.

Lewis, T. (2000). Technology education and developing countries. *International Journal of Technology and Design Education, 10*, 163-179.

Lieberman, A. E. (2003). *Taking ownership: Strengthening indigenous cultures and languages through the use of ICTs*. Retrieved January 2, 2005, from http://learnlink.aed.org/Publications/Concept_Papers/taking_ownership.pdf

Mammo, T. (1999). *The paradox of Africa's poverty: The role of indigenous knowledge, traditional practices, and local institutions: The case of Ethiopia*. Lawrenceville, NJ: The Red Sea.

Maybury-Lewis, D. (2002). *Indigenous peoples, ethnic groups, and the state* (2nd ed.). Boston: Allyn and Bacon.

McGovern, S. (1999). *Education, modern development, and indigenous knowledge*. New York: Garland.

McLoughlin, C., & Oliver, R. (2000). Designing learning environments for cultural inclusivity: A case study of indigenous online learning at tertiary level. *Australian Journal of Educational Technology, 16*(1), 58-72. Retrieved December 19, 2004, from http://www.ascilite.org.au/ajet/ajet16/mcloughlin.html

Miller, B. G. (2003). *Invisible Indigenes: The politics of nonrecognition*. Lincoln, NE: University of Nebraska.

Mosha, R. S. (1999). *The heartbeat of indigenous Africa: A study of the Chagga educational system*. New York: Garland.

Mundy, P., & Compton, J. L. (1995). Indigenous communication and indigenous knowledge. In D. M. Warren, D. Brokensha, & L. Jan Slikkerveer (Eds.), *The cultural dimension of development: Indigenous knowledge systems* (pp. 112-123). London: Intermediate Technology.

Reiser, R. (2001). A history of instructional design and technology: Part II: A history of instructional design. *Educational Technology Research and Development, 49*(2), 57-67.

Reynar, R. (1999). Indigenous people's knowledge and education: A tool for development. In L. M. Semali, & J. L. Kincheloe (Eds.), *What is indigenous knowledge: Voices from the academy* (pp. 285-304). New York: Falmer.

Robyn, L. (2002). Indigenous knowledge and technology. *American Indian Quarterly, 2*(6), 198-220.

Semali, L. (1999). Community as classroom: Dilemmas of valuing African indigenous literacy in education. *International Review of Education. 45*(3-4), 305-319.

Semali, L. M., & Kincheloe, J. L. (1999). Introduction: What is indigenous knowledge and why should we study it? In L. M. Semali & J. L. Kincheloe (Eds.), *What is indigenous knowledge: Voices from the academy* (pp. 3-57). New York: Falmer.

Sillitoe, P. (1998). The development of indigenous knowledge: A new applied anthropology. *Current Anthropology, 39*(2), 223-252.

Sillitoe, P. (2002). Globalizing indigenous knowledge. In. P. Sillitoe, A. Bicker, & J. Potteir (Eds.), *Participating in development: Approaches to indigenous knowledge* (pp. 108-138). London: Routledge.

Sonaike, S. A. (2004). The internet and the dilemma of Africa's development. *The International Journal for Communication Studies, 66*(1), 41-61.

Viergever, M. (1999). Indigenous knowledge: An interpretation of views of indigenous people. In L. M. Semali & J. L. Kincheloe (Eds.), *What is indigenous knowledge: Voices from the academy* (pp. 333-343). New York: Falmer Press.

Wangoola, P. (2000). Mpambo, the African multiversity: A philosophy to rekindle the African spirit. In G. J. Dei, B. L. Hall, & D. G. Rosenburg (Eds.), *Indigenous knowledge in global contexts: Multiple readings of our world* (pp. 265-277). Toronto, ON: University of Toronto Press.

Case Study V

Computer Technology and Native Literacy in the Amazon Rain Forest

Gale Goodwin Gómez, Rhode Island College, USA

Education programs among indigenous peoples throughout South America vary greatly in terms of content, instructional objectives, quality and level of instruction and the nature of the participants as well as the educational setting. This case study describes a relatively new component of an ongoing education program that involves Yanomami communities in the Amazon rain forest of northern Brazil. While the use of information technology (IT) in the classroom has become standard in most of the so-called "developed" world, the use of computers in remote indigenous villages is surprising to many observers. In the case of the Brazilian Yanomami, IT represents simply the latest stage in the process of acquiring Western means, such as written language, to strengthen their languages and culture and to provide access to information and knowledge of the outside world. IT is a potentially very powerful tool in their struggle to preserve their economic, political and cultural autonomy and ultimately to ensure their survival in a rapidly changing, globally interconnected world.

What makes the use of IT among the Yanomami so incredible is the rapid pace at which participants mastered reading and writing in their native languages and applied those skills to acquire computer literacy as well. In a few years, members of numerous Yanomami communities have moved from being monolingual speakers of traditional oral languages with limited knowledge of the outside world to employing software programs (designed for highly literate, technologically advanced societies) to produce literacy materials adapted to the needs of learners in remote rain forest villages. The Yanomami are among the largest remaining indigenous groups in the Americas that still live on their traditional lands and practice their traditional, semi-nomadic, hunter-horticulturalist way of life.

The Yanomami Intercultural Education Program (PEI) was begun in Brazil in 1995 by the Pro-Yanomami Commission-CCPY and was closely linked to the village health program instituted five years earlier by the same non-governmental organization. The preparation of educational materials for both of these programs involved, from the beginning, the collaboration of village leaders and reflected the desires and interests of the community. The initial educational goal of the pilot project was native language literacy in a single village of 100 inhabitants and much of the content of those original pedagogical materials related to hygiene and health education issues. At that time, high infant mortality and outbreaks of malaria and epidemics of communicable diseases were major concerns.

Within a mere decade since its inception, the PEI has developed into a regional, indigenous teacher-based program that currently serves over 400 students in 32 village schools (Pro-Yanomami-CCPY, 2004, p. 4). The curriculum has also expanded over time to include a wide range of subjects, including mathematics, geography, history, ecology and cartography. Instruction in the Portuguese language is an important additional aspect of the indigenous teacher training component of the education program. Bilingual literacy has also proved valuable to the training of indigenous medical technicians in a separate but related program.

The latest innovation in the PEI involves teaching applied computer skills to the Yanomami teachers. The goal is to enable them to use solar panel-powered computers in the village schools to produce teaching materials, texts and newsletters and for them to develop an instructional manual in their native languages to be used as a reference to teach other Yanomami about computers. The fact that village newsletters and pedagogical materials are now being self-published with the help of computer software, such as MS Word, PageMaker and Adobe Photoshop, illustrates the application of technology to literacy skills at a truly grassroots level. Futhermore, courses specifically designed for Yanomami teachers on "Computer Skills and Developing Educational Materials" have been offered in recent years by the Pro-Yanomami Commission-CCPY with equipment and technical support furnished by the Roraima State Office of Education in the capital city of Boa Vista (Pro-Yanomami-CCPY, 2004, p. 4). Funding for computers and related hardware for use in five villages was obtained in collaboration with cultural survival in Cambridge, Massachusetts, through an educational exchange program that involved American students, who raised awareness as well as donations in their respective schools, and three Yanomami, who travelled to Cambridge to meet with them.

Literacy and education have fostered inter-village communication and cooperation. Indigenous assemblies are held to discuss political and economic issues and strategies for dealing with local and national government agencies as well as immediate problems relating to increasing encroachment from outsiders, such as incursions into their lands by gold miners and ranchers. These assemblies are documented in letters and petitions translated into Portuguese by bilingual native teachers and sent to the appropriate authorities. Literacy is providing the Yanomami with a means to share ideas and newly-acquired knowledge of the outside world among non-neighboring communities and with opportunities to come together as a united group to protect their common interests.

The results of the Yanomami Intercultural Education Program represent a dramatic transformation for a largely monolingual and still remote society that is attempting — through its representatives — to actively engage the outside world in order to promote its own survival. The ultimate goal of the program is to enable the Yanomami to take responsibility for education and health care among their own people, and to advocate on their own behalf vis-à-vis the national society. They are by no means there yet, but what may have seemed totally inconceivable in the not-so-distant past is becoming a reality. No one in 1995 could have imagined that Yanomami teachers would one day prepare and print out their own pedagogical materials in their own villages, using state-of-the-art informational technology!

Note

For additional information about the Yanomami and current updates on their situation, visit the Pro-Yanomami Web site at http://www.proyanomami.org.br

Reference

Pro-Yanomami-CCPY. (2004, June). Yanomami teachers take computer course. *Boletim Pró-Yanomami*, *49*, 4. Retrieved June 28, 2005, from http://www.proyanomami.org.br/v0904/index.asp?pag=boletim

Case Study VI

Toi Whakaoranga: Maori and Learning Technology

Terry Neal, Institutes of Technology and Polytechnics, New Zealand

Andrea Barr, Tairawhiti Polytechnic, New Zealand

Te Arani Barrett,
Te Whare Wānagna o Awanuiārangi, New Zealand

Kathie Irwin, Awanuiarangi ki Poneke, New Zealand

In early 2004, the Institutes of Technology and Polytechnics of New Zealand (ITPNZ) received funding from the New Zealand government for a project "Critical success factors for effective use of e-learning with Maori learners." A group of individuals passionate about the potential for e-learning to transform learning experiences for everyone, including Maori, developed the project's approach.

Maori, the indigenous peoples of New Zealand, have long felt disempowered by traditional western approaches to education. Our challenge was to build an environment that enabled genuine partnership between Maori and e-learning experts who are predominantly from a western culture. As non-Maori project leaders, we were convinced that M ā ori, whose improved learning was the focus of the project, should play key roles in decision making at all stages.

We began at the management level by approaching leading Maori educationalists to form a group to co-direct the project. This group's active support ensured appropriate decisions were made and cultural protocols were followed, provided a robust framework, gave integrity and credibility to the project and provided access to networks which have been critical to the success of the project.

We demonstrated partnership at the first stage of the project by recognizing the importance of the two baskets of knowledge — e-learning and Maori pedagogies — and by recognizing the importance of their synthesis. First, we commissioned two reports summarizing the existing literature on "What is crucial for effective Maori teaching and learning?" and "What is crucial for effective e-learning?" These latter reports confirmed our assumption that there is little published literature on the use of e-learning with Maori learners. We also commissioned a report analyzing government statistics to understand the present use of e-learning by Maori learners in New Zealand.

To explore where e-learning and Maori pedagogies intersect, we ran a hui (workshop) of 30 individuals, invited because of their expertise in e-learning or Maori education. The aim of this hui was to build on the knowledge shared in the reports by enabling individuals with expertise in one basket of knowledge to build some awareness of the other basket of knowledge. Next, over two days, we processed the two baskets of knowledge together to build new understandings of what is critical for effective use of e-learning with Maori learners. A key factor in the success of this workshop was co-facilitation by two leading lights in their field — a female Maori educationalist and a non-Maori male e-learning expert. We, therefore, achieved partnership at a range of levels.

One of the main themes to emerge from the hui was a positive sense that e-learning provides a vehicle to achieve Maori aspirations, in their fullest expression, and will be utilized to the fullest extent. Harnessed in positive ways, e-learning was identified as a development which could make a vital contribution to nation building in Aotearoa. People shared practical examples of how this was already being achieved. A Web site has been developed by one whanau (family) to help them to stay in contact and to engage the age-old wisdoms associated with whakawhanaungatanga (the process of creating or reaffirming relationships) and genealogy. Other examples related to the ability to gather traditional knowledge and store it for future generations in increasingly sophisticated ways. This includes the use of Maori language and culture in every aspect of the e-learning so that e-learning is experienced as a transformational educational experience.

Those at the hui were adamant, however, that e-learning should not be allowed to become the new vehicle for the promotion of monoculturalism or monolingualism. Worse still, the main threat identified was that e-learning could function as another tool in the colonization of our people. At issue was the legacy of colonization and the political/cultural agenda of assimilation and social control which dominated our past. It took over a century to turn such policy around and to launch a successful cultural renaissance that has seen Maori reclaim education. Losing momentum with this vital social project is a prospect that our people will never countenance again.

We wanted to understand the student experience as well as the perspective of the educators. On advice from the reference group, we organized several focus groups of Maori students engaged in e-learning, seeking to understand their experiences and what worked and did not work for them. We ensured a culturally safe environment by working with a Maori facilitator who understands Maori protocols.

Such energy and interest was generated at the hui that it has led to the development of a new course for educators wishing to upskill in the area of Maori and e-learning. Again, we used a partnership model, bringing together a team consisting of a Maori education expert, an e-learning expert and someone with expertise in both fields. This course will use a blended delivery approach. We are presently developing an online "toolbox" which includes online material to support learners through the online part of the journey, a guide for professional developers to use the online resources and supplement these with face-to-face activities and advice for technicians to install the electronic material in their systems.

The governance groups were keen that the benefits of the research continue beyond the life of the project. We therefore plan to offer the course in partnership between two institutions — a mainstream polytechnic with a strong commitment to Maori learning and a wananga (learning institution) delivering learning based on traditional M ā ori approaches.

Long-term we plan to build on the single course and develop a post-graduate teaching diploma. As well as attracting national interest in New Zealand, we anticipate that there may be international interest in the course.

The reports from this project are available from the New Zealand government's eLearn site: http://www.elearn.govt.nz/elearn/elearn.portal

Case Study VII

Multimedia Curriculum Development Based on the Oral Tradition

Ella Inglebret, Washington State University, USA

Susan Rae Banks, Washington State University, USA

D. Michael Pavel, Washington State University, USA

Rhonda Friedlander, Oneclaw Speech Therapy Services, USA

Mary Loy Stone, Browning School District, USA

Responsiveness to cultural background has become a dominant theme associated with efforts to increase the effectiveness of human service delivery, both in educational and medical settings (Battle, 2002). As a consequence, service providers are in need of educational materials that accurately portray cultural factors impacting their interactions with members of culturally diverse groups. To address the need for materials pertinent to indigenous peoples in the Pacific Northwest (American Indians and Alaska Natives), an interactive, multimedia educational unit, titled "Diverse Voices: Native Perspectives in Human Service Delivery," was developed with funding from the U.S. Department of Education (HO29K70133). A collaborative endeavor among faculty and students at Washington State University in partnership with members of nearby indigenous communities, this project sought to provide an information source for non-indigenous students and professionals, while simultaneously using a culturally congruent pedagogy — the oral tradition.

A participatory action research framework (Reason & Bradbury, 2001) was used to establish the unit's content. Topics to be addressed by the educational unit were identified through small group discussions involving seven indigenous faculty members and students, in collaboration with four indigenous service providers. So that diverse perspectives would be considered, these participants represented five Northwest tribes and native villages and came from various human service professions, including education, speech-language pathology, counselling psychology and tribal administration.

In order to center the curricular pedagogy on the oral tradition, three additional enrolled members of indigenous nations were videotaped as they participated in individual interviews. These interviews were structured to address the themes identified in the small group discussions. Segments from these videotapes then became the focal point for presentation of the curricular content. Consistent with the intent of promoting self-determination for indigenous peoples, the video medium provided a powerful means for native peoples to be seen speaking for themselves. Again, emphasis was placed on recognizing the diversity existing among indigenous communities by presenting various perspectives. While interviewees shared similarity in that they all had extended experience serving indigenous communities, their experiences had been framed through three different professions, including educational administration, special education and speech/language pathology, and through their membership in three different indigenous nations in the Northwest.

Conversion of the videotaped segments into a cohesive, interactive, multimedia curriculum unit was guided by the principles of iterative software design and development. The first author and two computer science students formed a software design team to coordinate editing and digitizing of the videotaped segments and to design the software architecture and associated components. The miroVideo CD20 plus software (miroVideo Computer Products, Inc., 1997) was used for video capturing, digitizing and editing. Adobe Photoshop (Adobe, 1999) was used to create animated images, graphics and activation buttons, while Macromedia Director 8 Shockwave Studio software (Macromedia, 2000) was used to build the interactive, navigational architecture for the software and to incorporate text and music. The user interface was modeled after a common tool, a videotape player, to foster ease of use. This interface allowed users to select topics and speakers of interest and to move among these using individually determined routes.

A key element of iterative software design is continual review and evaluation of the product as it evolves (Barnum, 2002). Thus, the team was involved in prototype testing throughout all stages of development. After an integrated system had been constructed, the software underwent a holistic, integrative evaluation by the interviewees and graduate students of indigenous background. As a result, related modifications were made. The end-product then went through one more level of evaluation. One group of intended users, 22 graduate students in human service delivery fields, participated in usability evaluation of the multimedia educational unit. In this case, usability evaluation was implemented through judging the performance of the software relative to ten predetermined criteria (Barnum, 2002). Results suggested that the software met the usability standards. The finished product was made available for use as a two-disc, CD-ROM package.

This case study serves as an example illustrating how current multimedia technology can be used to center curricular pedagogy on the oral tradition. Historically, cultural beliefs and philosophies shared orally have provided the cornerstone for perpetuating the collective identities of indigenous communities. The video medium in this project provided a means for extending this tradition and allowed indigenous peoples to be seen speaking for themselves. Thus, it provided a means for both fostering self-determination and personalizing the presentation of pertinent information. Rapid changes occurring in digital media and software authoring systems are bringing about decreased costs and increased ease of use. Therefore, multimedia technology is likely to become more readily accessible for further development of curricular materials based on the oral tradition.

References

Adobe. (1999). *Adobe Photoshop*. San Jose, CA: Adobe Systems.

Barnum, C. M. (2002). *Usability testing and research*. New York: Longman.

Battle, D. E. (2002). *Communication disorders in multicultural populations* (3rd ed.). Boston: Butterworth-Heinemann.

Macromedia. (2000). *Macromedia Director 8 Shockwave Studio*. San Jose, CA.

miroVideo Computer Products, Inc. (1997). *miroVideo DC20 plus*. Palo Alto, CA.

Reason, P., & Bradbury, H. (2001). *Handbook of action research: Participative inquiry and practices*. Thousand Oaks, CA: Sage.

Case Study VIII

The Indigenous Pre-IT Program

Stephen Grant, University of Technology, Sydney, Australia

Max Hendriks, University of Technology, Sydney, Australia

Laurel Evelyn Dyson, University of Technology, Sydney, Australia

From January 12-24, 2004 the Faculty of Information Technology, at the University of Technology, Sydney (UTS), conducted the first Pre-IT program for indigenous students in Australia. The program was run successfully for a second time in July 2005, with a another planned for 2006. The Pre-IT grew out of the Indigenous Participation in Information Technology (IPIT) Project which began at UTS in 2002. The purpose of the IPIT Project is to increase the participation of indigenous Australians in IT studies and careers (Robertson, Dyson, Norman, & Buckley, 2002).

The design of the Pre-IT is modeled on the Pre-Law course at the University of New South Wales, which over 100 indigenous students have completed since 1995, with most proceeding to undergraduate law studies. Before the Pre-IT, there was no equivalent tertiary preparation course for indigenous students to enter Information Technology (IT) at any Australian university. The Pre-IT course extends indigenous access beyond the established study areas of law, education, business and health into a new field in which very few indigenous Australians have participated to date, namely information technology.

This article describes the Pre-IT, focusing on the first offering of the course, including the curriculum design, marketing strategy, background of students recruited and an evaluation of the course against the quality indicators contained in the original course proposal.

Development of the Pre-IT

In February 2003 curriculum development began. First, the objectives of the course were identified:

- to raise awareness of IT as a career and study option for indigenous Australians;
- to act as a feeder program for entry of indigenous students into tertiary IT courses; and
- to prepare indigenous students for tertiary studies.

The course was intended to provide indigenous students with the opportunity to sample some information technology that might whet their appetite for pursuing tertiary studies and a career in this field (an opportunity to "taste and see"). The course was designed to be two weeks long, with modules chosen to express the range of subjects offered in IT degree programs and as practiced in IT careers and professions: computer fundamentals, Web design, Internetworking, introduction to programming and information systems development.

It was decided to make the course project-based. This allowed for the integration of all modules to a central focal point — a single project on which participants would work throughout the course. The curriculum content, delivery and assessment were all built around this project model. Project-based learning has proven successful in indigenous technology education: It moves away from the non-integrated approach to knowledge presented in much of Western education in favour of a holistic view in which knowledge is integrated into social and practical contexts and outcomes (Seeman & Talbot, 1995).

The major item of assessment for the Pre-IT course is the development of a Web site involving the application of skills and knowledge from all five course modules. Students choose the topic of their Web site and work together in small groups of two or three. Elements of the project include:

- stakeholder analysis and the drawing of rich pictures (Bell & Wood-Harper, 1998);
- design and co-editing the Web pages in HTML;
- application of usability principals to evaluate screen design;
- programming of a simple game in VB.net for access from their Web sites;
- display of the Web site on a network that they have implemented; and
- presenting the design to their fellow students at the end of the course using PowerPoint.

Classes run five days a week, six hours a day over the two-week period, with interactive sessions involving presentation of the curriculum by the lecturer, whole class and small group discussions, hands-on laboratory work and student presentations. In addition there is an "IT in Action" session that showcases various technologies, such as Bluetooth wireless technologies, computer animation, AI technologies like Robot Puppy Soccer, video conferencing and interactive creative technologies.

Marketing and Recruitment

A multi-pronged campaign was adopted to maximize recruitment, given that student demand was uncertain and there was no prior knowledge of the course in the indigenous community. Marketing of the course was intensive, contracted to a six-week period due to the short time interval between approval and launch of the course. The marketing campaign for the first Pre-IT resulted in 13 applicants, 12 of whom were offered places, with 11 students commencing. Successful recruiting strategies (as identified by student questionnaires) included the placing of advertisements in the main indigenous Australian newspaper, contacting Aboriginal Liaison Officers at Technical and Further Education (TAFE) Colleges, visiting indigenous tertiary colleges and community centres, advertising on the Faculty Web site, and internal canvassing of indigenous UTS staff and students. The results of the campaign confirmed that recruitment for a new, untried course must be conducted using as many different indigenous sources as possible.

Background of Students

Most students in the first Pre-IT were tertiary educated but had mainly taught themselves how to use computers. All had used computers in their work or study, and two were currently working or had worked in the IT industry.

Evaluation

In-Course Evaluation

Several methods were used to evaluate the course:

- student focus-group evaluation of the course;
- completion of a questionnaire that focused on the students' attitudes toward further IT study and career goals;
- individual informal consultations with students by Pre-IT lecturers during the course to gauge student satisfaction, progress towards learning outcomes and future plans in IT; and
- debriefing with the Pre-IT lecturers.

The results of the evaluation show:

- a high rate of completion (only one out of 11 students dropped out of the first Pre-IT, with three out of 14 dropping out of the second Pre-IT);
- an enthusiastic response from the completing students with all stating they intended to pursue further studies in IT, five at university level;
- high commendations from the Pre-IT lecturers for the standard of work achieved; and
- agreement by most students and all the lecturers that the two-week course was too short and should, if possible, be extended.

Follow-Up Evaluation

Following the course, informal contact was maintained with the students to find out if they had continued with their IT studies or gained work in the industry.

Positive outcomes of the first Pre-IT included:

- one student enrolled in an MSCE (Microsoft Certified Systems Engineer) preparation course immediately upon finishing the course and then proceeded to complete a TAFE diploma in systems administration;
- two students enrolled in Certificate III in Web Design at TAFE, with one of these students enrolling in the Bachelor of Adult Education (Indigenous Education) at UTS; and
- two students opened an Internet café.

Positive results from the second Pre-IT included the recruitment of three students directly into the undergraduate IT degree program at UTS.

The Future of the Course

Given the success of the course, the faculty will continue it into the future. The only issue is that of funding, since the full cost of the course comes from the faculty's budget, subsidised with volunteer work by lecturers. This situation was exacerbated for the second Pre-IT course when a lack of funds prevented the payment of accommodation costs for potential students who were resident outside Sydney; this resulted in several applicants withdrawing. Even some Sydney residents, expressing an interest in the course initially, did not have enough money to pay for their daily travel and so failed to enrol. This emphasises the fact that, to be successful in the future, this program requires a guaranteed level of funding, possibly from government sources.

Conclusion

The indigenous Pre-IT program has been highly successful. Enrolments have exceeded the original target of eight to ten: Given the short marketing timeframe of the first Pre-IT, this shows that there is definitely an unmet demand for programs of this type. Moreover, there has been a high retention rate in the course. The completion of learning outcomes, the standard of work achieved by the students on their group projects and the level of student satisfaction all indicate that the course has been extremely successful.

A significant finding was the number of students who have continued on to IT studies and work, expanding their goals as a result of taking part in the Pre-IT program. This represents the strongest evidence of the success of the course. Unlike some other indigenous tertiary preparation courses, which have been described as "bridges to nowhere" (Keefe, 1992, p. 163), the Pre-IT has shown itself to be a bridge to new opportunities for indigenous Australians.

Acknowledgments

The authors acknowledge the expertise of Andrew Johnston, Paul Kennedy and Andrew Litchfield in the development of the indigenous Pre-IT program, and acknowledge their contribution to its successful implementation. The authors further acknowledge the work of Ray Leslie in the continuance of the program beyond its first implementation.

References

Bell, S., & Wood-Harper, T. (1998). *Rapid information systems development: A non-specialist's guide to analysis and design in an imperfect world* (2nd ed.). London: McGraw Hill.

Keeffe, K. (1992). *From the centre to the city: Aboriginal education, culture and power*. Canberra, Australia: Aboriginal Studies Press.

Robertson, T., Dyson, L. E., Norman, H., & Buckley, B, (2002, June 23-25). Increasing the participation of indigenous Australians in the information technology industries. In T. Binder, J. Gregory, & I. Wagner (Eds.), *PDC '02, Proceedings of the Participatory Design Conference* (pp. 288-294). Malmö, Sweden.

Seeman, K., & Talbot, R. (1995). Technacy: Towards a holistic understanding of technology teaching and learning among aboriginal Australians. In *Prospects, 25*(4), 761-775.

Case Study IX

Problem-Based Online Learning and Indigenous Tertiary Education: Reflections on Implementation

Rosemary Foster, University of Queensland, Australia

Michael Meehan, University of Queensland, Australia

In a degree program traditionally offering problem-based-learning (PBL) in a classroom setting, we began to explore how information technology could improve tertiary education for indigenous Australians. As a result, problem-based-*electronic*-learning (PB*e*L) was devised, piloted and implemented online from 2003. This case study allows reflection on the problems and possibilities associated with this change to the learning environment for the indigenous-majority student population.

The Centre for Indigenous Health of the University of Queensland (UQ) has a history of success with indigenous participation in a PBL methodology embedded throughout the Bachelor of Applied Health Science in Indigenous Health (BAppHSc(IH)) degree curriculum. Contributing to this success has been the small-group classroom setting that acknowledges learning as a cultural activity and fosters cultural security through respect, student-led discussion, self-discovery and traditions of oral communication and story-telling. In changing the context of the learning activity, how could these characteristics be maintained online?

The need for off-campus access was evidenced by the growing market of remotely located indigenous applicants seeking flexible alternatives to full-time internal mode study. Advances in information technology appeared to provide the pathway by which these people could be assisted. Real-time chat sessions, short video, voice-overs and hyperlinks to relevant interactive resources could all be easily located within a constructivist learning theory, promoting student-directed learning within their own social and cultural context (Biggs, 1999; Brockbank & McGill, 1998; McLoughlin & Oliver, 2000; Turnbill, 2000). Despite this apparent mesh between the available technology, current learning theories and desired student outcomes, development of a practical model that incorporated the technological features for PB*e*L proved difficult. Limitations in design included concerns about student Internet access and computer capacity to run large multimedia programs, together with development costs of technologically advanced programs.

The PB*e*L Model

A typical PBL package for the BAppHSc(IH) describes a health situation that indigenous health professionals may encounter. As students progress through the scenario, they solve a series of problems presented in three sequential "blocks." Phases of student activity for each "block" are group discussion of the problems, self-directed "research" and peer education. Online, students access the "blocks" (text-based materials) from the PB*e*L Web site situated within UQ's WebCT *e*learn platform. Individually, they prepare a series of hypotheses and learning objectives that are then shared with the group by posting to an electronic notice board. Following self-directed research, their findings are disseminated to the group by the same mechanism.

PB*e*L Implementation

A piloting of the PB*e*L model was conducted in first semester 2003. Two groups were run simultaneously, one online (on-campus in the student computer lab) and the other face-to-face in the classroom. The groups alternated their study mode for the following PB*e*L. Both qualitative and quantitative feedback was collected as students completed the PB*e*L process. Responses indicated that the model was easy to use and provided a flexible yet interesting way to learn. Comparable grades were achieved by students across both pilot groups. A very high standard of work was produced during the pilot, however, such standards have not continued.

Problems and Possibilities

Computer access off-campus continues to be one of the most prominent problems for implementing tertiary education online for indigenous students. Many of the remote students are employed by government organisations, and this was seen as a possibility to significantly increase access to the PB*e*L sites and resources. However, no great advantage has been conferred and adequate computer access continues to be a problem. Where students are able to access the 24 hour student computer lab on-campus, participation rates are promising.

Student engagement with *e*learning varied as expected with age and computer experience. Generally, younger students, and those using computers at work, were adept at using the technology, whilst those with little computer experience required support and in some cases individual tutoring.

Currently the PB*e*L model relies on text as the predominant mode of communication. This is a significant change, since previously verbal discussion and visual demonstration were the practiced mode. Accordingly, students for whom English is not their first language or for whom the use of aboriginal English dialect is the cultural norm have experienced difficulties translating the spoken word to grammatically correct written word. Such difficulties have been exposed by the change to text-based PB*e*l and are reflected in student grades for communicating self-directed "research" findings.

Expectations of both students and facilitators have been renegotiated in the new online learning environment. Whilst the PB*e*L pilot program had been designed with regular "checkpoint" times to emulate the face-to-face PBL practice of the student group progressing at the same rate, online students exploited the flexibility of the media, negotiating progress at their own pace. From a facilitator's perspective, the intended "checkpoint" times were a means of demarcating time spent online. Most facilitators maintain this schedule of logging on to the PB*e*L site, although the increasing flexibility with which students progress has created a higher expectation (up to 50%) of facilitator availability online responding to students needs.

To maintain the intended phases of student activity throughout either mode of PBL, submitted work is assessed. However, due to the difficulty of facilitating and assessing meaningful group discussion occurring in an asynchronous manner online, only the initial posting of identified learning objectives and the final posting of "research" findings are assessed. Consequently, the information sharing online has appeared to lose the depth and quality of classroom discussions, where rich personal experiences are related to course materials in a story-telling manner and understanding is developed through considered debate. As one student commented during PB*e*L pilot evaluation, *"I think I'd rather speak to people than try to converse through the computer"* (Centre for Indigenous Health, 2003).

Implications for PB*e*L and Online Learning

The challenge identified through the PB*e*L experience is to balance the accessibility of the technology with the quality of the learning environment created by it. Despite the initial vision for PB*e*L, the current model utilises little of the multimedia and online technologies that may accommodate a variety of cognitive styles. Understanding that off-campus computer access issues are not likely to be resolved in the short-term, recent development of the PB*e*L model now includes a combination of classroom and online components drawing on the elements each offers to maximise the quality of the learning experience.

References

Biggs, J. (1999). What the student does: Teaching for enhancing learning. *Higher Education Research and Development, 18*(1), 57-75.

Brockbank, A., & McGill, I. (1998). *Facilitating reflective learning in higher education.* Buckingham: The Society for Research into Higher Education.

Centre for Indigenous Health (2003). *PBeL pilot evaluation.* Brisbane, Australia: University of Queensland.

McLoughlin, C., & Oliver, R. (2000). Designing learning environments for cultural inclusivity: A case study of indigenous online learning at tertiary level. *Australian Journal of Educational Technology, 16*(1), 58-72.

Turnbill, J. (2000, December). From face-to-face teaching to online distance education classes: Some challenges and surprises. In *Learning In Tertiary Education 2000 Conference Proceedings*. Coffs Harbour, Australia: Australasian Society for Computers.

Case Study X

Student Technology Projects in a Remote First Nations Village

Tish Scott, University of Victoria, Canada

This qualitative case study focuses on community members' observations and perceptions of student multimedia technology projects produced in a grade 6/7 class, particularly in relation to what they affirm is important for their children's education. The projects are community-based and rooted in the First Nations culture of a remote village in northern British Columbia (Canada).

Community

Members of this small village (population ~ 300) live at a subsistence level. One of the most noticeable qualities of these diverse people is their willingness and determination to help each other out. Relationships are important in the family, extended family, tribe, nation, and with other nations. Many people still fish and hunt for their food, though Eurocentric culture has brought much change here.

First Nations schooling in Canada has been controlled by Church and State for over a century. First Nations people in this village were seized and sent to a variety of church-run residential schools, including one now enmeshed in litigation over numerous sexual abuse charges and allegations. These are the grandparents of the students now attending school. Their children, the parents of current students, experienced schooling in their own villages in their own school district, mainly controlled by the provincial government. Many do not know or speak their native language. They did not learn it from their parents who were not allowed to use it.

The process of language and cultural recovery for both students and adults in the community has gained importance with the resurgence of interest in the culture. Community drumming and dancing groups gather to celebrate traditional events, people are making their own ceremonial regalia and their efforts to learn and preserve the language are increasing. Community members have hired a cultural director to assist them in relearning some of the protocols that have been forgotten. People are interested in both traditional and contemporary culture and are finding new ways to practice and preserve their cultural heritage. One way includes the use of computerized and digital multimedia technologies.

Researcher Position

This inquiry developed specifically from a hands-on totem pole carving and multimedia project (www.gingolx.ca) done in the first year of the teacher/researcher's stay and relationship with the village and community. More generally, it came from a lifetime passion for learning and teaching in ways that are meaningful, interesting and participatory.

Student Technology Projects

The student technology projects were a culmination of research and field trips carried out over a period of a few months in the spring of 2003. Following students' engagement with the totem pole carving project and Web site creation, a community member wondered if we could do something similar on the treaty because he felt that everyone needed to know more about it. Students focused on various features of a treaty agreement with their nation, learned some of the history and interviewed an elder about an area that interested them. Based on these interviews, as well as classroom presentations, learning simulations and field trips, students created short multimedia pieces to present to the community. Six projects were completed by fourteen students including a video, a comic strip done as a PowerPoint presentation and several posters and essays narrated and made into slide shows that combined archival and contemporary photographs taken by students.

Study Method

Open-ended interviews were conducted and videotaped with twenty-five community members and school district personnel in 2003. Initial interviews explored issues of education, language and culture. Following the presentation of the student projects, interviews about impressions of the projects and how they fit with these issues were conducted with thirteen of the original study participants. Other data included videotapes of community meeting speeches from the student presentation, field notes, student technology projects as well as oral history interviews with elders and community members conducted by student researchers. Categories and themes were identified through reiterative review and analysis of the data.

Conclusion

Themes that arose from questions about the importance and purpose of education included achievement and level of attainment, employability and culture. Culture is perceived as essential to education, and education is seen as a route to success and employment. Education must also be relevant to students and their communities and include contemporary technologies.

Elder support for the student technology projects is evident in the words of one participant attending the community presentation:

... Elders ... were saying in their own language how pleased they were that the students are able to do that, because in their words, that is what we need to do now. And that is what I was saying earlier, in order for our culture to survive, we need to get it down somewhere. Technology is one of the ways to go because not everyone is going to be speaking our language all the time, even though that is what we want. (Individual interview transcript, Mac)

These projects are considered beneficial to students and community members both in the process that is used to develop, do and present them as well as the contribution they make to community cultural resources. Using digital technologies actually makes space for culture to be acknowledged, recognized, learned, practiced, preserved, revitalized and shared.

Cultural historical activity theory (Demmert & Towner, 2003) provides a way to look at some of the relationships and processes involved in culturally based education (CBE) initiatives such as the student technology projects. Similar work points to the potential for CBE programming to lead to increased levels of student achievement and success in other areas (Barnhardt & Kawagley, 2003). The projects may also bridge the gap between local and global educational requirements, with increased engagement in learning more likely to meet with increased achievement. The positive responses of community members in this study provide reasons for continued exploration of strategies that integrate hands-on, participatory learning based on community interests, traditional cultural practices and innovative uses of information technology.

References

Barnhardt, R., & Kawagley, A. O. (2003). Culture, chaos and complexity: Catalysts for change in Indigenous education. *Cultural Survival Quarterly, 27*(4). Retrieved July 17, 2004, from http://www.culturalsurvival.org/publications/csq

Demmert, W. G., Jr., & Towner, J. C. (2003). *A review of the research literature on the influences of culturally based education on the academic performance of Native American students (information analysis).* Portland, OR: Northwest Regional Educational Laboratory.

Case Study XI

Draw-Talk-Write: Experiences and Learning with Indigenous Australians that are Driving the Evolution of Word Recognition Technology

Russell Gluck, University of Wollongong, Australia

John Fulcher, University of Wollongong, Australia

A draw-talk-write (DTW) process evolved as one of the authors (Gluck) worked with indigenous Australians who had stories to tell, and encountered extreme difficulty in putting them into text that met the requirements of their audience, their discipline and, most of all, themselves. DTW enables literacy inefficient, visually strong and orally proficient people to journey to mastery of the language and discourse of any discipline. The process is rooted in Gardner's (1983) multiple intelligence theory and Vygotsky's (1978) zone of proximal development and (1962) ideas of thought and language.

Collaboration between indigenous students, the School of Information Technology and Computer Science and the Learning Development Unit at the University of Wollongong has generated a human computer interface (HCI) focused on enhancing indigenous students' literacy efficiency through drawing, talking and writing.

The heart of the draw-talk-write process consists of four related tasks:

1. talking with the learning facilitator about the assignment topic and relating it to their personal experience;
2. utilizing that personal experience to draw, decipher and tell a detailed story or create a scenario that can be used to fulfil the requirements of the assignment topic or area of inquiry;
3. researching the topic and determining a theoretical perspective that supports the story as an example suitable for the assignment topic; and
4. refining the assignment through revisiting steps one through four. (Gluck, Draisma, Fulcher, & Worthy, 2004)

The HCI is based on experimentation with electronic whiteboards, tablets, scanners, digital voice recorders, computers and word recognition engines to enable people to utilize their spatial and oral intelligences to record and investigate elements of their lived experiences. Work is being pursued that will allow students to simultaneously produce visual, oral and text records of DTW tasks two, three and four (Gluck & Fulcher, 2006).

The DTW platform is built around a speech recognition engine, but unlike conventional (commercial, off-the-shelf) packages, does not produce written text output, but rather images; obviously the former would be entirely inappropriate for text illiterate users. Accordingly, the basic pattern recognition task is performed by artificial neural networks (ANNs), in preference to the de facto speech recognition technique of hidden Markov models. As far as the ANN is concerned, it is simply classifying input patterns into 1-of-n output classes (images in this case). Standard preprocessing techniques are used to convert the raw speech input into a form suitable for inputting to the ANN classifier (such as noise filtering, conversion from the time to the frequency domain and acoustic feature extraction).

To date a simple multilayer perceptron/backpropagation ANN has sufficed for our purposes. An ongoing investigation is underway to develop an *optimum* ANN model for this task. A more critical consideration is the determination of a minimum yet sufficient number of images (n) for a single DTW user. Work on this aspect also continues.

It should be emphasized that the n output images can be pre-stored, scanned from drawings and/or captured in real time using a graphics tablet. The DTW system allows for the simultaneous playback of the user's (pre-recorded) speech associated with each such image. Moreover, the system can learn over time to strengthen such associations. Written text ("subtitles") can also be simultaneously displayed on the screen along with images, which further enables the learning of literacy skills (in other words, reinforcement learning).

The HCI provides a suite of tools that enables students to engage with the language and theories of a discipline in the context of their drawn, oral and textual records. Visual, oral and textual products of the DTW process are stored sequentially. Students can import verbal, visual and text records from any source and combine these with their lived experiences. The HCI provides a platform for students to engage with and intertwine the language and theories of their discipline with their lived experience, to make meaning and produce products that meet course requirements. The sequential record of manipulations also provides students and facilitator with a rich resource to reflect on how drawing, talking and writing lived experiences can be a key to students acquiring and mastering the language of a discipline.

DTW recasts students as multimedia designers as they combine visual, oral and textual records of their lived experience with the language of the discipline. The multimedia focus allows students to utilize their dominant intelligences to experiment with issues, language and theories of disciplines in ways that support and are consistent with their lived experiences and culture of their community. Students come to know how theory can relate to their community and how their experience and stories can embody theory. DTW provides a learning process in which it is safe to play with, construct, review, demonstrate and reformulate meaning, and to present learning at all levels of study — prevocational through to undertaking a PhD thesis.

Automation and storage enable students and facilitator to stand back from what they are doing and listen to their process of making and communicating meaning. They provide a mechanism for taking a detached view of what and how meaning is being co-constructed. The record of conversation, image and text provides rich data to reflect on as meaning is being constructed.

DTW allows students to use their own language to tell their stories and shape their experiences in the same moment they engage others and themselves as their audience. In summary, multimedia patch-working of DTW facilitates students access to the language of others (discipline, community, facilitator and fellow students), and through access to the language of others to build understanding.

References

Gardner, H. (1983). *Frames of mind: The theory of multiple intelligences.* New York: Basic Books.

Gluck, R., Draisma, K., Fulcher, J., & Worthy, M. (2004, November). Draw talk write. *Proceedings of the 6th Biannual Language and Academic Skills in Higher Education Conference* (pp. 109-116). Adelaide, Australia: Student Learning Centre, Flinders University.

Gluck, R., & Fulcher, J. (2006). Literacy by way of speech recognition. In J. Fulcher (Ed.), *Advances in applied artificial intelligence* (pp. 68-119). Hershey, PA: Idea Group Publishing.

Vygotsky, L. (1978). *Mind in society.* Cambridge, MA: Harvard University Press.

Vygotsky, L. (1962). *Thought and language.* Cambridge, MA: MIT Press.

Section III

Cultural Preservation and Revitalisation

Chapter IX

Ara Irititja: Towards Culturally Appropriate IT Best Practice in Remote Indigenous Australia

Martin Hughes, Smart Works, Australia

John Dallwitz, Ara Irititja, Pitjantjatjara Council Inc., Australia

Abstract

The creation of a digital archive database system for the Pitjantjatjara and Yankunytjatjara people in Central Australia has been a challenging information technology (IT) project requiring unique thinking about database design, implementation and deployment. What might seem like sound, standards-based IT practice in a typical urban or academic location becomes unworkable in the physical realities of remote Australia and in the context of indigenous Australian cultural sensitivities. Based on the experience of the Ara Irititja Project, this chapter outlines the central issues facing the development of archive databases for indigenous peoples in remote Australia and points towards the need for a new approach to IT best practices in this context.

Introduction

In 1991, Anangu (Pitjantjatjara and Yankunytjatjara peoples of Central Australia) celebrated the 10th anniversary of the granting of the *Pitjantjatjara Land Rights Act 1981* (South Australia). As part of the celebrations, John Dallwitz was engaged by the Pitjantjatjara Council to create a display of historically significant photographs.

During the research for this display, it became clear that there was a vast amount of historic and culturally significant material (not only photographs but also films, videos, sound recordings, documents and artefacts), held in private and public collections completely inaccessible to A<u>n</u>angu. However, the 3,000 Anangu on the Anangu Pitjantjatjara Yankunytjatjara Lands (referred to in this chapter as "the Lands"), in northwestern South Australia, live in communities and homelands spread over more than 102,630 square kilometres of spectacularly beautiful and challenging country (see Figure 1). In this harsh environment, it would be very difficult to provide Anangu access to the physical materials whilst ensuring each item's longevity for future generations.

Figure 1. Map of the A<u>n</u>angu Pitjantjatjara Yankunytjatjara lands (Printed with permission from A<u>r</u>a Irititja and Rightside Response Pty Ltd)

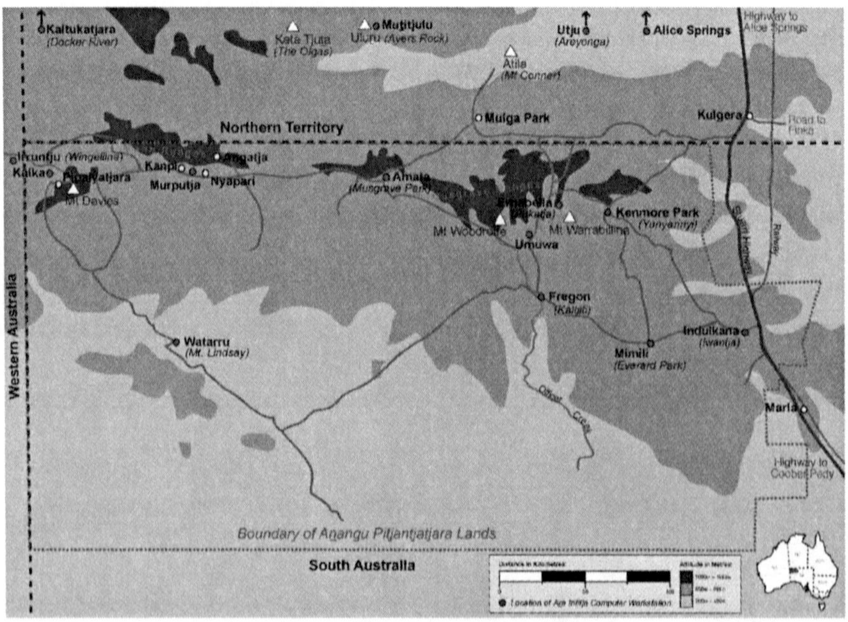

In 1994, Ara Irititja was established to develop a response to this dilemma when John Dallwitz, along with anthropologist Ushma Scales and Anangu Schools teacher Ron Lister, received the first funding from Pitjantjatjara Council Inc. This chapter outlines the central issues facing the design, implementation and deployment of archive databases for indigenous peoples in remote Australia and points towards the need for new thinking around information technology (IT) best practices in this context.

The Ara Irititja Project

Ara Irititja encompasses five main activities:

1. tracking down and negotiating for the retrieval of materials significant to Anangu;
2. attending to the storage of materials to archival standards;
3. creating digital copies of these materials;
4. returning the digital versions of the materials to Anangu, via an interactive digital archive developed specifically for this purpose (the Ara Irititja software); and
5. collecting information about these materials, from donors and Anangu working with the Ara Irititja software.

It is the last two points that make Ara Irititja unique as an archive. The fundamental intention of the project is to place access to the materials back into the hands of their rightful owners — Anangu — not just to view, but also for Anangu to create, manage and control their own archive.

As of June 2006, the Ara Irititja software holds information about more than 60,000 archived items. It is installed in ten permanent locations on the Lands. It is also installed in eight other Anangu locations outside the Lands including: Irrunytju (Wingellina WA), Mutitjulu (Uluru NT), Utju (Areyonga NT), three in Alice Springs, three in Adelaide and two at Port Augusta prison.

From the outset, it was hoped that the software might also provide a platform for other groups to start their own archives. In 2002 it was reworked into English (from Pitjantjatjara) and is now also being used by the:

- Central Land Council based in Alice Springs, and installed in communities within its region;

- Family History Unit of the Koorie Heritage Trust as an archive for the Koorie people of Victoria;
- Nepabunna community in South Australia;
- Ngaanyatjarra Council in Western Australia;
- Northern Territory Library and Information Service for installation in ten community libraries in "The Top End" of Australia;
- Peppimenarti community in the Northern Territory; and
- St. John of God community in Broome in Western Australia.

The Essence of the Conundrum

From an IT perspective, the Aṟa Irititja software is a straightforward database with two main functions:

1. a "viewer" for a rich media library of still images (photographs and digital images of documents, cultural artefacts and art objects), film, video and sound recordings;
2. a "metadata collector" for the items in the library. That is to say, a system that allows people to enter information about each item such as dates, the names of people and places in a photograph or movie or the name of the person who created an object, the stories that accompany it and the cultural restrictions that may limit its access.

The resulting Aṟa Irititja software is a fundamentally simple database system with less than 15 fields for data entry, spread over three primary tables with ten ancillary tables. Described like this it might seem particularly inefficient that this system has taken more than 2,000 hours over ten years to develop. Clearly, the work has not been in the data structure.

To understand the challenge of this project, it needs to be understood that the two technical database functions are only secondary to the software's primary purpose. Aṟa Irititja is a cultural repository for the Pitjantjatjara and Yankunytjatjara peoples.

"Aṟa Irititja" means "stories from a long time ago" and this is understood by Anangu to be *their* stories, in *their* words, about *their* people and *their* places. To this end the Aṟa Irititja software was created as an "interactive archive" to allow Anangu to add the necessary metadata that, more often than not, only they can provide. The archive materials may have value in and of themselves, but their full significance is only clear with the story (metadata) that explains their historical and cultural context.

Interface Design

The primary issue has been designing and implementing an appropriate user interface. From the outset, the design of the user interface had the overall brief that "it can't look like something Microsoft would make." By this, it is meant having a Eurocentric, business-styled interface. Instead, the user interface had to be designed to support and communicate the system's primary purpose: that it was for and by Anangu. Without this, the system would never achieve the necessary acceptance.

However, the demands on interface design have been much more than aesthetic. The people most likely to hold the necessary information about the archived material are older Anangu who have had no previous experience with computers. This meant that the user interface had to be user-friendly in the extreme. In addition, desert conditions make poor eyesight endemic to older residents. Consequently, the user interface had to use large print, bright, clear colours and large, easily recognisable icons. The current version includes all these features and is far from the generic business-styled interface usually adopted by large software manufacturers (see Figure 2).

Figure 2. Data entry screen in the Ara Irititja software (Printed with permission from Ara Irititja)

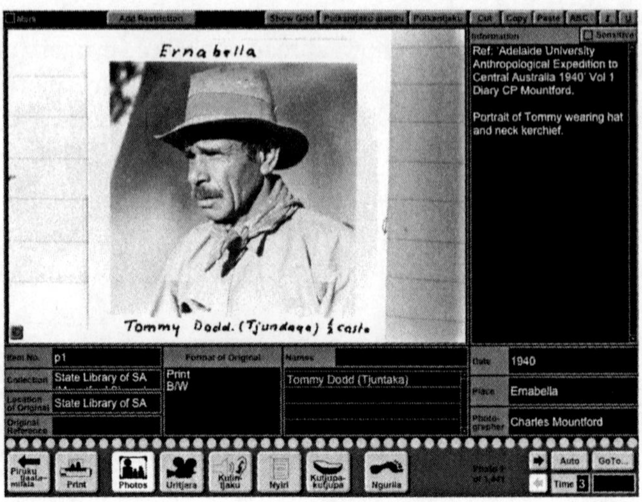

Designing the interface has never been a simple, single process from brief to approval. It is an organic, iterative process, requiring extensive fieldwork (and the funding to support it) to gather direct feedback from Anangu regarding their hands-on experience.

For example, some Pitjantjatjara language is used in the interface to give Anangu a greater sense of ownership. To achieve this, it was necessary to demonstrate different versions of the software to Anangu and then translate the action of a button or the purpose of a field rather than seeking an impossible, direct, translation of English computer terminology. The English words that remain in the system are words like "photo" that have been accepted into Pitjantjatjara usage, or words like "print," for which there are no matching Pitjantjatjara words, and only a wordy definition of the concept could take its place.

The length of time needed for this process has, in fact, been important to allow Anangu to develop a level of understanding about Aṟa Irititja and for the review process to work at their pace rather than with external deadlines that communicate outside purposes. For Aṟa Irititja to be a growing, perpetual, interactive archive, not just a fixed catalogue to be "delivered" to Aṉangu, it had to be absorbed into Anangu life.

Whilst all this may appear overly pedantic, it is perhaps one of the primary reasons for its success and longevity. Aṟa Irititja has never been presented to Anangu as a "service" designed and delivered from outside, but something that

Figure 3. First day of delivery of Aṟa Irititja to Watarru, July 9, 2003 (Courtesy of the photographer, John Dallwitz)

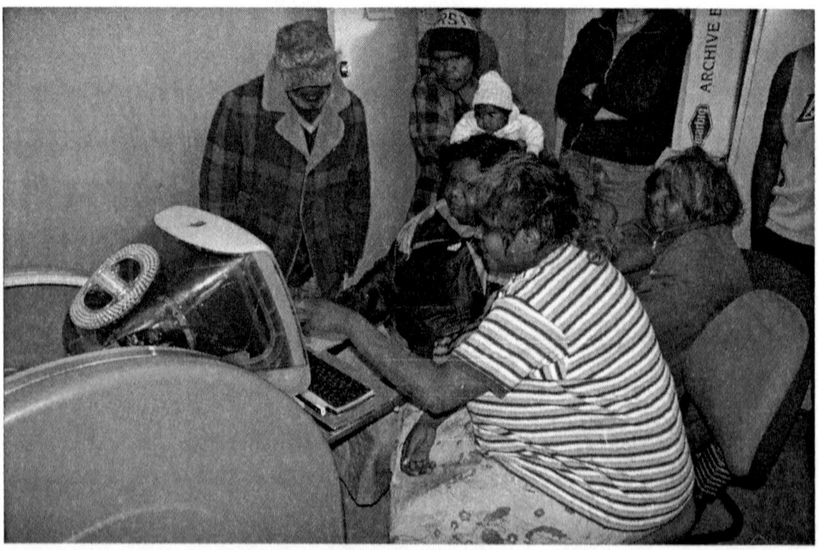

is wholly owned by Anangu. Indeed this is not just a matter of presentation, but fact. Copyright in the software and all other products of A̲ra Irititja are the inalienable property of the Pitjantjatjara and Yankunytjatjara peoples. Employees and contractors working on A̲ra Irititja do so with that understanding.

Success in these terms is hard to measure, but the archive software has been so popular in Anangu communities that a peculiar method of data entry has developed where only one hand is ever used on the keyboard. This is because if users take their other hand off the mouse, then it has become the custom that this relinquishes control of the computer to any one of the number of people usually gathered around, waiting for their turn (see Figure 3).

Security vs. Structure

Aboriginal cultures typically have a complex system of restrictions regarding access to significant places, objects and information. There is also a strong sensitivity to naming, discussing and viewing images of people who have recently passed away. Typically, these restrictions are based on sensitivity ("sorrow"), gender (men's and women's "business") and seniority (initiated or not). Archive material held in private and public collections is often a mixture of restricted and unrestricted items, thus the archive software must be able to deal with all levels of Anangu restrictions.

However, in terms of metadata, there is little or no difference between the record of a restricted item and that of a non-restricted item. Indeed, there are some cases where the restriction is only temporary. This is the case with images of people who have recently passed away. Such images are not allowed to be viewed for a certain length of time. However, the precise length of the time is not standardised in any way but is decided by the family of the deceased and is dependent on many things including family attitudes, the relative tragedy of the death and the stature of the deceased.

From the perspective of the data analyst, it would be logical to design a database for this metadata where all records reside in one system and "simple" security protocols are put in place to "hide" restricted items from unauthorised viewing based on user access privileges.

In the case of a database system for an Anangu archive, this solution was totally unacceptable. For Anangu and other Australian indigenous groups, it is essential that restricted men's objects cannot occupy the same physical space as women's or non-restricted objects. This requirement is held for the physical object itself as well as images and any recorded or written information about it.

As a result, the Ara Irititja archive data is currently split between three structurally identical databases: one for non-restricted ("open") items, one for men's and one for women's. This is despite the fact that all items across all databases are still regarded as being part of one archive, with item numbers reflecting the provenance of the item and not its digital location. For example, when a collection from a public or private source is returned to Anangu, it is digitised and entered into the archive database and each item in the collection is given a sequential number. This is all standard procedure for a well-organised archive. However, as any collection is likely to contain items with different restrictions, they must be separated into different physical locations and databases.

In addition, while Anangu elders allow the open database to be installed on the same computer with the men's or women's database, in no location on the Lands have both restricted databases been installed on the same computer. This deliberate structural redundancy would seem to contradict accepted database design standards, but it has been the only option available.

It is worthwhile stressing here that the consequences of a breach of these security requirements for Anangu are in no way similar to the consequences of a breach of security in a normal business IT application. With a "normal" business IT system, if someone gains access to restricted information it may result in lost income for the business and exposure to liability for the business and/or person. With Ara Irititja, if Anangu gain access to restricted information, it would be a breach of traditional Anangu law. This would incur the threat of prescribed punishments that, in very serious cases, can include the threat of personal physical injury, illness or damage to property. This makes security issues for Anangu totally non-negotiable and even very difficult to talk about. To tell someone explicitly about a particular restriction and to describe the rules that govern that restriction can be seen to breach that restriction. The fact that Ara Irititja has been able to achieve success in this area is a testament to the respectful and careful negotiation the Ara Irititja team have managed with Anangu elders.

Indeed Anangu elders have noted the particular facility that the Ara Irititja software offers them for managing security issues. With the click of a button it is now possible for them to immediately change the restriction on an item and, if necessary, remove the item from sight. This kind of immediacy is hard to replicate when dealing with physical objects.

Deployment Issues

Looking at the Ara Irititja software, and its dispersed deployment over a very wide geographic area, would lead most IT professionals to the same "logical" conclusion: "Why not have a centralised database served over a wide area network, perhaps via the Internet?" This may represent good IT practice with standard business systems in urban locations, but with indigenous knowledge systems it is culturally unacceptable, and in remote Australia it is impractical.

Despite assurances from government departments and others, our experience is that the current IT&T infrastructure in at least half the Lands simply doesn't have the capacity to support access to a high resolution, media-rich digital archive via the Web. Even if the multimedia content was held locally and only text information was served over the Internet, the current IT&T infrastructure would be inadequate. If access to the archive were only allowed from those communities with reliable power and telephone, this would be a significant limitation, as there are so many communities in the Lands without these services. This is the case for the majority of indigenous communities throughout Australia. According to the Australian Bureau of Statistics (ABS, 2001), there were 1,216 discrete indigenous communities in Australia in 2001. Of these 1,030 (85%) were categorised as being located in "very remote regions" (p. 13), and 956 communities (79%) were not on the state electricity grid nor did they have transmitted power. Instead, most of these communities use community or domestic generators, solar power or a hybrid of the two. Eighty communities (7%) had no "organised" power at all (p. 13).

In addition, the meeting places chosen for large groups of Anangu to view the archive are often completely unserviced. For example, a favourite meeting place for Anangu is in dry creek beds, typically some distance from any settlement. The soft sand of the creek bed is comfortable to sit on and the natural amphitheatre of the creek banks allows for better acoustics (portable generators are brought in to run the computer equipment).

To address some of the more rudimentary of these issues, a unique mobile workstation was developed to house a computer (with monitor, keyboard and mouse), a data projector, a printer and an uninterruptible power supply (see Figure 4). The design of the workstation had to protect its contents from the onslaught of mice, sand, all-pervading dust, inquisitive children and spillages. In addition, it also had to be mobile, so that it could be easily moved from community halls to classrooms to bush camps to dry creek beds. Specific inflatable wheels were selected that could travel just as easily over floorboards as stony or sandy ground. The dimensions of the workstation had to take into account standard door widths and allow it to be loaded into the back of a Toyota "troop carrier" (a common vehicle on the Lands) for longer trips. The first mobile workstation was delivered in March 2001, and by August 2003 another six workstations had been delivered to Anangu communities. Anangu call these workstations "Niri-niri," the Pitjantjatjara word for a scarab beetle (derived from the noise they make when flying at night).

In regard to the Internet, the potential is there to overcome the current technical realities, but even if this can be done in a financially viable way, Anangu have

Figure 4. Niri-niri (Courtesy of the photographer, John Dallwitz)

major concerns about security and privacy. From the beginning, Anangu made it very clear that their archive images and information were not to be made available on the Web. Likewise, many of the other communities that have taken up the A̲ra Irititja software have also been very anxious to confirm that data held in the archive software cannot be accessed via the Web.

Based on bad press early in the history of the Web, the general perception amongst Anangu and other indigenous peoples is that the Internet is not at all secure. There is also the assumption that the "World Wide Web" means "worldwide access." With this as the underlying perception, it is not hard to see how Anangu might be uncomfortable with the idea of putting their communities' private stories and images on the Web.

Scaling It Up?

As IT professionals, we are trained to think big — to test our designs and implementations against large scale scenarios to ensure they will stand up to a client's potential growth. It is clear from the success of A̲ra Irititja, and the interest in indigenous knowledge centres generally around Australia, that there is potential for all the aboriginal groups in Australia to start collecting their cultural material into similar archives. This prospect would make any IT professional worth their salt salivate at the opportunity to establish some kind of standard to which all these archives should conform, so that, at the very least, it would be possible for communities to share data and, perhaps, ultimately consolidate all the information into one centralised database repository. What a tremendous resource for all Australian indigenous peoples to enjoy! Even more, what a fabulous way to bring understanding of indigenous culture to the wider Australian (nay, worldwide) audience! It's not just a database; it's a tool for reconciliation!

It is easy to get excited, but, removing the hyperbole, this strategy might seem perfectly sound. There is only one problem — it will not work! For Anangu and many indigenous groups in Australia, it is totally inappropriate.

Australian indigenous peoples see themselves as many independent "nations" and not one diaspora waiting to be drawn back together. In fact, there are many hundreds of these nations distinguished not just by geography but also language, culture and religious differences. Each group regards itself as sovereign, with considerable distrust between some groups. Any attempt to combine different groups' culturally specific information in one repository would meet serious resistance.

Place this in the context of the indigenous experience of White Australia, and it is understandable why any strategy that has the ultimate aim of centralising information would meet with strong resistance from indigenous Australians. In the development of the software for A<u>r</u>a Irititja, we have been constantly reminded of the concern of indigenous peoples that the final result will not reduce protection, control, rights over and local ownership of their cultural material. The concern is whether the new technology is going to open their culture to more abuse and misappropriation of the kind historically suffered by most Australian indigenous peoples (Janke, 1998).

Any IT strategy dealing with cultural material must avoid any perception of technological colonisation and loss of local ownership. This point is worth stressing, as this single cultural difference between standard IT practice and indigenous sensibilities is the primary risk to the success of IT projects with indigenous Australians.

Even the use of seemingly essential IT language such as "scalability" needs to be modified to meet this sensitivity. To be clear, scalability refers to a computer system's ability to handle an increase in volume, either in the quantity of data or the number of simultaneous users. Indigenous communities are all too aware that the number of simultaneous users (let's say greater than 100) is not likely to be a true issue for community-based archives accessed only by their own people. Of the 1,216 indigenous communities in 2001, 889 (73%) had populations of less than 50 and only 145 (12%) had more than 200 people (ABS, 2001). IT strategies regarding community archives that pay too much attention to scalability, as it refers to number of users, are likely to cause concern for indigenous people about the true intentions of those strategies.

Concerns about scalability, even in terms of volume of records, suggest an assumption about an ongoing budget to fund the collection, storage, digitising and management of a large number of archive items. For A͟ra Irititja, and perhaps any indigenous IT project, this assumption would be naive. There is no ongoing single source of funding for this work. Whilst A͟ra Irititja has managed to find funding for continuous operation for over ten years, it has been a continuous battle requiring enormous labour from the A͟ra Irititja team and the future is always precarious.

It is easy for those of us who are aficionados of technology to see IT as some kind of panacea that will change historical relationships and have indigenous communities sharing information with other communities and cultural organizations. This kind of sentiment is likely to communicate naivety, arrogance and disrespect to indigenous people.

Conclusion

The development of the A͟ra Irititja software has uncovered many discrepancies with what might seem to be good IT practice in other contexts. The experience throws up the challenge that there is a different kind of IT best practice with indigenous communities. If so, then we are only at the beginning of understanding what that best practice might be. Even to contemplate it as a single problem with a single solution seems inadequate and inappropriate. However, a good place to start is to take everything we think we know, believe is essential or take for granted as axioms, and set them aside. Question anything we would like to hold on to about standards. Keep our technical ability and our sense of humour and add plenty of humility. Be prepared to think laterally not linearly. Be creative, passionate and prepared to wait. Then use the only tools that will have any positive result in this context: our eyes and ears, being open to the idea that there is no standard response — only community and individual requirements. We don't decide. They do.

Finally, this "us" (IT professionals) and "them" (indigenous peoples) assumes that the two are mutually exclusive. According to the 2001 census figures, 257 indigenous peoples recorded that they worked as computing professionals compared to 125,816 non-indigenous (ABS, 2001a). Therefore, whilst this might be the case in Australia now, clearly a solution to many of the problems outlined in this chapter would be to have more indigenous peoples providing IT for themselves.

Acknowledgments

This chapter has been written with the approval of the Pitjantjatjara and Yankunytjatjara communities through their ongoing liaison with the Ara Irititja project.

The topical information and examples in this chapter have derived from the first hand experience of the current Ara Irititja project team: John Dallwitz (artist, photographer and consultant to indigenous cultural projects since 1977); Ushma Scales (anthropologist and member of the Pitjantjatjara tribe since 1973); Ron Lister (teacher in Anangu communities since 1971, and Aboriginal Studies curriculum writer); Dora Dallwitz (artist and consultant to Ara Irititja since 1996); Martin Hughes (database developer since 1990 and developer of Ara Irititja software since 1997); Julia Burke (historian, NPY Women's Council Research Officer 1995-2002, and Ara Irititja Project Officer since 2002).

References

ABS (Australian Bureau of Statistics). (2001). *Housing and infrastructure in aboriginal and Torres Strait Islander communities*. Canberra, Australia: Commonwealth of Australia.

ABS (Australian Bureau of Statistics). (2001a). *2001 census*. Canberra, Australia: Commonwealth of Australia.

Janke, T. (1998). *Our culture our future: Report on Australian indigenous cultural and intellectual property rights* (prepared for the Australian Institute of Aboriginal and Torres Strait Islander Studies and the Aboriginal and Torres Strait Islander Commission). Surry Hills, Australia: Michael Frankel & Company, Solicitors.

Chapter X

Digital Songlines: Digitising the Arts, Culture and Heritage Landscape of Aboriginal Australia

Brett Leavy, CyberDreaming, Australia

Abstract

Digital Songlines is a software toolkit being developed by the Australasian Cooperative Research Centre for Interaction Design. It consists of an applied set of protocols, methodologies and a software program for the collection and sharing of indigenous cultural heritage knowledge. Regular consultation with indigenous traditional owners and representative groups is an essential component of the development process. This article provides an overview of the components of the Digital Songlines toolkit, and illustrates the development of the cultural heritage system in its current prototype. The system employs virtual reality tools to enable aboriginal communities to digitally preserve, protect and promote their arts, culture and heritage. The 3-D visualisation will allow users to appreciate the land as central to the culture, stories and lives of indigenous peoples.

Introduction

Australian aboriginal culture is one of the oldest surviving in the world. Aboriginal communities have occupied Australia for over sixty thousand years, with some estimates from research arguing that this timeframe could be extended.

Before 1788, when English settlement commenced in Australia, there were approximately 600 languages spoken, with an estimated indigenous population over 750,000 people. Today indigenous peoples comprise only 2% of the entire Australian population (about 410,000 people). Most knowledge about aboriginal culture is derived from the research of anthropologists, historians, researchers and interpretative centres, but also from Aborigines who survived the impact of European colonisation.

Digital Songlines is a software toolkit which is being developed by the Australasian Cooperative Research Centre for Interaction Design (ACID) to aid in the protection, preservation and promotion of Australian indigenous culture, its practices, myths and legends. It aims to assist the re-vitalization of the aboriginal culture through the visualization of its most prized asset—the land. The software will allow for the creation of a virtual landscape, containing oral histories, mythological stories and the eternal sense of land and spirituality, so that it can be understood and experienced by the broader community.

The software will encompass a toolset for recording aboriginal heritage, including a content management system. It will utilise virtual reality software in a multi-user virtual heritage environment (MUVHE) for the presentation of cultural knowledge of indigenous custodians, leaders and communities from throughout Australia. Digital Songlines includes a set of protocols and methodologies in addition to the software prototype. A service will put the content creation development toolkit into the hands of the communities and empower them to add to the body of knowledge.

Background: Indigenous Cultural Heritage

Aboriginal culture was passed on through oral traditions, art, dance and rituals. Aboriginal legends served an important purpose for teaching, understanding and interpreting the connection of aboriginal people to the land they relied upon to survive in the world they lived.

These oral traditions are vivid, dramatic, educative and informative yarns that served multiple purposes, including educating the receiver about social, environmental and cultural facets of aboriginal life. This collective oral tradition ensured the ongoing survival, socialisation and future prosperity of the clans as well as the deep and ancient connection of the people to the landscape.

These yarns are thematic, mythical and poetic in nature and quality. Some have a child-like simplicity whilst others contain complex relationship and instructional wisdom that span all the sciences. Character depictions draw upon a shrewd understanding of basic human behaviour and motivations to educate, inform and shape social, economic and political behaviour.

Because of their close connection to the land, aboriginal people know that the stories, songs and culture are inextricably linked to the clan's survival and the preservation of the environment. Rose (1996) says, "There is no place without a history; there is no place that has not been imaginatively grasped through song, dance and design, no place where traditional owners cannot see the imprint of sacred creation." She notes that aboriginal people talk about country as if they were talking about a person. For them, country is a living being — conscious and willing towards life. It is home, nourishment and peace.

Aboriginal culture survives today with these stories still being told. However, as the elders pass on, the culture is being diluted through external influences, and younger people, lost in the mainstream culture, forget their traditional one. On the other hand, some strive to learn and understand their cultural roots, while others seek to embrace western values but do so in combination with their own heritage. In most cases we need to protect and preserve these traditions before they are lost.

Digital Songlines

Digital Songlines is a tool for the creation of indigenous virtual worlds which detail a rich and diverse landscape that can be explored, as well as presenting the spiritual, the mythic, the magic and the superstitions within it. Not only will the landscape be presented as a traditional hunting and gathering ground, the hallowed place of worship and the vehicle for the livelihood of all aboriginal clans will also be represented.

Protocols

A set of protocols were written, adopted and applied to assist in dealing with indigenous communities whilst working towards developing the system. These were developed through the assistance of ACID and informed by protocols recommended by the Department of Aboriginal and Torres Strait Islander Policy

(1998), Mellor and Janke (2001) and Museums Australia (1998). These protocols provide guidelines for consultation with custodial owners and a framework for capturing the geographic and social heritage possessed by members of the indigenous communities throughout Australia.

This is our model and set of protocols for dealing with the intellectual property and copyright issues regarding aboriginal cultural knowledge. It is intended to ensure that respect and recognition of such knowledge occurs, and to guarantee the protection from abuse of such information. Protocols that direct our practice include:

1. that the stories of Traditional Owners be recognised as a "body of knowledge" that may be tens of thousands of years old;
2. that the stories are sourced from the Traditional Owner, who represents the country of which that story might originate;
3. that the communities make their own decision on what stories they want to have represented in Virtual Heritage;
4. that an approval process be implemented and approved by communities;
5. that the story represents the community and clan and is specifically placed geographically;
6. the nominated traditional owner group or community council holds ownership and copyright in the story and content;
7. that the community approves the content of the Virtual Heritage application, including artist styles, at all key production stages;
8. that the story provided by the community is not modified unless approved and endorsed by the Traditional Owner representative of that community;
9. that the community be paid industry standard rates and receives royalties from revenue earned from any capitalization and commercialisation; and
10. that indigenous peoples design and participate in the creation of the Virtual Heritage application development at all stages of planning, design and production.

About the Multi-User Virtual Heritage Environment

The system will communicate cultural information through a multi-user virtual heritage environment (MUVHE). This tool will be used for indigenous heritage and could also communicate issues of sustainability, land and water use, detail development issues and provide a means for describing contested narratives relating to the indigenous heritage values in native title areas. While the primary purpose of this toolkit is for cultural heritage recording and preservation, it also could be a presentation tool for museums, and science, cultural and interpretive centres. Because it uses a game engine approach, it could appeal to younger people and therefore has potential educational applications. The capacity exists to deliver either a low cost single-user system or a high-end visualisation theatre or planetarium experience.

The toolkit capacity includes:

1. terrain based modelling — the 3-D landscape in the toolkit is based on satellite imagery taken from global positioning system (GPS) level datasets with accuracy to 30 metres;
2. ability to set weather, time of day or progressive time, etc.;
3. user level tools to manipulate the landscape and add finer detail at a micro level;
4. ability to create scenarios/stories and control these through scripts;
5. Unique camera positions at first person and third person (tracking and bird's eye) view;
6. ability to create journey paths through the landscape, control the speed and direction along a path and allow for acceleration;
7. ability to add flora and fauna related to the area from a database/catalogue of objects;
8. ability to add ambient audio (wind in trees, bird calls, etc.), audio voice-over for significant locations (explaining the significance of a place to the viewer, explaining our presence to the spirits, etc.) and oral history (automatic or selected avatar);
9. ability to link to data attributes for presentation of educational material (e.g., select information about flora with botanical data, medicinal or bush tucker uses, artefact information such as the making of implements for food gathering or use as weapons); and
10. ability to participate in serious gaming strategies as applied to virtual heritage.

Technical Specifications

Auran, a game software company and partner of ACID, developed railway simulator software (known as Trainz) based upon its JET 2 game development engine. This software allows for fast prototyping. ACID researchers and assistants working on the Digital Songlines project have re-skinned this software and developed it as an indigenous cultural heritage toolkit, providing fast prototyping of virtual heritage landscapes and the delivery of indigenous virtual heritage information in a 3-D virtual landscape. A new indigenous look and feel

Figure 1. Main menu image © ACID 2006 (Used with permission)

has been applied to the menu (see Figure 1) and so a "new" simulator software is the result. This software permits developers to focus strongly on the content instead of on the software infrastructure.

The software is Microsoft Windows-centric, however with a port to Linux, Apple OS/X and the SGI PRISM (a newly released Itanium2-based visualisation system). The graphics code is OPENGL and the audio support changed to OPENAL so that cross platform support is enabled as well as the ability to present audio in full 3-D.

Large geographical distances exist between places of significance throughout Australia. This toolkit will cater to this while preserving high quality detail at ground or high-level perspectives. An established mechanism to import digital terrain models has been adopted to deal with large geographical areas. The project uses geo-spatial data, or data that is prepared for use in geographic information systems (GIS) software for accurately mapping the cultural heritage landscape for specific areas (see Figure 2).

The terrain data, in vector or raster-based formats, can be layered with spatial attributes to identify geographic features most relevant to the indigenous cultural heritage landscape. It is envisaged that this geo-spatial dataset will make up a cultural heritage metadata file set whose vector data could represent trade routes or Songlines. A database will store the artefacts that belong to significant places based on their spatial relationship to country, including indigenous names for sites, watercourses, hunting grounds, scar trees, artefacts and other significant aspects of the cultural heritage landscape. These items and objects could be placed correctly in the 3-D world, assisted via GPS coordinates.

Figure 2. Virtual reality landscape image © ACID 2006 (Used with permission)

In addition, native vegetation for specific areas can be treated in this 3-D world so that flora and fauna surveyed and photographed can then be modelled and included in the virtual environment.

About the Prototype

The area on which the finished prototype will be based is a 40 square kilometre space at Mt. Moffatt in Carnarvon Gorge, Queensland. The modelling of this space will demonstrate the capabilities and identify any potential limitations of the system and the methodology.

Figure 3. Mt. Moffatt cave paintings, "The Tombs" (Archaeological excavations have shown that Aboriginal people inhabited the sandstone rock shelters for some 16,000 years)

Some areas of interest include the sandstone cliff faces with numerous aboriginal stencil art paintings that are over 19,000 years old (see Figure 3). This significant rock-art site has been specially photographed so that a photogrammetry technique can be used to showcase how the software could represent the irregularities of the rock face and the art on it in 3-D.

Archaeological excavations have shown that aboriginal people inhabited the sandstone rock shelters for some 19,500 years.

We will also integrate avatars and animated sequences into the virtual world to tell the stories and represent other cultural heritage information. Some animated aboriginal dreamtime sequences will be included and made to be as seamless and transparent as possible within the virtual tour. Some rendered scenes will play as animations on the various textures in the software representation, and these animated objects will be triggered as the user travels near significant spaces whilst following defined invisible tracks.

Developing the artworks for the animations requires 3-D objects to be modelled that contain cultural significance (see Figure 4). This means that special consultation with indigenous storytellers, artists and cultural custodians must occur. Such consultations will happen at the origin of the content and we will respect protocol in the collation of these yarns.

A "tiered" model of content development is used where content "layers" can grow as these are identified, so that each links into the virtual model of the physical place. Such a model enables the conception of the (virtual) landscape as an interface through which the more traditional dynamics of content creation can be accessed. This layered model allows for participants in the indigenous knowledge to collaborate at a number of levels.

The content can be layered to support virtual heritage applications and narratives (such as land ownership issues, spiritual knowledge and historical and oral stories). The system can also serve as a community content development and

Figure 4. Screenshot of animated fish with representative indigenous art work image © ACID 2006 (Used with permission)

Figure 5. Schematic diagram of the proposed software architecture

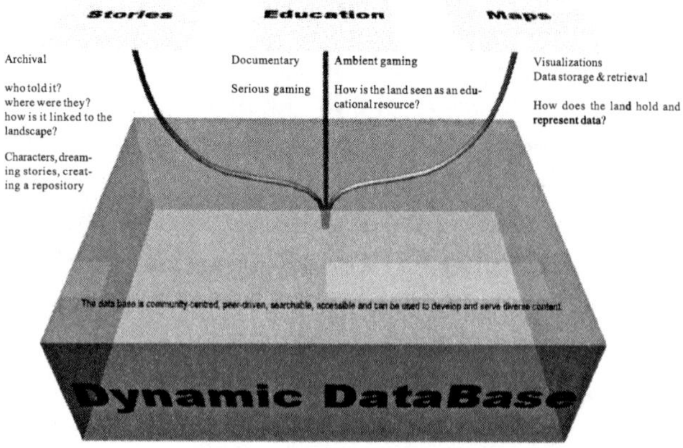

archiving tool (re-populating the virtual spaces with indigenous content). Such uses will facilitate entertainment, communal display, community consultation and educational outcomes (such as museum and cultural centre displays as the "languages walk," "bush tucker walk" or "oral history lesson"). All developed notions require the landscape-as-interface where the (virtual) land is layered with information and cultural practices that can be explored in the virtual.

Digital Songlines can be conceptually defined in use as comprising three separate and interconnected sources of knowledge presentation — Stories, Education and Terrain/Maps (see Figure 5).

These categories loosely capture the scope of the project, including the different classes of potential users. The information layers represented in the Terrain/Maps, for example, are shown in Figure 6.

Figure 6. Information layers of the Terrain/Maps Knowledge category

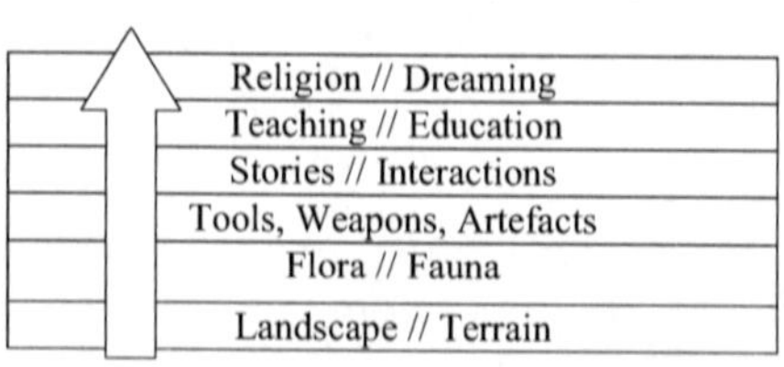

Conclusion

A major objective of this project is the development of an online networked infrastructure that will facilitate indigenous community-based content contribution and interpretation of indigenous culture and heritage. Through a network of contributors, the information system will enhance and accelerate the sharing of indigenous knowledge based on an ever-expanding virtual keeping space. Such a network would present diverse means of producing, accessing and presenting indigenous knowledge collaboratively and interactively. The result will be a rich knowledge resource accessible by the indigenous community as well as the broader community of researchers, educators, archivists, government and non-government organizations and more.

Digital Songlines is a system that focuses on the evolving knowledge flows and methods that will facilitate virtual communication and digital storytelling. Its development involves an ongoing refinement and consolidation of existing forms of knowledge like film, print, 3-D animation and game technologies. The system acknowledges that communication begins with the recognition of the landscape as the ideal and essential metaphor for presenting indigenous culture and heritage whilst providing a base for indigenous virtual heritage to be displayed. It will be a new means for accessing and displaying the combined cultural knowledge of indigenous peoples to support their voices.

Digital Songlines will facilitate access to information whilst simultaneously providing valuable indigenous content for the display of aboriginal arts, culture and heritage within a virtual indigenous world. While the primary purpose of this toolkit is for cultural heritage recording and preservation, it has many potential market applications such as education, information management, tourism and the entertainment markets.

References

Department of Aboriginal and Torres Strait Islander Policy. (1998). *Protocols for consultation and negotiation with aboriginal people.* Brisbane, Australia: DATSIP. Retrieved November 11, 2005 from http://www.indigenous.qld.gov.au/resources/cultures.cfm

Mellor, D., & Janke, T. (2001). *Valuing art, respecting culture: Protocols for working with the Australian indigenous visual arts and craft sector.* Sydney, Australia: National Association for the Visual Arts. Retrieved November 11, 2005, from http://www.visualarts.net.au/nv/articles/value.pdf

Museums Australia. (1998). *Taking the time — museums and galleries, cultural protocols and communities: A resource guide.* Brisbane, Australia.

Rose, D. B. (1996). *Nourishing terrains: Australian aboriginal views of landscape and wilderness.* Canberrra, Australia: Australian Heritage Commission.

Case Study XII

The Use of Information and Communication Technology for the Preservation of Aboriginal Culture: The Badimaya People of Western Australia

Katina Michael, University of Wollongong, Australia

Leone Dunn, University of Wollongong, Australia

Information and communication technology (ICT) has been applied successfully to numerous remote indigenous communities around the world. The greatest gains have been made when requirements are first defined by indigenous members of the community then pattern matched to an ICT solution.

Adoption of ICT By Indigenous Persons in Very Remote Areas

In Australia ICT adoption by indigenous communities in very remote areas is very low; at home in 2001 only three percent used a computer and one percent used the Internet (ABS, 2001). The cost of foregoing online services such as e-government, e-banking, e-procurement and e-employment is still perceived to be relatively low by indigenous communities. One could hypothesise that, for the greater part, government agencies have taken on the servicing of indigenous needs rather than encouraging communities to participate themselves. An application of ICT that could have particular usefulness for indigenous peoples is a system for cultural preservation.

ICT Solutions for the Preservation of the Badimaya Culture

The discussion below shows the potential uses of ICT in key areas fundamental to the continuing presence of the Badimaya culture. The Badimaya people traditionally occupied a large area around Lake Moore in Western Australia. Their language is classified as a member of the Kardu sub-group, of the southwest group of Pama-Nyungan languages.

Geographical Information Systems: The Portal Framework

A vector-based map in a geographic information system (GIS) could be used to show where different generations of the Badimaya lived and what languages are spoken today by their descendents. The interactive map, which could also serve as the portal front-end, would identify that the Badimaya people traditionally occupied a large area around Lake Moore, Ninghan Station and Paynes Find. Various map layers could pinpoint important sites, streets/paths/trails and traditional locations and provide additional information on each upon querying. Graduated thematic maps could also show that the Badimaya today are scattered in towns throughout the Murchison Region in Mullewa, Cue, Mingenew, Mt. Magnet, Yalgoo, Carnarvon and Meekatharra. Hotspots on the maps would allow users to trigger the selection of photographs of people, places and things from the region. Theme maps could also show which languages are spoken by various communities today, such as

Watjarri, otherwise known as the "Murchison" or "Yamaay" language. The GIS could also be used to provide evidence for native title land claims.

Multimedia Clips: Content Management

The Badimaya people interviewed by Dunn in the 1980s were all concerned about the potential for the Badimaya language to become extinct. They were pleased to hear that their language was being recorded, as many feared that over time it would be entirely lost. Joe Benjamin (now deceased), who was acknowledged at the time of recording the language to be one of the last speakers, was the principal source for the material gathered. While a Badimaya dictionary including phonetic pronunciation was documented by Dunn (1982, 1989), multimedia footage of Badimaya speakers conversing has not been captured. In 1982 there were only about 50 people claiming Badimaya descent. Apart from Dunn, Douglas (1981) and Gratte (1968) have documented a few Badimaya nouns.

The lexicon compiled from these authors would act as a directory source to corresponding multimedia clips of Badimaya culture. These clips could even show sacred locations, people participating in traditional rituals and live song and dance performances. Today, most of the Badimaya live in remote towns and non-traditional communities, so providing them with access to multimedia recordings is important in helping them maintain a link with their traditional culture.

Digital Document Archives: Knowledge Management

Although written historical accounts of the Badimaya are scarce, surviving documents could be digitally scanned and made available for access to the community. The majority of material that remains today dates back to the mid-19th century when Europeans first had contact with the Badimaya. There was the Badimaya experience with the missionaries during the 1840s, the pastoralists/explorers during the 1850s and the gold prospectors during the 1890s. Without a doubt, there are mixed perspectives of the benefits and costs of these periods to the Badimaya people. The Badimaya culture was under pressure to change, especially the use of language for communicating with the Europeans. Some have favourable impressions, others do not. Some believe that the interplay between the two cultures caused the Badimaya to fragment as a people, forcing families onto stations and children into non-traditional schools. In other descriptions, the Badimaya are said to have worked in partnership with prospectors in the goldfields.

Digital photographs from these periods — showing artwork, artefacts, people interacting at work and Badimaya in their natural surroundings — could be used to inform future generations. In addition, recordings of members of the community talking about the changes that took place over time, and recordings of myths and stories that have only survived through oral transmission, would be enriching to modern-day Badimaya people.

Preserving Culture Takes More Than ICT

Culture encompasses such things as language, art, music, food, spirituality, craftsmanship, history, ancestry and geography. The inherent problem with ICT is that while it is good at preserving tangible knowledge, it has difficulty with how to treat tacit knowledge. ICT output, no matter how well represented, is usually one-dimensional. Digital archiving of information (encompassing text, audio, graphics and video) is only the first step to cultural preservation. The second is placing the information in a meaningful knowledge management system where it can be accessed via community technology centres (CTCs): These centres can be re-used by educational institutions and maintained by the community itself. The third step is in defining relationships around that content through various collaborative tools relying on wireless or other networks, of which email and bulletin boards are only the beginning. Herein lies another problem for ICT, that of confidentiality: There are obvious "secrets" that belong to initiated males and females, and these are only passed down orally to other selected members of the community.

Cultural preservation cannot be achieved by ICT alone: It requires the spiritual element behind the history to be actively reinvigorated into a community to make its presence felt in a long-lasting manner. Culture is something that is alive and ever-changing. In brief, it is not machinery that reforms society, repairs institutions, builds social networks or produces democratic culture; it is people who make this happen. What has been presented in this paper is a way forward. By getting communities involved in the development of applications, ICT adoption by its members is likely to follow, bringing with it myriad benefits.

References

ABS. (2001). Use of information technology by aboriginal and Torres Strait Islander peoples. *Year book Australia*. Retrieved November 14, 2005, from http://

www.abs.gov.au/Ausstats/abs@.nsf/94713ad445ff1425ca25682000192af2/1b07e8e4c0161548ca256dea000539e3!OpenDocument

Douglas, W. (1981). Watjarri. In R. M. W. Dixon & B. J. Blake (Eds.), *Handbook of Australian languages* (vol. 2, pp. 196-272). Canberra, Australia: ANU Press.

Dunn, L. J. (1982). *Badimaya: A Western Australian language*. Unpublished master's thesis, University of Western Australia.

Dunn, L. (1989). Badimaya: A Western Australian language. *Monographs in Australian Linguistics, 17*. Canberra, Australia: ANU Press.

Gratte, S. (1968). *Notes and tapes on the Badimaya language*. Geraldton, WA: Geraldton Historical Society.

Chapter XI

Indigenous Language Usage in a Bilingual Interface: Transaction Log Analysis of the Niupepa Web Site

Te Taka Keegan, University of Waikato, New Zealand

Sally Jo Cunningham, University of Waikato, New Zealand

Mark Apperley, University of Waikato, New Zealand

Abstract

In this chapter we investigate the extent and characteristics of use of the Maori language, the indigenous language of Aotearoa (New Zealand), in a large bilingual Web site. We used transaction log analysis to investigate whether Maori was utilised by users of the Web site and how usage characteristics differed between users of Maori and users of the more commonly spoken English language. We found that Maori language was used in one quarter of all active sessions, and that in these sessions users were more likely to browse the Web site, whereas users working in the non-indigenous English were more likely to use the search facility. We also identified a new category of user of bilingual Web sites: the bilingual user.

Introduction

To analyse indigenous language participation in a Web site, one must be aware of how many potential indigenous language users there are. Approximately 14% of the total resident population of Aotearoa (New Zealand) is Maori and about one in four of these is able to converse in te reo Maori (the Maori language) (Te Puni Kôkiri, 2003). When we consider that 65% of Maori have never accessed the Internet, the potential users of a te reo Maori language interface is perhaps 1-2% (40,000-80,000) of the population of Aotearoa. In contrast, potential English-speaking users of the Web site in Aotearoa alone represent approximately 51% of the population (2,040,000) (Te Puni Kôkiri, 2001).

However, as well as potential user numbers, one must also consider the content of the Web site and whether the information available favours a particular language; in this case the odds shift back to the indigenous language. The Niupepa (Maori for "newspaper") Web site makes available over 17,000 historic newspaper pages collected from 35 periodicals published between the years 1842 and 1933, the time period when most te reo Maori periodicals were published. The number of publications in te reo Maori diminished after this time, and it was not until the latter part of the twentieth century when a resurgence of interest in Maori language led to a renewed interest in texts written in Maori. In 1996 the Alexander Turnbull Library published "Niupepa 1842-1933," a 407-page microfiche set containing facsimiles of the pages of these periodicals that had been preserved in libraries throughout Aotearoa. In 2002 the Computer Science Department at the University of Waikato made the collection available on the Internet through the bilingual Niupepa Web site (see Apperley, Keegan, Cunningham, & Witten, 2002), on which the study in this chapter is based. As 70% of the pages are exclusively in te reo Maori, and 27% are in both English and Maori, the content is most suited to users who are literate in te reo Maori.

While there have been articles written describing minority language use on bilingual Web sites (see Cunliff, 2003; IBIS, 2000; Warschauer, El Said, & Zohry, 2002) and publications produced on transaction log analysis (see Jones, Cunningham, McNab, & Boddie, 2000; Koch, Ardö, & Golub, 2005; Pikow, 1997) this chapter is unique in that transaction log analysis is used to determine indigenous language usage and characteristics in a bilingual Web site.

Limitations of This Type of Analysis

While every endeavour has been made to ensure that the data used is as accurate and as meaningful as possible, log file analysis does have shortcomings, in particular the effect of Web caches. A Web cache intervenes between a Web server and a Web client; it will note requests from the client and saves copies of the server's responses. If it detects a request to which it already has a copy of the response, it will supply the response directly and the request is not passed on to the original server. This saves time and reduces network traffic. However, as the original server (in this case the Niupepa server) does not receive the request, it is not recorded in its Web log file and so this user action is not included in the transaction log analysis.

There are two main types of Web cache; a browser cache, which is handled by a user's browser software, and a network (or proxy) cache, which is configured within a local area network. Both types of caches have the effect of masking repeated requests for the same data from a single user appearing in the transaction log; however, a network cache will also mask duplicated requests from different users within the same local-area network.

Other limitations of log file analyses include false hits due to Web robot activity, caused by server upgrades and maintenance and the inability to accurately delimit individual user sessions. We describe our efforts to deal with these limitations below. The analysis presented in this chapter, as with all transaction log analyses, must be viewed with the knowledge that not all user activity will appear in the Web logs because of the effect of Web caching.

The Niupepa Collection

The Niupepa Collection is currently delivered by the Greenstone software of the New Zealand Digital Library (NZDL) at: www.nzdl.org/niupepa (for a description of the Greenstone software, see Witten & Bainbridge, 2002). For a comprehensive explanation regarding the process of delivering the Niupepa on the Web, see Apperley et al. (2002). The software provides three methods of accessing the newspapers in the collection: full text search, browsing the newspapers by series and issues and browsing the newspapers by a timeline.

The newspaper pages themselves may be viewed as extracted text, or in either of two facsimile forms: a low resolution image that downloads quickly for previewing, or a high resolution image that takes longer to download but which is possible to read on the screen.

While the content is a mixture of Maori and English text (primarily Maori, see above), the interface to the collection can be presented in either Maori or English, and this language can be switched at any time. The default (starting) language of the collection is set to Maori (see Figure 1).

Figure 1. Niupepa Web site with the interface set to Teo Reo Mâori (Printed with permission from The New Zealand Digital Library Project, University of Waikato)

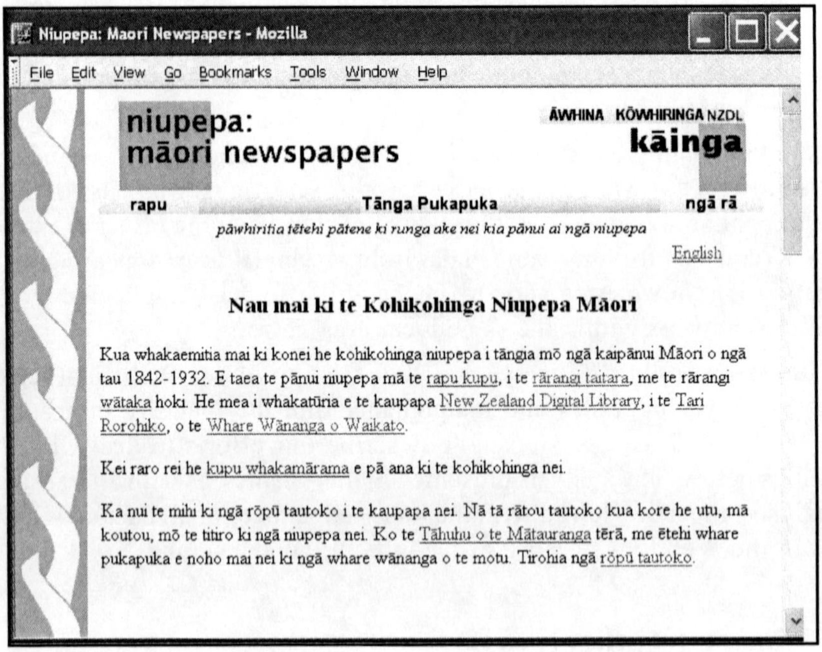

Gathering the Data

All user activity on the Niupepa Web site is logged. Every individual access event or "hit" is recorded with details such as the page requested, the language currently set in the interface, the time of the request, the nature of the request, the previous action, the IP address of the requester and other various user preferences that are currently set.

The data used for analysis in this report are from a log of 187,215 hits on the Niupepa site for the year 2004, recorded from 12:17 a.m. January 1, 2004, to 11:41 p.m. December 31. This average of more than 500 hits per day shows the strong usage of the site. The log represents usage from within New Zealand only, as all off-shore requests were handled by a Web server located at the University of Lethbridge in Alberta, Canada, and so are not included in the log.

The raw Niupepa transaction log data was filtered to remove unwanted hits. These included known Web robot hits (338), hits where the IP address was not defined (495), hits from the local research team (1,565) and hits where the interface language setting could not be determined (3,578).

Filtered Hits by Language

The resulting filtered Niupepa log totalled 181,239 hits, comprising 145,596 hits (80.3%) where the interface language was set to English, and 35,643 hits (19.7%) where the interface language was set to Maori, as shown in Figure 2.

Defining Sessions

To improve the usefulness of the data and to make it more relevant to the actual usage of the Niupepa Web site, hits in the filtered log were grouped into sessions, where we define a session as a sequence of two or more hits originating from a single user, with no more than a 60-minute gap between successive hits. Log analyses usually define sessions as having successive hits separated by no more than 30 minutes (see Pikow, 1997, p. 1348); however, because Niupepa users might be expected to spend extended periods examining a single newspaper page, and because the gap between hits might be exaggerated by Web caching (which could mask intermediate hits), we felt that for our analysis it was appropriate to extend the maximum spacing to 60 minutes.

In order to identify sessions, we needed to associate hits with individual users. For this purpose, two methods were available. The first is to identify users by the IP address of the computer responsible for the request, as recorded in the transaction log. The second method involves the use of cookies (see Pitkow, 1997, p. 1343); when a user begins a session, a cookie is created on their machine which includes the IP address of the computer and the time that the cookie was

Figure 2. Filtered hits by language

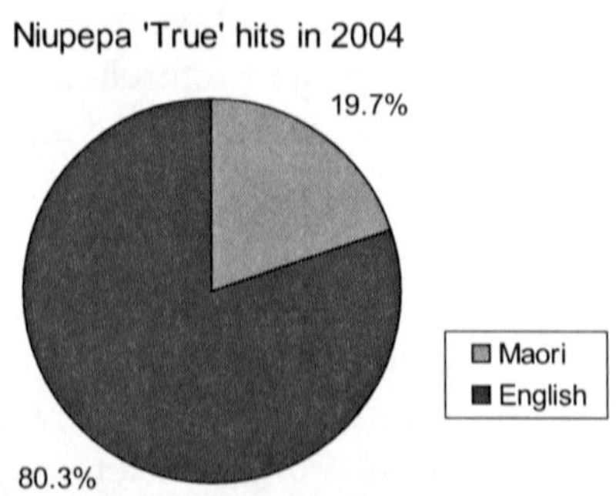

Figure 3. Classification of extended sessions

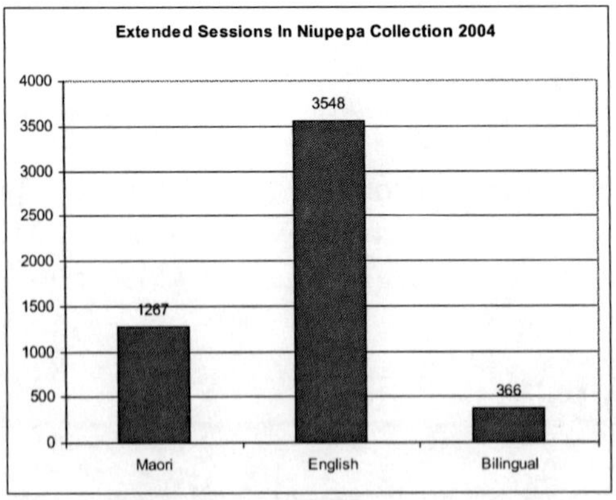

created. This information is included as the z argument in each transaction log record. Note that the z argument cannot distinguish between two people using the same login to a given computer (for example, if two or more people use a public library computer to access a collection).

Both techniques have their drawbacks. The IP address is machine specific, but not user specific; consequently, if multiple users share one computer in sequence, then several quite distinct sessions with different users might be seen as a single session in the log. People connecting through a shared dialup connection may also have a common IP address, and again multiple users' activities might be logged as a single session. Using the z argument to define users greatly reduces the problem of multiple users being recorded as a part of the same session; however, session activity of users who disable cookies will not be logged. We chose to use the z argument to identify sessions although this reduced the data set by 17% (sessions where cookies were disabled), as we were more confident that each identified session related to an individual user.

The sessions were identified and then classified into one of two groups: *Exploratory* sessions were defined as those where the user accessed only the homepage, the help page and/or the preferences page. No documents in the collection were accessed and no searches were undertaken. *Extended* sessions were defined as those involving queries and/or retrieval of documents from the Niupepa collection.

Our objective in analysing sessions was to determine if there were observable differences between those carried out in te reo Maori and those carried out in English. However, closer examination of the session data revealed that there was a third category of user: the bilingual users, who conducted their sessions using a mix of the Maori and English interfaces. For the purposes of our analysis, we defined a te reo Maori session as one that used the Maori interface for at least 80% of its logged events, and did not involve more than two interface language switches. An English language session was defined as a session that used the English interface for at least 80% of its logged events and did not involve more than two interface language switches. We defined a bilingual session as one that involved three or more interface language switches and/or where there was at least 20% of the log activity in each language.

Of the 5,653 individual sessions identified, 472 were exploratory. Because this represents such a small number of hits, there is little to be gained from the analysis of exploratory sessions. There were 5,181 extended sessions: 1,267 te reo Maori sessions, 3,548 English language sessions and 366 bilingual sessions (see Figure 2). The next section discusses the analysis of the extended sessions.

Analysis of the Extended Sessions

Table 1 shows the general statistics for the extended sessions, grouped according to the three language categories previously defined. Most of the sessions, 3,548 (68.5 %), are in English, with 1,267 (25.4%) in Maori and the remaining 366 (7.1%) making significant use of both languages. In general terms, the English sessions are more sustained, with longer sessions and more hits per session.

Table 1. General statistics for extended sessions

	Māori	English	Bilingual
Sessions:	1,267	3,548	366
Total session %:	24.5%	68.5%	7.1%
Unique users:	2,174	1,057	1,239
Page hits:	29,055	108,479	7,845
Mean (hits):	22.9	30.6	21.4
Median (hits):	7	15	9
Longest session (hits):	408	679	182
Shortest session (hits):	2	2	2
Std deviation (hits):	33.0	44.7	28.0
Mean (min):	18.7	25.2	16.3
Median (min):	7	8	5
Longest session (min):	390	711	241
Shortest session (min):	<1	<1	<1
Std deviation (min):	31.8	45.4	27.6

Extended Session Analysis: Accessing and Viewing of Newspaper Pages

The transaction log records indicate whether the newspaper pages accessed were the result of a search or by browsing by newspaper series or date. This analysis is shown in Table 2, where it can be seen that in all three categories, more document pages were retrieved by searching than by browsing.

Table 3 shows the manner in which these retrieved pages were viewed: in the form of extracted text, as a preview facsimile page or as a full-size facsimile page. Viewing the extracted text is the most common way to view a page, but then this is the default display following a search. However, the users in the Maori session show a greater tendency to view the full facsimile image (21.5%) than those in the English sessions (5.6%) or the bilingual sessions (9.9%).

As well as delivering newspaper pages, the Niupepa Collection makes available two other types of information: commentaries which include bibliographic details, background, subject matter and accessibility, written mostly in English; and abstracts written in English, which summarise the periodicals. If we look at the 15 most popular pages by hit count (Figure 4) in each language category, it can be clearly seen that Maori session users most commonly access actual newspaper pages, while English session users more commonly access the commentary information. This seems logical, as the users are accessing information that is available in the chosen language of the session.

Table 2. Niupepa pages retrieved by search, by series and by date

	Māori		English		Bilingual	
Pages viewed from search:	14,564	72.4%	64,125	83.3%	2,686	67.8%
Pages viewed from series:	3,782	18.8%	6,838	8.9%	761	19.2%
Pages viewed from date:	1,532	7.6%	4,818	6.3%	363	9.2%
Other:	234	1.2%	1,194	1.6%	149	3.8%

Table 3. Viewing of text pages, full images and preview images

	Māori		English		Bilingual	
Text pages viewed:	14,724	73.2%	50,746	65.9%	2,740	69.2%
Full images viewed:	4,310	21.4%	4,300	5.6%	391	9.9%
Preview images viewed:	1,014	5.0%	21,752	28.3%	801	20.2%
Undefined:	64	0.3%	177	0.2%	27	0.7%

Figure 4. Top 15 page type by hit count

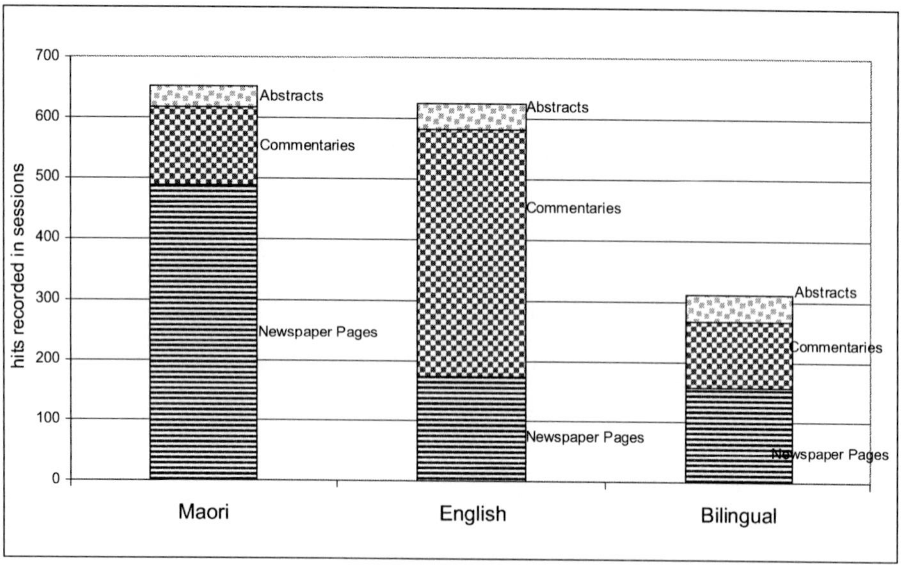

Session Analysis: Time Statistics

The extended sessions were also plotted against time (Figure 5). This shows a lower number of sessions in the New Zealand summer holiday months of December and January.

Figure 5. Extended sessions per day 2004

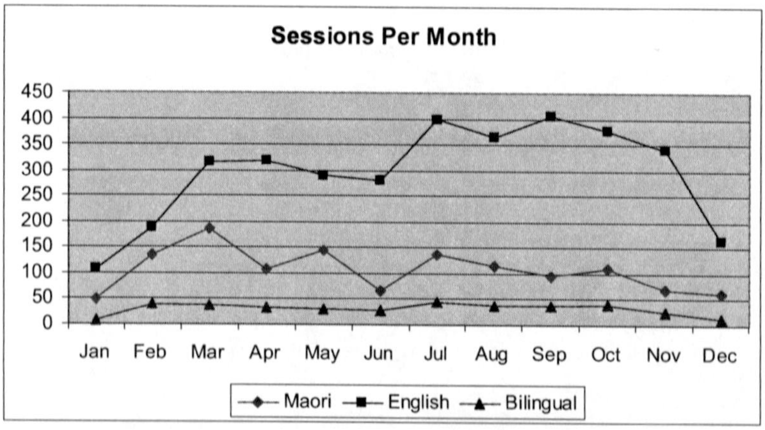

Breaking this down to daily usage (Figure 6), we see that while the sessions are reasonably consistent in the start and middle of the week, they taper off towards the end of the week. There are more sessions occurring on a Sunday than on a Saturday.

An examination of hourly exploratory sessions (Figure 7) shows that the majority of the sessions are occurring during the 9-5 work hours, with some further activity occurring in the evenings.

Figure 6. Extended sessions per hour 2004

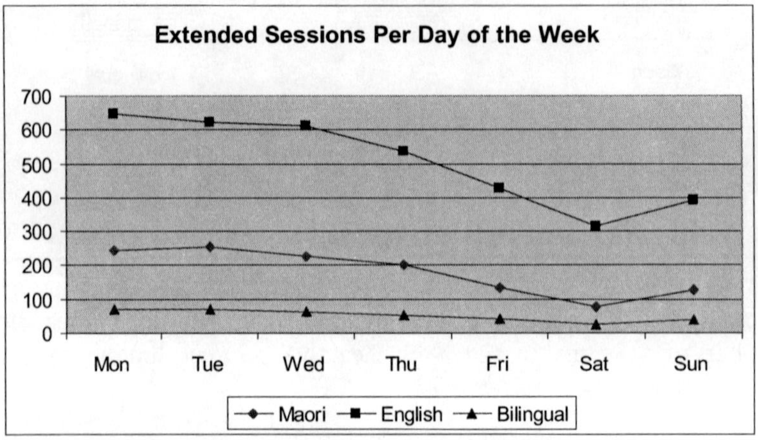

Figure 7. Extended sessions per hour 2004

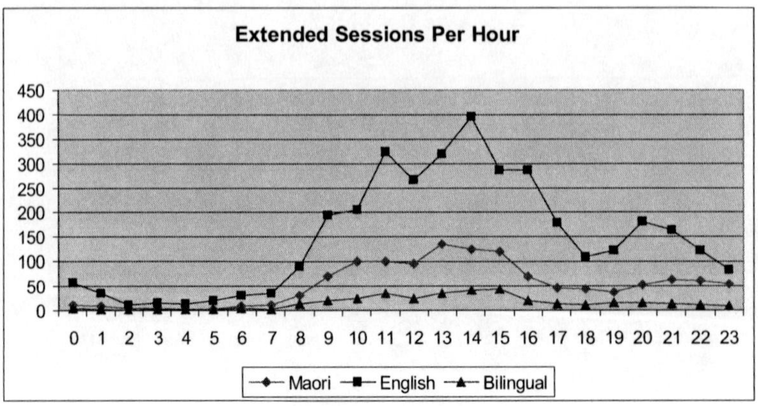

Extended Session Analysis: Searching

Statistics on searching conducted in extended sessions are presented in Table 4 This shows an average of three or four searches per session, and that 30-40% of all sessions involves three or more searches.

The number of terms used in searches is similar across the three extended session types, averaging just under two terms per search for all three session types (Table 5). Approximately half of all searches undertaken use just one search term.

We examined the top 50 searches that were submitted in the extended sessions using the different language interfaces. The search terms were manually examined and sorted into categories: people, e.g., Apanui; place, e.g., Parihaka; action, e.g., poroporoaki (farewell); object, e.g., Matariki (star constellation) and uncertain, e.g., Ngarakau (could be a name of a person or a place). The Maori extended session searches were reasonably spread across the four topics, while the English extended sessions were primarily concerned with people and places (Figure 8). The bilingual extended sessions showed results that were between the Maori and English sessions.

Table 4. Extended session searching activity

	Māori	English	Bilingual
Number of searches:	4,289	16,888	1,127
Average searches per session:	3.4	4.8	3.1
Std Deviation of Queries:	3.06	2.45	2.66
0 search sessions:	35.4%	24.8%	37.2%
1-2 search sessions:	29.4%	30.7%	31.7%
3+ search sessions:	35.2%	44.4%	31.1%

Table 5. Extended session searching terms

	Māori	English	Bilingual
Average terms per search:	1.8	1.9	1.9
STD DEV of search terms:	0.33	0.36	0.45
Searches with 1 term:	53.3%	47.0%	51.9%
Searches with 2 terms:	26.2%	32.6%	27.4%
Searches with 3+ terms:	20.5%	20.4%	20.7%

Figure 8. Top 50 search topics

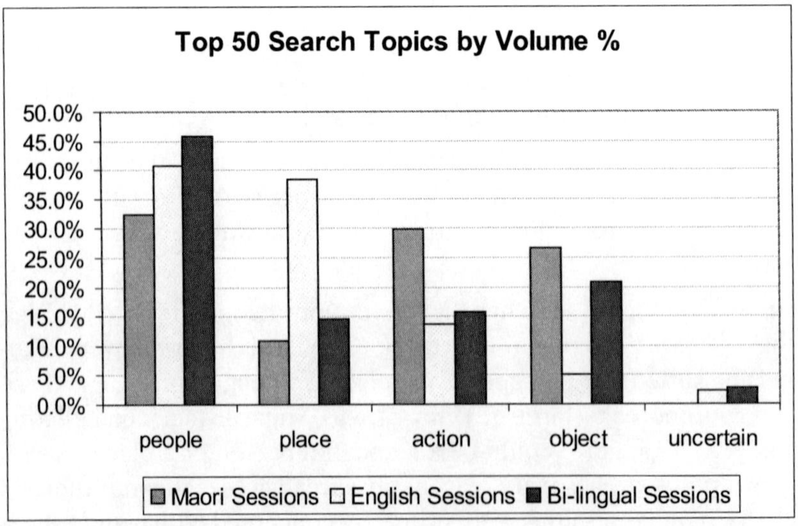

Extended Session Analysis: Language Switching

We also carried out an analysis to find out at what point in the sessions users chose to switch the interface language. The results are displayed inFigure 9, and clearly show that language switching in the English sessions occurs mostly

Figure 9. Position where language switching occurs in a session by percentage

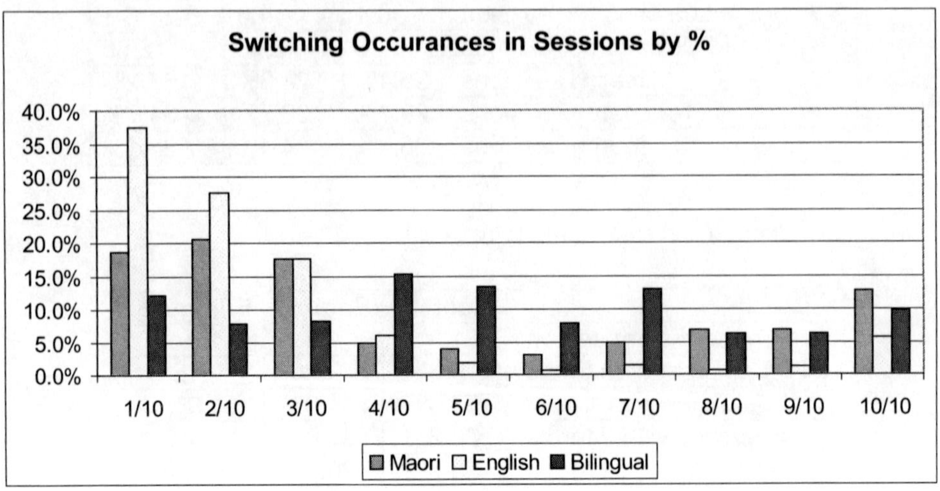

(82.8%) in the first 30% of the session. In te reo Maori sessions, language switches are more evenly distributed, with only 28.3% in the first 30% of the sessions. The language switching in the bilingual sessions is distributed evenly, with no clear peak or trough. This gives us an indication that this particular user group will switch the language of the interface at any point in the session.

Conclusion

The transaction log analysis of the bilingual Niupepa Web site has uncovered three important findings that have relevance to the usage of information technologies by indigenous peoples.

The first, and most important, conclusion drawn is that even though the potential number of users of a bilingual Web site in an indigenous language such as Maori is very low (1-2% of Aotearoa's population) the Web site is still used considerably in the indigenous language (approximately one in four of all active sessions). The decision to offer the Niupepa Web site in Maori has been justified by active use of the Web site in te reo Maori. When we consider that 99% of all Maori speakers are in fact Maori, then the usage statistics inform us that this particular Web site has active participation by Maori people.

The second finding is that session analysis suggests some important usage differences between indigenous and non-indigenous users. The Maori session users show a greater tendency to access the information by browsing, to download full size images (presumably for online reading) and when undertaking searching, tend to search for a wide range of topics (as opposed to English searching which is predominantly for names and places). While some of these usage differences may be explained by the language of the content, it does appear that indigenous users of this bilingual Web site are using a wider variety of information retrieval and display options than non-indigenous users.

The third significant outcome of this research is the discovery of another category of user that has not previously been considered when analysing usage of a bilingual Web site. This is the bilingual user, a user who conducts a significant proportion of the session in each language. This user is likely to switch languages at any time during a session. A characteristic noted of this user is a higher use of browsing strategies, taking advantage of browsable material available in both languages, with a subsequent lower dependence on the usage of the search engine.

References

Apperley, M. D., Keegan T. T., Cunningham S. J., & Witten, I. H. (2002). Delivering the Maori newspapers on the Internet. In J. Curnow, N. Hopa, & J. McRae (Eds.), *Rere Atu Taku Manu! Discovering history language and politics in the Maori language newspapers* (pp. 211-36). Auckland: Auckland University Press.

Cunliffe, D. (2003, April). Promoting minority language use on bilingual Web sites. *Proceedings of the 1st Mercator International Symposium, Aberystwyth*. Retrieved November 3, 2005 from, http://www.aber.ac.uk/~merwww/english/events/mercSym_03-04-08.htm

IBIS. (2000). *Interfaces for bilingual information systems project reports*. Retrieved November 3, 2005, from http://weblife.bangor.ac.uk/ibis

Jones, S., Cunningham, S. J., McNab, R. J., & Boddie, S. (2000). A transaction log analysis of a digital library. *International Journal on Digital Libraries, 3*(2), 152-169.

Koch, T., Ardö, A., & Golub, K. (2004). *Log analysis of user behaviour in the Renardus Web Service*. Poster session presented at the Libraries in the Digital Age Conference, Dubrovnik and Mljet, Croatia.

Pitkow, J. (1997). In search of reliable usage data on the WWW. Selected Papers From *The Sixth International Conference On World Wide Web*, Santa Clara, CA (pp. 1343-1355).

Te Puni Kôkiri. (2001). *Maori access to information technology*. Wellington, New Zealand: Te Puni Kôkiri.

Te Puni Kôkiri. (2003). *Speakers of Maori within the Maori population*. Wellington, New Zealand: Te Puni Kôkiri.

Warschauer, M., El Said, G. R., & Zohry, A. (2002). Language choice online: Globalization and identity in Egypt. *Journal of Computer-Mediated Communication, 7*(4).

Witten, I. H., & Bainbridge, D. (2002). *How to build a digital library*. San Francisco: Morgan Kaufmann.

Case Study XIII

Language, Identity, and Community Control: The Tagish First Voices Project

Kate Hennessy, University of British Columbia, Canada

Patrick J. Moore, University of British Columbia, Canada

To all my children, we are losing our language. You are our future leaders; you must learn our language. It is the root and heart of our culture. I pass you our language. You must learn our language. — "A Message to our Children," Tagish First Voices Web site.

From the turn of the century into the early 1970s, the Choutla Anglican residential school at Carcross in the Yukon Territory was home to generations of Tagish and Tlingit children. Victims of an assimilationist educational ideology that separated them from their families for at least ten months of the year, many children were denied the teachings of their elders, the right to speak their native language and, as a result, many aspects of their identity as native people. The Tagish and Tlingit community at Carcross has since come to terms with the pain and loss associated with the Choutla school and has become empowered to move beyond the extreme paternalism of the residential school era to greater self-determination and a deep sense of cultural identity. It is symbolic that in the very place where the native languages were aggressively decimated by the residential school policies, members of the local community are taking control of information technology to ensure the revival of the Tagish language. Control over technology has in this case facilitated the assertion of authority over every way their language is represented and made it possible for their cultural values and practices to define the nature of such representations.

In early 2004, the Yukon Government entered into a partnership with the First People's Cultural Foundation of British Columbia (FPCF). The Tagish-Carcross First Nation was invited to become a part of their FirstVoices project, a language archiving and teaching database. Tagish is considered the most endangered Yukon native language, with only a single fluent speaker. Its documentation and preservation is a fundamental priority for members of the Tagish community, who see the revitalization of their language as inextricably tied to the continuity of their knowledge, values and traditions. According to elder Clara Schinkel, "The language is our identity, it's who we are. If you give up your language, you give up who you are." Control of the technology associated with the Tagish FirstVoices Web site is seen by the community as essential to the articulation of the connection between Tagish language and identity.

The work of the Tagish project team entails a set of internal and external social relations that reflect the First Nations' desire to achieve local control of language and culture representation. The project team consists of elders and young adults from the community, who work together to record Tagish words and sentences directly into a computer and to add the files to their language archive. The First Nation took the initiative to access outside expertise in order to acquire the most suitable equipment for work on the First Voices Web site and, in collaboration with the First People's Cultural Foundation, also supported technical training for its members, ensuring that the local team is able to manage the language database. Written text is placed on the Web site with language recordings so that users are able to read the native language while they listen to it. Significantly, the First Nation has decided to abandon the more recent Leer Tlingit writing system in favor of the established Naish/Story writing system, which had been phased out of use in other Yukon language education initiatives. In addition to feeling that they were not adequately consulted about the change from Naish/Story to Leer, Tagish elders and other community members assert that the old system connects them to neighboring Tlingit in Southeast Alaska, with whom they have strong linguistic, social and cultural ties. The elders also saw wisdom in maintaining their original writing system to give their people continued access to all previously developed language materials. This system is further supported by a Unicode font and keyboard that was developed for use with Yukon languages by the

FPCF, bringing control over the representation of written Tagish literally into the hands of the First Nation.

For the Tagish FirstVoices Web site team, as in all other areas of Tagish cultural life, elders play a central role in teaching the younger members of the team about Tagish values and traditions. While respect for elders as cultural and linguistic authorities defines the team's working relationship, a keen awareness of Tagish's critical status as an endangered language has brought new meaning to the importance of transmitting knowledge from elders to youth. Technology like that being used by the Tagish FirstVoices team is now placed at the center of a vital process of language, identity and culture revival. Far from being alienated by the strong focus on Information Technology, elders see their involvement in the FirstVoices project as creating an essential connection between the ancestors and present and future generations. This understanding is clearly expressed in "A Message to our Children" (as seen above) which welcomes viewers to the Tagish Web site, and in the multi-generational images of Tagish community members that are shared on the site.

More than a tool for language archiving and learning, the Tagish FirstVoices project places language at the very center of wider discourses of knowledge, power and authority. It constitutes a significant assertion of identity that reclaims control of the representation of the Tagish language, and counteracts the loss of power associated with the Choutla residential school. According to elder Norman James, "Before abuse [associated with the residential school system], I think they [the Tagish people] were based in the teachings... to be honest, to respect.... After the abuse set in, everything is gone, nobody understands what is what... The language will bring it back. If you start using the language, it will bring it back."

Case Study XIV

Towards an Indigenous Language Knowledge Base: Tools and Techniques from the Arwarbukarl Community

Daryn McKenny, Arwarbukarl Cultural Resource Association, Australia

Baden Hughes, University of Melbourne, Australia

Alex Arposio, University of Newcastle, Australia

The Arwarbukarl Cultural Resources Association (ACRA)[1] is a leading indigenous cultural representation and coordination body in the Hunter Valley region of New South Wales, Australia. A particular focus of ACRA is language revitalisation — made more difficult since only a smattering of documentary evidence of the language exists from the 1830s. In 2005, the number of individuals involved in learning the Arwarbukarl language was 20. While indigenous language documentation and revitalisation efforts are by no means unique to the Arwarbukarl context, this particular indigenous community has made significant progress in the development of software tools for language analysis. Here we briefly consider a number of the important aspects (technological, functional, cultural and social) that have contributed to the success of this project.

Many indigenous cultural organizations involved in language documentation and revitalisation find commonly used linguistic analysis tools inaccessible because of the complexity of the learning curve needed to operate them and because they were not initially designed to serve language communities as primary users. Consequently, such organisations tend to either fail to realise the benefits of computational approaches to language analysis and data systematisation, or develop esoteric solutions in isolation of wider consensus as to particular methods and approaches that are grounded in the broad discipline of documentary linguistics. The linguistic knowledgebase application developed and used by ACRA is even more important in the context of the omission from a majority of linguistic analysis software of concern for the non-linguistically-trained user in terms of interface design and usability by non-experts (i.e., language learners as opposed to linguists).

The development of database software for the Arwarbukarl language is a prime example of linguistic knowledge management software that addresses the particular needs of indigenous language development work by providing a simple user interface for the analyst, yet powerful analytical capabilities, combined with an approachable user interface for the language learner. A variety of interfaces to the language data repository, including a multimedia dictionary and indexing

Figure 1. Analytical interface for language worker (Used with permission from Arwarbukarl Cultural Resource Association Incorporated)

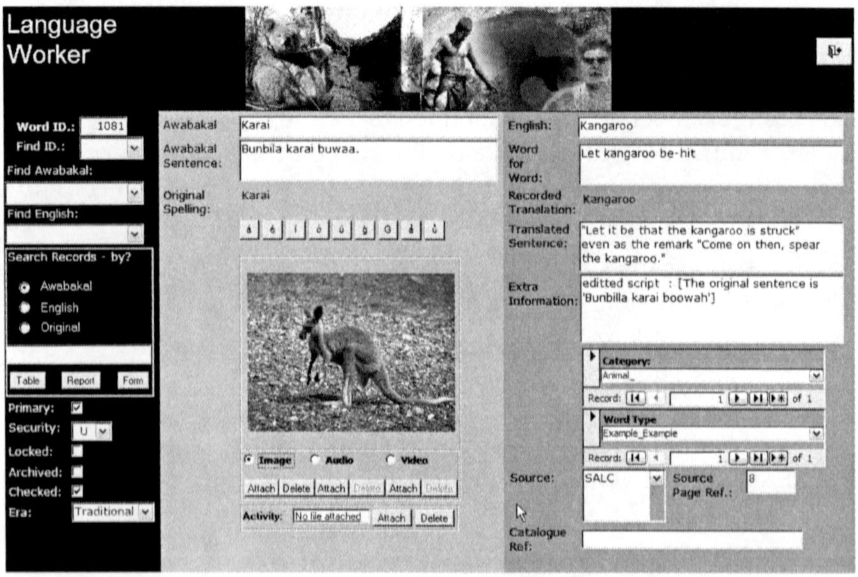

Figure 2. Learning Awabakal (Used with permission from Arwarbukarl Cultural Resource Association Incorporated)

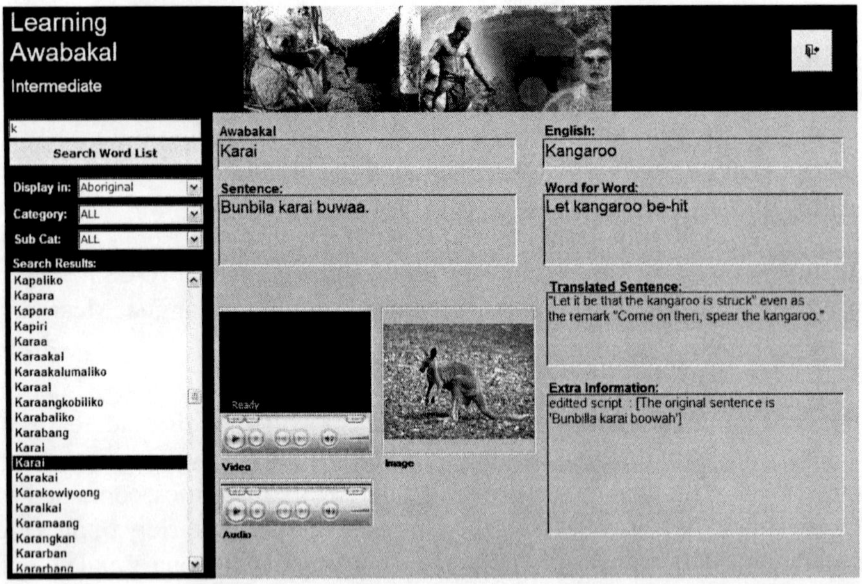

by linguistic/cultural features, are complemented by the ease of producing printed materials such as word lists and illustrated dictionaries. The inclusion of rich multimedia content in addition to textually based materials is an obvious advantage in attracting language learners. The provision of an analytical interface to the database (see Figure 1), which can be distributed on CD to language centres, together with an interactive learning area Web site (see Figure 2) available to the general public and all based on the same materials, allows interaction with language materials independent of network connectivity and conditions.

The ACRA software is strongly integrated in the vertical dimension: Larger scale projects at a state level (e.g., NSW Aboriginal Languages Research and Resource Centre Database)[2] and the national level (e.g., the Australian Institute of Aboriginal and Torres Strait Islander Studies AustLang Database)[3] provide a framework for language resource collation and assessment. The ACRA software complements these larger scale endeavours by providing the functionality most requested by indigenous cultural heritage organizations — enabling basic linguistic analysis and the ability to create language resources for revitalisation and pedagogy. The ACRA database therefore meets another strategic need for such smaller indigenous cultural organizations, and allows ease of integration with larger indigenous language resource management frameworks.

The ACRA database project complies with international best-practice standards for the creation and management of linguistic data and metadata (e.g., guidance provided by EMELD[4], DoBeS[5] and HRELP[6]), which ensures that significant initial effort invested in the initial creation of language materials has a long-term benefit in terms of ensuring that future generations of the Arwarbukarl community can access the data.

As with many cultural heritage organisations, ACRA is dependent on government funding for the majority of its activities. The approach adopted by ACRA in terms of enabling a broad cross-section of the indigenous community to contribute to the development of the database application and its contents has numerous benefits. Collaborative development of information technology infrastructure as well as linguistic content allows involvement of community language and education workers to contribute from the initial phases rather than simply acting as the recipients of the product at the end of a software development cycle. This holistic approach has benefits for both the software developers and the community, and encourages ownership of the final product, an outcome difficult to achieve simply by funding external parties to fulfil software development tasks.

In conclusion, the experience of the Arwarbukarl Cultural Resources Association in the development and deployment of linguistic knowledgebase software demonstrates how indigenous communities can effectively leverage information technologies to directly support their activities. Critical to the success of the ACRA project is ownership of the software development process by the indigenous cultural organisation. Subsequently, ACRA is disseminating the knowledgebase software framework to other language centres and communities, offering in-house customisation services and ongoing support. Further, as an information technology service provider, ACRA reaps the benefits of the software development process and an increasing return on investment. Vocational linkages from language documentation and revitalisation to information technology opportunities provide valuable pathways for younger generations of indigenous peoples in the local Newcastle area. In summary, the adoption by ACRA of information technology for language work has pervasive technological, functional, cultural and social impacts which will stretch beyond the current generation, ensuring a vibrant, engaging indigenous community in the Hunter Valley region of New South Wales.

Endnotes

[1] ACRA (Arwarbukarl Cultural Resources Association). (n.d.). Retrieved April 28, 2006, from http://www.arwarbukarl.com.au

[2] NSW Aboriginal Language Research and Resource Centre. (n.d.). Retrieved April 28, 2006, from http://www.alrrc.nsw.gov.au

[3] Australian Institute of Aboriginal and Torres Strait Islander Studies (AIATSIS). (n.d.). Retrieved April 28, 2006, from http://www.aiatsis.gov.au

[4] EMELD (Electronic Metastructures for Endangered Language Documentation). (n.d.). Retrieved April 28, 2006, from http://www.emeld.org

[5] DoBeS. (n.d.). Retrieved April 28, 2006, from http://www.mpi.nl/DOBES

[6] HRELP (Hans Rausing Endangered Languages Project). (n.d.). Retrieved April 28, 2006, from http://www.hrelp.org

Case Study XV

Ndjébbana Talking Books: *A Technological Transformation to Fit Kunibídji Social Practice*

Glenn Auld, Monash University, Australia

Members of the Kunibídji community are the traditional landowners of the land and seas around Maningrida, a community in Arnhem Land in Northern Australia. With very few exceptions, Ndjébbana is only spoken by the 150 Kunibídji community members of Maningrida, although Maningrida is also home to indigenous Australians who speak other languages. Ndjébbana is the preferred language of communication between members of the Kunibídji community. Ndjébbana is a minority indigenous Australian language.

The learning of Ndjébbana language and Kunibídji social practice by Kunibídji children is supported by Maningrida School in the teaching carried out in the Ndjébbana Two-Way Learning Program. When computers began to be used in the classrooms, Ndjébbana talking books were created to mediate Ndjébbana stories to Kunibídji students. Ndjébbana talking books integrate texts, sound and pictures in a multimedia format. When a page from a talking book is opened, the sound plays and each word of the text on that page is highlighted as it is read. There are three buttons at the bottom of each page, two for turning the page and one to stop the book. Ndjébbana talking books are designed to promote access to the Ndjébbana stories by Kunibídji children who have a variety of reading abilities.

With community participation, 96 Ndjébbana talking books were created. Some Kunibídji adults who could not read were able to participate in ways they could not with printed texts. For example, some adults were recorded speaking the names of animals that were consequently linked to the pictures and printed text to produce a talking book read by a respected community member. The Ndjébbana talking books were the first form of digital texts that represented Ndjébbana language and Kunibídji social practices. The production of the Ndjébbana talking books provided Kuníbidji children with a contextual resource that supported their threatened language.

The talking books were distributed on touch screen computers in homes of Kunibídji children. Each time the computer screen was touched, it was as if the mouse had been clicked, making the computers an appropriate technology for the dusty conditions. Embedded in the multimedia program was the capacity for the computer to record the number of times the screen was touched. As the pages were turned or a book selected from the 96 available, the computer recorded the interaction. Three touch screen computers were made available to Kunibídji children in different homes, displaying only Ndjébbana talking books. After an average of 27 days access to each computer, members of the Kunibídji had tapped the screens over 110,000 times (Auld, 2002). Kunibídji children had previous access to the Ndjébbana talking books as part of a qualitative study and the touch screens had intermittently been in the community for over two years before this data was recorded. An important feature of the high frequency of the taps was the children who had problems with attendance and achievement at school and were independently choosing Ndjébbana talking books at home.

Gee's (1996) concept of primary and secondary discourses is a good way of framing the transformations associated with the Ndjébbana talking books. Primary discourses are acquired by groups without formal teaching in contexts where everyday social practices occur. Secondary discourses, on the other hand, tend to be learned through overt instruction that involves explanation and analysis and some metaknowledge about the matter (Gee, 1996, p. 138). The Ndjébbana talking books were designed, produced and distributed to match the primary discourses of Kunibídji children. The technology that was commonly used to support the secondary discourses at the school was transformed. Computers connected to the Internet for individual student use were transformed to stand-alone touch screens that promoted collaborative readings of the Ndjébbana talking books amongst groups of Kunibídji children. The technological configuration of the touch screen computer in Kunibídji homes displaying talking books was not "led purely by the capabilities of the latest technical innovation" (Levy, 1997, p. xi).

A critical approach to technology was embedded in the provision of Ndjébbana talking books for Kunibídji children. Feenberg (2002) suggests the basis for a critical approach to technology is the "social values placed on design, not just the use of technological systems" (p. 14). The Ndjébbana talking books were designed to value the everyday social practices and language of the Kunibídji community. The design of the technological configuration provided the children with access to the texts and valued the manner in which the children collaboratively negotiate new meanings in their social environment. The design and use of the Ndjébbana talking books attempted to overcome some of the marginalisation facing Kunibídji children.

In minority indigenous Australian language contexts, care should be taken not to use technologies to exclusively support majority languages that are mainly associated with secondary discourses. Technology should not be used just to support the social transformation of community members to fit emerging technological practices used in other social contexts. Instead, technology can be transformed to fit everyday social practices of speakers of minority indigenous Australian languages.

As part of their human rights, speakers of minority indigenous Australian languages have a right to have their threatened languages and social practices represented by new technologies. They also have the right to access texts at home where they can tinker with new technological configurations and negotiate where these may fit in their everyday social practices. Kunibídji children enjoy reading the Ndjébbana talking books. They are also celebrating their linguistic human rights in reading digital texts in their first language at home.

References

Auld, G. (2002). What can we say about 112,000 taps on a Ndjebbana touch screen? *Australian Journal of Indigenous Education, 30*(1), 1-7.

Feenberg, A. (2002). *Transforming technology: A critical theory revisited.* New York: Oxford University Press.

Gee, J. P. (1996). *Social linguistics and literacies: Ideology in discourses* (2nd ed.). London: Falmer Press.

Levy, M. (1997). *Computer assisted language learning, context and conceptualisation.* Oxford: Clarendon Press.

Case Study XVI

A Talking Dictionary of Paakantyi

David Nathan, University of London, UK

This case study outlines the development of one component of the interactive multimedia CD-ROM *Paakantyi* (Hercus & Nathan, 2002), emphasising the value of community consultation throughout the project lifespan.[1] In our initial consultations with members of the Paakantyi community of NSW, Australia, about producing a CD-ROM to support their new language revival efforts, community members put forward the idea of a "talking dictionary." The value that many aboriginal people place on dictionaries as symbols of a language's significance is well-known, and, particularly following the publication of the (text-only) Kamilaroi/Gamilaraay Web Dictionary (Austin & Nathan, 1996), we had heard many people in many places express a preference to simply *hear* the words.

So, we set out to develop the first comprehensive interactive talking dictionary of an Australian indigenous language. This promised to be a challenge. Not only was the design of a good speaking dictionary initially unknown, but the very serious degree of language loss in the community meant that we were unsure how many words we would even be able to include.

We did know that protocol required that recordings be made with Paakantyi language consultants whose authority to use language was recognised by the community. As we set out on our second field trip, we discussed methodologies for recording words for the talking dictionary. My co-researcher Luise Hercus, a prominent field linguist who had worked with the Paakantyi community over a period of forty years, wanted to make "authentic" recordings using traditional elicitation methods to both populate the talking dictionary and to further her research on the language. As the multimedia developer, I was more focused on recording enough words to create a reasonable-sized dictionary, and felt that due to limited language knowledge in the community we might need to "stage" many of the recordings by asking people to read words from lists.

The consultants themselves argued for authenticity; they invariably commented that if they were prompted with words that they were not familiar with (and, in the later editing process, their judgements governed the inclusion or otherwise of words). Nevertheless, the outcome surprised all the participants, researchers and community members alike. The number of words recorded (and other materials, see below) was beyond what any of us had expected, probably as a result of the unbridled enthusiasm of the consultants and our shared attention to methodology. During the three fieldwork visits, our "team" evolved comfortable working styles and the consultants found it increasingly easier to recall and pronounce words and expressions that they had not heard or used for decades. And as other community members saw the draft CD taking shape, they also offered to record with us.

We not only recorded many more words than anyone had thought possible, but also discovered important parameters for the talking dictionary's design among the patterns of the consultants' contributions. For example, our main consultants (Renie Mitchell, Lottie Williams, John Mitchell and Badger Bates) would often follow Paakantyi words with English glosses and explanations, and possibly some expressions to illustrate usage. For example, John Mitchell provided the recorded entry for the word *murarta* "fast, quick" (as in Hercus, 1993). He said: *mura-mararta,* "hurry up"... *Mura-mararta thikalanaapa,* "hurry up, I'm going home." To accommodate such contributions, several non-trivial linguistic and functional design decisions needed to be made, including the following:

- Paakantyi speakers sometimes used forms that were different from those in the published dictionary. In some of these cases, the new data led to revision/correction of the dictionary; however, in most cases we simply juxtaposed the published (upper part of screen — see Figure 1) and the speaker's (lower part of screen) forms. It is up to the user of the CD to choose the form that appeals to them.

- Originally we had assumed that the voices in the talking dictionary would be solely speaking Paakantyi. But the "mixed" pattern (Paakantyi followed by English gloss) was pervasive across speakers and recordings. We realised that including the English commentary offered useful design and pedagogical advantages, since it makes the sound content independent of the written entries and therefore accessible to young children, or people with poor eyesight or who are sitting away from the computer.
- For some words, several usage examples were provided. We used a database to manage the assignments of examples to entries,[2] and designed a presentation interface with numbered access buttons that, when clicked, reveal the usage example text and play its sound (in Figure 1, there is only one usage example).

The usage examples are a crucial linguistic asset of the CD. They address a pervasive problem in language revival situations: the vast, increasingly empty space between dictionary and grammar, where people no longer know how to express ordinary, everyday meanings (cf. Pawley & Syder, 1983).

The preferences of the consultants and the types of materials they contributed had a defining influence on the design of the talking dictionary interface. Ultimately, the CD included three dictionaries: a full Paakantyi dictionary (an

Figure 1. Paakantyi CD: Design of the "Talking Dictionary" interface

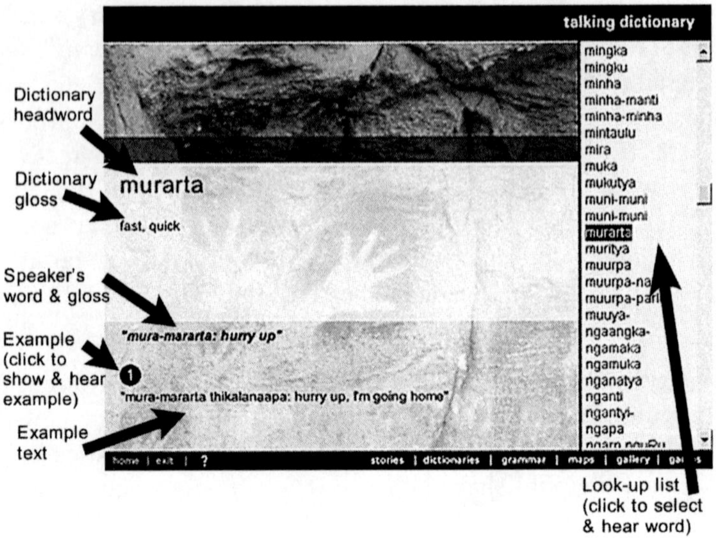

update of Hercus, 1993); an English to Paakantyi dictionary (recognising that for most Paakantyi people the access to Paakantyi words is via English); and the talking dictionary described here, which was presented as a self-contained dictionary so that community members could easily find the resource that they had fostered.

Thus the talking dictionary was more richly structured and populated than all had initially expected, and when we finally presented the Paakantyi CD to community members they told us that it was exactly what they had wanted! Elsewhere (Nathan, 2006), I describe how the distribution of art used throughout the CD mirrors the kinship relationships between the speakers and the artists represented, which resulted, like the talking dictionary, from the ongoing engagement with community members in development and the regular presentation of working drafts to show people how the product was evolving.

References

Austin, P., & Nathan, D. (1996). *Kamilaroi/Gamilaraay Web dictionary.* Retrieved November 10, 2005, from http://coombs.anu.edu.au/WWWVLPages/AborigPages/LANG/GAMDICT/GAMDICT.HTM

Hercus, L. A. (1993). *Paakantyi dictionary.* Canberra: L. A. Hercus.

Hercus, L. A., & Nathan, D. (2002). *Paakantyi.* Multimedia CD-ROM. Canberra, Australia: ATSIC.

Nathan, D. (2005). Developing multimedia documentation. In P. K. Austin (Ed.), *Language documentation and description* (Vol. 2, pp. 154-168). London: SOAS.

Nathan, D. (2006). Thick interfaces: Mobilising language documentation. In J. Gippert, N. Himmelmann, & U. Mosel (Eds.), *Essentials of language documentation* (pp. 363-379). Berlin: Mouton de Gruyter.

Pawley, A., & Syder, F. (1983). Two puzzles for linguistic theory: Native-like selection and native-like fluency. In J. Richards & R. Schmidt (Eds.), *Language and communication* (pp. 91-226). London: Longman.

Endnotes

1 The CD was produced by Luise Hercus of the Australian National University and David Nathan (then) of the Australian Institute of Aborigi-

nal and Torres Strait Islander Studies, together with Paakantyi language consultants Mrs. Renie Mitchell, Mrs. Lottie Williams, Badger Bates and Mr. John Mitchell (also Doreen and Julie Mitchell).

2 Described in Nathan (2005).

Case Study XVII

Building the Dena'ina Language Archive

Gary Holton, University of Alaska Fairbanks, USA

Andrea Berez, Wayne State University, USA

Sadie Williams, Eastern State University, USA

As the world's indigenous languages continue to be threatened with extinction, technology can play an important role in indigenous language revitalization, maintenance and preservation (cf. Buszard-Welcher, 2001). The emergence of electronic language archives provides an unprecedented opportunity to both preserve and provide access to often obscure and inaccessible endangered language data. Indeed, the relative ease of use of new electronic tools has made digital archive projects within reach of even modestly funded language communities. However, the ability of these data to endure in electronic format hinges crucially on attention to accepted standards of digital preservation. Lack of attention to open formats can lead to "digital carnage" (Bird & Simons, 2003). Similarly, lack of attention to proper digital storage — for example, by relying on CD-ROM for data preservation — can also lead to data loss (Bradley, 2004).

With these caveats in mind, the Dena'ina Language Archive was begun as an effort to create an enduring digital archive of the Dena'ina Athabascan language of Alaska. By incorporating best practice methodologies in the digital preservation of digital data, we hope that it will serve as a model for future digital language archive projects.

The Archive is being built under the aegis of the Dena'ina Archiving, Training and Access (DATA) project, funded by the United States National Science Foundation grant NSF-OPP 0326805. Initially organized by The LINGUIST List and the Alaska Native Language Center, DATA is a collaborative effort between linguists, language technologists and community members.

Like most of the indigenous languages of Alaska, Dena'ina is no longer spoken by children and no longer functions as a language of daily communication. However, there is a keen interest in language revitalization and language learning within the community. While there are relatively few publications in or about the Dena'ina language, a wealth of documentation has been gathered by speakers and linguists over the past few decades. This documentation includes field notes, word lists, grammatical information, transcribed texts and audio recordings. While some of this material has been circulated in limited form as mimeographs, little of it is extant and accessible within the Dena'ina community. Fortunately, much of this material can be found in the Alaska Native Language Center (ANLC) Archive. However, the ANLC Archive is located in Fairbanks and is not readily accessible from the Dena'ina community.

The primary goal of the DATA project is to create archival digital copies of existing Dena'ina language materials. The project began by creating digital copies of more than 200 audio recordings and approximately 250 documents housed at ANLC, following digitization standards established by the U.S. Library of Congress. Audio recordings are archived as WAV files, and documents are archived as TIFF files. These files are then preserved on a digital mass storage system at the Arctic Region Supercomputing Center, ensuring long-term preservation.

While digital storage using open formats ensures preservation, access to these digital data requires both an electronic catalogue and an electronic interface. In many cases it was necessary to enrich existing archive metadata in order to provide useful search capabilities. This included standardization of names and dates, as well as titling of files which were originally created without publication in mind.

Given sufficiently rich metadata, resource discovery can be facilitated by a variety of means. One approach is to expose metadata via the protocols of the Open Language Archive Community (http://www.language-archives.org) so that it becomes discoverable via established Open Archives Initiative service providers (e.g., http://linguistlist.org). This approach has the advantage of maximizing interoperability between various indigenous language archives. However, an interface devoted exclusively to the Dena'ina language may do more to promote indigenous language appreciation and thus enhance language revitalization efforts. The DATA project incorporates both approaches.

Access to the Archive is embedded within a Web portal, the Dena'ina Qenaga Web site (http://www.qenaga.org). The Web site is designed to be a flexible and ever-changing portal to Web-based community language initiatives. It contains general information on the Dena'ina language and community as well as authenticated access to the Archive. The Web interface allows users to search the Archive across people, titles, dates, dialects and subject areas. Resources can be accessed and downloaded directly via hyperlinks.

One of the benefits of digital archiving is that it can facilitate new ways of accessing material. The DATA project will leverage digital technology to bring at least two new types of products to the community. First, transcriptions of traditional Dena'ina stories with English translations are being time-aligned to the corresponding audio in archival XML formats, which are then transformed to user-friendly HTML displays for distribution in the community. This is the first time Dena'ina heritage speakers have had access to united text and audio. The project is also developing a facility for easy conversion of the XML transcriptions, so that community members may produce the displays themselves. Second, existing lexica are being converted to archival XML format which can be browsed and searched electronically.

Crucially, underlying every presentation format for use in the community is an archival-quality version designed to endure well into the future. Languages are endangered, data on those languages are endangered and the data can be difficult to access. That means linguists and archivists need to pay as much attention to the methods they use as to what gets produced.

Finally, technology training is integrated into every phase of the DATA project, with the goal of training a core of Dena'ina language learners to assist with the evolution of Dena'ina Language Archive into the future. The Archive alone will not save the Dena'ina language, but with careful attention to emerging standards of best practice in digital preservation, the Archive can provide an enduring resource for Dena'ina language revitalization.

References

Bird, S., & Simons, G. (2003). Seven dimensions of portability for language documentation and description. *Language, 73*(3), 557-582.

Bradley, K. (2004). *Guidelines on the production and preservation of digital audio objects* (IASA TC-04). International Association of Sound and Audiovisual Archives.

Buszard-Welcher, L. (2001). Can the Web help save my language? In L. Hinton & K. Hale (Eds.), *The green book of language revitalization in practice* (pp. 331-345). San Diego: Academic Press.

Section IV

Applications Transforming Communities

Chapter XII

Ethnocomputing with Native American Design

Ron Eglash, Rensselaer Polytechnic Institute, USA

Abstract

This chapter shows how culturally situated design tools can be developed to support traditional culture and individual creativity in Native American communities. The software allows students to simulate traditional craft designs as well as their own creations. By translating the indigenous mathematical concepts and practices embedded in craftwork into the formal mathematics of the school curriculum, students can see math and technology as a bridge to native culture, rather than a barrier. Evaluation of one of the tools has shown statistically significant improvements in students' mathematics performance as well as an increased interest in information technology.

Introduction

The term "ethnomathematics" refers to mathematical concepts embedded in indigenous practices. Examples range from purely numeric (e.g., counting systems) to geometric (sculpture and textiles) and even various uses of logical relations (such as indigenous kinship diagrams). In discussing my previous work on fractal structures in African material culture (Eglash, 1999), Matti Tedre of the University of Joensuu in Finland suggested the term "ethnocomputing," which seems a better fit, given that many of the examples made use of computer simulations in order to "translate" between indigenous practices and western technical concepts. My efforts are primarily focused on using these computer simulations of indigenous designs to aid in mathematics education of secondary students (primarily those whose heritage is based in those traditions). In the fall of 2001 our team at Rensselaer Polytechnic Institute received funding from Housing and Urban Development, the Department of Education and the National Science Foundation that allowed us to include some new efforts in Latino and Native American designs as well. We have titled this suite of simulations "Culturally Situated Design Tools" (CSDTs); they are available as free applets online at http://www.rpi.edu/~eglash/csdt.html. This paper will review the development and evaluation of CSDTs created in collaboration with Native American communities and discuss how our activities attempt to navigate through the potential dangers and rewards of this potent hybrid of information technology, traditional culture and individual creativity.

The Virtual Bead Loom

In the summer of 2000 I was invited by Professor James Barta at the University of Utah to discuss the ethnocomputing approach with the educational community on the Shoshone-Bannock reservation in southern Idaho. Key tribal members included Drusilla Gould, an instructor in American Indian studies at Idaho State University and Ed Galindo, science teacher at the reservation junior-senior high school. Our first attempt, the virtual bead loom, turned out to be one of the most successful tools in our entire repertoire.

There were several aspects of the beadwork that made it seem like an important candidate for one of the CSDTs. First, it offered a bridge between historic tradition and contemporary culture. All too often, components of what constitutes "tradition" have — whether by the colonial experience or neocolonial forces like tourism — become "museumified" into static forms that have little engagement with contemporary community members. But Native American beadwork in general, and Shoshone-Bannock beadwork in particular, has not suffered this fate. It maintains direct ties from pre-contact practices, in which beading was an important form of personal adornment, to contemporary hybrids in which military insignia and other representations decorate everything from cigarette lighters to Wacom® digital stylus pens (Eglash, 2004). Second, the rows and columns of the loom are analogous to the deep design theme of four-fold symmetry in Native American cultures (which will be explained momentarily). And third, the two axes of the loom offer an analogue to the Cartesian Coordinate system, and thus provide a good match for standard school curricula.

The Web page for this virtual bead loom (VBL) begins by showing the four-fold symmetry theme that can be seen in a wide variety of native designs: Navajo sand paintings, Yupik parka decoration, Pawnee drum design and other geometric manifestations of the "Four Winds" or "Four Directions" concept (which can also be seen in the prevalence of base four or sub-base four counting systems, temporal patterns of four in drumming rhythms, etc.). We then introduce the students to the analogy between the Cartesian Coordinate system and these four-fold symmetries. This is a crucial step in ethnomathematics, and we initially gave a great deal of consideration to it. For example, we show how the Yupik parka designers use a two-finger length to count over from left or right of the centerline — in other words, there is actually a quantitative grid employed here, so that it is not merely a metaphor to call it a Cartesian system. In contrast to our excitement in finding good evidence for an indigenous Cartesian system, we have found that math teachers, even those at reservation schools, are typically far less interested in claims for indigenous knowledge, and more focused on whether or

Figure 1. Comparison of uneven steps in VBL triangle, and even steps in Shoshone-Bannock beadwork

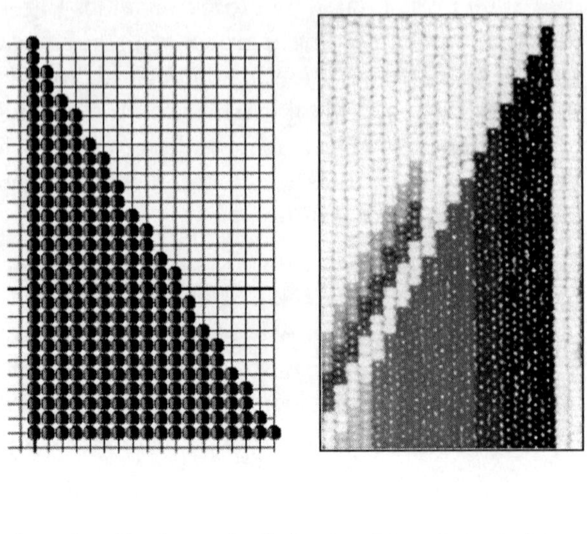

not students can actually learn mathematics by using this software. The good news is that both goals seem to work in concert: the students not only express excitement in using it, but also show statistically significant increases in their performance on math evaluations.

The first prototype allowed the creation of a pattern with only single beads added one by one. This was clearly too tedious, so we introduced shape tools: for example, you enter coordinate pairs for the two endpoints to make a line, or coordinate pairs for opposite corners to make a rectangle. Following the same logic, we created a triangle shape tool, in which the user enters the coordinate pairs for the three vertices to get a triangle. However, a problem arose because these virtual bead triangles often had uneven edges — the original Shoshone-Bannock beadwork always had perfectly regular edges (Figure 1).

The original program used a standard "scanning algorithm" — filling in any specified polygon — for the task of generating these triangles. But somehow the traditional beadworkers had algorithms in their heads that were better. After a few conversations with them, we realized that they were using iterative rules—e.g., "subtract three beads from the left each time you move up one row." We developed a second tool for creating triangles, this time using iteration (Figure 2).

Figure 2. Triangle iteration example (This is actually several triangles overlaid to produce the change in colors)

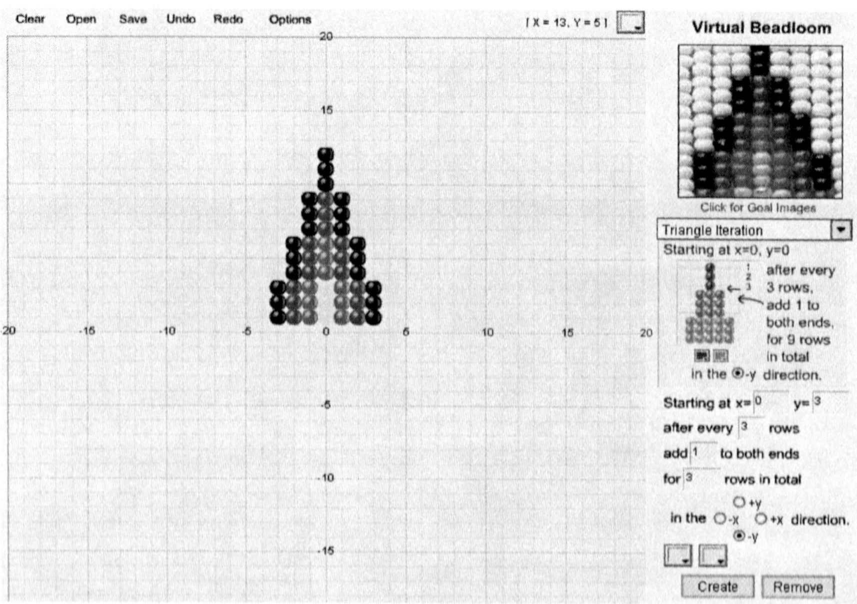

We also retained the original triangle tool, so that students could see the contrast between the two. This has provided a powerful learning opportunity: claiming that there is such a thing as a "Shoshone algorithm" can evoke skepticism, but a comparison between the standard scanning algorithm with that used by the Shoshone beadworkers makes the existence and strength of the indigenous computing quite clear.

Art teacher, Mimi Thomas, working at a school serving the northern Ute reservation in Utah, has introduced new collaborative efforts between art and math instruction using the VBL. Figure 3 shows one of the examples from her classroom in which students created virtual designs using the VBL, transferred the pattern to paper for use in math class and then created physical beadwork in art class based on that same pattern.

The most recent tribal connection has been with the Onondaga Nation in upstate New York. Following discussions with their school's cultural counselor, Frieda Jacques, we began to develop additional historical material. An exciting contribution from their group was the important historical connections with the development of the US constitution. They also suggested creating an option to work with wampum, rather than spherical beads. Joyce Lewis, a tribal member and math teacher at a nearby high school serving the reservation population, investigated traditional wampum and found that their height to width ratio was about 2:1 — thus disrupting the one-to-one mapping of beads to integer coordinates which had made the current VBL work so well in math classrooms. We decided to offer two wampum choices, one with traditional dimensions and a modified bead with a 1:1 height to width ratio — a sort of hybrid bead whose reconstructed identity echoed the cultural hybridity inhabited by many of the students. (See Barta, Jette', and Wiseman (2003) for further discussion of this VBL).

Figure 3. Ute students create physical beadwork based on the VBL

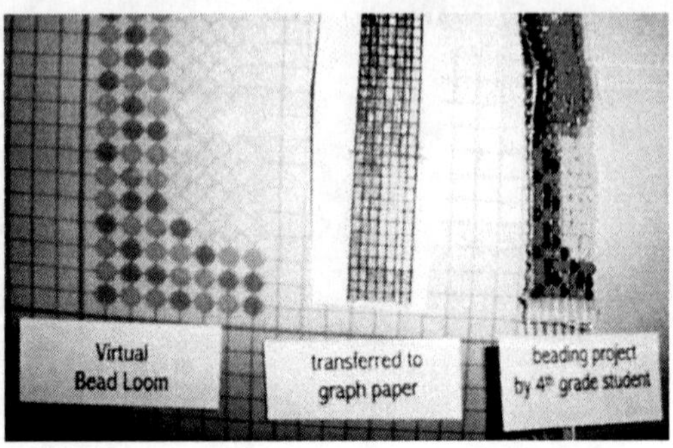

SimShoBan: Simulation of a Cultural Ecology

Back at the Shoshone-Bannock reservation in Idaho, discussions with science teacher Ed Galindo led to a project the Shoshone students dubbed "SimShoBan" — a simulation of pre-colonial life, both social and biological. The development of the SimShoBan CSDT has been described elsewhere (see Eglash, 2001). While the project began with a very broad scope, conversations with students and faculty at the reservation school eventually lead to a focus on simulations of four indigenous technologies: the fish weir in the spring, the camus root gathering basket in the summer, the tipi in the fall and the pine nut winnowing basket in the winter. The gathering basket simulations resulted in some particularly interesting creations by the students. Figure 4, for example, shows two gathering basket simulations; the one at left was made by one of the older students (age 16). Younger students (age 12-14) tended to create simulations that look less recognizably "traditional," such as the one on the right. This was enabled by the particular software prototype used at the time, which allowed them to manipulate computer graphic parameters (such as resolution) as well as parameters that would correspond to physical features (such as basket depth). The age difference may have been due to the context of a science summer camp, in which the older students were constantly asked to set an example for the younger, but it also matches research that suggests that minority ethic/racial self-identity makes a dramatic (i.e., non-linear) shift in this age range (cf. Forbes & Ashton, 1998). The names that students used to title their work also revealed playful creativity,

Figure 4. "Munchie Basket" by 16-year-old student at left; "Invincible" by 14-year-old at right

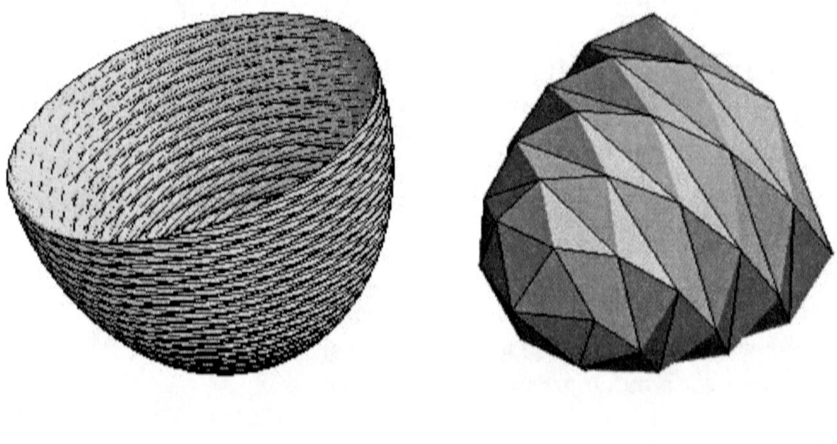

Figure 5. The Black Bullet

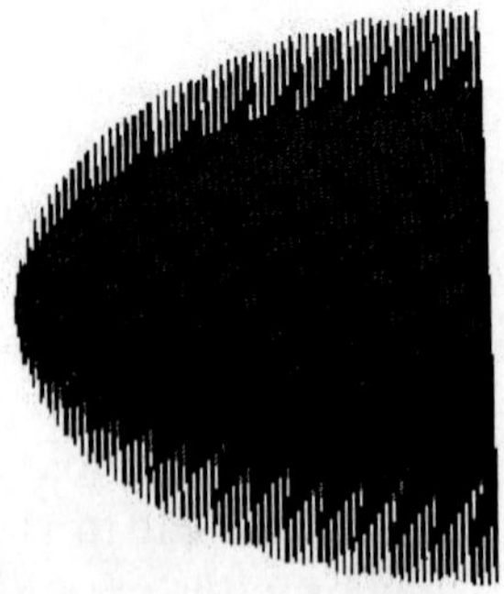

including irony or parody (as the titles “Munchie Basket” and “Invincible” invoke), even for the older students who were more serious about the concepts of indigenous knowledge.

The basket simulation in Figure 5, “The Black Bullet,” is particularly interesting: This student tried to generate a basket with one million strands, causing the laptop to crash. He re-booted it and tried again at 900,000; gradually decreasing the number until he found the maximum it could tolerate. We had a striking sense that he felt he had mastered the machine in this process of discovering its limits.

Yupik Simulations

Native researcher Claudette Engbloom-Bradley has been working on Yupik star navigation for a number of years (Bradley, 2002), and developed a board game for the purpose of teaching both the skill (much needed for survival when snowmobiles or Global Positioning Systems (GPS) fail) and the mathematics embedded in its practice. With her help we created an online version of this game, with the hope that although it is not really “design” per se, it might open the door to the development of other Yupik CSDTs. In March 2003 I accompanied Engbloom-Bradley on a trip to the village of Akiachak in the Kuskokwim delta near the Bearing Sea. The children at the local school greatly enjoyed reading the cultural background section, which named Fred George, the Yupik navigator, with whom they were all familiar. They were happy to engage in the game once or twice, but soon grew tired of it. That is partly because we only finished the first “level” of the game; presumably adding on additional levels will allow us to extend their interest. But it is also a drawback of the lack of creativity involved in playing a game as opposed to the act of design: the design tools often engage the children for a much greater span of time.

Figure 6. One of Fred George's granddaughters creating a 3-D simulation of her grandfather's fish weir.

Fred George and his family generously invited us to a dinner one night, and afterwards I showed them the simulations from SimShoBan. Fred did not speak much English, but was excited about the Shoshone fish weir, and showed us a traditional Yupik weir that he made for catching blackfish (*Dallia pectoralis*). Although there were considerable differences between the two, we created a new version of the Web page on the spot, substituting an image of Fred with his weir for the Shoshone image. The following day we tried it at the school and the children were delighted — it had both the name recognition of Fred George and a more creative component in its design capabilities (Figure 6). Adults we spoke to suggested that we develop a Yupik-specific design, and expressed interest in the possibility of a cross-cultural exchange between the Shoshone and the Yupik.

Evaluation

There are several advantages to the use of culturally situated design tools, but one of the most important is the possibility of boosting children's mathematics achievement. Our best quantitative data to date come from evaluations of the VBL. Middle school teacher Adriana Magallanes, who has both Native American and Latina heritage, ran a quasi-experimental study of the VBL for her master's thesis. She compared the performance of Latino students in two of her pre-algebra classes, one using the beadloom, and the other using conventional teaching materials. She found a statistically significant improvement ($p<.01$) in the math test scores of students using the beadloom. Other teachers have used pre-test/post-test comparisions on a single classroom, and also found statistically significant improvement using the VBL. We expect to find similar positive results with the other design tools. We have also examined the impact of design tools on attitudes towards information technology careers with minority students, using the Bath County Computer Attitudes Survey. Using workshops with Latino and African American students, we found statistically significant ($p<.05$) increases over baseline values for that local population. This indicates that it may also be possible to raise interest in technological careers for Native American students using the design tools.

Conclusion

CSDTs offer an exciting convergence of both pedagogical and cultural advantages. Unlike many other ethnomathematics examples, we can modify the interface to allow a close fit to the math curriculum, which makes it easy for teachers to incorporate into their class. At the same time, their ability to move between virtual and physical implementations allows use in the arts; and their historical connections provide teaching opportunities in history and social science. Most importantly they allow for a flexible, creative space in which students can reconfigure their relations between culture, mathematics and technology.

Acknowledgment

This material is based upon work supported by the National Science Foundation under Grant No. 0119880.

References

Barta, J., Jette', C., & Wiseman, D. (2003). Dancing numbers: Cultural, cognitive, and technical instructional perspectives on the development of Native American mathematical and scientific pedagogy. *Educational Technology Research and Development, 51*(2), 87-97.

Bradley, C. (2002). Travelling with Fred George: The changing ways of Yup'ik star navigation in Akiachak, Western Alaska. In I. Krupnik, & D. Jolly (Eds.), *The earth is faster now: Indigenous observations of Arctic environmental change.* Fairbanks, AK: Arctic Research Consortium of the United States.

Eglash, R. (1999). *African fractals: Modern computing and indigenous design.* New Brunswick, NJ: Rutgers University Press.

Eglash, R. (2001). *SimShoBan: Computer simulation of indigenous knowledge at the Shoshone-Bannock school.* Retrieved September 20, 2005, from http://www.aaanet.org/committees/commissions/aec/simshoban.htm

Eglash, R. (2004). The American Indian computer art project: An interview with Turtle Heart (pp. 181-206). In R. Eglash, J. Croissant, G. Di Chiro, & R. Fouché (Eds.), *Appropriating technology: Vernacular science and social power.* Minneapolis, MN: University of Minnesota Press.

Forbes, S., & Ashton, P. (1998). The identity status of African Americans in middle adolescence: A reexamination of Watson and Protinsky — 1991 — response to M. F. Watson and H. Protinsky, *Adolescence*, vol. 26, p. 963. *Adolescence, 33*(132, Winter), 845-9.

Chapter XIII

Cut from the Same Cloth: The United States Bureau of Indian Affairs, Geographic Information Systems, and Cultural Assimilation

Mark H. Palmer, University of Oklahoma, USA

Abstract

The construction and implementation of geographic information systems (GIS) within the United States Bureau of Indian Affairs (BIA) is yet another attempt to assimilate American Indians into the greater American society. Historically, the BIA collaborated with Christian missionaries to assimilate indigenous Americans. The United States federal government implemented the reservation and boarding school systems, and promoted the English language and Christianity while effectively suppressing indigenous languages and religions. Today the BIA collaborates with new missionaries who are distinctly technical and corporate. This particular BIA/GIS implementation strategy can have homogenizing and universalizing impacts upon American Indian cultural landscapes, geographic knowledge and native languages.

Introduction

Recently, there has been a push by government and non-government organizations to develop and implement geographic information system (GIS) technologies within indigenous communities around the world. Computer-based information technologies such as GIS are "transforming basic cultural concepts and experiences such as those of time, space, reality, privacy, and community and ... also affecting fundamental shifts in cultural practices" (Brey, 2003, p. 55). Technological determinists argue that GIS are a way for indigenous communities to attain progress by replacing old, traditional views of geographic knowledge with new, progressive, scientific and technological ways. However, technological determinists fail to acknowledge that information technologies like GIS are not endemic to indigenous societies. Like all technologies, GIS are socially constructed within the historical contexts of some institutions (Chrisman, 1993), and some institutional histories are filled with conflict, military action and the colonization of indigenous peoples throughout the world. One such institution currently involved in the promotion of GIS within indigenous communities is the United States Bureau of Indian Affairs (BIA).

The BIA was officially created on June 30, 1834. At first, the bureau was under the administration of the Department of War and later moved to the Department of the Interior (DOI). Historically, the bureau implemented and carried out the United States government policies of extermination, assimilation, termination and self-determination on American Indians and their land resources (Jackson & Galli, 1977). One former BIA administrator stated that, "The two main functions of the BIA through most of its history have been (1) to help Indians adjust to the society that gradually surrounded and engulfed them; (2) to exercise trust responsibility for Indian land and resources as long as that was required by law" (Taylor, 1984, p. 45). Some American Indians see these objectives as a product of colonialism, and assimilationist and paternalistic in nature.

To fulfill its mission to assimilate American Indians, the BIA often collaborated with Christian missionary groups. Missionary groups and administrators, "largely viewed the BIA as somehow their bureau, with the assimilation process being their responsibility to guide and shape" (Daily, 2004, p. 35). Through their relations with the U.S. federal government, missionaries gained access to American Indian people through the reservation system, boarding schools and the development of churches in Indian Country; all of which promoted the implementation of the English language and westernized education. Through these social structures, missionaries assisted in the cultural assimilation of many American Indians. American Indian scholar and activist Vine Deloria "argued that it is because Indians perceive themselves as sovereign that they resisted assimilation, fought termination, and preserved their cultures as much as possible" (Deloria, quoted in Gross, 1989, p. 8).

In this article, I will argue that GIS are yet another means by which the BIA seeks to assimilate American Indians and their natural resources into the greater American society. My objective is to explain how the homogenizing and universalizing characteristics associated with the construction and use of GIS can have adverse affects upon the diversity of American Indian cultural landscapes, geographic knowledge and languages. Contemporary BIA mapping and technology projects are one-way exchanges of knowledge. BIA officials, technical consultants and corporate GIS vendors are the new missionaries and Indian agents. What I am suggesting is that the coming of the information age to Indian Country is a reproduction of an already experienced reality. And once again, American Indian communities have very little say in how geographic information is constructed at the BIA.

Assimilation in GIS and Society

This article contributes to the literature on GIS and society, and more specifically to Robert Rundstrom's work on assimilation, North American Indians, cartography and GIS. Cultural assimilation is the total absorption of an ethnic group into the larger, more central host society. However, cultural assimilation is not inevitable. It is only one strategy implemented into the construction of GIS. Robert Rundstrom stated that, "Assimilationist practices can and do emanate from the ways in which cartographic technology (including GIS) is used, and from the cartographers' erstwhile desire for an easier job" (Rundstrom, 1993, pp. 22-23). These cartographic and GIS practices can affect the diversity of indigenous languages (Rundstrom, 1993), and intentionally or inadvertently map indigenous people, places and language out of existence — a process referred to as the silences and secrecies of maps (Harley, 1988), that reinforce social, cultural and political values (Monmonier, 1996). Historically, the diverse indigenous knowledge of places was effectively left out of colonial and imperialistic inscriptions such as maps (Craib, 2000). Moreover, these systems alter the way indigenous peoples use "their own language, not just in writing but in speech, on the ground and in their very sense of the world around them" (Godlewska, 1995, pp. 16-17). This attack upon the cultural landscapes of indigenous peoples is likened to the civilizing mission in which Christian missionaries and government agents infiltrated the homelands of indigenous peoples and affectively suppressed cultural traits such as language, religion and symbology. Current cartographic and GIS mapping practices are undertaken with the "zeal" of contemporary missionaries and government agents (Rundstrom, 1995).

GIS Relations between the Federal Government and American Indian Tribes

There are a few articles that focus upon the implementation of GIS within tribal communities. GIS enters American Indian tribal governments through various governmental and non-governmental organizations, and also through academia. Some of the more visible American GIS technology transfer institutions are the BIA, the Environmental Protection Agency (EPA), Bureau of Land Management (BLM), United States Geological Survey (USGS) and National Aeronautics Space Administration (NASA) among others. Over the last couple of decades, there has been a slow, but steady, stream of GIS articles pertaining to North American Indians. Often, these papers focus upon the use of GIS for land claims (Duerden, 1992), water rights litigation (Marozas, 1991) and the documentation and protection of culturally sensitive sites (Williams, 1994). Others have considered the idea of culturally appropriate (Natel, 1999) and culturally relevant GIS to be deployed in North American Indian communities using government data sources (Marozas, 1993).

Some tribal governments revealed that in the early 1990s, the BIA controlled many of their important forestry and natural resource GIS applications (Marchand & Winchell, 1992). The BIA also maintained control of the Colville Confederated, Warm Springs and Flathead reservations' GIS applications and vast storage of data. All three tribal governments made a request for the development of independent, locally-controlled GIS, but were originally denied by the BIA (Adam, 1999). Other tribes, like the Cherokee Tribe of Oklahoma, have successfully used the BIA as a "springboard" for jumping into the GIS arena and developing local, tribally-controlled GIS (Bond, 2002). Although these studies provide important insights, they are conventional accounts of the implementation process, and with the exception of Marchand and Winchell (1992), do not critically examine issues pertaining to GIS, cultural assimilation or colonialism.

Corporate GIS, the Federal Government and American Indians

In an era of rising neo-conservatism and neo-liberal economic policies in the United States, a new kind of technical missionary has emerged in Indian country. Over the past two decades, GIS software corporations have knowingly or unknowingly entered into the complex cultural, social, political and economic relationships between the United States federal government and American

Indian tribes. As with past missionary activities, federal Indian policies and present GIS technology, these corporate to government relationships are contradictory in nature. For instance, the GIS software corporation, Environmental Systems Research Institution (ESRI), helped produce a GIS overlay map of "Zuni Lands Taken Since 1846" and "was created to aid the Zuni in a land claim against the United States" (Warhus, 1997, p. 217). In another instance, plaintiffs in the Cobell v. Norton multimillion dollar lawsuit against the DOI for alleged mismanagement of tribal funds used ESRI's ArcView GIS software and BIA GIS data sets to analyze trust land assets (Dizzard, 2003) to prove their case. Yet at the same time, ESRI supplies western governments and transnational corporations with GIS software that affectively assimilates and may ultimately colonize indigenous peoples on a global scale. Although ESRI may declare a neutral position and label such activities as "conservation GIS," these activities are in themselves very political acts.

GIS at the BIA Geographic Data Service Center

The BIA Geographic Data Service Center (GDSC) began operations in Lakewood, Colorado in the mid 1980s. The GDSC is the GIS technology transfer department for the bureau, staffed by approximately 20 GIS technical consultants and one federal government director. The GDSC provides GIS services such as GIS software and hardware training, technical support, data acquisition and selected GIS applications (Bureau of Indian Affairs, 2003). According to the GDSC, its mission is: the establishment and promulgation of policies, procedures, standards, goals and objectives for all spatial data technologies and applications throughout Indian Country (Bureau of Indian Affairs, 2004). As with past BIA activities, outside collaborators support the agency's mission. This time it is GIS software corporations.

From the late nineteenth century to around 1933, Christian missionary groups and the BIA often supported one another politically to meet the standards of US federal Indian policy that the BIA was to implement. For missionaries, this cooperation would give them direct access to American Indians on the reservations through the establishment of churches and through the administration of government-funded boarding schools. In the relationship between the BIA and missionaries, "missionaries offered their political support for the ongoing work of the BIA in exchange for the BIA's extension of unique privileges to Christian workers. This relationship was further grounded in a larger belief that America enjoyed a unique calling as a beacon of Christian civilization" (Daily, 2004, p. 79).

Since 2002, the ESRI/BIA relationship has some similar characteristics to the missionaries. On December 20, 2002, the DOI (BIA's parent administrative unit) and ESRI signed a three-year GIS software blanket purchase agreement (ESRI, 2003). This collaborative effort supports the Bush Administration's E-Government Act that was signed on December 17, 2002, as a part of the larger Presidential Management Plan. ESRI stated that "GIS is the glue for government management in the future" (Sinha, 2003), a standardized network of homogeneous software and hardware that will connect the world. In turn, the DOI was subsequently supported politically by ESRI when the corporation presented its President's Award for Exemplary use of GIS to the DOI on July 7, 2003 (Department of the Interior, 2003), thus reassuring the Office of the President and Congress that the DOI is reading the right "road map." This quid pro quo relationship beckons back to the partnership between the pre-New Deal missionary and the BIA. The act of GIS corporations collaborating with the BIA and promoting the free-market agenda of the current administration of the United States may place fiscal discipline upon tribal governments participating or conforming to GIS licensing agreements, and have a homogenizing effect upon American Indian culture.

Universality and GIS

Universalism refers to the idea of "a unitary and homogeneous human nature which marginalizes and excludes the distinctive characteristics, the differences" of indigenous societies (Ashcroft et al., 1999, p. 55). Some governmental and non-governmental organizations often proclaim the benefits of universalism as a means of bringing people, places and things closer together. When the English language, western mathematics (Bishop, 1990) and science and technology (Adas, 1989) are seen as the progressive and superior methods of seeing the world, then the universalism promoted by institutions and organizations take on imperialistic characteristics (Ashcroft et al., 1999). Universalism is a kind of social, cultural, political and economic monopoly. Christian missionaries allied with the BIA to promote: (1) the universalizing religion of Christianity, (2) English over native language and (3) writing over oral traditions. Whether deliberate or inadvertent, many of these same processes of cultural assimilation can be found in BIA resource management and GIS documents. Except this time, science is the new religion.

Feathers, Tom-Toms and Scientific Management

American Indian knowledge, like the knowledge of other indigenous groups worldwide, is often seen and portrayed as mystic, irrational, "chaotic, and a threat to a Eurocentric sense of order and technique" (Rundstrom, 1995, p. 55). When confronting western scientific knowledge, indigenous knowledge is often pushed to the margins.

The natural resource department within the BIA Office of Trust Responsibilities initiated and funded the implementation of GIS at the BIA in the mid 1980s. One of the primary documents advocating the use of GIS is the Integrated Resource Management Planning (IRMP) Guidelines. The IRMP lays out the lineaments of scientific management principles and defines, "the policies and priorities land managers are to use to insure their actions move the tribe towards its vision for the reservation" (Bureau of Indian Affairs, 1998, p. 1). Throughout the IRMP document are bits and pieces of "traditional" statements by American Indians regarding management of the natural environment. The statements are sprinkled in like inscribed subliminal messages on a page consisting of pure scientific management practice. Italicized wisdom is placed at the corner of pages and presented as fragmented contributions that are not integrated into the overall management scheme or policy of the IRMP and accompanying GIS.

As with past BIA policies, this GIS and scientific management practice affectively "de-worlds" knowledge by taking it out of its original context, allowing for distant control (Feenberg, 2003). The visions referred to in the document are not dreams. Rather the visions are clearly that of a technoscience that excludes the particular, non-scientific worldviews of American Indians in the management of their own natural resources. Is this an issue of digital divide or yet another attempt to divide and conquer?

Silencing People and Places

The cartographic silencing (Harley, 1988) of American Indian languages and places is consistent with the way the BIA, Christian missionaries and government boarding schools collaborated in suppressing Indian languages and worldviews. The BIA incorporated similar assimilation practices into the construction of nineteenth and twentieth century maps. Historically, American Indian place-names rarely appear on BIA constructed maps (Cole, 1993). Although BIA maps are supposed to be cartographic representations of American Indian landscapes, the content consists primarily of reservation infrastructure, natural resources and tribal land holdings (Kelsay, 1977). Most traces of native language and vernacular place-naming are not present. Indigenous naming systems are replaced in GIS by more standardized, colonizing systems such as the Geographic Names Information System (Rundstrom, 1995) and the BIA GDSC's own GIS Database Organizational Guidelines (DoG) which propose to create a GIS "standard structure" that can be "portable across reservations" (Bureau of Indian Affairs, 1997, 1). This kind of GIS model can have an adverse effect upon the diversity of American Indian cultural landscapes and the subsequent interpretations of these landscapes. Within this kind of universalized GIS, a tree is a tree, a mountain is a mountain, and a river is a river uniformly explained across all American Indian land areas, regardless of the different cultural meanings ascribed to these features.

Deskilling Elders

For some American Indian elders, GIS may represent another attempt by outsiders to colonize their "lifeworlds" (Habermas, 1984). This kind of tension has moved one tribal GIS manager to state,

There still is that legacy of thought, the colonials thinking: it's resource driven and it's based on the extraction of resources, value that's given to the resource. How do we apply that to traditional usage areas where the value of the land has nothing to do with money? (First Nations GIS, 1999)

Often, elders wonder why young GIS managers are suddenly interested in talking to them about the past and the old ways. One tribal elder stated,

You walk the walk or talk the talk, choose something. I know what it boils down to — it's all about money. I know it...we've been faced with the same line of questions for so long about: what is your basis for occupying this land, how do you define the extent of your territory...is this really your territory...can you prove it or can you not? When we talk of standards, like those required of federal funding agencies...it sometimes frightens me because it brings me back again to the way we are applying GIS is a method that's based on resource extraction...values that are quantified by resource extraction and availability (First Nations GIS, 1999).

This reflexive voice recognizes the marginalizing effects of colonial technoscience, and its potential to disenfranchise tribal elders.

Tribal elders are respected as leaders in American Indian communities. In the recent revival of American Indian languages in tribal communities, elders provide the direction that the younger generation needs to continue maintaining their ever-fragmenting cultural landscapes. Yet the introduction of GIS can have a contradictory affect. On the one hand, young American Indian GIS managers integrate fragments of native language and sacred places into GIS. On the other hand, such inscriptions may not be welcomed by tribal members struggling to maintain oral traditions. This can seriously transform the relations between tribal elders and the more computer savvy tribal GIS managers. This is because GIS and digital computers in general can deskill people. For instance, social historian David Noble (1984) tells of how industrial automation led to the deskilling of artisan workers and the empowering of white-collar management and technicians through the introduction of digital computers in the post-World War II era. Similarly, though in a different social context, GIS supports the authority of computer technicians' explicit knowledge at the expense of the local, particular knowledge of tribal leaders and elders councils. The deskilling and de-worlding of American Indian people was the main objective of missionary-BIA led assimilation efforts in the late nineteenth and early twentieth centuries. The undisciplined introduction of GIS into American Indian tribal relations can have the same deskilling/de-worlding impact.

Conclusion

Information technologies, such as GIS, are shaped and conditioned within the historical context of some institutions (Chrisman, 1994). Bureaucracies such as the BIA are conservative and tend to repeat past practices. In the past, the BIA collaborated with Christian missionaries in an effort to assimilate American Indian people into the greater America society. Cultural assimilation had a negative impact upon the diversity of American Indian cultural landscapes, geographic knowledge and native languages. The BIA constructed and maintained systems such as reservations and boarding schools to carry out the processes of assimilation. Historically, this meant suppressing native languages and religions and implementing English and the universalizing religion of Christianity.

Today, the BIA collaborates with a new kind of technically oriented missionary in their efforts to diffuse GIS further into Indian County. By examining various textual documents, it is possible to reveal some of the homogenizing and universalizing affects that BIA GIS can have upon American Indian cultural landscapes. As has happened throughout history, indigenous knowledge is once again pushed to the margins in favor of westernized, scientific management practices that are thought to be the best practice for tribes. Yet tribal GIS managers are asking, why GIS? This is because they understand past colonial experiences and the strain such technology can place upon local social relationships between young technocrats and tribal elders.

There should be more IT and GIS research examining the governmental transfer of IT and GIS technology into indigenous societies. Multiple case studies of other governmental and non-governmental organizations are needed. Furthermore, there are many questions to be asked. What happens to GIS once it enters indigenous communities? How does IT and GIS affect local social relations between members of indigenous communities? How are indigenous communities using these technologies? Who owns GIS and IT in indigenous communities? Empirical evidence from such studies could reveal the extent to which indigenous communities are being assimilated or the extent to which they are assimilating GIS into their own cultures.

References

Adams, S. I. (1999). *GIS on the rez: A case study of GIS implementation on the Colville Indian Reservation*. Unpublished Masters thesis. University of Washington.

Adas, M. (1989). *Machines as the measure of men*. Ithaca, NY: Cornell University Press.

Ashcroft, B., Griffiths, G., & Tiffin, H. (1999). Universality and difference. In B. Ashcroft, G. Griffiths, & H. Tiffin (Eds.), *The post-colonial studies reader*. New York: Routledge Press.

Bishop, A. J. (1990). Western mathematics: The secret weapon of cultural imperialism. *Race and Class, 32*(2), 71-76.

Bond, C. (2002). The Cherokee Nation and tribal uses of GIS. In W. Craig, T. Harris, & D. Weiner (Eds.), *Community participation and geographic information systems* (pp. 283-294). London: Taylor and Francis.

Brey, P. (2003). Theorizing modernity and technology. In T. J. Misa, P. Brey, & A. Feenberg (Eds.), *Modernity and technology*. Cambridge, MA: MIT Press.

Bureau of Indian Affairs. (1997). *Database organization guidelines*. Lakewood, CO: Geographic Data Service Center, Office of Trust Responsibilities.

Bureau of Indian Affairs. (1998). *A Tribal executive's guide to integrated resource management planning*. Washington, DC: Office of Trust Responsibilities.

Bureau of Indian Affairs (Office of the CIO). (2003). *GIS in the BIA*. Lakewood, CO: Geographic Data Service Center.

Bureau of Indian Affairs (Office of the CIO). (2004). *2004 GDSC GIS users conference: Enterprise GIS proceedings.* Lakewood, CO: Geographic Data Service Center.

Chrisman, N. R. (1993). Beyond spatio-temporal data models: A model of GIS as a technology embedded in historical context. *Proceedings AUTO-CARTO 11* (pp. 23-32).

Chrisman, N. R. (1994). *A geography of geographic information systems*. Unpublished manuscript.

Cole, D. (1993). One cartographic view of American Indian land areas. *Cartographica, 31*.

Craib, R. B. (2000). Cartography and power in the conquest and creation of New Spain. *Latin American Research Review, 35*(1), 7-36.

Daily, D. W. (2004). *Battle for the BIA*. Tucson: The University of Arizona Press.

Department of the Interior. (2003). *ESRI international honors Department of the Interior with President's Award for exemplary use of GIS*. Washington, DC: Office of the Secretary.

Dizzard, W.P. (2003). Border analyses by GIS could untangle Indian trust fund assets. *Government Computer News, 22*(7), 1.

Duerden, F. (1992). GIS and land selection for native claims. *The Operational Geographer, 10*(4), 11-14.

Environmental Systems Research Institution (ESRI). (2003). *U.S. Department of Interior selects as its standard for enterprise GIS*. ESRI Press Release. Redlands, CA.

Feenberg, A. (2003). Modernity theory and technology studies: Reflections on bridging the gap. In T. J. Misa, P. Brey, & A. Feenberg (Eds.), *Modernity and technology*. Cambridge, MA: MIT Press.

First Nations GIS. (1999). *GIS 99 – First Nations GIS*. Retrieved September 20, 2005, from http://www.nativemaps.org/conferences/GIS99/frank.html

Godlewska, A. (1995). Map, text and image — The mentality of enlightened conquerors — A new look at the Description de l'Egypte. *Transactions of the Institute of British Geographers,* (20), 5-28.

Gross, E. R. (1989). *Contemporary federal policy toward American Indians*. New York: Greenwood Press.

Habermas, J. (1984). *The theory of communicative action, Volume 2: Lifeworld and system: A critique of functionalist reason*. Boston: Beacon Press.

Harley, J. B. (1988). Silences and secrecy: The hidden agenda of cartography in early modern Europe. *Imago Mundi, 40*, 57-76

Jackson, C. E., & Galli, M. J. (1977). *A history of the Bureau of Indian Affairs and its activities among Indians*. San Francisco: R. & E. Research Associates.

Kelsay, L. E. (1977). *Cartographic records of the Bureau of Indian Affairs*. Washington, DC: National Archives and Records Service.

Marchand, M. E., & Winchell, R. (1992). Tribal implementation of GIS: A case study of planning applications with the Colville Confederated Tribes. *American Indian Culture and Research Journal, 16*(4), 175-183.

Marozas, B. A. (1991). The role of geographic information systems in American Indian land and water rights litigation. *American Indian Culture and Research Journal, 15*(3), 77-93.

Marozas, B. A. (1993). A culturally relevant solution for the implementation of geographic information systems in Indian Country. *Proceedings of the Thirteenth Annual ESRI User Conference: Vol. 1.*

Monmonier, M. (1996). *How to lie with maps*. Chicago: University of Chicago Press.

Nantel, M. (1999). *So as to hold many sheep: Towards a culturally appropriate GIS*. Unpublished Masters thesis.

Noble, D. (1984). *Forces of production: A social history of industrial automation*. Oxford: Oxford University Press.

Rundstrom, R. A. (1993). The role of ethics, mapping, and the meaning of place in relations between Indians and whites in the United States. *Cartographica, 30*(1), 21-28.

Rundstrom, R. A. (1995). GIS, indigenous peoples, and epistemological diversity. *Cartography and Geographic Information Systems, 22*, 45-57.

Sinha, V. (2003). Geographic information systems find their place in federal sector. *Government Computer News*. Retrieved September 20, 2005, from http://www.gcn.com

Taylor, T. W. (1984). *The Bureau of Indian Affairs*. Boulder, CO: Westview Press.

Warhus, M. (1997). *Another America: Native American maps and the history of our land*. New York: St. Martin's Press.

Williams, J. M. (1994). *Documenting and protecting traditional cultural landscapes using geographic information systems*. Paper presented at the 90th Annual Meeting of the Association of American Geographers, San Francisco.

Chapter XIV

Representations of Tribal Boundaries of Australian Indigenous Peoples and the Implications for Geographic Information Systems

Andrew Turk, Murdoch University, Australia

Abstract

This chapter explores the concepts of boundary ("limit of country") held by indigenous Australians and how they might be represented in computer-based information systems, especially geographic information systems (GIS) and digital cadastre databases. The impact of these representational issues on native title processes and determinations will also be discussed. The analysis provides a partial understanding of the nature of tribal boundaries, especially variations which occur in the physical definition of boundaries and their (intentional and unintentional) indeterminacy. The chapter goes on to draw some conclusions regarding the representation of indigenous boundaries in the property cadastres of Australian States and Territories. If such "official" boundaries are to do justice to indigenous law and culture, they must reasonably reflect the ontology and epistemology of the concepts of boundary held by indigenous Australians. Hence, there is a significant interaction between constraints imposed by particular information technology (IT) practices and indigenous concepts of place.

Introduction

To optimize the design of geographic information systems (GIS), and to facilitate interoperability, it is necessary to understand the relationships between the ontology and epistemology of spatial concepts and representations of spatial phenomena. This should lead to improved formal models on which to base digital representations, for instance, within a property cadastre database. It should also aid in establishing a sounder basis for the design of GIS which reflect the fundamental notions of space held by users, including an improved understanding of spatial uncertainty (Mark et al., 1997).

This chapter concentrates on concepts of boundaries. It seeks to illuminate (and perhaps extend) common notions of boundary by an exploration of the nature of the boundaries of indigenous Australian tribes. Since many geographic features have boundaries, this will make some useful contribution to the overall objective stated above.

The author (in collaboration with Kathryn Trees) has been involved in IT-related activities over many years with people from the Ngaluma and Yindjibarndi tribes in the Pilbara region of Western Australia, and he witnessed processes involved in their native title land claim (Trees & Turk, 1998; Turk, 2003; Turk & Trees, 1998a, 1998b, 1998c, 1999a, 1999b, 2000). This chapter draws on that experience.

Boundary as an Individual Concept and a Social Construct

Lakoff (1987) suggests that one of the first concepts that a person achieves is that of "insideness" and "outsideness" ("the container schema") — i.e., boundaries are fundamental to individual consciousness. However, boundaries are also social constructs, since they are limits to territories we share with others, and they often define where groups of individuals have particular rights and responsibilities. Dear (in Benko & Strohmayer, 1997) explains that social processes and spatial concepts interact — "Social relations exist to the extent that they possess a spatial expression: they project themselves into space, becoming inscribed there, and in the process producing that space itself. Thus, social space is both a field of action and a basis for action" (p. 56).

Beyond the initial body-experience basis for the boundary concept there is a vast array of meanings formed in our mind which are shaped by the social processes we engage with. These are mediated by the ontology and epistemology of our culture, with language playing a key role in this process. When we specify or describe boundaries we should do so within their social context. Hence, if a representation is to do full justice to the notion of a boundary, it needs to incorporate consideration of:

- the basis for the boundary concept involved — e.g., the law on which it is based;
- the people who have rights, responsibilities or interests related to the area of land enclosed by that boundary — e.g., an indigenous tribe;
- the way in which the boundary concept is operationalised to enable its location on the ground — e.g., a definition of "Mean Low Water" and the survey methods and data sets needed to locate it; and
- any physical manifestations (natural or placed/constructed) of the boundary location on the ground — e.g., natural features, such as rivers, or constructed markers, such as surveyors' pegs.

Why Examine Indigenous Concepts of Space

Watson-Verran and Turnbull (1995) suggest that cross-cultural comparisons of knowledge systems are receiving renewed interest from researchers in the field of science and technology studies "... as fresh insights are gained from the intersections of the social study of science with anthropology, postmodernism, feminism, postcolonialism, literary theory, geography, and environmentalism" (p. 115). Unfortunately, indigenous knowledges have often previously been thought to be merely of interest within a particular anthropological context. However, such a restricted view is giving way to one which encourages a respectful examination of local knowledges within the global context.

"Ethnophysiography" is a newly-defined ethnoscience of landscape which seeks to document and compare terms used in various languages and cultures to refer to the natural landscape and its parts, and to compare the meanings of those terms (Mark & Turk, 2003, 2004). Research to date indicates that there are significant differences in concepts of landscape in different cultures which must be taken into account when developing cross-cultural GIS for land-use planning, etc.

Postmodernism, Postcolonialism, and GIS

Postmodernism and postcolonialism present related challenges to developers of information systems, especially GIS. In the case of GIS involving indigenous communities, there must be an appropriate recognition of alternative ontological and epistemological positions, that is, a recognition that knowledge is local and particular.

GIS is a strong example of "technological determinism," and developers of such systems need to become especially aware of social and ethical questions (Prickles, 1995). Miller (1995) discusses the relationship between GIS and current social theory, which he describes under the "rubrics" of deconstruction, postmodernism and structuration. He notes that these philosophical developments have had little impact on GIS — " ... the current empirical and positivist basis of GIS has led to a general dismissal of the idea that the theoretical debates rocking the human sciences have any relevance for 'practitioners' or 'applied geographers'" (p. 98). This tendency could be said to arise from the technological training of most practitioners and their desire to represent the physical facts of the observable world (to particular quality standards) within a realist tradition.

The development of GIS technology was hailed as an opportunity to break free from the tyranny of the multipurpose (multi-user) series map conventions — an opportunity to provide hard-copy *or* ephemeral maps (from a generic database with many different themes) for a specific user and use, as required. In this sense, GIS were, from the very beginning, seen as potentially postmodern tools, although their technical nature has led more naturally to a positivist approach.

Interactions between Concepts and Representations of Boundary

Traditionally, indigenous peoples represented boundaries in ephemeral performances, such as song and dance, and, when in more permanent form (e.g., paintings or carvings), in an abstract or metaphorical manner (Muecke et al., 1984; Turnbull, 1989). This meant that the representations did not transfer their inevitable limitations to the concepts of boundary, since they were in modes that matched the vagueness of the concepts. However, the act of boundary representation in a fixed and (seemingly) exact way can misrepresent the true boundary concept, and may also influence future versions of the boundary concept itself (Rundstrom, 1995). Many other ethical issues arise regarding the appropriateness of using GIS technology to represent indigenous concepts, and a set of ethical principles and practices should be adopted to suit any specific project, through a reflective and close engagement with the people affected by the system (Turk & Trees, 1999b). The use of multimedia approaches can also assist in more adequately representing indigenous concepts.

The native title determination process for indigenous Australians can also impact on the relationship between concepts and representations of tribal boundaries. Producing maps of indigenous boundaries has become an inherently political (though necessary) process, placing heavy burdens on the shoulders of cartographers:

> *... publishing a map of Aboriginal country of any kind is becoming an increasingly onerous responsibility. Some would argue that such a mapping exercise is, at least in part, characterised and invalidated by the post-colonial relationship between the cartographer and the "natives". On the other hand, some Aboriginal people actively pursue the recording of their geographical knowledge by anthropologists and others, including themselves. Also, the Aboriginal land claim tribunals in this country would all find it extremely difficult, if not impossible, to hear and assess claims that lacked any spatial documentation.* (Sutton, 1995, p. 47)

The Nature of Australian Indigenous Tribal Boundaries

Davis and Prescott (1992) attempt an extremely ambitious task in their book (and accompanying map). They seek to describe and locate the boundaries (limit of territory) of most of the "extant" indigenous peoples of Australia. They begin by noting the considerable debate over the nature of such boundaries and briefly summarise attempts to locate them (dating back to the earliest days of European settlement).

In a very real sense, the country of any particular indigenous group does not belong to that group, rather, the group belongs to the land. They have sets of rights within the area and, more importantly, they have responsibilities for "keeping the land healthy" through conducting rituals. The way that indigenous tribes and clans were formed, and responsibility for land assigned (and maintained), is described by Davis and Prescott (1992) as follows:

Aboriginal people generally believe that each sociopolitical group variously described in the literature as a clan or tribe was made corporate by its birth from ancestral beings upon an area which became identifiable as a territory at the moment of birth of the group with whom the territory is identified. The acts of ancestral beings in conferring territories and giving birth to each group established for all time the identity of those groups and the boundaries of the territories with which they are identified. (p. 132)

Primary rights in territories accorded to Aboriginal groups by the ancestral beings are contingent upon the Aboriginal custodians continuing to care for the territory by singing the songs and performing the ceremonies associated with the territory as well as caring for the sacred objects and places. Subsidiary rights may be held by other people who ... most often claim affiliation to the territory through uterine relatives of the patrilineal descent group. (p. 134)

The boundaries of these territories are not fixed in written treaties and not usually indicated by special boundary markers on the ground — "Rather, they are defined in oral traditions, through songs, ceremonies, and non-permanent symbolism such as body painting, bark painting and ground designs" (Davis & Prescott, 1992, p. 134). The boundaries between groups have been subject to change because harsh living conditions lead from time to time to a diminishing of descendants appropriate for the continuation of the proper process of caring for country. This leads to succession to territory.

Although some of the general statements about indigenous Australian boundaries (such as those quoted above) found in Davis and Prescott (1992) are widely supported, there has been considerable disagreement with the details provided in the book and accompanying map. Sutton (1995), with the support of more than forty anthropologists, linguists and geographers, has provided a detailed review and critical analysis of Davis and Prescott's work. The details of boundaries for many particular tribes are criticised, through reference to anthropologists' work with those groups. Sutton's analysis also points to a number of important issues regarding the location and representation of indigenous boundaries. Such boundaries may display some or all of the following features:

- An exact location of the boundary may not exist unless some physical feature of the landscape (such as a river) is there to define it.
- Watersheds can form boundaries between tribes and/or clans. Similarly, creeks and rivers can be boundaries, as can changes in vegetation. Boundaries can also include areas of sea.
- A group's country may consist of non-continuous areas and may consist of "… clusters of sites and surrounding areas" (Sutton, 1995, p. 13).
- Tribal boundaries can change location when one tribe takes over responsibility for an adjacent area, either through long-lasting "succession" or where it is held temporarily in trust ("regencies" or "trusteeships"):

... the process of succession to deceased Aboriginal estates may go on for a generation or so. It may be a case of waiting, in relative unanimity, for a suitable replacement to emerge from another group. It may be a case of long negotiations and even disputation. (Sutton, 1995, p. 53).

- There may be a boundary zone of transition of responsibility from one tribe to the next. This may be related to "hand over points" along shared "Dreaming tracks" (songlines). Davis and Prescott (1992) term these zones of transition between the country of tribes as "frontiers," rather than "boundaries".
- The boundary may have one location when approached from one direction and a different location when travelling in another direction.
- Boundary concepts may vary between people of different gender or cultural seniority:

It is noticeable, at least in north-central Australia, that men and women have partly overlapping, partly complementary and partly different ways of reckoning who are the right people for what land. Briefly, men will tend to place more stress on site-focused ceremonial knowledge and agnatic relations (related by descent from a common male ancestor) while women will tend to place more emphasis on cognatic relationships (related by descent from a common maternal ancestor), in generating a picture of groups responsible for particular tracts of land. (Sutton, 1995, p. 60).

- Boundaries may, of course, be disputed:

Debates and disputed succession are integral to land tenure systems under Aboriginal tradition, not a sign of their decay. To assert that disputed land succession is outside Aboriginal tradition is like asserting that litigation over disputed property settlements in European Australian law is extraneous to Australian law. (Sutton, 1995, p. 59)

Within any boundary location or depiction project, it is important to understand which of these (and possibly other) features may apply to particular tribal boundaries and to use appropriate formats for data storage and representation. Indeed, the indigenous community may not wish a specific location for a boundary to be depicted. For instance, in their native title land claim, the main group representing the Ngaluma and Injibarndi peoples decided not to identify the boundary between their tribal areas but rather to pursue a joint claim for the whole area (Jones, 2002).

It is also important to note that the simplistic notion of a specific group having a fixed set of rights over a particular territory does not apply to indigenous Australians. Within a tribe individuals will have different sorts of rights to different places (within the general tribal area) because of factors such as: the special country of their father and that of their mother, the place where they were born and places where they have spent large periods of their life. Sutton (1995, pp. 44-5) provides an example of this complexity:

... the Warlpiri of north-central Australia (and many others) assert equivalent possessory connections to the same land by both its kirda (people inheriting land interests from the father, in their own patriline) and its primary kurdungurlu (people inheriting land interests from the mother, in their mother's patriline). Actually these possessory relationships do not control "Warlpiri country" (a recognised but very large entity). Rather, they are asserted in respect to the region's small "countries" defined by rights and interests in sites on localised Dreaming tracks, or to portions of far-travelling Dreaming tracks and in the local land surrounding them. ... Because some Warlpiri female kirda have children from marriages with non-Warlpiri men, some countries belonging to Warlpiri kirda thus also belong to, or at the very least come under the religious and political custodianship of, kurdungurlu with non-Warlpiri fathers. And some countries have dual linguistic affiliation because they are co-owned by kirda of different languages ... A tribal map which asserts that the Warlpiri are the group holding political responsibility for a monolithic bloc of country, separate from those affiliated to other languages, simply ignores the facts of the kirda/kurdungurlu relationships which, above all, is concerned with the exercise of responsibility for land.

The particular rules will quite possibly vary from one tribe to another. Hence, a more complex IT solution is required to properly indicate the relationships between individuals and groups, and their rights and responsibilities for country. In a GIS this may be represented by overlapping polygons coded to correspond to particular aspects of association with "country." The meaning of these associations could be explained via attached multimedia materials.

Tribal Boundaries and Native Title Claims

In the Mabo (1992) case, the High Court of Australia recognised native title. The court found that, although Australia is a settled colony, it was not "terra nullius" (land without laws) when European settlers arrived two centuries ago. Hence, the international common law doctrine of "native title" was applicable when British sovereignty was extended over Australia. The Crown could extinguish that native title providing the appropriate legislation or executive act embodied "a clear and plain intention" to do so.

Because of the way that "valid government acts" since colonisation (e.g., the granting of freehold title) have been held by the High Court to extinguish native title, there are only a patchwork of land parcels now available for claim (mainly "unallocated/vacant crown land") (Reynolds, 1992). In the desert areas, these may cover huge areas such that tribal boundaries may fall within such a parcel. However, in settled areas, the claimable land may be a scattering of small parcels, whose boundaries bear no relation to indigenous boundaries (Turk, 1996; Turk & Mackaness, 1995; Turk, Mackaness, & Tinlin, 1995). Thus the legally adopted "boundary" of a native title parcel is usually the cadastral boundary of the adjacent (extinguishing) parcel.

The current practice, for the relatively few native title cases which have so far been decided, is to incorporate these interests in the digital property cadastre in the same manner as non-native title boundaries — i.e., as a set of "vector" lines, between locations with specified coordinates. This is certainly administratively convenient and may be sufficient where there is no boundary between adjacent indigenous peoples involved. However, where such cases do arise, a more complex solution is required to do justice to the true nature of indigenous boundaries. For instance, this could involve digital representation of a boundary zone and/or indication of varying levels of positional accuracy. The Native Title Act does allow for the detail of boundaries to be updated if necessary. Hence, if a more adequate way of expressing indigenous boundaries is found, then the property cadastre could, at least in theory, be upgraded accordingly.

Indigenous GIS

In North America the use of GIS by indigenous peoples is much more advanced than in Australia. Although this was initiated by relevant government departments, with attendant issues of the level of indigenous "ownership" (Rundstrom, 1995), it is now being embraced enthusiastically by many tribes as part of an approach to enhanced self-management of tribal land. This has led to calls for the development of "indigenous GIS," which more faithfully reflect the ontology and epistemology of the local people. Alvin Warren, a Tewa elder from the Santa Clara Pueblo, suggests that, "Now, a new generation of indigenous mappers, academics and practitioners alike, are endeavoring to reform and redefine the use of mapping by indigenous peoples... (via) ... strategies for improving understanding of different conceptualizations and representations of place" (Warren, 2004). Ethnophysiography research (Mark & Turk, 2003, 2004) supports the possibility of indigenous peoples using GIS technology in a culturally-appropriate way by identifying indigenous concepts and terminology for landscape features.

Such research also increases the opportunity for enhanced interoperability between indigenous and non-indigenous forms of GIS, covering the same area. This may be linked to the exercise of rights awarded in native title cases. For example, the Australian Federal Court has recognized the native title rights of the Ngarluma and Yindjibarndi peoples of Western Australia (NNTT, 2003). This decision is expected to lead to an enhanced joint management agreement covering land use and environmental issues for the Millstream National Park, which includes very significant sacred sites. Joint management of cultural and natural resources would be facilitated by interoperable companion GIS (or complementary layers within a single GIS), one using English terminology and national mapping feature codes (AUSLIG, 2003) and the other using Yindjibarndi terms and concepts for landscape features (Mark & Turk, 2003). Such an approach would also need to incorporate indigenous concepts of boundary.

Conclusion

The discussion above provides an introduction to some aspects of the concept of boundaries held by indigenous Australians. Clearly, key aspects of the boundary concept call for representations which allow for indeterminacy of various types, boundaries which are not lines but zones (perhaps with complex strength/decay functions) and portrayal of the overlapping interests of various stakeholders.

To do justice to the complexity of boundary constructs, it is suggested that the digital representation would also need to incorporate information concerning: the basis for the boundary concept; the people who have rights, responsibilities or interests related to the area of land enclosed by that boundary; the way in which the boundary concept is operationalised to enable it to be physically located; and any physical manifestations (natural or placed/constructed) of the boundary location on the ground. Perhaps a taxonomy of boundary types could be established where at least some of this information could be standardised.

It is not the purpose of this chapter to suggest any particular technical solution which would incorporate these requirements. However, one option is the use of a metadata file (attached to the boundary file), as is sometimes used to convey information about data quality.

The discussion in this chapter clearly indicates that the relationship between indigenous concepts of space, place and boundary need to be clearly understood, and respected, if an IT system is to properly represent them. This has important practical consequences for determination and registration of native title land rights and for the design of cross-cultural GIS for land use planning and management.

Acknowledgments

The author would like to acknowledge the assistance of the Ngaluma, Injibarndi and Banjima peoples and his research collaborator, Dr. Kathryn Trees.

References

AUSLIG, (2003). *Feature codes used by the Gazetteer of Australia*. Retrieved June 23, 2004, from http://www.ga.gov.au/map/names/featurecodes.jsp

Benko, G., & Strohmayer, U. (Eds.). (1997). *Space and social theory: Interpreting modernity and postmodernity*. Oxford: Blackwell.

Davis, S., & Prescott, J. R. V. (1992). *Aboriginal frontiers and boundaries in Australia*. Melbourne, Australia: Melbourne University Press.

Jones, C. (2002). *Aboriginal boundaries: The mediation and settlement of aboriginal boundary disputes in a native title context* (National Native Title Tribunal Occasional Paper Series No. 2/2002). Perth, Australia: National Native Title Tribunal, Commonwealth of Australia.

Lakoff, G. (1987). *Women, fire, and dangerous things: What categories reveal about the mind.* Chicago: University of Chicago Press.

Mabo. (1992). Australian High Court decision in "Mabo v Queensland" (No. 2) (1992) 175 CLR 1 [which led to the passing of the "Native Title Act" 1993 (Cth)].

Mark, D. M., Egenhofer, M. J., & Hornsby, K. (1997). *Formal models of commonsense geographic worlds* (NCGIA Technical Report No. 97-2). Buffalo: National Center for Geographic Information and Analysis, State University of New York, Buffalo.

Mark, D. M., & Turk A. G. (2003). Landscape categories in Yindjibarndi: Ontology, environment, and language. In W. Kuhn, M. F. Worboys & S. Timpf (Eds.), *Spatial information theory: Foundations of geographic information science* (LNCS 2825, pp. 31-49). Berlin: Springer.

Mark, D. M., & Turk, A. G. (2004, October). Ethnophysiography and the ontology of the landscape. *Proceedings of the Third International Conference on Geographic Information Science, GIScience 2004,* MD (pp. 152-155).

Miller, R. P. (1995). Beyond method, beyond ethics: Integrating social theory into GIS and GIS into social theory. *Cartography and Geographic Information Systems, 22*(1), 98-103.

Muecke, S., Benterrak, K., & Roe, P. (1984). *Reading the country: An introduction to nomadology*. Fremantle, WA: Fremantle Arts Centre Press.

NNTT. (2003). *Australian National Native Title Tribunal — Report on recent decisions*. Retrieved June 23, 2004, from http://www.nntt.gov.au/media/1057275393_2456.html

Prickles, J. (Ed.). (1995). *Ground truth*. New York: Guilford Press.

Reynolds, H. (1992). *The law of the land.* Ringwood, Vic: Penguin.

Rundstrom, R. A. (1995). GIS, indigenous peoples, and epistemological diversity. *Cartography and Geographic Information Systems, 22*(1), 45-57.

Sutton, P. (1995). *Country: Aboriginal boundaries and land ownership in Australia* (Aboriginal History Monograph 3). Canberra: Department of History, Australian National University.

Trees, K. A., & Turk, A. G. (1998). Culture, collaboration and communication: Participative development of the Ieramugadu Cultural Heritage Information System (ICIS). *Critical Arts, 12*(1-2), 78-91.

Turk, A. G. (1996). Presenting aboriginal knowledge: Using technology to progress native title claims. *Alternative Law Journal, 21*(1), 6-9.

Turk, A.G. (2003). Digital divide remediation: An Australian indigenous community case study. *Southern Review, 36*(1) (Special Issue re Wired Communities and Information Poverty), 48-63.

Turk, A.G., & Mackaness, W.A. (1995). Design considerations for spatial information systems and maps to support native title negotiation and arbitration. *Cartography, 24*(2), 17-28.

Turk, A. G., Mackaness, W. A, & Tinlin, W. (1995). Designing maps to support native title negotiation and arbitration in Australia. *Proceedings of 17th International Cartographic Conference, ICC'95,* Barcelona (Vol. 1, pp. 1109-1115).

Turk, A. G., & Trees, K. A. (1998a). Ethical issues concerning the development of an indigenous cultural heritage information system. *Systemist 20* (Special Issue), 229-242.

Turk, A. G., & Trees, K. A. (1998b). The role of information systems in sustaining indigenous communities: The Ieramugadu Cultural Project. *Proceedings of the 42nd Annual Conference of the International Society for System Sciences* [CD-Rom], Atlanta, GA.

Turk, A.G., & Trees, K. A. (1998c). Culture and participation in development of CMC: Indigenous cultural information system case study. In C. Ess, & F. Sudweeks (Eds.), *Proceedings of the international cultural attitudes towards technology and communication — CATaC'98*, Science Museum, London (pp. 219-223). Sydney, Australia: University of Sydney.

Turk, A. G., & Trees, K. A. (1999a). Culturally appropriate computer mediated communication: An Australian indigenous information system case study. *AI and Society*, *13*, 377-388.

Turk, A. G., & Trees, K. A. (1999b). Ethical issues concerning the use of geographic information systems technology with indigenous communities. *Proceedings of the Australian Institute of Computer Ethics Conference, AICEC99,* Melbourne, Australia (pp. 385-398).

Turk, A. G., & Trees, K. A. (2000). Facilitating community processes through culturally appropriate informatics: An Australian indigenous community information system case study. In M. Gurstein (Ed.), *Community informatics: Enabling communities with information and communication technologies* (pp. 339-358). Hershey, PA: Idea Group Publishing.

Turnbull, D. (1989). *Maps are territories: Science is an atlas*. Geelong, Australia: Deakin University Press.

Warren, A. (2004, November). *Becoming our own cartographic masters*. Keynote presentation to the AIATSIS Conference: Indigenous studies — Sharing the cultural and theoretical space, Canberra.

Watson-Verran, H., & Turnbull, D. (1995). Science and other indigenous knowledge systems. In S. Jasanoff, G. E. Markle, J. C. Petersen, & T. Pinch (Eds.), *Handbook of science and technology studies* (pp. 115-139). Thousand Oaks, CA: Sage Publications.

Chapter XV

E-Community-Based Tourism for Asia's Indigenous People

Roger W. Harris, Roger Harris Associates, Hong Kong

Doug Vogel, City University of Hong Kong, Hong Kong

Lars H. Bestle, UNDP's Asia Pacific Development Information Programme - Bangkok, Thailand

Abstract

Indigenous peoples are good for national tourism development in Asia because they present an exotic image that helps to differentiate countries from each other. However, tourism is far from being good for indigenous peoples, as they are often excluded from the revenues that tourism generates and are subjected to the environmental degradation and cultural pollution that mass tourism inflicts upon them. information and communication technologies (ICTs) in the hands of such people can help alleviate some of this imbalance. By catering to the rising demand for authentic travel experiences that do not damage the environment, and in a manner that is under the control of the indigenous peoples themselves, ICTs empower local communities to operate small-scale tourism on their own terms. Once familiar with the ICTs, such people can go on to apply them to their special needs, in accordance with international conventions concerning the well-being of indigenous peoples.

Introduction

Indigenous peoples are often used to promote tourism destinations. Their images and cultures are showcased as major attractions by national tourism authorities. Often, the indigenous peoples themselves have no control over or participation in this process, either in how their cultures are represented to the outside world, or in a fair share of the incomes that tourism generates. When visitors encounter indigenous peoples, they often bring with them images that are stylised and outdated, and they expect their hosts to live up to such falsehoods. Furthermore, by the time they reach their destination, tourists have paid their expenses to travel agents, tour operators and transportation services that have little or no connection with the indigenous inhabitants of the destination, who are left to scrape what meagre incomes they can from sales of handicrafts and light refreshments or from performing stylised versions of their traditional rituals. "Tourism has turned us into performers," remarked one Kadasan/Dusun inhabitant of Sabah, one of the East Malaysian states on the island of Borneo.

Community-based tourism (CBT) is emerging as a mechanism for fostering locally based tourism operations, as opposed to those whose financial interests are located away from the tourist destination. CBT is already operating among a number of Asia's indigenous minorities, including the Tay and H'mong of northern Vietnam, the Gurung of Nepal, the Kelabit of Sarawak, Malaysia, the Kadasan/Dusun peoples of Sabah, Malaysia, the nomadic herders of Kyrgyzstan and the multitude of indigenous ethnic minorities in northern Thailand, the Lao PDR and south-western China.

Concurrent with the growth of CBT, information and communication technologies (ICTs) in the form of telephones, computers, the Internet and radio, are increasingly being deployed in rural and even remote locations across the developing world. Innovative rural ICT programmes are being planned or implemented across Asia, bringing a wide range of benefits to poor people, among them being better health care, agricultural support, government services, enterprise creation, distance education and e-commerce. Such programmes are usually deployed in the form of shared facilities in community centres, often called telecentres.

Electronic commerce for CBT, or e-CBT, operated from shared community telecentres, places ICTs in the hands of poor communities with the potential and capacity to provide satisfying experiences to tourists. Currently, there are very few examples where this is happening, as the concept is new. However, the Kelabit people of Bario on the island of Borneo are pioneering their use of community ICTs for e-CBT. Evidence from regular contacts with the residents points to significant increases in tourism activity and incomes since their e-CBT operations began, although a detailed study has yet to be conducted.

Tourism and International Development

Tourism is one of the world's largest industries, generating an estimated 11% of global gross domestic product, employing 200 million people (Roe & Urquhart, 2001). World tourism receipts amounted to just US$102 billion in 1980 and in 2003 they reached US$523 billion (WTO, 2002). Between 1950 and 1998, international tourist arrivals increased 25-fold, from 25 million to 635 million. Approximately two million people currently cross an international border each day, compared with only 69,000 in 1950 (French, 2000). World tourism enjoyed exceptional years in 2000 and 2001, growing by an estimated 7.4% in 2000, its highest growth rate in nearly a decade and almost double the increase of 1999 (WTO, 2002). The fastest developing region in 2000 was East Asia and the Pacific, with a growth rate of 14.7% and some 14 million more tourists than 1999 (WTO, 2002). The World Tourism Organization (WTO) forecasts that international arrivals are expected to reach over 1.56 billion by the year 2020.

Tourism offers huge opportunities for developing countries to increase incomes from the growing number of arrivals that land on their shores. Tourism is a principal export for developing countries and the least developed countries (LDCs). It is growing rapidly and is the most significant source of foreign exchange after petroleum (WTO, 2002). There is a general shift of tourism arrivals towards developing countries. Growth rates of international tourism receipts during the 1990s were, on average, 50% higher in the major developing country destinations in comparison to the major developed country destinations. China, Thailand and Indonesia together generated 40% of all international tourism receipts accruing to developing countries in 1996.

Despite the contribution that tourism makes to national economies, it has relatively little impact on poverty reduction. The value added by international tourism intermediaries, who are often no more than marketers and information handlers, and who rarely own or manage physical tourism facilities, can be as high as 30% or more, thus controlling general terms and conditions throughout the whole value chain. Where tourism brings revenues into areas populated by the poor, they are usually restricted to deriving any benefits from the margins of the industry, such as in low paid, low-skilled jobs and with street-level handicraft sales. For example, tourism in the town of Sa Pa in northern Vietnam has boomed in recent years. Yet the many ethnic communities in the surrounding mountains who are visited by tourists receive little benefit. According to one account, "Tourists spend very little money in the villages. Most of the economic benefits of tourism are received in Sa Pa, Hanoi or further afield and it is well known that there are few economic returns to the local people" (SNV).

Community-Based Tourism

Community-based tourism (CBT) occurs when decisions about tourism activity and development are driven by the host community. It involves cultural exchanges where tourists meet with local communities and engage with aspects of their lifestyle. It provides incentives for natural and cultural conservation and generates paid employment for people from a variety of backgrounds and with various skills and experiences, especially women.

Typically, with CBT, the community runs all of the activities that a tourist engages in: lodging, food, guiding and craft sales. Benefits include economic growth in rural regions, the distribution of tourism revenue, which can foster improved welfare and equity in the industry, improved resource conservation by local people and diversification of the regional and national tourism product (Sproule, 1996). For rural communities, CBT offers a range of attractions:

- farming and tourism development are often complementary in scope;
- the conversion to services and tourism activities is easier for farmers, even smallholders and poor farmers, than for industry workers, as farmers worldwide have an independent and entrepreneurial capacity and a greater potential for personal initiatives;
- tourism can enhance human occupation or re-colonise rural spaces that now have easier access to global information sources. In this way, tourism can decrease or stop the rural exodus by providing new economic and job opportunities in rural areas; and
- tourism can bring empowerment and cultural revival to local, isolated and remote populations. (di Castri, Sheldon, Conlin, Boniface, & Balaji, 2002)

CBT is a tool for natural and cultural resource conservation and community development that is closely associated with ecotourism. Eco-tourism also emphasises observation and learning by the tourist, alongside economic and cultural conservation, and the delivery of benefits that ensure long-term sustainability of communities and natural resources (Allcock, 2003). CBT is operated in many developing countries, often in support of wildlife management, environmental protection and/or development for indigenous peoples.

Travel, Tourism and the Internet

The Internet is having a profound impact on the travel and tourism industry. The Internet is restructuring tourism distribution channels and the tourism industry itself (Sheldon, 2002). The use of the Internet in developed countries for purchasing tourism products is increasing dramatically. Of the total e-commerce sales of US$64 billion in 1999, travel, transport and hotel reservations as a group represented the largest category of Internet transactions, accounting for 38.5% of all online sales (UNCTAD, 2000). According to a report by the United Nations Conference on Trade and Development (UNCTAD, 2001), the tourism industry is among those sectors quickly adopting the Internet as a business medium. The hard reality in the tourism industry today is "that if you are not on-line, you are not on sale" (WTO, 1999).

Now, as ICTs reach into the remotest regions of the world, even small or remote destinations and products with well-developed and innovative Web sites can have equal access to international markets. Marketing is a strategic tool for community-based tourism advocacy and sustainability. Marketing can enhance the success of CBT by identifying market segments, defining the products based on the tourism objectives and inputs from market studies, bringing the products to a wide audience and helping to clarify what products are the most viable. The Internet is the ideal technology to handle the information and marketing aspects of community-based pro-poor tourism.

Information and Communication Technologies in Developing Countries

Governments and the international and bilateral aid agencies are becoming increasingly enthusiastic about the potential for ICTs to alleviate poverty. Among many similar initiatives, the United Nations Development Programme (UNDP) has launched the Digital Opportunity Initiative (DOI), a public-private partnership to help developing countries put in place national e-strategies.

A common form of providing public access to ICTs in developing countries is the Multi-purpose Community Telecentre; also known as information kiosks, information centres or just telecentres. Telecentres are springing up all over the developing world, as grassroots projects driven by communities, non-government organisations or research bodies or as pilot projects intended by governments as precursors to wider infrastructure projects designed to close the digital divide between better-off people in the cities who can more easily get access to the Internet and their poorer compatriots in rural areas.

For communities that are able to mobilise themselves toward community-based tourism and are provided with access to the Internet, electronic commerce for community-based tourism, or e-CBT, can become a pump-primer for introducing telecentres into rural communities, which can subsequently be used to foster the other forms of development that ICTs make possible. Moreover, there is a continuing debate concerning the financial sustainability of development telecentres (Harris, Kumar, & Balaji, 2003). Telecentres that target income-generating opportunities from the outset are more likely to survive after the initial start-up funding dries up.

The Target Market for E-CBT

The market for e-CBT is the same as that for CBT, but the introduction of ICTs means it is well matched to an identifiable type of consumer. A growing area of consumer research has identified what is known as the "neo-consumer," reflecting the research in the USA that identified the "geo-tourist" (National Geographic Traveler, 2004). Neo-consumers represent a quarter of the population in developed countries, but control half the discretionary spending power of the economy (Honeywill, 2002). They possess the following characteristics that are relevant to e-CBT:

- seeking more experiential tourism;
- not interested in mass market information;
- a preference to stay in villages; and
- a desire for encounters with the authentic. (Honeywill, 2002)

CBT has the potential to satisfy many of the lifestyle needs of neo-consumers and geo-tourists, and e-CBT represents an appropriate form of engaging with them for promotion, marketing and information exchange as well as for sales transaction processing.

As a platform for community development, e-CBT has the potential for realising the fullness of the promise of a pro-poor approach to tourism for at least two important reasons:

- it reverses the prevailing pattern whereby much of the tourism industry is controlled by financial interests located away from tourist destinations (Heyendael, 2002); and
- it fosters micro-enterprise tourism which acts as a catalyst to complement and promote community fisheries, traditional agriculture, handicraft production and conservation practices, as well as helping to enhance the quality of natural and cultural resource utilisation (di Castri et al., 2002).

ICTs and Indigenous People

Indigenous peoples are good for tourism; they appear in the publicity material of most of the countries in which they can be found. However, it is highly questionable if tourism is good for indigenous peoples. Whilst CBT is capable of directing tourism revenues more towards small-scale rural village tourism operators, outside interests are still capable of exerting undue influence and control over the distribution of such revenues by controlling the flow of information, visitors and the terms under which they make their visit. ICTs that are under the control of local people remove dependency on outside interests by connecting operators directly to their target market. Moreover, in addition to this disintermediating effect on the tourism value chain, ICTs can be put to further use in support of the social and economic development of rural poor populations, including, of course, the indigenous minorities that are often found to share unequally in national development.

Alongside the potential for desirable developmental outcomes from e-CBT, difficulties may exist. Setting up the technology facilities is always a challenge in rural and remote locations where telephony can be sparse and electricity supply unreliable. Problems with the transfer of ICT and tourism skills to rural residents often require close co-operation from support institutions, both government and non-governmental. In some cases, the political climate may not favour providing indigenous minorities with telecommunications capability that would allow them to freely communicate globally. Finally, tourism can carry negative impacts. These issues need to be addressed when e-CBT is introduced.

With a carefully planned e-CBT implementation, ICTs can be used to empower indigenous peoples toward achieving the aims of important international declarations and conventions that seek to protect their rights. These include:

- The Convention (No. 169) concerning Indigenous and Tribal Peoples in Independent Countries by the General Conference of the International Labour Organisation (1991)[1];
- The United Nations Commission on Human Rights' Draft Declaration on the Rights of Indigenous Peoples[2]; and
- Declaration on the Rights of Persons Belonging to National or Ethnic, Religious or Linguistic Minorities, UN Doc. A/47/49 (1993).[3]

These international conventions and declarations contain obligations that can be readily fulfilled with the help of ICTs that are embedded into the social and economic fabric of communities. Table 1 indicates how.

Table 1. The contributions of e-CBT to the fulfilment of international conventions

Obligation Agreed to in One or More International Convention/Declaration	Contributing Role of e-CBT
Promoting the full realisation of the social, economic and cultural rights of these peoples with respect for their social and cultural identity, their customs, traditions and institutions.	e-CBT encourages Indigenous peoples to create their own cultural Websites that present a picture of themselves to the outside world that they themselves have formulated and agreed upon and which is not subject to outsider misinterpretation or misrepresentation.
Assisting the members of the peoples concerned to eliminate socioeconomic gaps that may exist between Indigenous and other members of the national community, in a manner compatible with their aspirations and ways of life.	As a pro-poor ICT implementation, e-CBT introduces ICTs to minority communities and thereby fosters other improved public services and enterprise opportunities, countering the negative effects of the digital divide.
Establish means by which these peoples can freely participate, to at least the same extent as other sectors of the population, at all levels of decision-making in elective institutions, administrative and other bodies responsible for policies and programmes that concern them.	Once ICTs have been introduced for e-CBT, communities can use them to become empowered with a voice in decision-making that affects them. Grass-roots advocacy is enhanced when ICTs are deployed.
Establish means for the full development of these peoples' own institutions and initiatives, and in appropriate cases provide the resources necessary for this purpose.	Having deployed ICTs for e-CBT, communities can learn to use them to initiate further development activities and to facilitate the mobilisation of additional external resources.

Table 1. continued

The improvement of the conditions of life , work and levels of health and education of the peoples concerned, with their participation and cooperation shall be a matter of priority in plans for the overall economic development of areas they inhabit.	CBT is often accompanied by improvements in sanitation and hygiene, necessary preconditions for attracting visitors. Not only does this in itself benefit the residents, but the ICTs that are deployed for e-CBT can also be further used for achieving improvements in health and education, which are among the principal achievements of pro-poor ICTs.
Governments shall take measures, in co-operation with the peoples concerned, to protect and preserve the environment of the territories they inhabit.	e-CBT fosters environmental protection by providing incentives for inhabitants to do so.
Indigenous peoples have the right to practise and revitalize their cultural traditions and customs. This includes the right to maintain, protect and develop the past, present and future manifestations of their cultures, such as archaeological and historical sites, artefacts, designs, ceremonies, technologies and visual and performing arts and literature, as well as the right to the restitution of cultural, intellectual, religious and spiritual property taken without their free and informed consent or in violation of their laws, traditions and customs.	ICTs allow Indigenous peoples to take back control of their cultures from outside interests that commonly misrepresent or even exploit them. ICTs can help establish customary rights and intellectual property ownership.
Indigenous peoples have the right to establish their own media in their own languages. They also have the right to equal access to all forms of non-Indigenous media.	Commonly, Indigenous peoples lack the resources required to express themselves through traditional media, requiring external interpretation to gain a national or international voice. ICTs democratise access to contemporary media, allowing low cost global publishing.
Indigenous peoples have the right to determine and develop priorities and strategies for exercising their right to development. In particular, Indigenous peoples have the right to determine and develop all health, housing and other economic and social programmes affecting themselves and, as far as possible, to administer such programmes through their own institutions.	ICTs are capable of bringing previously excluded people into the mainstream of national development planning, as well as fostering ground-level initiatives that need not be dependent on passive acceptance of top-down processes.
States should consider appropriate measures so that persons belonging to minorities may participate fully in the economic progress and development in their country.	Without ICTs, full and equal participation of the rural poor, which make up the majority of Asia's Indigenous minorities, in national development will be impossible.

Conclusion

With developing countries enjoying something of a boom in world tourism, there are emerging opportunities for diverting more of the income that tourism can generate towards the indigenous communities that often attract the expenditure in the first place, but who have not enjoyed a fair share of the benefits. The changing nature of the tourism and travel industries, which are becoming increasingly based on new information technologies, combined with the increasing availability of such technologies for rural people, present a powerful opportunity for empowering poor indigenous peoples with the ability to exploit the natural assets under their custodianship for their own betterment and also for the preservation of those assets. World tourism is a highly lucrative and therefore competitive marketplace. E-CBT has the potential for balancing market conditions more in favour of small local operators who can promote their sought-after products to global niche markets on equal terms with large corporations. Being small, individualised and not mass-market oriented, local operators have an advantage over larger organisations when targeting appropriate consumers: ICTs allow such operators to exploit that advantage in a manner that is wholly suited to their market. With the additional opportunities that ICTs bring, e-CBT becomes a powerful catalyst that carries the potential for propelling indigenous peoples toward new levels of prosperity and well being.

References

Allcock, A. (2003). *Sustainable tourism development in Nepal, Vietnam and Lao PDR*. Vientiane, Lao PDR: SNV, Netherlands Development Organisation.

di Castri, F., Sheldon, P., Conlin, M., Boniface, P., & Balaji, V. (2002). Introduction: Information, communication and education for tourism development. In F. di Castri & V. Balaji (Eds.), *Tourism, biodiversity and information* (pp. 423-429). Leiden, The Netherlands: Backhuys.

French, H. (2000). *Vanishing borders: Protecting the planet in the age of globalization*. WA: Worldwatch Institute.

Harris, R. W., Kumar, A., & Balaji, V. (2003). *Sustainable telecentres? Two cases from India. ICTs and development: New opportunities, perspectives and challenges*. Aldershot: Ashgate Publishers.

Heyendael, A. (2002). Sustainable tourism within the context of the ecosystem approach. In F. di Castri & V. Balaji (Eds.), *Tourism, biodiversity and information* (pp. 25-44). Leiden, The Netherlands: Backhuys.

Honeywill, R. (2002, June 5). Cash in on the neo consumer. *Traveltrade*. Retrieved June 16, 2005, from http://www.maryrossitravel.com/whoweare/news/pdf/traveltrade_jun2002.pdf

ICT for development. (2002, August 28). *The Rising Nepal* (English Daily).

National Geographic Traveler. (2004). Retrieved June 16, 2005, from http://www.tia.org/survey.pdf

Roe, D., & Urquhart Khanya, P. (2001). *Pro-poor tourism: Harnessing the world's largest industry for the world's poor*. UK & South Africa: IIED.

Sheldon, P. (2002). Information technology contributions to biodiversity in tourism. In F. di Castri & V. Balaji (Eds.), *Tourism, biodiversity and information* (pp. 449-456). Leiden, The Netherlands: Backhuys.

SNV (Netherlands Development Organisation). *Sustainable tourism development in Nepal, Vietnam and Lao PDR: Experiences of SNV and partner organisations*. Retrieved June 16, 2005, from http://www.snvworld.org/cds/rgTUR/documents/snv%20docs/SNV%20Tourism%20Azie.2002.pdf

Sproule, K. W. (1996). Community-based ecotourism development: Identifying partners in the process. In *The ecotourism equation: Measuring the impacts* (Bulletin Series, Yale School of Forestry and Environmental Studies No. 99) (pp. 233-250). New Haven, CT: Yale University.

United Nations Conference on Trade and Development (UNCTAD). (2000, September 18-20). *Electronic commerce and tourism: New perspectives and challenges for developing countries*. Expert Meeting on Electronic Commerce and Tourism, Geneva. Retrieved June 16, 2005, from http://r0.unctad.org/ecommerce/docs/ecomtour.pdf

United Nations Conference on Trade and Development (UNCTAD). (2001). *E-commerce and development report 2001*. New York & Geneva: United Nations. Retrieved June 16, 2005, from http://r0.unctad.org/ecommerce/docs/edr01_en/edr01pt0_en.pdf

United Nations Development Programme (UNDP). (2001, July 2001). *Creating a development dynamic: Final report of the Digital Opportunity Initiative*. Retrieved June 16, 2005, from http://www.opt-init.org/framework/DOI-Final-Report.pdf

World Tourism Organization (WTO). (1999). *Marketing tourism destinations online* (p. 4).

World Tourism Organization (WTO). (2005). *Tourism, microfinance and poverty alleviation*. Recommendations to small and medium-sized enterprises (SMEs) and to microfinance institutions (MFIs) (p. 10). Madrid, Spain: World Tourism Organization.

Endnotes

1 http://www.unhchr.ch/html/menu3/b/62.htm

2 http://www.unhchr.ch/html/menu3/b/62.htm

3 http://www1.umn.edu/humanrts/instree/d5drm.htm

Case Study XVIII

Computerised Tests of Brain Function for Use with Indigenous People

Sheree Cairney, Menzies School of Health Research, Australia

Paul Maruff, CogState Ltd., Australia

An assessment of brain function (or cognitive function) has become an important process with applications in a growing number of areas including medicine, psychiatry, occupational selection, law and education. The most sophisticated, direct and precise measurements of brain function are obtained using brain imaging techniques (e.g., fMRI, MRI and PET). However these hospital-based techniques are expensive and immobile and are therefore not appropriate for use in many applications. When brain imaging techniques are not appropriate, cognitive tests have been shown to provide accurate measures of brain function that can be interpreted within robust brain-behaviour models, based on extensive research with healthy humans, primates and humans with specific brain lesions. Thus, carefully measured behaviour is an accepted surrogate marker of brain function. An assessment of cognitive function provides information about the efficacy of a person's thought processes. For example, a cognitive assessment may include tests of psychomotor speed, attention, problem solving, working memory, learning, inhibition and executive function.

Often cognitive assessments use language, stimuli or normative data with a cultural bias towards western populations, and therefore may produce misdiagnosis among those from other cultures. Performance deficits on these tasks that suggest brain dysfunction may actually arise from cultural determinants such as socio-economic status, language or expectations of the assessment experience. At present there are few, if any, assessments of brain function that are relevant to indigenous Australians. Consequently, indigenous people do not access the same opportunities and services in this area as other Australians. Here we describe a solution to this problem that involved developing and validating computer-based and culturally-appropriate cognitive assessments that can be used in indigenous groups across Australia.

For over 10 years, we have studied the neurological and cognitive effects of substance abuse and mental illness among indigenous people from remote aboriginal communities in Arnhem Land, Northern Australia. Specifically, investigations have been conducted on brain dysfunction associated with abusing petrol (sniffing), kava, alcohol and cannabis, as well as in people with specific neurological problems and psychotic syndromes (see www.menzies.edu.au for a list of publications). Before this, there had been very little investigation or understanding about the effect on the brain and behaviour of substances like petrol that are almost exclusively used among indigenous groups from remote regions, because there were not appropriate tools. In some of the communities where this research was conducted, road access is limited and the only access to the communities may be through light aircraft when weather permits. In addition, many people from these communities have no previous experience with psychological or educational testing and many speak only very little or no English. Many people have never used a computer before. To measure brain function in these indigenous groups, it was therefore necessary to use validated tests of brain function that do not rely on language but are still capable of identifying cognitive deficits independently from underlying movement disorders. Portable tools are also important for mobile use in remote and isolated communities.

To perform this research we developed and validated a series of neurological, eye movement and cognitive assessments. For example, our assessment protocol included tests of basic motor function, an eye movement assessment that utilised infrared reflectance oculography to generate computer signals of precise eye movement position and motion as well as touchscreen-based computerised cognitive assessments. This assessment protocol was used successfully to gain a thorough understanding about the effects of petrol sniffing on the brain. However, the equipment used for these assessments was expensive, immobile and difficult to operate. Moreover, analysis of the data was labour intensive and required considerable expertise. While these assessments were therefore appropriate for research programs that are funded and coordinated by those with technical and medical expertise, they are not appropriate for clinical and community applications, especially in remote indigenous populations.

The next step was to devise a novel and appropriate test of brain function specifically for use among indigenous populations that can be administered and interpreted by indigenous people, with little training necessary. Previously we noted that many indigenous people enjoyed playing, and were familiar with card games. We therefore removed the chance aspect and modified the rules of such games to generate valid tests of memory, attention and executive function. These can be downloaded from an internet Web site (CogState Ltd, www.cogstate.com) and administered on any computer. On mobile notebook computers, CogState assessments have been performed successfully by indigenous people in remote communities to test for the effects of cannabis and petrol sniffing, and also for indicators of mental illness. Sometimes this involved home visits to participants where computerised assessments were performed in many unusual locations including under a tree, on people's verandas or on the beach. Many participants who had never used a computer before performed the assessment effectively after a practice period of familiarisation. Interpreters were used where necessary to explain the basic rules although due to the automated instruction process of the assessment tool, even people who did not understand English did not usually require further instruction. The CogState assessment was therefore successful for use among indigenous people living in remote communities and the knowledge generated through this approach has been validated among the scientific community. At present, we are exploring and establishing its use for indigenous people among a wider range of settings including community applications, prisons, schools, legal services, medical and research services where it can be used by clinicians, educators and researchers, or for self-monitoring.

Because playing cards are universally recognisable, CogState assessments have been adopted effectively for other areas of research in the wider population including for sports-related concussion, cardiac surgery, Alzheimer's disease, clinical drug and alcohol studies, and CogState has been purchased for use by many international research and drug companies (see www.cogstate.com). CogState is sensitive to brain dysfunction caused by substance abuse, mental health problems or neurological injury. CogState is therefore a rare example of a tool that was designed for use among indigenous Australians and has then been recognised internationally and adopted for the wider population.

Case Study XIX

Alliance Project: Digital Kinship Database and Genealogy

Shigenobu Sugito, Sugiyama University, Japan

Sachiko Kubota, Hiroshima University, Japan

This study has three main aims:

1. to develop software for an indigenous kinship database and genealogy using a cross-platform Java engine;
2. to contribute to a kinship study, which will serve as a fieldwork support tool for anthropologists; and
3. to assess the importance and potential of the kinship database and genealogy in IT-based indigenous knowledge management.

Regarding the third aim, we would like to emphasize the importance of kinship data in the post-colonial era, and the need for kinship data in land rights issues and the recognition of indigenous identity, as well as the possibility of the autonomous use of this visualized kinship database by indigenous peoples in the future.

The Alliance Project, which is named after the alliance theory by C. Levi-Strauss (1969), started as the management of a kinship study for the Yolngu people of Eastern Arnhem Land, Northern Territory, Australia, and was later extended to the study of kinship in general. Alliance software is downloadable from the following website: http://study.hs.sugiyama-u.ac.jp/alliance/

Alliance Project

The main purpose of commercial genealogy software is to record a person's genealogy and display his/her relationship in one family tree. This means a database is basically managed as one data set per family and is based on a monolineal concept, reflecting a Eurocentric image of kinship. In contrast, Alliance's original dataset is for the Yolngu kinship, composed of a genealogy of 3,700 people. The Yolngu have traditionally had a very complicated marriage system and great social importance is placed on affinal relationships, that is, relationships by marriage. Commercial genealogy software has never been appropriate to this kind of genealogy because their kinship system is not isolated but complexly interconnected. In other words, the number of kinship relationships is too numerous for the commercial genealogy software. Complex data management has, therefore, been necessary for these kinds of genealogies and databases.

The Alliance Project has chosen to develop a new kinship database and genealogy which can display the large genealogies and affinal relationships using a multiple window system. The system can also switch between patrilineal or matrilineal lines, according to one's analytical focus. As a result, this system is suited to other kinship systems as well as the Yolngu system.

Records of kinship and genealogy are fundamental for anthropologists in the field, and immediate crosschecking of kinship data will provide a valuable tool for these fieldworkers. Laptop computer technology provides easy access to the records and is an ideal means for crosschecking the kinship database and genealogy. Initially, the Alliance Project invested a lot into the development of a standalone type of software for multiple platforms, called Alliance. Subsequently, a Web version of Alliance, known as WebAlliance, was developed. WebAlliance does not need to be installed into your computer, but can be used on the Internet as a server-side Java operation.

Figure 1. Personal record entry in card image

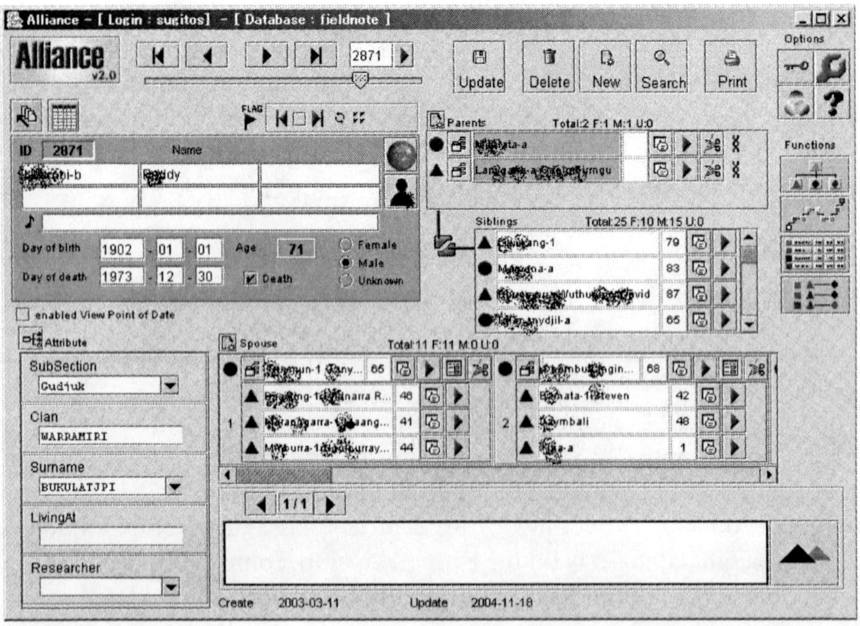

Alliance Database

The database is composed of a card-like image for each personal entry (Figure 1). The personal relationship allocates linkages with parents and spouses in a particular personal entry. Alliance will immediately draw the desired genealogy. Users can also input personal details for specific entries, thereby increasing the power of the database.

Genealogy: Standalone Alliance

Alliance allows its multi-window system to draw kinship genealogies. The number of windows that are available depends on your CPU and physical memory size. Patrilineal (Figure 2) or matrilineal (Figure 3) images are colour coded to indicate personal details, such as their clan affiliation and so on. The "trace route" function (Figure 4) is convenient for searching the relationship between two specified people.

Figure 2. Patrilineal genealogy

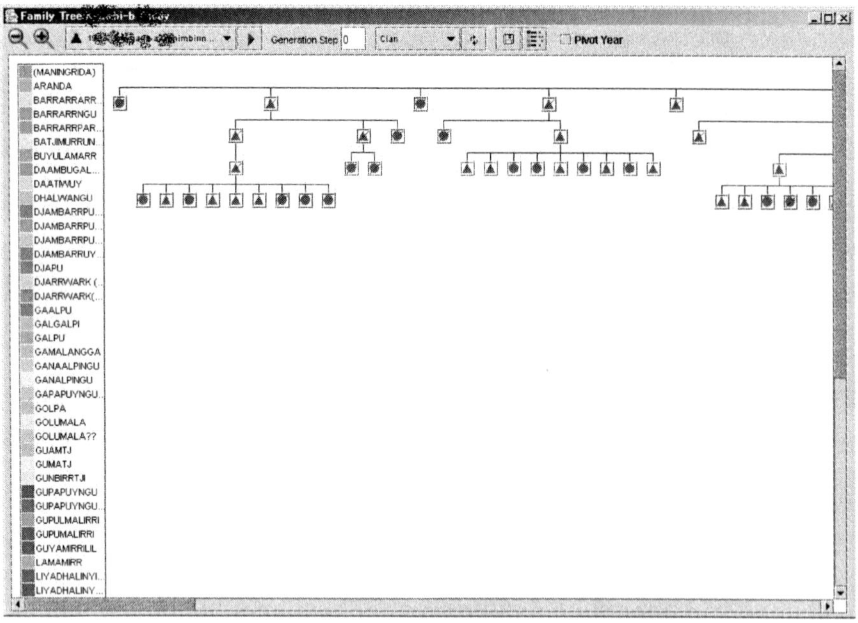

Figure 3. Matrilineal genealogy

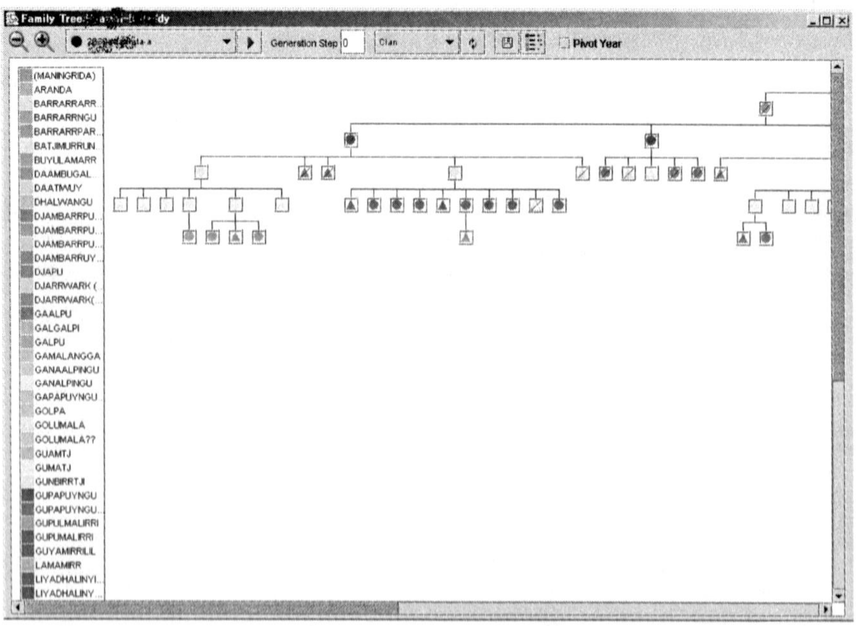

Figure 4. "Trace Route" function for two specified persons

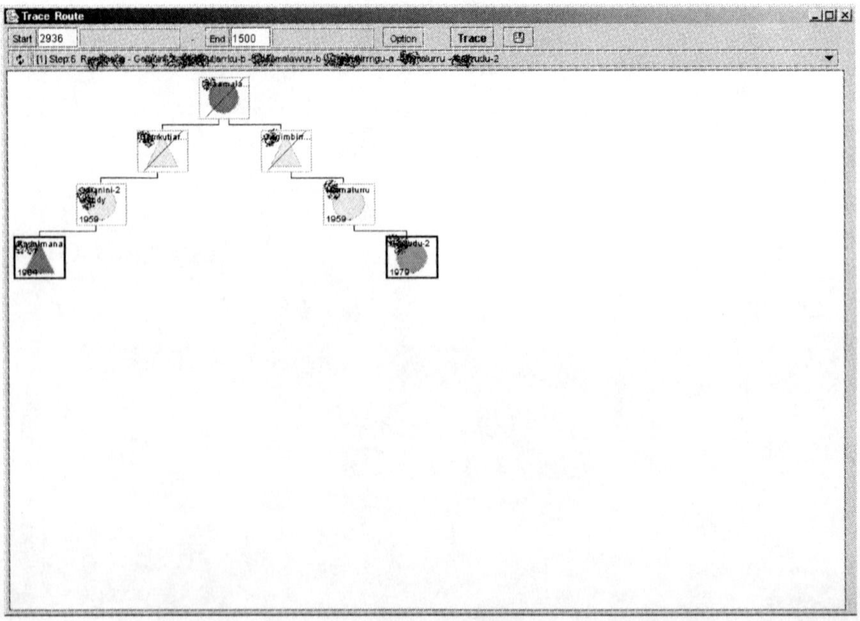

Genealogy: WebAlliance

WebAlliance is a simplified software for Alliance. Although its servicing functions are more limited, it has been developed as an educational tool for genealogy. The system allows multi-user entry to the system at the discretion of the registered users. This function can be productively operated in a classroom setting.

Discussion

The Alliance Project has developed Alliance for building kinship databases and genealogies, and a simplified Web version tool for the same purpose, WebAlliance. The project still has minor technical problems and an upgrade will be necessary in order to allow cognatic (any combination of matrilineal and patrilineal) kinship analysis.

Moving away from technical-related issues, we would like to offer some final thoughts and suggestions:

1. Protection of personal information is an important issue in any country, and a kinship database is no exception. This bank of personal information, however, is of high cultural and political value, especially as indigenous knowledge. We urge that the possibility of exempting such information from certain privacy laws be considered.
2. Keeping kinship knowledge is, in general, a very important and strategic option for the indigenous peoples themselves. For this purpose, we must develop the tools to educate people about kinship knowledge and genealogy. The use of the database will be advantageous for sharing kinship knowledge. Although further development of this software is still required, WebAlliance offers one educational tool option.
3. We would like to propose a conference on indigenous knowledge to move us along the path of achieving our aims.

Acknowledgments

The Alliance Project would like to acknowledge support, in the form of Grant-in-Aid for the Scientific Research, provided by the Japan Society for Promotion of Science, as well as the assistance of the following people: Patrick McConvell (AIATSIS), Nicolas Peterson (ANU), Luke Taylor (AIATSIS), Shuzo Koyama (ex-NME), Masatoshi Kubo (NME), Masakazu Tanaka (Kyoto University) and the many others who have supported the Alliance Project. The project also sends a special thanks to the Yolngu people.

Reference

Levi-Strauss, C. (1969). *The elementary structures of kinship*. Boston: Beacon Press.

Case Study XX

Agreements Treaties and Negotiated Settlements Database

Marcia Langton, The University of Melbourne, Australia

Odette Mazel, The University of Melbourne, Australia

Lisa Palmer, The University of Melbourne, Australia

The Agreements Treaties and Negotiated Settlements (ATNS) database (www.atns.net.au) is an online gateway and resource that links current information, historical detail and published material relating to agreements made between indigenous peoples and others in Australia and overseas. Designed for use by indigenous and other community organisations, researchers, government and industry bodies, the ATNS database includes information on agreements not only relating to land, but those made in the areas of health, education, research, policy and indigenous relations. Since its public launch in 2003, the database has become an important research facility and is the only resource of its kind in Australia that demonstrates the range and variety of agreement making with indigenous peoples in various jurisdictions.

As governments, industry and indigenous peoples are using agreements as the major policy and governance tool for the conduct of their relationships, the database's significance lies in its utility as a public resource. In Australia, as in other settler states, agreement making with indigenous peoples is becoming increasingly important. Since the first land use agreements signed under the provisions of the federal statute, *Aboriginal Land Rights (Northern Territory) Act 1974* more than twenty years ago, there has been a proliferation of agreements between indigenous peoples and other parties including local, state and federal governments; proponents of major infrastructure projects; farming and grazing representatives; universities and other institutions and agencies (see Figure 1). The Australian High Court decision in *Mabo v Queensland (No 2)*, the subsequent native title decisions of the courts and the federal statute, *Native Title Act 1993* (*NTA*) have all influenced the culture of agreement making and have placed parties under an obligation to negotiate and mediate proposals for land, sea and resource use.

While some agreements have statutory status, are registered under the terms of the *NTA* or result in determinations of the Federal Court of Australia, others are more simple contractual statements, service delivery agreements, memoranda of understanding or statements of commitment or intent. The ATNS database developed as an innovative and communicative tool to capture the diverse range of agreements made within different social, historical and legal settings, involving a wide variety of parties and seeking to address very different issues. Made

*Figure 1. The number of agreements with indigenous peoples in Australia by year recorded on the ATNS Database**

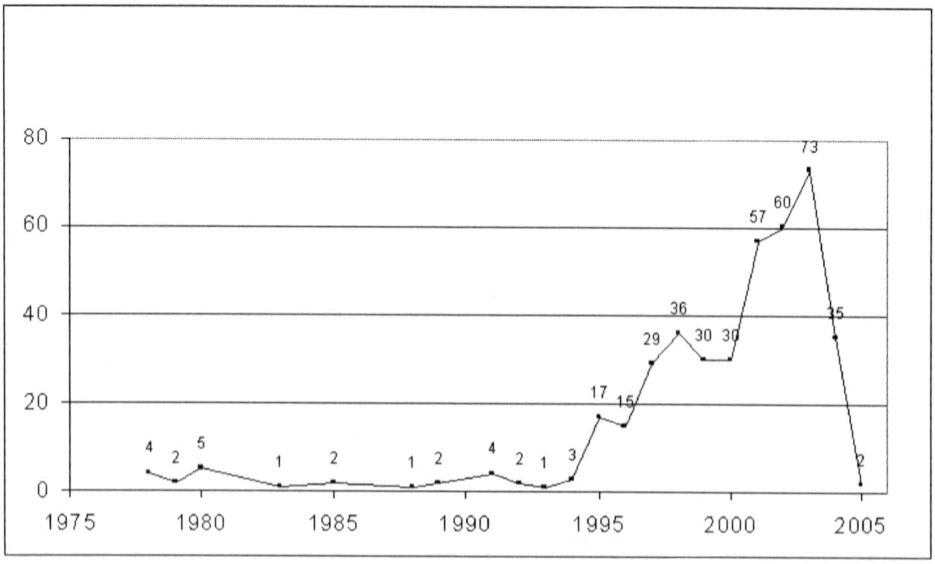

* *This chart details agreements that have been recorded on the ATNS database as of April 2005 and does not intend to be a comprehensive representation of all the agreements made in Australia between Indigenous peoples and others.*

Figure 2. ATNS home page

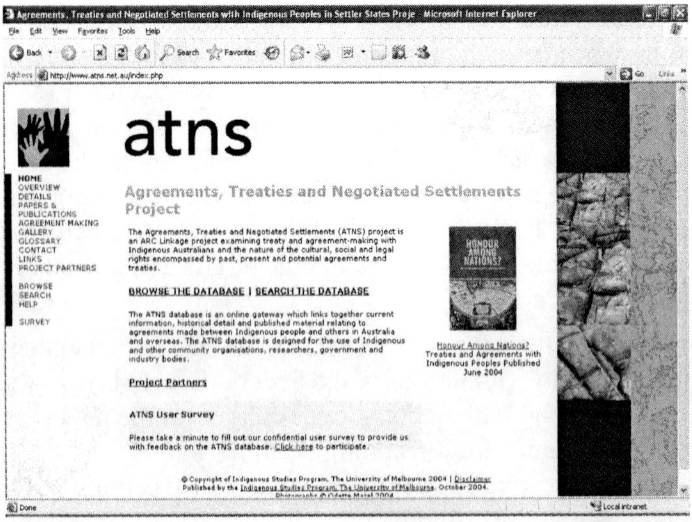

available via the Internet, the database provides information on agreements in a comprehensive and accessible format (see Figure 2).

Information included in the ATNS database is gathered from a range of published materials, including newsletters, journals and periodicals, as well as from material and documents provided by the organisations and agencies that are involved in the agreement making process. Synthesised and arranged to provide a comprehensive and coherent body of material reflective of the current state of agreement making in both the Australian and international contexts, this information can be browsed and searched by category, type, subject matter, date, location or more specifically through a key word search (see Figure 3). Each data entry is presented complete with essential summary information and more detailed notes where the information is necessary and available. In addition, details on agreement provisions, such as employment and training, education, business opportunities and cultural awareness programs, are provided, along with links to information about parties, related agreements, organisations and events. Direct access to relevant published and online resources is provided, and geospatial maps detailing the position and boundaries of agreements are gradually being introduced. While access to actual agreements is often constrained due to the fact that they are made on a commercial basis and in confidence, in some cases, where we have the consent of all parties, the full text of agreements is available on the database (no confidential information is made available on the database).

Figure 3. Searching the ATNS database

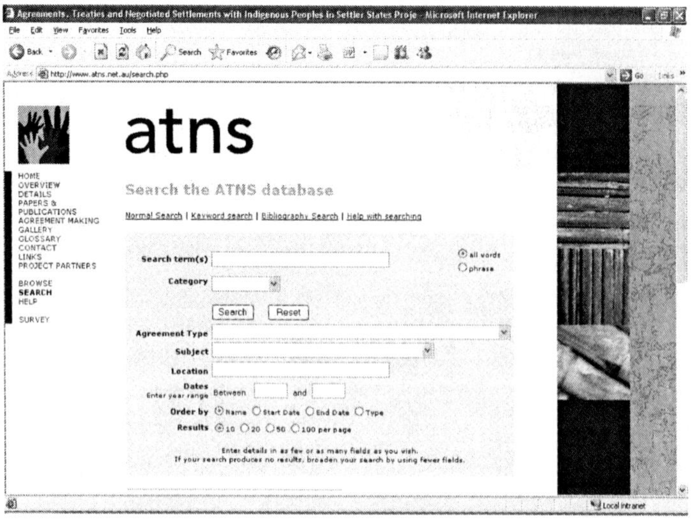

The ATNS database is already assisting indigenous communities and the organisations and agencies involved in indigenous affairs with planning for economic and social development through agreement making. As a resource base with an average of over 20,000 visits per month (the amount of times the site is entered), it contributes to the body of knowledge concerning non-litigated pathways to the recognition of the rights and entitlements of indigenous peoples. These include matters amenable to negotiated settlements such as land use, resource management, community governance, heritage protection and co-existing rights. Because of this, the database has the potential to inform future negotiations and settlements and increase awareness about the nature and scope of agreement making in a way that enhances both social and economic outcomes for indigenous peoples. The inclusion of international developments in agreement making, particularly in Canada and New Zealand, provides material of comparative relevance for Australian circumstances.

The ATNS database is part of a wider Australia Research Council Linkage Project, "Agreements, Treaties and Negotiated Settlements with Indigenous People in Settler States: Their role and relevance for Indigenous and other Australians," which began in March 2002. Further major initiatives of the project include the publication of *Honour Among Nations? Treaties and Agreements with Indigenous People* (2004), and *Settling with Indigenous People: Case Studies in Agreement Making from Australia, Canada and New Zealand* (in press), both edited collections of international papers which examine wide ranging issues affecting indigenous peoples including sovereignty, land rights, self-determination, treaty and agreement making and their implementation. Along with our industry partner, the Office of Indigenous Policy Coordination, this project involves researchers from both The University of Melbourne (Professor Marcia Langton, Chair of Indigenous Studies, Associate Professor Maureen Tehan of the Faculty of Law and Dr Lisa Palmer, Postdoctoral Research Fellow) and The University of Technology, Sydney (Professor Larissa Behrendt of the Faculty of Law and Jumbunna Indigenous House of Learning). The project is also supported by the Australian Institute of Aboriginal and Torres Strait Islander Studies, the Minerals Council of Australia, and Rio Tinto Pty. Ltd.

References

Aboriginal Land Rights (Northern Territory) Act. (1976). Commonwealth.

Agreements, Treaties and Negotiated Settlements (ATNS) Database. (2004). Retrieved May 11, 2006, from http://www.atns.net.au

Langton, M., Mazel, O., Palmer, L., Shain, K., & Tehan, M. (in press). *Settling with indigenous peoples: Case studies in agreement making from Australia, Canada and New Zealand*. Annandale, Australia: The Federation Press.

Langton, M., Palmer, L., Tehan, M., & Shain, K. (Eds.). (2004). *Honour among nations? Treaties and agreements with indigenous people*. Carlton, Australia: Melbourne University Press.

Mabo v. Queensland, No. 2, 175 CLR 1. (June 3, 1992).

Native Title Act. (1993). Commonwealth.

Section V:

Linking Communities and Improving Access

Chapter XVI

The Diffusion of New Technologies: Community Online Access Centres in Indigenous Communities in Australia

Anne Daly, University of Canberra, Australia

Abstract

This chapter presents data from the 2001 Census of Population and Housing to highlight the low levels of computer and Internet usage by indigenous Australians. This result is not surprising, given the well-documented connection between education, income, location of residence and use of these technologies. One possible way of addressing the digital divide between capital city dwellers and other Australians is through the development of community online access centres. Using evidence from the literature and from fieldwork in New South Wales, the chapter considers some factors that are likely to make these centres more successful. These include a strong commitment by the community to the development of a centre and a close integration of the centre with community activities. It is important that significant funds be budgeted to training for all involved including centre staff and community members.

Introduction

There has been a general concern that particular groups have been left behind in the diffusion of new information and communications technology (ICT) and the related skill development, and that this may have long term implications for the ability of these people to participate in society. indigenous Australians, both aboriginal and Torres Strait Islanders, are among those at risk. Earlier research by Lloyd and Hellwig (2000) looked at the determinants of the take-up of the Internet. They found that educational qualifications and income were the major determinants of access to the Internet at home. Living outside a major urban area was also associated with lower levels of computer and Internet usage. On the basis of all these indicators, indigenous Australians were expected to fall on the wrong side of the digital divide. Education levels and income are lower for this group than for non-indigenous Australians (Altman, Biddle, & Hunter, 2004). In addition, a larger proportion of indigenous compared to other Australians live outside the capital cities. Access to the Internet has been less reliable and more costly in these areas than in the cities (Besley, 2000; Regional Telecommunications Inquiry [RTI], 2002).

The 2001 Population Census was the first census to ask Australians about their access to computers and the Internet. The results show that while 30% of non-indigenous Australians had access to the Internet at home, less than 10% of indigenous Australians did. Other research has also documented low levels of computer access at home for school-aged indigenous Australians (Dyson, 2003). The purpose of this chapter is to examine the census evidence on computer and Internet usage for indigenous Australians and to consider whether the development of community online access centres can help to bridge the digital divide between indigenous and other Australians. It highlights the indicators of success and the limitations these centres have faced using evidence from the literature and fieldwork conducted in New South Wales (NSW).

Computer and Internet Access for Indigenous Australians

The 2001 Census provides a useful aggregate picture of home access to computers and the Internet and includes information on indigenous Australians for the first time. Several studies have used these data to investigate the use of new technologies by indigenous Australians. Lloyd and Bill (2004) developed a model for explaining the determinants of home computer and Internet usage. They found that Australians with higher levels of educational attainment and incomes were more likely to access the Internet at home than those less qualified and with lower incomes. Their results show that people with poor English language skills, indigenous Australians and those living in remote areas were less likely to use a home computer or access the Internet than a non-indigenous urban married man working in a white-collar job with no children and no tertiary qualifications. While the probability of the latter person using a computer at home was 43.8%, a person with identical characteristics, except that they were indigenous, only had a probability of home computer usage of 20.3% — a gap of 23.5 percentage points. There was also a substantial gap of 22.5 percentage points in the predicted probability of using the Internet for the non-indigenous male compared with an indigenous person with otherwise identical characteristics. According to Lloyd and Bill's results, being indigenous was one of the most important negative determinants of computer and Internet usage.

Biddle, Hunter, and Schwab (2004) have used the census data on Internet access to analyse indigenous participation in education. Based on a detailed geographical analysis of those data, they found that access to the Internet at home raised the probability of educational attendance. They interpreted this variable as an indicator of educational attainment in a household and support for educational participation. Their analysis shows substantial differences between indigenous and other Australians in their access to the Internet, particularly in remote areas.

The census data are used here to present a broad picture of computer and Internet access; for more detailed tables see Daly (2005). Table 1 summarises the census evidence on access to a computer at home for indigenous and non-indigenous Australians for each of the Australian States and Territories (hereafter referred to as "States"). It shows that the proportion of the total indigenous population that used a computer at home was well below that for the non-indigenous population in each State. The Australian Capital Territory (ACT) had the highest proportion of computer users among both the indigenous and non-indigenous populations. The two States that stand out as having the lowest ratio of indigenous to non-indigenous computer users in the population were Western Australia and the Northern Territory, where the ratio of indigenous to non-indigenous users was less than one-third. When State data are divided between the capital city and the rest of the state, they show that only 8% of the indigenous population of Western Australia and 3% of the indigenous population of the Northern Territory living outside the respective capital cities had access to a computer at home (Daly, 2005).

While about two-thirds of non-indigenous Australians who used a computer at home also had access to the Internet, the figure was closer to a half for indigenous Australians. Table 2 focuses on access to the Internet at home for both indigenous and non-indigenous Australians. The data show that less than 10 per cent of the indigenous population of Queensland, South Australia, Western Australia and the Northern Territory had Internet access at home. The ratio for Internet access at home was particularly low for indigenous people in Western

Table 1. Proportion of indigenous and non-indigenous populations that used a computer at home, by state, 2001 (Source: 2001 Census of Population and Housing)

	Indigenous (1)	Non-Indigenous (2)	Ratio (1)/(2)
New South Wales	0.22	0.43	0.51
Victoria	0.28	0.45	0.62
Queensland	0.18	0.44	0.41
South Australia	0.17	0.42	0.40
Western Australia	0.13	0.46	0.28
Tasmania	0.31	0.39	0.79
Northern Territory	0.06	0.43	0.14
Australian Capital Territory	0.41	0.59	0.69

Australia and the Northern Territory compared with the non-indigenous population.

Table 3 includes all sources of access to the Internet. This is comprised of the census categories home (the focus of Table 2), work and elsewhere (for example schools, libraries, friends' homes and community online access centres). A comparison of Tables 2 and 3 highlights some interesting results.

While indigenous Australians were less likely to use the Internet than other Australians, the gap was smaller if all usage of the Internet was the focus rather than Internet usage at home. A shift of focus from home usage to usage from all sources doubled the proportion of indigenous people accessing the Internet in South Australia, Western Australia and the Northern Territory but from a very low base (see Tables 2 and 3). The inclusion of other access points was particularly important outside the capital cities in Queensland, Western Australia, South Australia and the Northern Territory (Daly, 2005).

The census data are now three years old and, in this area of rapid change, there has probably been substantial growth in computer and Internet usage in the Australian population. Given certain characteristics of the indigenous population — relatively low levels of educational attainment, low incomes and location outside the capital cities — it seems likely that they continue to exhibit levels of computer and Internet access well below the national average.

Table 2. Proportion of indigenous and non-indigenous populations that had access to the Internet at home, by state, 2001(Source: 2001 Census of Population and Housing)

	Indigenous (1)	Non-Indigenous (2)	Ratio (1)/(2)
New South Wales	0.11	0.29	0.38
Victoria	0.16	0.33	0.48
Queensland	0.08	0.29	0.28
South Australia	0.07	0.27	0.26
Western Australia	0.06	0.31	0.19
Tasmania	0.15	0.23	0.65
Northern Territory	0.03	0.29	0.10
Australian Capital Territory	0.24	0.41	0.59

Table 3. Proportion of indigenous and non-indigenous populations that used the Internet, by state, 2001 (Source: 2001 Census of Population and Housing)

	Indigenous (1)	Non-Indigenous (2)	Ratio (1)/(2)
New South Wales	0.18	0.38	0.47
Victoria	0.26	0.40	0.65
Queensland	0.15	0.38	0.39
South Australia	0.17	0.37	0.46
Western Australia	0.12	0.41	0.29
Tasmania	0.28	0.35	0.80
Northern Territory	0.07	0.42	0.17
Australian Capital Territory	0.40	0.57	0.70

The Role of Community Online Access Centres

Policymakers have been concerned about the development of a digital divide based on location for some time. There have been two recent Commonwealth government enquiries into the state of communications systems outside the capital cities (Besley, 2000; RTI, 2002) and a report focusing directly on remote indigenous communities, the Telecommunications Action Plan for Remote Indigenous Communities (TAPRIC) (Department of Communications, Information Technology and the Arts [DCITA], 2002). One recommendation of these reports has been the need to further encourage the use of community facilities to promote access to ICT in situations where private households are unlikely to pay for these services themselves. Remote indigenous communities fall within this category. Residents have low incomes and low levels of education and technical expertise. The physical environment is harsh, making maintenance of the equipment difficult.

There are potentially many benefits for remote communities from access to ICT. These technologies have the ability to increase access to goods and services, for example, Internet banking and health and education services, and to facilitate access to information and the preservation of local history and culture. There is also a negative side where opening a community to the Internet may increase the availability to residents of socially undesirable influences such as pornography and gambling. However, there are many examples of new technologies providing positive outcomes for remote communities (Daly, 2002; Farr, 2004). Government-funded centres are one way of bringing these services to remote communities and bridging the digital divide.

The Commonwealth government has used revenue from the partial privatisation of Telstra (the main telecommunications carrier in Australia) to fund almost 700 communications projects costing a total of $325 million in remote and regional Australia through Networking the Nation (NTN). It has included 60 projects worth $35.1 million of "exclusive or significant benefit to indigenous communities" (DCITA, 2002, p. 26). State governments also have programs designed to improve public access to the Internet outside the capital cities. These include the Community Technology Centres (CTCs) in NSW (CTC@NSW), the West Australian telecentre program and Tasmanian Communities Online. These programs are jointly funded by NTN and their respective State governments. They provide public access to computers, photocopiers, fax machines, the Internet and videoconferencing in small rural and remote towns. Public libraries and schools in all states also offer public access to the Internet in numerous locations (DCITA, 2003).

There are some important factors in creating successful community online access centres discussed in the literature and highlighted during fieldwork undertaken by the author in 2003 in NSW. In the fieldwork, visits were made to CTCs in Dubbo, Menindee and Wilcannia. Extensive discussions were held with the managers of these centres, members of the indigenous communities, employees of Commonwealth and State government departments, the Outback Telecentre Network and other service providers to indigenous communities. While indigenous communities in NSW may not face the same issues of geographical isolation as those in other Australian States, they often face major problems of social and economic isolation. In Australia, most of the centres have only been running for a short time, so an evaluation of their impact in their communities can only be partial.

The Role of Community Support

For these centres to be successful, it is important that community members are involved in their development from the initial stages of the project through to the ongoing operation of the centre. Several studies discussed by Farr (2004) emphasise the importance of local champions in establishing and maintaining centres. Further examples include the CTC in Dubbo that was run from a community centre providing a range of facilities for the local indigenous population, including health and education services; a management committee of community leaders oversaw the operations of the community centre and the CTC. On Cape York Peninsula, the Cape York Digital Network (CYDN) has been established through detailed partnership agreements with the Community Councils in each location.

One method of fostering community support is by using the centres for the preservation of local culture and history. For example, pictures, stories and artefacts of the Bawgutti people have been digitally recorded and archived at the Bowraville CTC. The information has been made generally available on CD-ROM. Where literacy levels are low, special strategies may be required to engage the community in ICT activities.

The Development Role of the Centres

Related to the previous point is the need to recognise the role of online access centres in the development of communities. If they are to be successful, they need to be integrated into other activities in the community. It is important that centres engage in outreach activities to show how they can contribute to community life and development. For example, the development of radio and Internet access has been used in the Torres Strait to disseminate more accurate and detailed weather forecasts that are critical for fishing activity. In the CTCs visited in NSW, facilities were used for local meetings, educational purposes and for organising community transport. The Wilcannia CTC planned to establish a small local museum in the same building and a driver reviver centre to encourage passing tourists into the building.

There are currently very few Australian examples of a community online access centre that has been used as a base for a successful business enterprise. One example was the CTC at White Cliffs in NSW that was successfully used as a call centre but was later closed down. Overseas examples show the importance of a skilled workforce to make these ventures successful (Farr, 2004).

Schwab and Sutherland (2003) have proposed a similar role for schools as part of indigenous learning communities at the centre of community activities. It is only by integrating these institutions with community life that they can offer real opportunities for people to enhance their skills and foster development in the communities.

Local Employment and Training in the Centres

There are considerable difficulties in finding local people with the relevant skills to work in an online access centre. It is important that ongoing training of community members is available in an attempt to build the skill base, and that centre managers are also given the opportunity to upgrade their skills. While there are some funds for training, in general the budgets of these centres are very small and there is not much scope for training expenditure. The CTCs visited in NSW had not been very successful in their attempts to employ local indigenous people in the centres. A major constraint was the limited budget under which these centres were operating. In addition, many of the people who were available through the Community Development Employment Projects (CDEP) scheme or Work for the Dole were not suitably skilled, and some of them were not acceptable for working with children for other reasons.

Community online access centres offer the opportunity to provide online training to people in remote areas who might otherwise not have access. Many centres offer basic training in computer skills for community members (for example the NSW CTCs, CYDN and PY Media in South Australia). Technical and Further Education (TAFE) Colleges are now developing a range of online courses and are able to provide interactive education sessions to dispersed groups of students. One example from the Northern Territory is a pilot of virtual business education where participants establish virtual businesses and interact online to learn how to run them. However, it is important that the courses recognise the existing levels of skills and the requirements of those they are planning to teach in order to be successful.

What Can the Centres Do for Youth?

Young people are very keen computer and Internet users and have been a primary focus of efforts to integrate online access centres into communities. While they may be interested in using the Internet chiefly for entertainment rather than conventional education purposes, access to Internet facilities can provide young people with reading and communication skills that they would otherwise not be acquiring.

An innovative example of the use of Web technology for young indigenous people is the dEadly mOb Web site run from the Gap Youth Centre in Alice Springs (http://www.deadlymob.org). The site displays artwork and information about youth activities in Alice Springs and surrounding communities. It also provides a mentoring service for young indigenous people interested in gaining work experience.

The New South Wales CTCs have also focused on the needs of this group, for example, by establishing homework clubs for students after school, holding a photo competition run throughout NSW and a videoconferencing session on healthy lifestyles that enabled interaction between participants in communities and some professional football players. A significant issue with respect to youth is the importance of supervision. Several community leaders expressed concern that young people should only be able to access suitable Web sites. This has also been a concern for CYDN (2004). Another important issue from the viewpoint of the financial sustainability of the online centres is that these young people are unlikely to have the income to pay for their use of the centres' facilities. There needs to be some way of cross-subsidising their access, and one potential solution, access to large government contracts, is discussed in the next section.

Use of Community Online Access Centres for Government Service Delivery

Several authors have argued that a way of making these centres financially viable is for them to establish contracts with government departments for the supply of services to remote communities. This idea is currently being explored in some detail and is beginning to be put into operation. For example, the Australian Tax Office has provided training to CTC@NSW managers in using their Web site and pays a retainer to CTC@NSW to provide ongoing support for individuals accessing the Web site through the CTCs. However there are significant problems that must be overcome before community online access centres could be used to deliver many services. For example, to use a centre for a legal or health consultation via videoconferencing would require a secure network connection and the privacy of a separate room to ensure the confidentiality of the consultation. Most of the centres do not have these facilities. The CTC@NSW policy has been to undertake negotiations on behalf of all the CTCs in NSW with Commonwealth and State government departments. The agencies have been supportive of the proposals but are concerned about possible customer resistance to videoconferencing and the need to protect the privacy and security of the service. The ability to use income from these sources to cross-subsidise community activities remains a long-term objective.

Technical Support

The experience in NSW, Western Australia and the CYDN shows that it is very important that there is a strong centralised technical support network for the centres. This support is necessary for dealing with technical problems, brokerage with government agencies and as a source of new ideas. If the centres are going to be successful in remote communities, support information must be timely and available in a form that is accessible to people in the communities.

Use of Appropriate Technology

The technology available in these centres must be appropriate for the conditions and requirements of the communities. This includes social, cultural and economic constraints as well as physical ones. Supplying the most up-to-date technology may not lead to the best outcomes. For example, in each of the CTCs visited in NSW, there were videoconferencing facilities available at very reasonable rates by commercial standards. They were, however, still too expensive for members of the local community and were under-utilised. Managers argued that most of the limited use that was made of this equipment resulted from its implementation being "Sydney-driven" rather than initiated in the communities. Any equipment that is provided to these centres needs to come with a budget for use and maintenance training. If the skills are not available in the community to keep the equipment operating successfully, then there is limited advantage in its being there.

Long-Term Sustainability

Under many of these government-sponsored programs there is a goal of long-term financial independence for each centre. All the evidence of developments in Australia and in remote communities overseas suggests that this is unlikely to happen for a long time in indigenous communities (Caspary & O'Connor, 2003; DCITA, 2003). The communities do not have the resources to make these centres financially self-supporting. In this context, the only way that the centres can be made self-supporting is if they can generate income from government or business sources to cross-subsidise community activities, for example youth support programs. Current movement in this direction has been slow.

In order to be sustainable in the long run, community online access centres must offer a range of services. One example from Canada is K-Net Services (http://www.services.knet.ca), a regional broadband network for First Nations which offers Web site and e-mail hosting, network services, videoconferencing and Web site and graphic design. On a less sophisticated level, this may involve running a café as well as a set of computer terminals. Centres seem to perform better where they are integrated with other key organisations in a community, for example, the health centre, the library and the school. While long-term experience with online access centres in Australia is limited, there is a much longer history in radio communications in remote communities, and the Broadcasting for Remote Aboriginal Communities Scheme (BRACS) has been reviewed on several occasions (Aboriginal and Torres Strait Islander Commission [ATSIC], 1999). One of the important lessons of the BRACS reviews has been the need for continuing technical support and a budget for ongoing skill development in the communities.

Conclusion

This chapter has presented the evidence from the 2001 Census on computer and Internet access for indigenous Australians. It shows that access to computers is well below that for other Australians, particularly in Western Australia and the Northern Territory. Home Internet access is even more limited for indigenous Australians with less than 10% of the population having access to the Internet at home. The census evidence confirms a digital divide between indigenous and other Australians.

One way of trying to bridge this divide is by the development of community online access centres. While the development of these centres is in its early stages in Australia, there are some factors that appear to be associated with likely success. It is important that the community actively supports the introduction of a centre and is closely involved with its development and management. Centres should take a developmental role in their community and focus on ways in which they can contribute to its future. The centre management must be actively involved in outreach activities to show residents how they can benefit from using the facilities. They can have a special role in developing the skills of young people in the community and expanding opportunities.

A lack of appropriate skills among the local population is likely to be a significant issue in developing these centres in remote indigenous communities. It is imperative that there is a budget available for training and upgrading skills and that the management has ready access to support from outside the community.

There are many important underlying reasons for the economic disadvantage apparent in remote indigenous communities. These include the lack of employment opportunities, high levels of welfare dependence and low levels of income and education. These underlying factors are of paramount significance in addressing the long-term disadvantage of indigenous Australians. The development of a successful network of community online access centres could contribute to a reduction in these underlying determinants of economic disadvantage.

Acknowledgments

I would like to thank all the people who gave me their time during the fieldwork in NSW that is used as a basis for this chapter, particularly Kerry Fraser and Susan Locke. I would also like to thank Boyd Hunter and Diane Smith for useful comments on an earlier draft.

References

Aboriginal and Torres Strait Islander Commission (ATSIC). (1999). *Digital dreaming, a national review of indigenous media and communications*. Canberra, Australia: ATSIC.

Altman, J. C., Biddle, N., & Hunter, B. (2004). *Indigenous socioeconomic change 1971–2001: A historical perspective* (CAEPR Discussion Paper No. 266). Canberra, Australia: Centre for Aboriginal Economic Policy Research, Australian National University.

Besley, T. (Chair). (2000). *Connecting Australia, report of the telecommunications service inquiry*, Retrieved September 19, 2005, from http://www.telinquiry.gov.au/final_report.html

Biddle, N., Hunter, B. H., & Schwab, R. (2004). *Mapping indigenous educational participation* (CAEPR Discussion Paper No. 267). Canberra, Australia:

Centre for Aboriginal Economic Policy Research, Australian National University.

Cape York Digital Network (CYDN). (2004). *Clean IT for Cape York*, media release January 28th. Retrieved September 19, 2005, from http://www.cydn.com.au/359.html

Caspary, G., & O'Connor, D. (2003). *Providing low-cost Information Technology access to rural communities in developing countries: What works? What pays* (OECD Development Centre, Working Paper no. 229). Paris: OECD. Retrieved September 19, 2005, from http://www.oecd.org

Daly, A. (2002). Telecommunications services in rural and remote indigenous communities in Australia. *Economic Papers, 21*(1), 18-31.

Daly, A. (2005). *Bridging the digital divide: The role of community online access centres in indigenous communities* (CAEPR Discussion Paper 273). Canberra: Centre for Aboriginal Economic Policy Research, Australian National University.

Department of Communications, Information Technology and the Arts (DCITA). (2002). *Telecommunications action plan for remote indigenous communities*. Retrieved September 19, 2005, from http://www.dcita.gov.au

Department of Communications, Information Technology and the Arts (DCITA). (2003). *Maintaining the viability of online access centres in regional, rural and remote Australia* (discussion paper). Canberra: DCITA. Retrieved September 19, 2005, from http://www.dcita.gov.au.

Dyson, L. (2003, June 19-21). Indigenous Australians in the information age: Exploring issues of neutrality in Information Technology. In C. Ciborra, R. Mercurio, M. De Marco, M. Martinez, & A. Carignani (Eds.), *New paradigms in organizations, markets and society: Proceedings of the 11th European Conference on Information Systems (ECIS),* Naples, Italy. Retrieved September 19, 2005, from http://www-staff.it.uts.edu.au/~laurel

Farr, P. (2004, September 5-7). *Achieving sustainability and "triple bottom line": Outcomes for community online access centres*. Paper presented to the International Telecommunications Society 15th Biennial Conference, Berlin.

Lloyd, R., & Bill, A. (2004). *Australia online: How Australians are using computers and the Internet* (Australian Census Analytic Program, cat. No. 2056.0). Canberra: Australian Bureau of Statistics.

Lloyd, R., & Hellwig, O. (2000). The digital divide. *Agenda, 17*(4), 345-58.

Regional Telecommunications Inquiry (RTI). (2002). *Connecting regional Australia: The report of the Regional Telecommunications Inquiry*. Retrieved September 19, 2005, from http://www.telinquiry.gov.au/rti-report.html

Schwab, R. G., & Sutherland, D. (2003). Indigenous learning communities: A vehicle for community empowerment and capacity development. *Learning Communities: International Journal of Learning in Social Contexts, 1*(1), 53-70.

Chapter XVII

Wireless Applications in Africa

Laurel Evelyn Dyson, University of Technology, Sydney, Australia

Abstract

This chapter examines wireless technologies in Africa, with special reference to indigenous minority populations. In a continent with limited infrastructure, itinerant populations, low literacy levels and little money to spend on technology, wireless is proving an effective solution. Four implementations are examined to demonstrate how new approaches to mobile design are producing culturally and environmentally appropriate technology: the Himba's satellite-based mobile telephone network, Cyber Sherpherd, Cybertracker and WorldSpace satellite Internet radios.

Introduction

Innovative wireless technologies are being implemented across Africa to address a range of information and communication needs. With low levels of computer ownership and Internet access, as well as inadequate basic electricity and telephone infrastructure (Nxasana, 2002), governments, non-government organizations (NGOs) and researchers are being forced to think imaginatively. Wireless devices such as mobile phones, personal digital assistants (PDAs), GPS (global positioning systems) devices, and satellite Internet radios are proving cost effective for delivering services across the continent and can operate where traditional infrastructure is lacking. Moreover, mobile devices answer people's communications needs better than fixed-line services, given the strong trend to itinerant work, the movement of people from rural areas to the cities (Marsden, 2002) and the semi-nomadic lifestyles of some indigenous Africans. The high cost of fixed-line services combined with deregulation in the cellular market has helped fuel the unexpected exponential growth (Research ICT Africa!, 2004). More than 70% of Africa's telecommunications services now consist of mobile technology, the highest ratio in the world (Lougheed, 2004). One in 11 Africans is a mobile subscriber and the continent is the fastest-growing market in the world, with an average annual increase of 58% (LaFraniere, 2005).

In this chapter, four wireless applications that have been implemented or are being trialed in Africa are examined, with particular reference to Africa's indigenous minorities.

Wireless Issues and Challenges

There are an increasing number of studies of wireless technology design, adoption and use, yet there are still many aspects that are poorly understood. Sarker and Wells (2003) note the lack of a clear understanding of the consumer's perspective in mobile device adoption. Preece, Rogers, and Sharp (2002) list the challenges of designing small interfaces, of developing software which can work with the limited memory capabilities of mobile devices and of dealing with environmental factors such as glare, noise and bad weather. Other design issues include the need for the devices to be operated with one hand since users are likely to be doing other things at the same time, and the issue of task sequencing since users may be interrupted by external events. One problem that Nokia has found with the design of innovative mobile devices is that "users will not necessarily have the vision of future possibilities" (Preece, Rogers, & Sharp, 2002, p. 467).

In reaching an understanding of wireless technology adoption in Africa, we also need to take into account factors specific to the region and to developing economies. Cost structures, rechargeability issues, network coverage, environmental challenges, literacy and user motivation for choosing mobile devices, services and design features may be very different.

Cost

Most commentators have been surprised by the growth in the mobile phone sector in Africa (Research ICT Africa!, 2004). Though the cost of cell phones and calls are high compared to average income, mobile calls save people money and time in travel because they can speak to family and friends over the phone instead. Also, shared usage of phones helps to spread the service without added cost: in South Africa over half of all mobile owners let members of their family use their phone for free, and a third do the same for friends (Cascio, 2005).

Rechargeability

Lack of electricity to charge mobile devices means that innovative approaches have to be found. There has been interest in developing a bicycle-driven charger, and solar power has already been implemented in some applications. However, for most people living in small villages, the solution is power supplied at a small cost by someone who owns a car battery (but not necessarily a car), which, in turn, they take by bus to the nearest town to get recharged when it runs down (LaFraniere, 2005).

Wireless Network Coverage

There are still large areas of Africa that do not have wireless coverage, and in some countries services are largely confined to major towns, tourism centres and transport routes (A. Gillwald, in Research ICT Africa!, 2004). However, the demand for mobile services coupled with deregulation is fueling a constant increase in coverage.

Environmental Challenges

Heat, dust and other environmental aspects must be taken into account when designing mobile devices for African users.

Literacy

Illiteracy in much of Africa requires new approaches to interface design. Indigenous languages prevent many Africans from using text-based applications in English or other dominant languages. Language issues also affect usage patterns; for example, text-messaging is much lower in Africa than it is in Western countries (Cascio, 2005). Computer skills become an issue with maintenance of equipment.

User Motivation

Most research into wireless technology has been conducted in Western and Asian consumer-oriented cultures and the results may not be applicable to user behaviour in developing regions such as Africa. A number of researchers have noted the effect of culture on usage patterns and design preferences of mobile technology (see, for example, Choi, Lee, Kim, & Jeon, 2005). A major motivating factor in Africa is the urbanization of the workforce: Families and friends are left behind in the villages while breadwinners move to the cities to find work. Mobile phones are important in maintaining contact. The phones may not be used very often, but are essential when there is important news to discuss (LaFraniere, 2005).

The Himba: Accessing Cultural and Community Services

The Himba people of the remote Kaoko region in north-western Namibia are maintaining their traditional semi-nomadic lifestyle while at the same time beginning to adopt modern technologies. A link between the Himba cattle herders and the outside world is being established using a wireless network and an information and communications technology (ICT) base station (Chesselet, 2004). This project is a collaboration between Doxa Productions (a documentary film company based in South Africa), UNESCO and the universities of Cape Town and Cologne. The ICT centre in Okanguati, a village in the region, will be managed by Cornelius Mukuena Tjiuma, a Himba translator and trainee teacher, who has completed his International Computer Driver's License in addition to training in internetworking and audiovisual techniques, and is working as an assistant producer in filming the oral histories of his people. The ICT centre will provide a platform where documentaries of Himba culture, that form part of the Kaoko Local Knowledge Living Archive

Project, can be stored on DVD and viewed (Chesselet, 2003). Moreover, it will provide community services such as telemedicine, veterinary information on cattle diseases and legal advice via the Internet. Himba people will be able to liaise with other indigenous peoples and organizations and gain the benefit of their experiences and survival strategies. The satellite-based mobile telephone network has already been installed and will be important in extending these services beyond the confines of the ICT centre, an essential component for a semi-nomadic people like the Himba.

Cyber Shepherd: Managing Livestock Sustainably

Gallé Aynabé, or Cyber Shepherd, is a project supported by Canada's International Development Research Centre (IDRC) and initiated by the Veterinary Science and Medicine School at Dakar (Sylla, 2004). Its aim is to help semi-nomadic herders in Senegal choose the best grazing land for their flocks of sheep, goats and herds of cattle as they move at the end of the rainy season to new pastures in the more fertile southern areas of the country and often end up in conflict with sedentary pastoralists and farmers. An important objective is to produce ecological outcomes by avoiding over-grazing. The project, still in its pilot phase, hopes to improve the standard of living of the population, who depend on their animals for at least half their income.

Several herders have been equipped with mobile phones to provide them with information about pastures and watering holes, and track other flocks moving in the grazing zone. Some herders have also been given information technology training so they have the skills to access a Web site showing maps of land already occupied with estimated carrying capacity, as well as information on animal diseases. Herders have been taught to prepare the maps themselves using GPS devices.

As the project moves into its second phase, researchers intend to simplify the approach, since issues have arisen during the pilot from the herders' low literacy levels and problems with maintenance of equipment.

CyberTracker at Work in Africa's National Parks

Researchers at the University of Cape Town have developed a field computer for gathering detailed data on animal behaviour and it as been used in several national parks in South Africa and the Congo (Blake, Steventon, Edge, & Foster, 2000). The device consists of a PDA with a graphical user interface on which options are selected by touching the screen with a stylus. Expert animal trackers use the system to record sightings of animals and a full range of behaviours, including drinking and feeding, the plant or animal species consumed, spoor information, etc. Because the trackers are illiterate or semi-literate, the interface text is supported by icons representing different species and animal behaviours. A GPS receiver attached to the top of the PDA allows automatic recording of the locations of observations, which are also automatically date and time stamped. The field computer is quick and easy to use and trackers produce more than 100 wildlife observations per day in the normal course of their work. The PDAs can hold up to one week's data before downloading onto the base station computers.

Park managers can then query the database to display information at varying levels of detail. Visualization is used to display animal sightings on a park map. The database stores information collected over a long period, well after the trackers have forgotten specific details, and therefore allows long-term monitoring of ecological trends.

The system also provides a social payoff since it allows the community to benefit from the expertise of the trackers. In turn, they have gained prestige since they are no longer viewed as unskilled workers. They now have an incentive to refine their traditional skills of animal observation which might otherwise die out in an age when the hunting of game animals is being replaced by conservation.

WorldSpace Satellite Internet Radios

The WorldSpace Foundation, a non-profit organization based in the USA, has established a satellite network to provide access to radio programs and the Internet for people in remote rural areas, including, although not restricted to, indigenous peoples. The network uses three satellites launched over Africa, Asia and America. The AfriStar Satellite has three broadcast beams, with each region in Africa receiving broadcasts from at least one beam (Lusaka, 2002). More than 40 different channels can be broadcast over each beam and the digital signals are captured by special portable radios. The radios operate off electricity, solar power, dry cell or car batteries; and the weather-resistant micro-dish receiver can be detached and placed outdoors to pick up the satellite signal while the radio is being used indoors. Users can search for programs by name, type or language, and programs can be stored on a tape recorder during the broadcast. Radios provide high quality audio, but can also be connected to a computer via a special modem so that text and images from selected sites on the Internet can be accessed.

As well as using the radios for entertainment, individuals can access much useful information. The Africa Learning Channel (ALC) occupies 5% of the broadcast bandwidth and provides environmental and agricultural information, a public health channel, information to foster micro-enterprises and conflict resolution and weather forecasts which include a famine early warning system (Ayieko, 2001). Organizations such as the Arid Lands Information Network — Eastern Africa, is using the ALC to provide information support to community development workers operating at a grassroots level and help them share experiences and make contact with potential collaborators. Moreover, the satellite network can be used for distance learning, with the Kenya Institute of Education and the Ethiopia Media Agency both having channels for broadcasting educational programs (Women of Uganda Network, 2002).

The main limitation of these radios for indigenous Africans is language: At present most broadcasts are in English. Even if local languages are adopted, they are more likely to be the language of the dominant national culture rather than the minority languages. This is particularly so, given the opposition by some governments in the region to "vernacular" languages (Mungai, 2000).

Conclusion

Africa is leading the way in introducing innovative wireless solutions to meet a range of needs. In a poor continent it is cheaper to buy and operate a mobile phone, PDA or satellite radio than to buy and install a desktop computer. For people living in remote regions where infrastructure is poor, wireless technology provides the ideal way of linking communities to the outside world and giving them access to services. Where indigenous peoples still practice semi-nomadic lifestyles, mobile devices offer portability to match their way of life and allow them to continue their traditions on the land while benefiting from modern access to information and communication. For indigenous peoples whose language skills are oral rather than written, mobile phones are an obvious communication tool.

New approaches to mobile systems design are showing how it is possible to produce screens which are usable by illiterate or semi-literate people with strong visual-pictorial cultural traditions. Moreover, the experience in Africa has shown that it is possible to develop wireless devices that are environmentally robust and can withstand heat, dust and rain. There is a real need to continue this investment in the development of culturally and environmentally appropriate mobile technologies.

Issues still remain regarding the cost of devices in addition to the lack of necessary expertise within indigenous communities to maintain equipment.

However, wireless technologies are a real option for indigenous peoples, not only in Africa but in other regions where remoteness, mobility of lifestyle and lack of infrastructure and money limit technology choices. Wireless implementations in Africa could well provide a model which other indigenous peoples in other parts of the world should be watching.

Acknowledgments

The author thanks Max Hendriks and Donna Walsh for their insightful comments and suggestions on the draught of this chapter.

References

Ayieko, F. (2001, October 19). Internet radios aid Africa. *BBC News*. Retrieved August 8, 2004, from http://news.bbc.co.uk

Blake, E. H., Steventon, L., Edge, J., & Foster, A. (2000). A field computer for animal trackers. *ACM SIGCHI South Africa Chapter*. Retrieved August 21, 2004, from http://pubs.cs.uct.ac.za/archive/00000041

Cascio, J. (2005, March 9). Mobile phones and development. *WorldChanging*. Retrieved September 9, 2005, from http://www.worldchanging.com/archives/002306.html

Chesselet, J. (2003). *The Kaoko local knowledge living archive project*. (Proposal to UNESCO under the ICTs for Intercultural Dialogue Initiative). Paris: UNESCO.

Chesselet, J. (2004). *Ochre and water project phase three: The Kaoko local knowledge living archive project*. (Report to UNESCO). Paris: UNESCO.

Choi, B., Lee, I., Kim, J., & Jeon, Y. (2005, April). A qualitative cross-national study of cultural influences on mobile data service design. *Proceedings of the SIGCHI Conference on Human Factors in Computing Systems* (pp. 661-670).

LaFraniere, S. (2005, August 26). Cell phone frenzy in Africa, world's top growth market. *The San Diego Union-Tribune*. Retrieved August 30, 2005, from http://www.signonsandiego.com/uniontrib/20050826/news_1n26phones.html

Lougheed, T. (2004). *Wireless points the way in Africa*. World Resources Institute. Retrieved September 2, 2004, from http://www.enn.com

Lusaka, N. (2002, August). WorldSpace: The information alternative in Africa's remote areas. *Science in Africa.* Retrieved August 21, 2004, from http://www.scienceinafrica.co.za/2002/august/radio.htm

Marsden, G. (2002, March-April). Subverting technology: Meeting user needs in a developing economy. *ACM SIGHI Bulletin*, p. 8.

Mungai, W. (2000, September 8). Radio interference: Why does the president of Kenya want to ban private vernacular broadcasting. *CPJ.* Retrieved November 2, 2005, from http://www.cpj.org/Briefings/2000/Kenya_sept00/Kenya_sept00.html

Nxasana, S. (2002). A bridge across the Africa divide. In R. Hurst (Ed.), *BMI-T communication technologies handbook* (pp. 38-42). Johannesburg, South Africa: BMI-Tech Knowledge.

Preece, J., Rogers, Y., & Sharp, H. (2002). *Interaction design: Beyond human-computer interaction.* Hoboken, NJ: John Wiley.

Research ICT Africa! (2004). *ICT sector performance in Africa: A review of seven African countries.* Retrieved September 9, 2004, from http://www.researchictafrica.net

Sarker, S., & Wells, J. D. (2003). Understanding mobile handheld device use and adoption. *Communications of the ACM, 46*(12), 35-40.

Sylla, C. (2004, August). A cyber shepherd at work in the Sahel. *Science in Africa.* Retrieved August 21, 2004, from http://www.scienceinafrica.co.za/2004/july/cybershepherd.htm

Women of Uganda Network (WOUGNET). (2002). *Report on WorldSpace Radio training held at Isis WICCE, Kampala, May 21, 2002.* Retrieved August 21, 2004, from http://www.wougnet.org

Case Study XXI

UHF-Based Community Voice Service in Ngannyatjarra Lands of Australia

Mehran Abolhasan, University of Wollongong, Australia

Paul Boustead, University of Wollongong, Australia

The Ngaanyatjarra land is located in the Gibson Desert in the state of Western Australia, and is the home of 12 major communities primarily made up of indigenous peoples. These communities are spread over a 250,000 square kilometre radius, with the population of each community ranging from 75 to 450.

The remote location of these communities, far from major rural centres, has limited the roll-out of advanced communication technologies. One area of concern has been the limited availability of personal communication services to provide communication links within and between these communities.

The Ultra-High Frequency (UHF) network, a project initiative of the Federal Government's Networking the Nation fund, was established in 1997 to provide an alternative networking strategy to the existing high frequency (HF) radio. The HF radios were unreliable and not very mobile due to the bulkiness of the transceivers. This restricted their use to vehicles and stations. The introduction of the UHF radios gave better mobility and flexibility through smaller handheld devices. These devices have proven to be very popular as they provide a cost effective and easy-to-use personal communication solution.

The community UHF network operates over 18 repeater towers, which supply coverage to most of the Ngaanyatjarra communities, except for Kanpa and Tjukurla. The UHF towers increase the area of coverage of the network to allow people to communicate in ranges of up to 50 km. Figure 1 illustrates a UHF repeater tower in the Warakurna community.

Currently, each Ngaanyatjarra community has a dedicated UHF channel which is used to communicate within their community. For example, in Warakurna, the UHF channel 1 is used for community general chats.

The UHF network has been a great success in these communities, as it provides an alternative mode of communication compared to global system for mobile communications (GSM) or code division multiple access (CDMA) mobile phones used in rural or metropolitan areas. The advantage of the UHF network is that there are no additional costs required by the user to access or communicate on this network, except the cost of the handset. One disadvantage of this

Figure 1. UHF repeater tower at Warakurna community

network is that it is currently experiencing significant levels of traffic as all community members talk on top of each other on the same channel. Furthermore, the current UHF network does not provide a private communication channel for individual users.

Case Study XXII

Cape York Digital Network

'Alopi Latukefu,
Australian Agency for International Development, Australia

Power comes in all manner of media — economic, legislative, industrial, cultural and social — with each level of power intertwined into a massive network of inter-relationships. The cliché, "knowledge is power," has been the catch cry of organisations and people from the disenfranchised to the elite, from community and civil rights activists to business and government over many years.

Information and communications technology (ICT) represents a marked departure from what has come before, by shifting the knowledge/power relationship away from centralised decision making to distributed consensus. The technology does this through low-cost internetworked distribution of information and knowledge in digital format using the standardised Internet protocol (IP) platform. It provides the opportunity for a fundamental shift in the dynamics of many traditionally dependent relationships, such as those of indigenous communities and individuals in the way they relate to the mainstream public and private sectors. With aboriginal people throughout Australia facing massive changes within the current political cycle in the way in which they are governed and their relationships to service providers, a number of organisations have seized upon this opportunity to develop commercial, political and bureaucratic partnerships within the information technology and communications sector with a view to establishing a modicum of self-determination and independence from the traditional government funding cycle, which has fundamentally underpinned the aboriginal economy, particularly within remote and regional Australia.

Through the Commonwealth Government of Australia's Networking the Nation program, a number of key aboriginal organisations came together to form a company limited by guarantee called the Outback Digital Network (ODN). This organisation provides the means to managing many of the different relationships involved in information technology and telecommunications, including governmental, commercial interests and industry/competition regulators. The resulting model, involving both commercial arrangements and public investment, utilises technology and other means to empower aboriginal communities. This has been achieved by establishing a managed network service that remote communities can use to take responsibility in areas such as governance and administration while achieving far greater access to the basic services that are their right as citizens of Australia. The ODN controls the technical know-how, intellectual property and ICT strategy of the network and also the development of applications running over and through the technology.

The Cape York Digital Network (CYDN) represents the first iteration of the ODN as an innovative approach to delivering ICT services into remote communities. Cape York, as with many remote parts of Australia, consists of a number of small to medium-sized indigenous communities distributed over very large distances. These communities are characterised by low literacy and numeracy, very little economic opportunity and socio-cultural degradation, as traditional practices and management have given way to welfare dependency and anomie within the community. The network meets the community needs for quality assurance in data and ICT services, including video-conferencing, with the challenge of providing these services in an operationally cost effective manner. The CYDN was built on the technical plans developed within the ODN process, while utilising the contracts for carriage demand aggregation as negotiated by the ODN with commercial carriers. CYDN provides a generic IP-based platform to distribute content and applications into remote communities through both terrestrial and radio-based technologies. The network is designed to account for the challenges facing remote communities namely:

- the tyranny of distance and remoteness;
- the barriers to economic independence and sustainability brought about by low disposable incomes;

- the difficulty in achieving economies of scale;
- the challenge of aggregating demand and negotiating better and more diverse services; and
- the need to improve access to quality assurance in products, services and service delivery and to establish realistic, meaningful and productive service level agreements with carriers.

A couple of examples of how the network is currently operating to service communities are given here. First, in 2004 the Indigenous Stock Exchange (ISX) won a laureate from the Museum of Technology in San Francisco for its innovative use of technology to empower indigenous people. Utilising the ODN network and skill base, the ISX brought together communities, indigenous business owners, business partners, potential investors and other groups from all over Australia and the world using video-conferencing and webstreaming: The aim is encourage investment by the business and charitable sectors into indigenous enterprises.

Secondly, on a more local level, applications such as Internet banking have become widely used within many of the CYDN access centres. This has had huge implications for people who, in the past, were required at times to travel substantial distances to the town branch to transfer money between family members.

Furthermore, in many of the communities in Cape York, access by elderly people to family members locked up in Lotus Glen prison has been an ongoing issue. The introduction of video conferencing in these communities and in the prison has provided some older members with their only access to family members, while for others who are fit enough to travel, it has resulted in the saving of time and money. This has been an important service that the CYDN has provided to the communities.

Cape York Digital Network, in partnership with the Outback Digital Network and Telstra (the main telecommunications carrier), has developed network services within the Cape York region. CYDN manages part or all of a community's network and computing infrastructure in seventeen communities stretching from Umagico in the region's north, to Kowanyama in the Southwest and Wujal-Wujal in the Southeast. The full gamut of services and applications is covered, providing holistic end-to-end network and infrastructure management, including basic network access, a help desk, desktop management, infrastructure building and maintenance, auditing and analysis of network performance, security, service application provision, troubleshooting, videoconferencing and other network functionality. CYDN has also established a team of community members employed to manage the community centres and provide practical and technical ICT support. The CYDN is designed to be scalable to manage a community's entire information technology and telecommunications needs and growth, both now and into the distant future. The network has given choice in areas that in the past severely lacked any real options, and is a testament to the aboriginal communities and their representatives, utilising technology to empower themselves and achieve some independence and self-determination for aboriginal people.

Case Study XXIII

Redfern Kids Connect

Ryan Sengara, Redfern Kids Connect, Australia

Redfern Kids Connect is a volunteer-based community project running each Saturday morning out of the Redfern Computer Centre in inner-west Sydney, Australia. The project has been running consistently since August 2002.

The Redfern-Waterloo suburbs of Sydney are widely considered a centre of urban aboriginal Australia and are often in the political and media spotlights. The area experiences high levels of socio-economic disadvantage and social problems, including high crime rates, high incarceration rates, domestic violence and a lack of extra educational and recreational opportunities for young people.

The Redfern Kids Connect project provides computer and Internet access to kids in the Redfern-Waterloo area with the help of a team of volunteers. Participation is completely voluntary and takes a drop-in format. The project has no set curriculum but attempts to foster positive interaction and relationships.

Common activities include surfing the Internet, listening to streaming audio and video, network gaming, multimedia production, Web page-building, sports and more. There are high levels of interaction between youth and volunteers, as well as within these groups during the course of every session. The project has averaged approximately fifteen kids and five volunteers at each weekly session.

Children participating in the community project have ranged in ages from five through fifteen-years-old and come from a variety of cultural backgrounds, including a large proportion of aboriginal and Torres Strait Islanders. The volunteer team is a mix of young adults and university students from a wide variety of backgrounds that on the whole are not similar to the backgrounds of kids participating. Most volunteers have high levels of computer literacy and have attained at least some level of post-secondary education. The volunteer team to date has not regularly included any formally-trained social or community workers, or any aboriginal or Torres Strait Islanders.

In its initial stages, the objectives of the community project were loose and untested. It was hoped that the project would bridge the "digital divide" with the disadvantaged kids of the community by providing computer access — the idea being that youth in the area lack access to technology. At the same time, the project was to facilitate "sharing cultures" between participants. At its outset, outcomes were irregular and hard to identify, as the project struggled to attract a regular turnout of kids, experienced high turnover of volunteers and did not run each week.

As the project achieved consistency, the level of interaction and activity grew. Consequently, the quantity and complexity of outcomes developed at a fast rate. The volunteer team has had to deal with many challenges and outcomes not initially considered which have made the project a sometimes intense and confusing experience. Challenges and outcomes have included:

- questions around authority, culture clash and dealing with confronting incidents both in the project and in the community;
- questions about the meaning of relationships formed and developed through the project;
- questions of contextualising how the technology available is used, navigating through technology content options (Internet, gaming and multimedia) and censorship (Is it okay that we're facilitating kids surfing the Net, playing games and listening to music rather than more formal activities?); and
- changes in conceptual thinking about the objectives, format and direction of the project. Why are we here? What should we be trying to achieve? How can technology play a part?

It has become obvious that the project's outcomes are more complex than "bridging the digital divide" and "sharing cultures.". In fact, these objectives have become obsolete in a sense as the project has progressed. Volunteers have shared reflections and thoughts through an e-mail list and through informal conversation to help better understand their experiences. Concepts that have been helpful have come from writings on the digital divide and technological determinism (Warschauer, 2003; Postman, 1992), books on social capital (Cox, 1995; Putnam, 2000), and work on pedagogy and intervention in marginalised communities (Freire,1996). In addition, Ryan Sengara, a volunteer of the project, has been completing a research thesis around the outcomes and experiences of the project to date.

References

Cox, E. (1995). *A truly civil society*. Sydney, Australia: ABC Books.

Freire, P. (1996). *Pedagogy of the oppressed*. London: Penguin.

Postman, N. (1992). *Technopoly: The surrender of culture to technology*. New York: Vintage Books.

Putnam, R. (2000). *Bowling alone*. New York: Simon & Schuster.

Warschauer, M. (2003). *Technology and social inclusion: Rethinking the digital divide*. Cambridge, MA: MIT Press.

Case Study XXIV

Community Computing and Literacy in Pascua Yaqui Pueblo

J. David Betts, University of Arizona, USA

In 1998, the U.S. Department of Commerce Telecommunications and Information Infrastructure Assistance Program funded the Pascua Yaqui Connection project. This grant initiative was created to address the Digital Divide. Programs were established to bridge this gap for communities traditionally behind in information and communications technology (ICT) and underserved by connectivity and access to the Internet and advanced computer systems. The Pascua Yaqui Community Resource Lab was established by the joint effort of the Pascua Yaqui Tribe of Arizona, Pima Community College and the University of Arizona (Betts, 2002).

The reservation community of New Pascua Pueblo is located 14 miles southwest of Tucson. Approximately four thousand Pascua Yaqui tribal members live in New Pascua, which is located within 60 miles of the Mexican border, where the tribe is originally from. Fourteen thousand or so members of the Pascua Yaqui Tribe of Arizona live in five separate communities around Tucson and Phoenix.

In 1999, the lab made high speed computing and Internet access available to the reservation for the first time. The lab was established in a portable building next to a house that had been converted into a neighborhood education center. After several delays in creating the infrastructure of phone, power and networking, the 20 workstations with T-1 Internet access saw steadily increasing use. The Tribe's department of education hired staff from the community. Their Office of Information Technology (IT) provided technical support once the lab was opened with help from IT specialists in various departments of the College and the University. At the end of the original grant support for the lab, the Tribe took on full responsibility for its operation.

Community members of all ages learned to used typical office software, in particular MS Word, Publisher and Explorer. Open workshops were offered for these programs. The youngest children, from pre-K programs such as Head Start, used interactive sing-along programs and learning games. Older children played knowledge and memory games and visited youth-centered online sites such as PBS.org, where they were able to participate in the activities by printing line drawings for coloring. Middle school boys were drawn to online music sites like MTC.com and hip-hop culture shopping sites. Many older youth and adults used word processing for a wide variety of purposes such as homework, job applications and home businesses.

In 2003, the lab was moved to a larger re-purposed Head Start building central to the community next to a new Hiaki Intel Clubhouse, a multimedia computer lab established with a grant from Intel Corporation. The new community activity center thus added 15 new computers with multimedia capability, including a music studio and workstations for robotics, graphics, video and animation to the community's ICT resources. The Intel Clubhouse ran a drop-in program for youth in the community to work with mentors in multimedia projects.

Theoretical Framework

The attractive new tools required for participation have enabled certain new kinds of literacy and learning on the part of the user (Alvermann, 2004; Zhang, 2003). New media spawn new language and literacy and have allowed us to create new mediating technologies. By establishing a physical connection and space for participation, new literacies have become part of the social practice of the community (Street, 2003). In after school programs (Heath, Soep, & Roach, 1998), like much of the lab's activity, that relationship between literacy and technology takes place in a dynamic and interactive human environment (Betts, 2002, 2003). Students can feel that they are part of the information age, and their cultural and affinity groups utilize all sorts of technology to establish identity (Gee, 2000).

Procedures

I visited the lab often and did participant observation, including videotaping of lab activities and interviews with participants. A 30-item User Registration Survey that captured demographic and attitudinal data was created and administered as part of the lab's user registration procedure. During the last year of the project, a streamlined 18-item post-test survey questionnaire, based on an item analysis of the results of the pretest instrument (see discussion below), was delivered to the lab in September 2001. All users, new and registered, were asked to complete the second survey. We asked people about how they used the lab and how they felt about it. Taken together these observations attempted to capture the atmosphere of the lab and its many uses.

Outcomes

Data were analyzed in an activity system framework (Engström, 1999) allowing us to consider the dynamic aspects of the social setting. We observed the activity settings in which users participated, the actions that were performed in pursuit of their goals and objectives and the operations that were learned and used to apply new tools to desired outcomes. Individuals worked toward goals using mediating tools. They created a culture with rules and a variety of roles to play. The staff and the community of users negotiated the lab's rules in the context of the Tribe's Department of Education. The culture of the community and the culture of the lab meshed in a unique way to this tribe.

We recorded the lab's unique sounds and images: the music online and children's sing-along CD-ROM games, the arrival of the middle school boys after school, the classes and the exploring that took place as part of the lab's regular use. People spoke in English, Spanish and Yaqui, the native tongue, as they got help and helped each other. New literacies, as Gee (1998) and others have described, were discovered, invented and adapted for the lab and the new media age it represented for the community.

There were higher post-test scores for attitude and perceived self-efficacy measures of lab users for the new communication and information gathering capabilities in their community. Observations recorded users of all ages talking about mastering new skills and literacies. There was an increase in training and learning opportunities for tribal members.

In interviews, teachers said that their students' work had improved due to their work in the lab. Community members and families supported the lab's outreach efforts by participating in the open house events, workshops and classes. The lab became known as a safe after school activity and this lead to its acceptance with the technology it contained.

Longitudinal Study

A longitudinal study has been proposed which focuses on case studies of children and adults identified in the initial study. It addresses these questions, among others:

- What do parents and family members report as effects of a neighborhood computer lab on school attendance, school success and literacy on the Pascua Yaqui Reservation? In what ways does the technology become situated in the day-to-day life of the reservation?
- How are the rules of use negotiated? What tools are used? What cultural considerations are made to accommodate Pascua Yaqui lifestyles?
- What new kinds of literacy are being developed? How are they distributed among the community members?

With the lab as a permanent part of the community, the Pascua Yaqui Tribe of Arizona is in the forefront of rural Native American technology infusion. It is anticipated that the dissemination of this tribe's experience will help other small rural communities that are interested in the possible effects of high technology on their communities.

References

Alvermann, D. E. (2004). Multiliteracies and self-questioning in the service of science learning. In W. Saul (Ed.), *Crossing borders in literacy and science instruction* (pp. 226-238). Newark, DE: International Reading Association.

Betts, J. D. (2002). *Pascua Yaqui connection: Community Resource Lab* (Report to U.S. Department of Commerce National Telecommunications and Information Administration). Retrieved September 19, 2005, from http://www.ntia.doc.gov/otiahome/top/research/exemplary/pima.htm

Betts, J. D. (2003*). Art and technology integration: A longitudinal study of the Multimedia Arts Education Program*. Paper presented at American Educational Research Association (AERA) 2003 Annual Meeting, Chicago.

Engström, Y. (1999). Activity theory and individual and social transformation. In Y. Engström, R. Miettinen, & R. Punamaki (Eds.), *Perspectives on activity theory* (pp. 1-38). Cambridge, MA: Cambridge University Press.

Gee, J. P. (2000). The new literacy studies: form "socially situated" to the work of the social. In D. Barton, M. Hamilton, & R. Ivanic (Eds.), *Situated literacies: Reading and writing in context* (pp. 180-196). Routledge: London.

Heath, S.B., Soep, E., & Roach, A. (1998). Living the arts through language and learning: A report on community-based youth organizations. *Americans for the Arts Monographs, 2*(7), 1-20.

Street, B. (2003). What's "new" in new literacy studies? Critical approaches to literacy in theory and practice. *Current Issues in Comparative Education, 5*(2), 1523-1615.

Zhang Y. (2003). Making meaning in a digital literacy club: Teachers' talk of beliefs about email communication in literacy and learning. In Y. Saito-Abbott, R. Donovan, & T. Abbot (Eds.), *Emerging technologies in teaching language and culture*. San Diego, CA: LARC Press.

Case Study XXV

Reunification of the Wendat/Wyandotte Nation at a Time of Globalization

Linda Sioui, Huron-Wendat Nation, Canada

In the 17th century, an important period of contact with Europeans, the Wendat nation (Iroquoian linguistic family) lived in the Georgian Bay area, close to Lake Simcoe, in Ontario, Canada. Its territory is located at the northern limit of southern Ontario's agricultural lands. Data vary regarding the total population at the beginning of the seventeenth century (the contact period), but it may be assessed to have been 29,000 souls on average (Trigger, 1976, p. 30). To start with, the Wendat nation comprised four nations distributed among several villages. A fifth nation joined later. The French called this semi-sedentary people "Hurons," thus referring to the tuft of hair on a wild boar's head the nation's warriors' hairstyle reminded them of.

According to the Wendat cosmovision, the first woman (Aataentsic) fell from the sky and landed on the back of a giant turtle, on which marine animals hastened to lay soil retrieved from the bottom of the sea. Once this "island" was created, Aataentsic gave birth to a girl who in turn brought forth two sons, Tawiskaron and Iouskeha, ancestors of good and evil. The Wendat called themselves "dwellers of the island, or peninsula." We have to locate them on the North American continent in the light of their cosmovision as this, to them, is the original natural and global ecological order (Hall, 2003, pp. 100-101).

Contact Period and Dispersal

Prior to contact, the Wendat had long been involved in a regional economic network with numerous neighbouring aboriginal nations, with whom they maintained good diplomatic relations. This accounts for the first significant influence of globalization because all the conditions were already in place for the extension of this commercial network to Europe: Therefore, the existing fur trade underwent an unprecedented increase (demand for beaver pelts especially). The introduction of Christianity to Huronia (namely by the Recollets and the Jesuits) laid the foundations for another globalization influence. These influences overcame the Wendat confederation's unity. Moreover, imported illnesses such as smallpox, against which the Wendat had no immunity, killed over half of the population (Heidenreich, 1978, p. 368). In 1649, the Wendat confederation segmented in several groups, found today in Oklahoma, Kansas and Michigan (USA) under the name Wyandotte (or Wyandot), and in Wendake (formerly known as Huron Village) outside of Quebec City (Quebec, Canada). Descendants are also found near Amherstburg, Ontario and in Ohio (USA).

Upon the destruction of the original homeland, the ancestors of the Quebec Wendat found refuge at "Gahoendoe" (Christian Island) and in the spring of 1650 they arrived in Quebec City under the guidance of Jesuit Father Joseph-Marie Chaumonot. They settled in various places such as Île d'Orléans, Sainte-Foy, Ancienne-Lorette, Beauport, and they finally established themselves at the present location of Wendake (formerly known as "Lorette" and later on as "Village-des-Hurons") in 1697. Slowly, they adapted to their environment and later intermarried with the French.

After 1649, the Wyandottes (or Wyandots) migrated around the Great Lakes and were later found in Detroit (Michigan, USA) as well as Amherstburg (Ontario, Canada). Some settled in Ohio where they had hunting territories. The signing of treaties as well as land cessions, and various American government policies such as the *Removal and Relocation Act* (1828-1887), brought them to Kansas and then Northeastern Oklahoma where their descendants can be found today.

Reunification

From 1649 to 1999, sporadic contacts were recorded, but it was in mid-August 1999, i.e., 350 years after the dispersal, that the Wendat/Wyandotte nation regrouped at the heart of the ancestral land to celebrate its reunion. In a ceremony formerly called "Feast of the Dead," participating members reburied the bones of ancestors whose initial cemetery had become the site of archaeological digs in 1947. The year 1999 marked a turning point in the history of this scattered people. The great reunion was punctuated by the four groups' political leaders, reaffirming the reunification of the people while appealing to peace and national solidarity.

The Wendat/Wyandotte: Cyberspace Indigenous People?

The Internet has allowed for daily communications following the reunion and the creation of bonds among scattered members of this people. The virtual group "Wendat Gathering" (on Yahoo) was created through this new "globalizing" technology. This group has since given way to another, called "Wendat Culture," where the most diverse subjects are discussed. It is first of all a platform where members exchange ideas on issues of identity, culture and language, and plan upcoming gatherings, cultural events and the acquisition of a territory within their ancestral land.

From discussions held in this forum, affinities have developed and other discussion groups emerged. These new groups tend to reconstitute in part the nation's basic cultural elements according to tradition. For instance, the "Wendat Longhouse" group, made up of some members of the Bear clan, discuss sensitive topics where wisdom and decisions are required. As for "Longhouse Women," its aim is to re-establish the decision making power of women within this former matriarchal/matrilineal society.

New information technologies unquestionably allow for quick communication and information exchange. Thus, it becomes easy for people to establish daily contact at an international, national and individual scale. These communications give rise to real and very interesting exchanges, and the Wendat can once again reassemble the pieces of their shattered confederation where they were left in 1649. Therefore, could they be referred to as cyberspace indigenous peoples?

Conclusion

The context of this indigenous diaspora partially fits Safran's description, quoted by Clifford, in several senses: The Wendat people were dispersed from an original "centre" into more than two peripheral places; they perceive the ancestral territory as a place to eventually return to at the appropriate time; they are committed to the maintenance or the restoration of this ancestral territory; and, finally, their group awareness and solidarity are defined in an important way by this ongoing relation with the ancestral land (Clifford, 1994, pp. 304-305).

Now that they try to steer away from colonialism in this era of globalization, the Wendat/Wyandotte fervently desire to define their distinct identity. We are therefore witnessing the birth of a Wendat/Wyandotte transnational movement from which emerge some archaic "residues" of the ancestral culture. The Wendat/Wyandotte people's identity probably resides at a crossroads of these e-groups. The creation of a virtual Wendat/Wyandotte community through the Internet may just well be the springboard for this indigenous people to reaffirm their national identity and pride, and where they can strive to become more Wendat/Wyandotte, not more American or Canadian, in this globalized world.

References

Clifford, J. (1994). Diasporas. *Cultural Anthropology, 9*(3), 302-338.

Hall, A. J. (2003). *The American empire and the fourth world.* Montreal: McGill-Queen's University Press.

Heidenreich, C. (1978). Huron. *Handbook of North American Indian: Volume 15*. Washington: Smithsonian Institution.

Trigger, B. (1976). *The children of Aataentsic — A history of the Huron people to 1660: Volumes I - II.* Montreal: McGill-Queen's University Press.

Epilogue

Future Directions

Laurel Evelyn Dyson, University of Technology, Sydney, Australia

Max Hendriks, University of Technology, Sydney, Australia

Stephen Grant, University of Technology, Sydney, Australia

This book has demonstrated that the use of information technology within indigenous communities and by indigenous peoples is no longer an issue of debate but a proven fact. It is no longer a dream of the future but is the reality of today.

The way that information technology is used by indigenous peoples around the world is hugely varied. It reflects their different cultures and their aspirations for themselves, their families and their nations. It reflects the special needs for each particular community at this particular time in history.

The use of information technology by indigenous peoples will definitely expand in the future as access is improved and new technologies come onto the market which better serve indigenous requirements. It is impossible to predict accurately what these technologies will be. However, current indications point to an increased role for mobile devices of all kinds, motes and sensor networks, GPS and satellite broadband delivery. The Internet and networking technologies of all kinds will link communities and overcome the disadvantage of their geographical isolation. The convergence of telecommunications, broadcasting and computer technology will have a huge impact on the lives of all indigenous peoples. Above all, the integration of graphics, sound, video and animation in multimedia applications has an enormous potential for indigenous peoples, whose cultures are rooted in ceremony, dance, music, art and oral language traditions.

Information technology will allow indigenous peoples to revitalize their cultures and redefine themselves in the 21st century. It will help them overcome the injustices of the past and serve indigenous goals for self-determination and a better standard of living. Residing in their communities but linked to the outside world, they will again become a vital part of the world community, sharing their culture and contributing their ancient ways of knowing to help solve the world's many problems, for which Western science has been unable to find all the answers. Information technology will help them to become once more nations of respect, knowledge and cultural vigour.

Glossary

Aboriginal and Torres Strait Islander Communities: Indigenous peoples who form part of the 500 indigenous nations belonging to Australia prior to European colonization.

Active Sessions: A session is defined as the series of requests that a Web user asks from a Web site in a given time period. An active session is a session where the user does more than just look at the home and explanatory pages, but either undertakes some searches or browses some of the content of the Web site.

Andragogy: The theory that there is a difference in the way that adults learn from how children learn.

Australian Educational Institutions: The various educational systems that educate Australians from early childhood through school age education, including technical colleges and higher education institutions.

Avatar: A graphical digital character in a computer game.

Back-End: Back-end aspects of educational technology are functions that occur "behind the scenes," processes invisible to the end-user such as database and network functions.

Cache: High speed memory storage allocated from main memory or a storage device.

Cadastre: The details of land parcel boundaries, property rights and ownership recorded by governments. This is known as a property cadastre.

Central Processing Unit (CPU): A computer silicon chip that processes the information required to run programs.

Clan: Within a tribe there will normally be distinct groups (which may well occupy specific areas of land) that would normally consist of a few (or possibly many) related families. The term usually adopted for such a group is "clan."

Community-Based Tourism (CBT): Community-based tourism occurs when the residents of the destination manage tourism operations, usually in the form of home stays and associated guiding, catering and handicraft sales activities. It usually involves some form of cultural exchange where tourists meet with local communities and witness and/or engage in aspects of their lifestyle.

Community Online Access Centres: Computer centres established with Internet access for indigenous community members.

Computer Simulation: A computer representation of a real world event.

Cookies: A file on a Web user's hard drive that is used by Web sites to record data about the user.

Country: The term "country" is used to indicate the territory of an indigenous tribe or clan.

Cultural Assimilation: The total absorption of an ethnic group into the larger, more central host society.

Cultural Construction of ICT: A perspective that looks at the relationships between culture and technology. It assumes that ICT is not comprised of neutral technologies, but is embedded in the cultural considerations of its users, in this case indigenous peoples.

Culture: Encompasses sets of learned rules and standards shared within a group that describe a range of behaviours and beliefs that are proper, acceptable, valid and promote the survival of the group. Cultures and traditions are constructed within specific sociopolitical contexts and they all share four basic components: symbols, language, values and norms. Components include technology, language, community, enculturation, religion, legend, aesthetics and politics.

Decentralized Contextualization: Refers to localization processes that rely on distributed user input. Rather than programming different versions themselves, technology developers design a process that allows end-users to customize their software individually.

Deregulation: A concept that describes the removal, reduction or elimination of government regulations, restrictions or policies regarding a particular market or industry.

Digital Divide: A term used to describe the discrepancy between those who have access to information and communication technology and those who do not. Also used to describe the discrepancy between those who have pertinent ICT skills and knowledge and those who do not. Used in contrast to those in certain geographical areas, higher socio-economic groups and with a formal education; and on a global scale, contrasting industrialized and developing countries.

E-Learning: Encompassing term that includes various instructional materials delivered via CD-ROM, networks and the Internet. It includes computer-based training (CBT), Web-based training (WBT), electronic performance support systems (EPSS), distance and online learning.

Electronic Commerce for Community-Based Tourism (e-CBT): Computer-based tourism (CBT) that is marketed by tourism operators using information and communication technologies (ICTs).

Ethnocomputing: Use of computer simulations in order to "translate" between indigenous practices and Western technical concepts.

Facsimile: A photographic reproduction of a page that is as true to the original as possible.

Front-End: Front-end aspects of educational technology are functions and attributes visible to the end-user, including interface and interactions.

Geographic Information Systems (GIS): A computer-based system for collection, storage, analysis and display of geographic data, usually as map overlays.

Geo-Tourism: Tourism that sustains or enhances the geographical character of the place being visited — its environment, culture, aesthetics, heritage, and the well-being of its residents.

Governance: This comprises the traditions, institutions and processes that determine how power is exercised, how citizens are given a voice, and how decisions are made on issues of public concern.

Health Informatics: The collection, storage, retrieval, communication and optimal use of health-related data, information and knowledge.

Indigenous Intellectual Property: Specific intellectual property laws that consider the cultural specificity of indigenous and tribal peoples.

Indigenous Learning Styles: The theory that indigenous peoples tend to learn using methods based on their traditional learning patterns. This style differs from that predominant in Western culture on which much educational practice is based.

Information and Communication Technology (ICT): Broadly defined as computers, software, networks, satellite links and related systems that allow users to access, analyse, create, exchange and use data, information and knowledge. The infrastructure that it creates brings together people in different places and time zones, with multimedia tools for data, information and knowledge management. Some researchers use it also to include radio, telephone, television, loudspeakers, newspapers and other hard copy formats.

Information Architecture: The organization, nomenclature and design of information in a Web site or multimedia application.

Information Marginalisation: Refers to the fact that indigenous populations have largely been excluded from access, control or ownership of information outlets.

Information Society: A notion that became popular in Europe in the mid 1990s to refer to the increasing importance of information in the global economy. Today it is used to conceptualise a global society based on information networks, products, flows and markets. It also refers to the social formations in civil society that base their work on networked information and communication technologies.

Instructional Design and Technology (IDT): IDT is a well-defined field with guidelines and models to direct the development of instructional sequencing. It encompasses the analysis of learning and performance problems, design, development, implementation, evaluation and management of instructional and non-instructional processes and resources intended to improve learning and performance. The instructional goals are accomplished through systematic procedures and a variety of instructional media.

Internet Banking: People who have a bank account can access their accounts via the Internet to do a range of transactions themselves.

Interoperability: The ability of different computer systems to be able to share data in a meaningful and valid manner.

IP Address: A 32-bit number that identifies each sender or receiver of information that is sent across the Internet. An IP address has two parts: the identifier of a particular network on the Internet and an identifier of the particular device (which can be a server or a workstation) within that network.

Log File: Electronic log book which records information regarding visitors to the Web site. It can also record the history of single user's visits to different Web sites.

Metadata: Data that is used to describe other data, such as a table or index.

Microfiche: A small sheet (4" x 6") containing microfilmed images of pages, read with a microfilm reader. Many pages of text fit onto a single fiche, and their major advantage is in saving shelf space.

Multimedia: The use of computers to present text, graphics, video, animation and sound in an integrated way.

Neo-Consumer: High yield consumers across all age and gender groups with a range of spending, attitudinal, behavioural and psychological characteristics including a desire to be in control of their own lives, a passion for authenticity, an urge for the hand-made, a desire for change and an appetite for technology. Travel is a must-have component of their lifestyle.

Networking the Nation: An initiative by the Australian Federal Government to fund projects which aim to improve the telecommunications infrastructure and services in rural and remote regions of the country.

Online Learning: The use of computing, telecommunications, and the Internet to create a learning and teaching community. Instructional materials are presented on the Web and on CD-ROM. E-mail, bulletin boards and chats are used for interaction.

Outcamps: Information communication technology learning centres based within isolated aboriginal communities.

Runtime: The period of time during which a program is being executed.

Self-Determination: Since the 1960s, indigenous leaders, advocates and activists have been calling for the acknowledgement of the basic right of self-determination for indigenous peoples. The principles of self-determination in international law refer not only to a number of specific human rights, but more precisely to the right of indigenous nations to have and manage their own distinctive politico-territorial identities. The very notion of an indigenous nation is intimately tied to the notion of territory, and indigenous groups have actively demanded their right to govern themselves and have a more proactive role in the decision-making instances that concern their political, economic and cultural future.

Self-Representation: The concept refers to the ways in which indigenous and Tribal peoples around the world choose to represent themselves in the public domain and through a variety of media, including television, film, arts and the Internet. In recent years it has become an essential aspect of the struggle for cultural survival in many indigenous movements worldwide.

The concept is linked to other rights demanded by indigenous peoples like self-determination.

Server: A computer which stores data, files and applications for many users.

Server Side: A program that resides on the server allowing a user to interact with it.

Three-Tier Architecture, Three-Tier File Structure: A three-tier file-structure separates the files that make up a piece of software into three layers. In general software parlance, these layers are divided such that the underlying database and processes are hidden from the end user. In order to create easily modifiable educational multimedia, layers are divided so that the complexity of the application is hidden from the teachers and students modifying the software. The first layer contains the multimedia application, connected by the second layer — a database: to the third layer, which contains the media files that are modified. Those media files are integrated into the multimedia application at runtime, so that teachers and students can make edits to individual images and texts without needing to understand how to operate the more complex multimedia application.

TIFF: Tagged Image File Format, a commonly used file format for images on computers.

Transaction Log Analysis: An analysis that is undertaken on the data that have been recorded in a Web log. A Web log will record all requests for pages, often called hits, that are made to a Web server.

Tribe: A range of different terms have been applied to groupings of indigenous peoples. At the larger end of social categories (describing hundreds or thousands of individuals) the most common term is "tribe." It is noted that some people feel that the term "tribe" can carry with it notions of primitivism. For these reasons (and others) the term "language-group" is sometimes used, although this does not necessarily refer to the same group of people as would the term "tribe."

Ultra-High Frequency (UHF): This refers to the radio frequency range from 300 MHz to 3 GHz.

United States Bureau of Indian Affairs: The United States federal government agency that fulfills the government's trust responsibility and promotes self-determination on behalf of tribal governments, American Indians and Alaska Natives.

WAV: File format for storing sound files, developed by Microsoft and IBM.

Web Browser: A software package that enables a user to display and interact with documents hosted by Web servers.

Web Cache: A Web cache fills requests from the Web server, stores the requested information locally and sends the information to the client. The next time the Web cache gets a request for the same information, it simply returns the locally cached data instead of searching over the Internet, thus reducing Internet traffic and response time.

Web Robot: Also known as a Web wanderer or Web spider, it is a program that traverses the Internet automatically by retrieving a document, and recursively retrieving all documents that are referenced. The data recorded in transaction logs by this type of activity is termed "non-human" and can lead to misleading results; consequently it must be removed when undertaking transaction log analysis.

Web Server: A Web server is a computer that runs Web server applications that allow access to Web pages for Web users. Every computer on the Internet that contains a Web site must have a Web server program.

Workplace Learning: A broad term that covers learning that takes place in the workplace both through practice and direct instruction.

About the Authors

Laurel Evelyn Dyson (BSc, Hons; BA, Hons; PhD; CELTA; GradDipABE; GradDipInfTech, Distinction; CCNA; CCAI; MInfTech) is a lecturer in information technology at the University of Technology, Sydney, Australia, where she is one of the founders of the Indigenous Participation in Information Technology Project. As part of this project, Dr. Dyson led the successful introduction in January 2004 of the first university information technology tertiary preparation course for indigenous people ever offered in Australia. Having lived herself on the other side of the digital divide until a few years ago, her mission is to assist others to master the tools of the information age. In this role, her teaching in recent years has included computer education programs for indigenous Australians, senior citizens, adult literacy students and prisoners. In total, her experience in university and adult education spans a period of over two decades, with a focus on language, study skills, university preparation courses and, lately, information technology. Her research interests are predominantly in the fields of indigenous people and information technology and Australian culture and the role of indigenous Australians in its development and history. She has published two books and a number of book chapters, journal articles, and research papers in these two areas, has been interviewed 13 times about her research for radio and the press, and has had 33 reviews of her work in the media. Currently she is leading the evaluation, for UNESCO, of their ICT4ID Project involving indigenous people and information and communication technologies in Africa and Latin America.

Max Hendriks lectures in information technology at the University of Technology, Sydney, Australia, where he is also currently completing a master's degree in Internetworking science. He has been an educator for over 35 years and taught all grades from pre-school through university postgraduate students, as well as holding senior executive positions in education. Over this time he has been a strong advocate for the rights of all peoples. He is involved in the Indigenous Participation in Information Technology Project at the University of Technology and took an active role in the development and delivery of the university's first indigenous Pre-IT program. This involvement is ongoing. His research interests are in Internetworking and how this technology can bridge the divide between all communities. Of particular interest are wireless technology and related security issues.

Stephen Grant holds an academic position at the University of Technology, Sydney, Australia, where he is in charge of mentoring indigenous students in the Indigenous Participation in Information Technology Project. This is the first project of its kind in Australia and aims to boost indigenous enrollments in IT courses and the number of indigenous Australians working in IT. Already the success of his work on the project has been recognized with a University Equity, Social Justice and Human Rights award. It has also been largely due to his efforts that the indigenous Pre-IT program has been so successful. He is one of a handful of qualified indigenous IT professionals in Australia, with qualifications and industry experience in engineering and IT as well as in indigenous affairs. Since joining the Faculty of Information Technology, he has added to his networking industry certification by becoming a qualified networking instructor as well as commencing a Master of Science in Internetworking part-time, making him one of three indigenous IT postgraduate students in Australia. His current research interests are mobile networks and embedded products.

* * *

Mehran Abolhasan received a BE in computer engineering (Hons) from the University of Wollongong, Australia (1999). He completed his PhD in the School of Computer, Electrical and Telecommunications Engineering, University Wollongong (2003). In July 2003, he started working as a research fellow with the Smart Internet Technology Cooperative Research Centre (CRC) and the Office of Information and Communication Technology (OICT) within the Department of Commerce in NSW. In July 2004, he joined the Desert Knowledge CRC and Telecommunication and IT Research Institute, where he is leading a project called Spare Ad hoc Network for Desert (SAND). His current research interests are: wireless ad hoc networking, sensor networking and 3G and beyond 3G networks.

Mark Apperley is a professor of computer science and dean of the School of Computing and Mathematical Sciences at the University of Waikato, Aotearoa (New Zealand). After completing his PhD in electrical engineering, he has been involved in computer science education and human-computer interaction research for the past 30+ years. His research publications cover interface implementation and design, usability studies, information visualization, computer-supported collaborative work and large shared interaction spaces. His particular interest in the Niupepa Project was fuelled, in part, by the fact that his great-grandfather was an editor of one of the newspapers in the collection.

Alex Arposio (alex@aboriginalhunter.com) is a PhD candidate in philosophy at the University of Newcastle, Australia, and works with the Arwarbukarl Cultural Resource Association in the area of language recovery and revitalisation.

Glenn Auld is a lecturer in language and literacy at Monash University, Australia. He has spent many years learning and researching with Kunibídji children, who live in Maningrida in the Northern Territory. Auld has submitted a PhD thesis on the literacy practices of Kunbiídji children on DVD. He is interested in the social applications of emerging technologies with reference to the linguistic human rights of speakers of minority indigenous Australian languages.

Susan Rae Banks, PhD, is an associate professor in the Department of Teaching and Learning at Washington State University, USA. Her specialties include curriculum development, assessment, special education and professional preparation of Native teachers. She is an enrolled member of the Arapaho Nation.

Andrea Barr is the manager of information services at Tairawhiti Polytechnic, situated in Gisborne on the East Coast of the North Island of New Zealand. She has responsibility for e-learning within the polytechnic and is committed to a vision of the polytechnic as a centre of excellence for e-learning, specialising in provision for Maori learners. She was part of a group that came up with the idea for the project "Critical Success Factors for Effective Use of e-Learning with Maori Learners" and has been involved in both governance groups, as well as providing advice and support for the project manager.

Te Arani Barrett joined the staff of Te Whare Wānanga o Awanuiārangi, a Maori tribal university in Aotearoa (New Zealand) following years of computer-related teaching in secondary and tertiary settings. She established the distance and e-learning framework which is now termed "e-Wānanga;" and this best describes the way in which delivery options are blended. Such blending requires particular cognisance and consideration for student audiences which are primarily Maori.

Andrea Berez is a research assistant with the LINGUISTList and the Dena'ina Archiving, Training, and Access Project. She has conducted documentary fieldwork with the Dena'ina language in Alaska and has investigated the role of middle voice in Athabascan languages. She is currently compiling a volume of Dena'ina texts with aligned audio.

Lars H. Bestle currently works as programme specialist for UNDP's regional programme on ICT for Development (ICT4D) called Asia Pacific Development Information Programme (APDIP). He spent three years in Vietnam, where he was the ICT4D programme officer for UNDP. During this time, he assisted the Vietnam government in its policy-making activities for ICT4D, among others, to develop their national ICT strategic framework. More recently, he has consulted with the Asian Development Bank in assessing the demand and readiness for ICTs to improve basic social services in the countries of the greater Mekong sub-region, and with UNESCAP as economic affairs officer on ICT4D issues relating to digital divides and ICT applications for achieving the Millennium Development Goals in the least developed and landlocked countries of Asia and the Pacific.

J. David Betts is an assistant professor of literacy and technology. His courses include literacy and technology, media and literacy, computers in language arts research, multimedia authoring for teachers, and literacy and the arts. His recent research in the integration of art and technology in education includes work with the Tucson Pima Arts Council, several local school districts and the Pascua Yaqui Tribe of Arizona. Dr. Betts is also a multimedia producer and videographer, working in the area of social change and the arts.

Paul Boustead is a senior research fellow at the Telecommunications and IT Research Institute at the University of Wollongong, Australia. He is currently leading projects within the Cooperative Research Centre (CRC) for Smart Internet Technology and recently led a project in the CRC for Desert Knowledge. He completed a PhD at the University of Wollongong in 2000 in the area of label switching protocols for high-speed networks. Dr. Boustead's current research interests include: network and server support for the delivery of distributed services over the Internet, network games, content distribution networks, dense multi-party communication, providing applications over ad hoc networks and developing cheap, reliable and sustainable communications technologies suitable for use in remote indigenous communities of Australia.

Fiona Brady has lived in a remote community in Cape York Peninsula for two decades and has many years' experience in education and training, and recently completed a Master of Learning Management from Central Queensland University. She works with indigenous communities in Cape York Peninsula and the Torres Strait of Australia. She is involved in community development and particularly interested in the use of ICT in remote indigenous communities. Currently she is taking part in an indigenous cultural archiving and revitalization project recording hymns in indigenous language and making them more accessible to the community.

Sheree Cairney is a post-doctoral fellow based in the Top End of the Northern Territory. She has worked among aboriginal Australians living in remote regions in Arnhem Land investigating the effects on the brain of using kava, cannabis or petrol. Dr. Cairney is currently investigating brain-behavioural relationships in mental health and substance abuse among aboriginal people and the development of creative and appropriate means of communicating these concepts with aboriginal people.

Sally Jo Cunningham received degrees in computer science and Asian studies from the University of Tennessee, and a PhD in computer science from Louisiana State University. She has been a lecturer with the University of Waikato, New Zealand, since 1990. Dr. Cunningham is a member of the New Zealand Digital Libraries research group. Her research interests include human-computer interaction, digital libraries, computer education and computer applications in textiles.

John Dallwitz has been an artist, photographer, educator, heritage consultant and cultural adviser, based in South Australia since the 1960s. Throughout his life, he has travelled and researched extensively in the Australian outback. The diversity of these experiences has come together during his past 14 years' liaison with the Pitjantjatjara and Yankunytjatjara people of the central desert. This has led to the successful development of the acclaimed A<u>r</u>a Irititja Project.

Anne Daly is an associate professor in economics at the University of Canberra and a visiting fellow at the Centre for Aboriginal Economic Policy Research at the Australian National University. Her research interests include the economic status of indigenous Australians, particularly women and families. This work has focussed on labour market issues and the relationship between work and the welfare system. She has also conducted research on telecommunications policy with a focus on the implications of technological developments for indigenous Australians. A future project will involve case studies of selected indigenous communities in Australia and their current access to telecommunications facilities and potential uses of new technologies in the daily lives of the people.

Deborah Danard is a doctoral student at the Ontario Institute for Studies in Education, Canada, specializing in indigenous studies. She is Anishinaabekwe/Ojibway nation, Rainy River First Nation, Treaty #3. Her research focuses on aboriginal identity and the role culture and spirituality play in education, including traditional approaches to teaching and curriculum development. She is the recipient of the University of Toronto/McMaster University Indigenous Health Research Development Program Graduate Scholarship, funded by the Canadian Institutes of Health Research-Institute of Aboriginal People's Health, for her research, "Finding Our Way: Culture as Resistance to Suicide in Indian Country." The chapter in this book is her first academic collaboration.

Michael Donovan is a Gumbaynggir man from the North Coast of NSW, Australia, but grew up in the Western suburbs of Sydney. He has worked in aboriginal education since 1992 in various fields from community education, school, to higher education. His professional involvement with the aboriginal community comes through his role as an aboriginal education assistant and through the Aboriginal Education Consultative Group, the primary advisory body on aboriginal education in NSW, where he has represented his community from local to State levels. He has a Bachelor of Teaching with First Class Honours, the first aboriginal male to achieve this at the University of Western Sydney. He has worked at Wollotuka School of Aboriginal Studies at the University of Newcastle since 1996, lecturing in aboriginal studies with a current focus on the use of online technologies as a teaching and educational tool that can support the maintenance of aspects of aboriginal culture, including the revitalisation of aboriginal languages.

Leone Dunn is a senior lecturer in the School of Information Technology and Computer Science at the University of Wollongong, Australia. She was awarded her PhD at the University of Queensland in 1992. Dr. Dunn also holds a Master of Arts in linguistics from the University of Western Australia (1985).

Ron Eglash holds a BS in cybernetics, an MS in systems engineering and a PhD in history of consciousness, all from the University of California, USA. A Fulbright postdoctoral fellowship enabled his field research on African ethnomathematics, which was published in 1999 as *African Fractals: Modern Computing and Indigenous Design*. He is now an associate professor of science and technology studies at Rensselaer Polytechnic Institute, USA. His current project, funded by the NSF, HUD and Department of Education, translates the mathematical concepts embedded in cultural designs of African, African American, Native American and Latino communities into software design tools for secondary school education. The software is available online at http://www.rpi.edu/~eglash/csdt.html.

Rosemary Foster is a lecturer at the Centre for Indigenous Health, University of Queensland, Australia, where she teaches research methods, applied research and project management courses in the Bachelor of Applied Health Science (indigenous health). Recently she has developed these courses with either substantial online components or for complete online delivery for a majority indigenous student population.

Rhonda Friedlander, MS, is a speech-language pathologist and owner of Oneclaw Speech Therapy Services. She has provided speech/language services to native communities across the Northwest United States for the past 19 years. Rhonda is an enrolled member of The Confederated Salish and Kootenai Tribes of the Flathead Nation.

John Fulcher is a professor of information technology and director of the Health Informatics Research Centre at the University of Wollongong, Australia. He holds a BEE (Hons) from the University of Queensland (1972), a Research Masters from LaTrobe University, Melbourne (1981) and a PhD from the University of Wollongong (1999). His 100 or so publications include a best-selling textbook on microcomputer interfacing, a recent monograph on applied intelligent systems and three chapters in a handbook on neural computing. His research interests include microcomputer interfacing, computer science education, artificial neural networks (especially higher-order ANNs), health informatics and parallel computing.

Bethalia Gaidan is a Torres Strait Islander. She lives on Dauan Island in the far north of Australia with her husband and three children. She is currently council clerk of the Dauan Island Community Council. Mrs. Gaidan likes reading thrillers, sewing and fishing.

Russell Gluck is a lecturer in learning development at the University of Wollongong, Australia. He has worked for more than 20 years in squatter camps, prisons and the Aboriginal Education Centre at the University of Wollongong. This wealth of experience has led to the development of an engagement process that enables literacy-inefficient people to draw, compose, write and read stories — sufficient in some cases to successfully complete university studies.

Gale Goodwin Gómez is a linguistic anthropologist and chair of the Department of Anthropology at Rhode Island College in Providence, USA. Her degrees include a PhD in anthropological linguistics from Columbia University and an MA in linguistics from the American University, Washington, DC. A Fulbright scholar in Brazil in 2001, Dr. Goodwin Gómez has engaged in field research and advocacy of the Yanomami Indians of northern Brazil for over 20 years.

Roger W. Harris has a PhD in information systems and lives in Hong Kong but works with rural communities in Asia, helping them get connected to the Internet and to use it for their own development. As an independent consultant since 2001, he has been involved with rural IT projects in more than 10 Asian countries, working for a variety of governments and international aid agencies. Dr. Harris founded Asian Encounters, an organisation that promotes the use of the Internet by rural communities who operate community-based tourism as a way of generating incomes.

Kate Hennessy is a PhD student in the anthropology of media at the University of British Columbia, Canada. She is working on a number of community and academic projects related to the use of digital technology in First Nations communities in the Yukon, Alberta and British Columbia. Using methods of participatory ethnography while facilitating community media projects as a videographer, trainer and multimedia producer, she is examining the role of digital archives and multimedia in these communities as tools for the repatriation of language materials and cultural documentation.

Gary Holton, PhD, is an associate professor of linguistics at the Alaska Native Language Center, University of Alaska Fairbanks, USA. His research interests include endangered language documentation and revitalization, with a focus on Athabaskan languages and the languages of Eastern Indonesia. He has worked to develop standards for digital language archiving through involvement with international organizations, including the Open Language Archives Community and the Digital Endangered Languages and Musics Archive Network.

Baden Hughes (badenh@cs.mu.oz.au) is a research fellow in the Language Technology Group in the Department of Computer Science and Software Engineering at the University of Melbourne, Australia.

Martin Hughes is somewhat accustomed to bridging cultural divides. In 1984, he completed a Bachelor of Education at Victoria College, Rusden Campus, Australia, with majors in mathematics, drama and dance. For 10 years after that, he worked as a professional dancer in Australia and overseas. Hughes continues to perform when he can. He has been working as a database developer and consultant since 1990.

Ella Inglebret, PhD, is an assistant professor in the Department of Speech and Hearing Sciences at Washington State University, USA. She has been involved in professional preparation of American Indian and Alaska Native (AI/AN) students in the fields of speech-language pathology and audiology for the past 16 years. Her research focuses on factors associated with AI/AN student success in higher education and speech/language service delivery to native communities.

Kathie Irwin (Dip Teacher Training, Dip Tchg, BEd, BEd, Hons., 1st Class; MEd, PhD) descends from Ngati Porou, Ngati Kahungunu, Scots, Orkney Island and Irish forebears. Irwin started her professional career in education in 1974, training as a primary school teacher, and has served over 20 years as an academic at Massey and Victoria Universities, Aotearoa (New Zealand). She has held several senior positions in education, including head of the department and inaugural director of He Parekereke, the Institute of Maori Research and Development, Department of Education, Victoria University. She was appointed as the inaugural chair of the New Zealand Teachers Council by the Minister of Education. Dr. Irwin specializes in Maori research, education and development and has published extensively in these areas. Her doctoral thesis is entitled *Maori Education: From Wretchedness to Hope*. She currently holds the position of director of academic programmes, Awanuiarangi ki Poneke.

Judy Iseke-Barnes is an associate professor at the Ontario Institute for Studies in Education of the University of Toronto, Canada, where she teaches courses in aboriginal and indigenous studies in education for graduate students and teacher training. She is a member of the Metis Nation of Alberta. Her research activities have also engaged groups of aboriginal educators in interactions on the Internet in a Canada-wide discussion of aboriginal issues. Her recent publications include a book (with Njoki Wane) *Equity in Schools and Society*, published in 2000, and several international journal articles on indigenous peoples and the Internet.

Robyn Kamira (Te Aupouri, Te Rarawa tribal areas) has presented around the world on technology, indigenous and Maori subjects and is an early proponent of indigenous guardianship models for information in the health sector. She is committed to moving Maori well-being forward using technology in strategic and constructive ways. Robyn is a member of New Zealand's national Digital Strategy Advisory Group and the National Kaitiaki Group for Maori women's health data. She is a founding trust member of the Society for Professional Maori Women in Information Technology (Te Waka Wahine Wa-Hangarau), and internationally, is secretariat member to both the CIRN (Community Informatics Research Network) and the Global Community Networks Partnership (GCNP). She holds academic qualifications alongside her practitioner experience. Robyn is director of Paua Interface Ltd — a technology and knowledge company, and Rangatiratanga Canvases Ltd. — a creative technology company involved in indigenous storytelling, multimedia and film.

Te Taka Keegan is of Waikato-Maniapoto and Ngati Porou descent. He received a diploma in computer engineering from the Central Institute of Technology in Wellington, Aotearoa (New Zealand), and spent six years as a hardware engineer. He was awarded a BA and an MA at the University of Waikato through the Tohu Paetahi (Maori language) stream. Since 1994 he has been lecturing computer science in te reo Maori at the University of Waikato. He was the project manager for the Niupepa Web site. His research interests are primarily involved with the use of the Maori language in the computing and Internet environments.

Wanjira Kinuthia is an assistant professor at Georgia State University, USA, where she teaches courses in instructional design and technology. Prior to that, she worked as an instructional designer in higher education and business. She has a PhD in instructional design and development, a master's degree in international affairs focusing on African studies and women's studies, and a master's degree in computer education and technology. She also has a bachelor's degree in international business. Dr. Kinuthia has a special interest in international and comparative education. Her research focuses on socio-cultural factors influencing e-learning in developing countries.

Sachiko Kubota, PhD, is an associate professor in the Department of Integrated Arts and Sciences, Hiroshima University (Japan), and a visiting researcher at the National Museum of Ethnology. She did fieldwork in Arnhem Land (1986-87) and is continuing this study. Also, she has started a comparative study in Canada since 2000. Her interests are: (1) the changes in women's roles in indigenous society, (2) gender issues, and (3) indigenous representations. In Japan, Dr. Kubota has published *Aboriginal Society from Gender Point of View* (2005), *Indigenous People in Multi-Cultural Society* (co-edited with Dr. Shuzo Koyama, 2003), and many other works.

Marcia Langton is the inaugural chair of Australian indigenous studies at The University of Melbourne, Australia. She is also a chief investigator with the research project on Agreements, Treaties and Negotiated Settlements. Professor Langton is a descendant of the Bidjara and Yiman nation of central Queensland. She was previously founding director of the Centre of Indigenous, Natural and Cultural Resource Management, and ranger professor of aboriginal studies at the Northern Territory University. She has worked for three of the major Aboriginal land councils and is a specialist in aboriginal land tenure and resource issues.

'Alopi Latukefu works with the Australian government through the Australian Agency for International Development (AusAID). Prior to taking up this role, he worked as chief executive officer of Goolarri Media in Broome and in various senior management roles within the Outback Digital Network, where much of the information for his case study was sourced. Formally, Mr. Latukefu did research in electronic commerce and other aspects of the information economy for groups including the Centre for Corporate Change (Australian Graduate School of Management, University of NSW), the National Office for the Information Economy (Commonwealth Government of Australia) as well as undertaking consulting work researching the methodology for knowledge assessment within Pacific Island Countries for the World Bank.

Brett Leavy is an indigenous Australian from the southwestern Queensland Kooma tribe, part of the Gungari-speaking people. He has served in senior positions in a federal government organisation, serves on the boards of a number of indigenous organisations, initiated a successful indigenous newspaper and is the CEO of a multimedia company called CyberDreaming, Australia. H recently swung his energy and time into the Digital Songlines project, developing capabilities to digitise the arts, culture and heritage landscape of aboriginal Australia in a joint venture with the Australasian Cooperative Research Centre for Interaction Design.

Carole Leclair is a new member of the Faculty of Indigenous and Contemporary Studies at Laurier Brantford, Canada, and plays an active role in further developing the indigenous studies curriculum. She completed her PhD on *Metis*

Environmental Knowledge: La Tayr pi Tout li Moonde. Dr. Leclair's academic interests include Aboriginal environmental thought systems, writing in English, gender and sexualities, radical democracy, cultural landscapes and women's activisms. Her personal time is well spent as affectionate referee between two pug dogs and a cat, assorted children and grandchildren, tons o' relatives and a husband with a great sense of humour (a house policy).

Daryn McKenny (daryn@aboriginalhunter.com) is an aboriginal person living in Newcastle, Australia, and is the manager of the Arwarbukarl Cultural Resource Association Incorporated. McKenny has led the development of software for the Awabakal community.

Paul Maruff is a full-time employee of CogState Ltd., head of the Neuropsychology Laboratory at the Mental Health Research Institute of Victoria, and a professor in the School of Psychological Science at La Trobe University, Melbourne, Australia. He is a neuropsychologist with expertise in the identification and measurement of subtle behavioural and cognitive dysfunction. Professor Maruff's research integrates conventional and computerised neuropsychological testing with cognitive neuroscientific methods to identify subtle neurocognitive impairment, and assesses the efficacy of pharmacological treatment, in Alzheimer's disease, mild cognitive impairment and the HIV dementia complex.

Margaret Mau is a Torres Strait Islander and lives on Dauan Island, Australia, with her husband and children. She is currently a chairperson of the Dauan Island Community Council and is an executive member of Torres Strait Regional Authority (TSRA) and Island Coordinating Council (ICC). Mrs. Mau holds the portfolio for women and families, and is a member of the Torres Strait Health Council. For relaxation she likes to fish, play volleyball, do puzzles and watch quiz shows.

Odette Mazel is a lawyer and research fellow with the research project on agreements, treaties and negotiated settlements. She is based in the School of Anthropology, Geography and Environmental Studies at The University of Melbourne, Australia.

Michael Meehan is a senior research officer at the Centre for Indigenous Health, University of Queensland, Australia. He manages the Centre's flexible delivery strategy and translates course and problem-based learning material for online delivery to the external and remotely located indigenous student base. His research interests focus on the development of culturally appropriate educational multimedia titles and the emerging literacy of new technology and its impact upon the indigenous student.

Katina Michael is a lecturer in information technology at the University of Wollongong, Australia. Her current research activities are focused on location-based services and the impacts of technology upon citizens. She was awarded her PhD in 2003 and received her Bachelor of Information Technology from the University of Technology, Sydney (1996). Most of her work experience was acquired as a senior network and business planner with Nortel Networks, where she gained expertise in the use of geographic information systems (1996-2001). Dr. Michael has also held positions as an analyst at United Technologies and Andersen Consulting.

Victor Giner Minana, born in Valencia, Spain, in 1977, holds a law degree from Valencia University. He pursued a Master of Science in Latin American studies at the Ortega y Gasset College at Madrid's Complutense University and a Master of Arts in international humanitarian assistance at Louvain's Catholic University in Belgium. In 2004, he collaborated as a consultant for UNESCO's Information and Communication Technologies for Intercultural Dialogue Program. He currently works as project manager for the Spanish International Cooperation Agency in Morocco.

Patrick J. Moore is an assistant professor in anthropology at the University of British Columbia, Canada. He received his PhD from the University of Indiana in 2002. He has studied the languages and narrative traditions of Northern Athabaskans, and lived for many years in Slavey and Kaska communities in northern Alberta and the Yukon. He is the author, with Angela Wheelock, of *Wolverine Myths and Visions*, and he edited *Dene Gudeji: Kaska Narratives*, a collection of Kaska narratives published by the Kaska Tribal Council.

David Nathan is director of the Endangered Languages Archive, part of the Hans Rausing Endangered Languages Project at SOAS, University of London. He has worked with computing applications for endangered (especially Australian aboriginal) languages, and taught courses in computing, linguistics, cognitive science, multimedia development and English at universities in Australia, Japan and the UK. His publications include the textbook: *Australia's Indigenous Languages*; papers on lexicography, indigenous people and the Internet, and multimedia; and multimedia CD-ROMs. He established several major Web sites, and was co-author (with Peter Austin) of the Web's first hypertext bilingual dictionary (for Gamilaraay/Kamilaroi).

Terry Neal is project manager of e-learning for the Institutes of Technology and Polytechnics (ITP) of New Zealand. She was part of the group that came up with the idea for the project "Critical Success Factors for Effective Use of e-Learning with Mâori Learners" and then managed the project. She led the implementation of e-learning initiatives in two ITPs in New Zealand. She has also worked with other ITPs to understand how e-learning fits with their strategic direction and how to establish it within their institutions.

Pauline Hui Ying Ooi graduated with a first class degree in information technology management from Multimedia University, Malaysia. She had worked for Motorola Malaysia as an intern prior to joining the University of Technology, Sydney, as a visiting scholar under the AIESEC International Graduate Traineeship Exchange Program in July 2004. She currently works for Intel Technology Penang, Malaysia. She is interested in intercultural interaction in information systems, mobility in creative and interactive art (music), business information systems and IT management.

Lisa Palmer is an Australian Research Council postdoctoral fellow with the research project on agreements, treaties and negotiated settlements. She is based in the School of Anthropology, Geography and Environmental Studies at The University of Melbourne.

Mark H. Palmer is a PhD candidate in the Department of Geography at the University of Oklahoma, USA. He is also a member of the Kiowa Tribe of Oklahoma. His research interests include geographic information systems (GIS) and society with an emphasis upon the impacts of these systems on indigenous communities in North America. His current research focuses upon the development and diffusion of GIS at the United States Bureau of Indian Affairs (BIA).

D. Michael Pavel, PhD, is an associate professor in the Department of Educational Leadership and Counseling Psychology at Washington State University, USA. His research focuses on American Indian and Alaska Native (AI/AN) education and native teacher preparation. He is the author of a series of AI/AN education reports published by the U.S. Department of Education, as well as the Ford and Kellogg Foundations. Dr. Pavel is a tradition bearer for the Skokomish Nation.

Christopher Robbins has worked as a designer and developer for organizations as diverse as the University of the South Pacific, Fiji; the Museum for African Art, New York City; the Union Bank of Switzerland, New York City;

the Children's Discovery Centre, London; and a Reuters "dotcom" joint-venture, London. He studied links between design and society in Japan, and developed cross-cultural instructional materials as a Peace Corps Volunteer in Benin, West Africa, before focusing on educational technology at the Media Centre of the University of the South Pacific. He is currently exploring physical interfaces to digital media at the Rhode Island School of Design (RISD) in the USA.

Juan Francisco Salazar is a Chilean anthropologist and media producer living in Sydney, Australia, since 1998. He holds a PhD in communications and today lectures in media studies and production at the School of Communication, Design and Media, University of Western Sydney. He has worked extensively in a wide range of cross-disciplinary research projects including consultancies for government and international non-governmental organizations. Dr. Salazar has published on media anthropology, Chilean cinema in exile and indigenous media in Latin America. He is associated with several transnational networks such as OurMedia and CLACPI, the Latin American Council of Indigenous Film and Video.

Tish Scott (tishscot@uvic.ca) is a doctoral student in education studies (curriculum and instruction) at the University of Victoria, BC, Canada. She is a teacher and curriculum developer. Her research interests include teaching and learning with educational technology, using technology to support and strengthen language and culture, online interactive curriculum development, health education, student motivation, assessment, evaluation, culture and participatory research.

Ryan Sengara has been the project leader of Redfern Kids Connect since August 2002. He first became involved in the project while on exchange from his home country of Canada and has since completed a research thesis on his experiences at the Centre for Culture Research (University of Western Sydney) titled: *Redfern Kids Connect: Technology and Empowerment.*

Linda Sioui was born in 1960 and is a Huron-Wendat from Wendake, Quebec. She holds a bachelor's degree in sociology from the University of Ottawa. She is presently a part-time student at *Université Laval*, Quebec, Canada, working on her master's in anthropology. In 1983, she worked on compiling the field notes of Quebec ethnologist Marius Barbeau (Huron-Wyandot Collection) for the Canadian Museum of Civilization. She has travelled extensively and worked for several Native organizations. She currently holds the position of cultural affairs advisor for the Huron-Wendat Nation's Council.

Mary Loy Stone, MA, is a speech-language pathologist for the Browning School District on the Blackfeet Reservation. She has provided speech/language services to native communities in Northwest and Southwest Regions of the United States. She is an enrolled member of the Blackfeet Nation.

Shigenobu Sugito is a professor in the School of Human Sciences, Sugiyama Jogakuen University, Japan. He has done fieldwork in Australia, mainly Arnhem Land, since 1984 and his concern is population study and social structure using information technology and aboriginal art. His most significant research is contained in the article "Marriage Rule as a Population Control Factor: A Computer Simulation Study" (1991).

Andrew Turk has undergraduate degrees in surveying, applied science (cartography) and arts (psychology and philosophy) and a PhD. In the 1970s and early 1980s he worked for the Australian government on the production of topographic maps. In 1983 he commenced research at the University of Melbourne concerning design and production of tactual (raised-line and low-vision) maps and other graphics for blind and partially-sighted persons. In 1992 he completed his PhD on human factors aspects of geographic information systems. Since 1993 he has worked at Murdoch University, where his teaching, graduate student supervision and research activities concern design and evaluation of computer applications (user interfaces, Web sites and interactive TV), including cultural and ethical considerations.

Doug Vogel is a professor of information systems at the City University of Hong Kong. He has been involved with computers and computer systems in various capacities for over 30 years, including the position of president of a 50-person manufacturing company. Professor Vogel's interests bridge the business and academic communities in addressing questions of the impact of management information systems on aspects of business process improvement, group problem solving, education and organizational productivity. Professor Vogel is widely published and has directed extensive research on aspects of business process improvement in conjunction with a series of research contracts and organizational applications.

Sandi Warren is a PhD candidate at Trent University, Canada, in native studies where her dissertation is entitled: *Respect, Responsibility, and Reciprocity: Examining Indigenous Knowledge Systems as Best Practices for Aboriginal Business Development.* Ms. Warren's career has followed a specialist route as a project lead and business strategist. In this capacity, she has contributed to projects in both the private and public sector. As an educator, she continues to instruct courses for human resources, public administration and native studies programs. Her academic interests include creating livelihood systems through the acknowledgment of indigenous knowledge as best practice models for a sustainable future.

Sadie Williams is a research assistant with the LINGUISTList and the Dena'ina Archiving, Training and Access project. She has assisted with the development of a language archive at the Alaska Native Heritage Center and has pursued research on the Dena'ina sound system.

Index

N

O

P